Economic Ideas and Issues

A Systematic Approach to Critical Thinking

Jerry Evensky

Department of Economics
Maxwell School of Citizenship
Syracuse University

41246

Prentice Hall, Englewood Cliffs, NJ 07632

Library of Congress Cataloging-in-Publication Data

Evensky, Jerry
    Economic ideas and issues: a systematic approach to critical thinking/Jerry Evensky
    Includes index.
    ISBN 0–13–223611–7
    1. Neoclassical school of economics.   I. Title.

HB98.2.E94 1990   89–8657
330.15′7—dc20   CIP

Editorial/production supervision: **Patrick Reynolds**
Cover design: **Jerry Votta**
Manufacturing buyers: **Laura Crossland** and **Peter Havens**
Cover photo: Bruegel, Pieter, the elder: *The Harvesters,*
July 1565. Oil on wood. 46½″ x 63¼″. The Metropolitan
Museum of Art, Rogers Fund, 1919.

 © 1990 by Prentice-Hall, Inc.
A Division of Simon & Schuster
Englewood Cliffs, New Jersey 07632

Printed in the United States of America

10 9 8 7 6 5 4 3 2 1

ISBN 0-13-223611-7

Prentice-Hall International (UK) Limited, *London*
Prentice-Hall of Australia Pty. Limited, *Sydney*
Prentice-Hall Canada Inc., *Toronto*
Prentice-Hall Hispanoamericana, S.A., *Mexico*
Prentice-Hall of India Private Limited, *New Delhi*
Prentice-Hall of Japan, Inc., *Tokyo*
Simon & Schuster Asia Pte. Ltd., *Singapore*
Editora Prentice-Hall do Brasil, Ltda., *Rio de Janeiro*

Contents

Preface   ix
Introduction   xi
Overview   xix

---

1. THE SUBJECT AND METHOD OF ECONOMICS   1

A. The Subject Matter of Economics   1

What Is Economics About?   1
The "Quandary of Choice" or the "Science
    of Scarcity"   2
Some Basic Economic Questions—Generally Stated   3

B. How Economists Go About Answering Their Questions   4

The Economist's Use of Models   4
Model Building   5
  • *The Basics*   5
  • *Where to Look for Flaws*   9
  • *What Makes Good Theory?*   10
  • *Choosing From Among Competing Theories*   11
The Approach We Will Follow—Building an Economic
    Model   12

---

2. AN ANALYSIS OF A SIMPLE SOCIETY AND THE FORCES THAT GIVE RISE TO COMPLEXITY   15

A. Assembling Our Tool Kit   16

The Consumption Side   16
The Production Side   21

iii

B. Model of a Simple Robinson Crusoe Society   25

The Basic Decision Rules   25
Adding a Time Dimension   32
A Note on Risk and Uncertainty   37
Concluding Our Analysis of a Simple Society   38

C. The Emergence of a Complex Society   39

Introducing the Complex Society   39
Factors That Give Rise to Complexity, Including the Division
   of Labor and the Gains from Trade   41
Role of Money in a Complex Society   45

**3. THE NEOCLASSICAL GENERAL COMPETITIVE
     EQUILIBRIUM MODEL OF A COMPLEX SOCIETY—
     EXCHANGE UNDER PERFECT COMPETITION   47**

A. Reviewing Our Assumptions   47

**B. How Markets Coordinate the Decisions of Individuals
   in a Perfectly Competitive Environment   49**

An Overview   49
The Demand Curve   52
The Supply Curve   53
Combining Supply and Demand   54

**C. Conditions that Determine Equilibrium in the Product
   Market   61**

Conditions That Determine Demand   61
   • *The Downward Slope of the Demand Curve   61*
   • *The Responsiveness of a Good or Service's Quantity Demanded
     to a Change in Its Own Price—Own Price Elasticity   63*
   • *The Responsiveness of a Good or Service's Demand and
     Quantity Demanded to a Change in Income or in the Price of a
     Related Good or Service—Income and Cross-Price
     Elasticity   70*
   • *Individual vs. Market Demand   73*
Conditions That Determine Supply   75
The Power of the Invisible Hand Under our Nice
   Assumptions   80

**D. Conditions that Determine Equilibrium in the Factor Market
   Given Our Nice Assumptions   81**

E. **Conclusion on the General Competitive Equilibrium Model   86**

Overview   86
Efficiency and Equity   88
Answering the Basic Microeconomic Questions Given Our
    Nice Assumptions   90

4. **RELAXING OUR "NICE " ASSUMPTIONS—GENERAL EQUILIBRIUM ANALYSIS   92**

A. **Market Power   93**

Introduction to Market Power   93
Naturally Occurring Market Power   94
Artificially Created Market Power   95
  • *Mobility—All Persons or Commodities Must Have Equal Access*
    to All Markets   96
  • *Information—All Persons Must Have Equal Access*
    to Information   96
Seeking Market Power   99
Conclusion   100

B. **Market Failure   101**
Externalities   101
Public Goods   106

5. **CONCLUSION OF OUR ANALYSIS OF THE MICROECONOMIC MODEL   107**

A. **The Role of Government in the Microeconomy: Policy Debate   107**

B. **An Example of the Complexity of Applied Microeconomic Analysis: Drug Policy   113**

C. **Conclusion   115**

6. **INTRODUCTION TO MACROECONOMICS   117**

A. **Overview   117**

B. **Defining Terms   120**

Introduction   120
National Product   120
Labor-Related Terms   121

Price Level: Inflation and Deflation   123
Real versus Nominal   127

7. BUILDING THE BASIC MACROECONOMIC MODEL   131

A. The Big Picture—Aggregate Demand/Aggregate Supply   131

B. Aggregate Demand   134

Aggregate Expenditure and Real Income—the Roots of
    Aggregate Demand   134
Deriving the Aggregate Demand Relationship   135
Aggregate Demand Shocks   140

C. Aggregate Supply   142

D. Combining Aggregate Demand, Aggregate Supply, and Long-Run Aggregate Supply   147

8. PUTTING THE BASIC MACROECONOMIC MODEL TO WORK: ANALYZING MACROECONOMIC SHOCKS AND MACROECONOMIC ADJUSTMENTS   152

A. Sources of Exogenous Aggregate Demand Shocks   152

How the Investment Level is Determined   153
    • *The Effect of Expectations on Investment—An Example*   *154*
How the Trade Balance Is Determined   156
How the Government's Budget Position Is
    Determined   165
Summary on Aggregate Demand Shocks   168

B. Sources of Exogenous Short-Run Aggregate Supply Shocks   169

C. The Working Model—A Summary   170

D. Macroeconomic Adjustments to Exogenous Shocks—the Micro/Macro Connection   171

Macroeconomic Adjustment Under the Nice Microeconomic
    Assumptions   171
    • *Condition 1: A GNP Gap*   *172*
    • *Condition 2: An Inflationary Gap*   *175*
Macroeconomic Adjustment in the Absence of the Nice
    Assumptions   178
Conclusion on the Micro/Macro Connection   179

9. MACROECONOMIC POLICY—THE TOOLS AND THE DEBATE 180

A. Background to Macroeconomic Policy 180
The Promise and the Problems 180
The Government's Role—Introducing the Debate 187

B. Monetary Policy 189
Introduction 189
How the Fed Influences the Money Supply 189
- *Open Market Operations and the Discount Rate* 189
- *On Banks and Reserves* 191
- *The Fractional Reserve System and the Multiplier Effect* 192

From Monetary Policy to Macroeconomic Results—
the Transmission Mechanism 196
Conclusion on Monetary Policy 200

C. Fiscal Policy 205

D. Trade Policy 214

E. The Problem With Policy 217

10. THE STATE OF THE NEOCLASSICAL THEORY 220

A. Historical Background—From J.B. Say to J.M. Keynes 220

B. The Current State of NeoClassical Theory 223

C. Resolving the Debate Within NeoClassical Theory—Problems 225
Overview 225
Theoretical versus Technical Definitions 226
Regression Techniques 230

D. Conclusion 231

APPENDIX: EXTENDERS 235

Index 349

Preface

The purpose of this book is to introduce you to the ideas that form the foundation of modern Western (NeoClassical) economic thought, to examine the basic framework (the model) that economists have built on this foundation, and to show how this model is applied to current issues facing individuals and society.

The book is rigorous, but it is not heavily mathematical. The only math skills you will need are basic algebra and geometry. The skills you will need to have carefully sharpened are the ability to reason and to follow the reasoning of others. The most important thing you can learn from this book is how to follow the thread of a powerful argument. By the time you finish it, you should understand and be able to explain and apply the fundamentals of Western mainstream (NeoClassical) economic theory.

There are a lot of parts to the theory, and each one can be studied in great detail. That is not our objective. We want to recognize the parts, to be able to identify their role in basic terms, and to explain how they all fit together. If we accomplish that goal, you will have an excellent foundation in NeoClassical analysis that you can apply to your study in other fields, to your everyday life as you read the newspaper, and to your participation as a citizen in our representative government. If you find the subject interesting, you will have an excellent foundation for further study within the field.

This book is the product of many hands. Professor Jerry Miner, Chairperson of the Syracuse University Department of Economics, has provided support in the form of resources and encouragement. Without his faith in the project, it would still be only a vision in my mind's eye. Dr. Robert M. Diamond, Syracuse University Assistant Vice Chancellor for Instructional Development, made available the services of the Center for Instructional Development. It was in the offices of CID and with the guidance of its staff that the vision became a design and the design became a product. My guide at CID was Chuck Spuches. Chuck encouraged, challenged, suggested, sup-

ix

ported, facilitated—in short, he made my sloppy handwritten scrawl on yellow legal pages into a book. When Chuck moved on to other challenges, Rob Pearson stepped in and did an excellent job of seeing the work to completion. As the book was being prepared for submission to the publisher, Alton Roberts provided valuable expertise in production of an appropriate manuscript. June Mermigos did all the word processing. Her lovely combination of professionalism and warmth made my life easier and more enjoyable. Martha Strain did all the original graphics. She has a wonderful ability to see with more than her eye. She captured the idea in each of my sketches and transformed it into a clear picture. Jesse Burkhead, the Maxwell Professor of Economics, generously donated his time to reading an earlier version of this text and offering constructive criticism. There are at this point several hundred students who also contributed to this book. Each semester as the development proceeded, they used the text and responded to my inquiries about it with very helpful constructive criticism. I have also benefited greatly from the excellent educational instincts and editorial eyes of the first group of Project Advance teachers to review this text. The last phase of the book's preparation brought me into contact with Bill Webber and Patrick Reynolds, at Prentice Hall. They have combined a solid professionalism with a human touch that I appreciate. I have been blessed with a very special support group. To all of these people I wish to express thanks.

I have tried to create a stimulating book that will serve as a valuable educational tool by informing you and then challenging you to think beyond the information it offers. If it is successful, it will be *our* success—yours for patiently working through the model presented, that of those people named above for their valuable contributions, mine for the effort I put into it, and my wife Celia's for supporting and encouraging me throughout that effort.

This book is dedicated to the memory of Mr. Herbert Behrend. Mr. Behrend taught me algebra, chemistry, and physics in high school, but more than that, he taught me the meaning of vision. He showed me that to study one dimension of human experience is valid only if that study is set into a vision of the many dimensions of experience. In his classroom I learned physics in the context of its history and its relationship to the development of the arts and literature. He was truly a man of vision. I hope that I have honored his memory by communicating some measure of that vision herein.

Introduction

It seems that a good place to begin this book is with what my wife refers to as a "taster." While I'm cooking dinner, she'll come in to ask for a taster—a little taste of whatever it is—so she can tell what dinner will be like. If the taster is good, it whets her appetite for more. If not, she prepares to endure dinner. Here I want to give you a taster of the power of economic theory and its relevance to your life that I hope will whet your appetite for economics.

Generally speaking, economics is about how you and I and everyone else makes choices, and how all of our individual choices affect one another. So the basic issue is choice. Economists assume that the basic motivation for your behavior is a desire to maximize the satisfaction (utility) you get out of life. Economists envision you as deciding each choice by making lightning calculations (generally unconsciously) of the consequences of each available option and the satisfaction you would receive from each set of consequences. You will, according to economists, choose the option that gives you the greatest expected satisfaction. The satisfaction (and dissatisfaction) associated with each available option are the incentives (and disincentives) to choose that option. Thus you and I make choices on the basis of the incentives we face—and so it is for everyone.

Let's take an immediate case in point. You have chosen to spend some of your time studying this book. (Remember the phrase "spend time." It should take on new meaning as you spend more time reading this book.) Why do you choose to spend your time studying?

When you were in the seventh grade, if you studied at all, it was probably at least in part because your parents either punished you for not studying or rewarded you for doing so. In other words, whatever studying you did was in response to the incentives you faced:

"If you don't have that report written, you're not going to the party on Saturday."

OR

"If the report is written by Saturday, we'll take you to the movies."

xi

You still respond to incentives, but now both you and the kinds of incentives you face have changed dramatically. You have toiled through many years of school, you are in the prime of your life, your parents have much less leverage over you—so why do you choose to go on to more pressure and more toil? Why are you in college, sitting here reading an assigned text? It's not required by law, your parents can't make you, and there are other good ways to spend your time. You could get a job, start earning a living immediately, and after supper you wouldn't have to hit the books. You could start enjoying life now. Why are you putting yourself through this grind instead?

According to economic theory, by making this choice, you have revealed that, of all the available options, you prefer college. This choice (college) must, therefore, give you more satisfaction (utility) than any of the available alternatives. Yet anyone who's been there knows that college can be an exhausting, nerve-wracking, even a brutal experience. Why would anyone "prefer" college?

Economists have an explanation that includes three parts. First of all, some people derive immediate satisfaction from exploring and learning new ideas, from meeting new people from places they've never been, from going to parties and athletic events, or from some combination of these elements of college life. If any one of these applies to you, then your attendance can be explained, at least in part, by these incentives. You are, in economic terms, consuming (deriving immediate satisfaction from) college.

There is also an investment aspect to attending college. School is like any other investment. You pay now in order to reap benefits (satisfaction) later. Your current payment is made in three ways. There's the direct payment (tuition, room, and board), there's the indirect payment (earnings you forgo by not taking a job immediately after high school), and there is the payment in kind (sweat and blood). Your benefit from the investment is the *likelihood* (remember, with any investment there is risk) that your future income and lifestyle, and therefore your future satisfaction in life, will be better than they would have been if you had started working directly out of high school.

Since it's unlikely that the consumption aspects alone attract most people to college, most of you are probably making an investment. The second and third parts of an economist's explanation of your decision relate to choice as an investment. Economists explain this investment in two ways:

1. *Human capital theory.* Human capital theory simply extends the logic of capital investment from machines to humans. We invest in education for the same reason we invest in machines; it makes us

more productive. Being more productive means high earnings. Thus we spend money directly (tuition) and indirectly (forgone earnings) now in order to make more money later. So long as the rate of the return on the human capital investment is enough to convince us to forgo current consumption—and is at least as good as alternative investments—we choose school.

2. *Signaling theory.* Those who hold this alternative view of the human investment process argue that school doesn't make us more productive, it just allows us to signal our superior productivity. According to this view, people who are more productive (owing to genetics, dedication, or determination) need a way to signal that difference to prospective employers. A college diploma serves as such a signal. If nothing else, it tells employers that you have the ability to stay at a long and sometimes difficult task until it is done.

Notice that the three parts of this explanation are not mutually exclusive. You may be in college to acquire productve skills *and* because you believe a college degree is a useful signal, *but* you may also be enjoying the process and the enviroment.

Thus economic theory of educational choice helps us understand why people choose school. Consider yourself. Why are you here? If you think about it, you'll probably find that the theory provides a very useful explanation of your own behavior. Even more impressive and useful is the fact that the theory can also help us predict behavior.

While an economist studying the behavior of prospective college students won't have a lot of information on any one individual, she can often get some basic information on a lot of individuals—a class or a generation. With this information and the economic theory of educational choice outlined above, an economist can often make some generally accurate and useful predictions about the behavior of the group as a whole.

For instance, if it is correct that most students think of college in large measure as an investment, then it must also be true that students' choices of majors will reflect their expectations about the kinds of jobs to which those majors will lead. Using the theory, we can predict, therefore, that as expectations about job prospects change, so will college students' choices of majors.

This is a simple application of the basic premise that choices are made on the basis of incentives. Clearly, as incentives change, choices will change. To continue our example, if getting a good job is a primary incentive for attending college and if job prospects change, then the major that students choose at college should change in response to the changed incentives. Evidence seems to support the theory.

In the 1960s the baby boom generation was moving into and through the public schools. That created a lot of teaching opportunities. In response to this incentive, college students flowed into departments of education, confident that plenty of opportunities awaited them when they finished. As the bulge of baby boomers passed out of the schools, the opportunities in education contracted. In response to this change in incentives, students entering college began to flow into departments other than education.

During the 1980s there has been a significant increase in the number of college students choosing business-related majors. This presumably reflects a perception on their part that there are good opportunities and salaries to be had in business. If this increasing supply of business majors expands faster than the demand, then eventually the number and quality of opportunities available to each graduating business major will decline. As that happens, other opportunities will begin to be relatively more attractive—in other words, the structure of incentives will change. When this new perception about future opportunities filters its way through college and high school campuses, students will adjust their behavior accordingly by moving into majors that lead to the newly blossoming opportunities. The chart below reflects the change in choice of majors from the early 1970s to the early 1980s.

'In' and 'Out' Degrees

The latest figures from the United States Department of Education on undergraduate fields of study confirm that today's college students are keeping their eyes glued to the job market. Business and management, which ranked behind education and the social sciences in the number of degrees awarded in 1974, surged ahead by 1984. Other large gainers were computer and information science, communications and engineering — degrees that can immediately result in jobs. Losers were traditional liberal-arts specialties, such as education, literature, language study, philosophy and religion.

Bachelor's degrees conferred by institutions of higher education

Program Areas	1973–74	1983–84	% Change*
Business and Management	131,766	230,031	75%
Communications	16,250	38,586	137
Computer and Info Sciences	4,756	32,172	576
Education	185,225	92,382	−50
Engineering	42,840	75,732	77
Foreign Languages	18,840	9,479	−50

Program Areas	1973–74	1983–84	% Change*
Health Sciences	41,394	64,338	55
English	55,469	33,739	−39
Library and Archival Sciences	1,164	255	−78
Life Sciences	48,340	38,640	−20
Mathematics	21,635	13,211	−39
Philosophy and Religion	9,444	6,435	−32
Physical Sciences	21,178	23,671	12
Psychology	51,821	39,872	−23
Social Sciences	150,298	93,212	−38

* Minus indicates declines *Source Center for Statistics. U.S. Department of Education* The New York Times, Aug. 3, 1986

By understanding the direction and degree of responsiveness individuals exhibit when their opportunities and thus their incentives change, economists are able to make predictions about an individual's or a group of individuals' response to a particular opportunity change. The ability to make that sort of prediction is often very valuable. Consider the military draft.

Right now the United States has no draft. When it did have one, the military could compel you to show up and serve your country. Since your option was to show up or to go to jail, the incentive to show up when called was strong. The military had no need to create a pay incentive to get you, the incentive to participate was a very effective stick (Fort Levenworth—the prison). There was no need for the military to offer a carrot (high pay). However, when the draft was eliminated, the situation changed dramatically. There was no longer a stick. In order to get men and women to join, the military had to make that choice appealing enough so that an adequate number of eligible young people would choose it over all other available opportunities.

When unemployment is high, recruiting is not very difficult. After all, during hard times, there are not many other decent opportunities for young people. However, when the national economy is strong, just the opposite is true. The military must compete with lots of good opportunities by offering better pay and benefits, and by advertising what a great job it is.

If the United States gets involved in another conventional war, the need for recruits will expand rapidly. In order to meet their requirements the military services will either have to increase the benefits of serving (which is very expensive), appeal to everyone's patriotism (which in most wars hasn't produced enough enlistments), or reinstate the draft. This prediction is based on economic theory. So, you see, even the draft—and most of you are draft age—has an economic dimension.

In fact, almost everything you do has an economic dimension. That would be true even if you lived all by yourself like Robinson Crusoe, because you would still have to make choices. The economic dimension of your life is all the more complex because, unlike Crusoe, you live in a world of human interaction; that is, your choices affect the choices made by others and vice versa. It is this pervasiveness of economics—the fact that it is such a fundamental part of our lives—that makes it such an interesting and important subject.

When you look out the window at the world, it seems so complicated. As you sit here, it may even seem scary. You have hopes and dreams. Surely your mind wanders from the immediate world to that imaginary world of what you'd like to be and do, and you wonder to yourself: "How do I get there from here? Am I wasting my time in school? What should I be doing?"

Well, the world is complicated and this text can't make it any less so. But it can help you understand the world a bit better and maybe if you understand it better you will be less threatened by it and more empowered to shape your own future. As the text will make clear, some forces are within your control (you are free to make some choices) and other forces are beyond your control (they constrain the opportunities from which you can choose). No human being can ever have absolute control over his or her destiny, but the more you understand about how the world works, the more effectively you can use the power you do have.

This book is written to help you understand "how the world works." Economics is not the whole story of how the world works; there are also social, political, ethical, and natural forces that move the world. It is, however, a very important part of that story.

At the end of the body of the text is a lengthy section called "Extenders." These are provided, as the name implies, to extend the content of the text. They were placed at the end of the book so they would not interrupt the flow of the logic developed in the body of the text. As you read through the text, you will see marginal notes that refer you to the extenders. The note will appear as shown in Figure 0-1. These notes provide an unobstrusive signal that the subject being covered is extended in the appendix.

Extender Number   *E*   *P*   Page Found On

FIGURE 0-1

There are three kinds of extenders:

1. *Technical:* These provide a more rigorous graphical analysis of a relationship derived in the body of the text. If you plan to take courses beyond the introductory level, you should master these techniques.

2. *Conceptual:* These present a more detailed look at a concept covered in the body of the text.

3. *Newspaper articles:* These show how the content of the text can be applied to reading the newspaper. The articles are not current—it is impossible for a publication other than today's newspaper to have today's news. Rather, they were chosen for their generic value. If you see how the content of the text applies in the articles examined, you should be able to do a similar application to issues making the daily news as you are reading the text. Buy the newspaper and try to do this as you read the text. If you master that application of your knowledge, the content of the text will be of permanent value to you.

Overview

This Overview is written to serve two purposes. As you begin, it gives you an impression of the course we will follow. Later, as we are making our way through that course, it will serve as your verbal map. You should reread the Overview as you work your way through the text in order to put each new issue we examine in a larger perspective, thus constantly orienting yourself.

In order to accomplish our purpose, we will follow the Western mainstream (NeoClassical) channel in economic thought. Our course will begin in general philosophy, move on to basic NeoClassical microeconomic theory, and then to basic NeoClassical macroeconomic theory. At the end of our journey we will look back and critically examine the NeoClassical model we have studied.

We begin with general philosophy because the first question we must answer is: Why do scientists build models? We are, after all, about to spend a lot of time examining one such model, so it is reasonable to begin with this question. Once we convince ourselves that model building is worthwhile, we will then spend some time examining how it is done. It is much easier to understand a model, to recognize its strengths and weaknesses, if you know how it was built.

When this very general philosophical background is complete, we will narrow our focus a bit and look at the specific issues involved in social science model building. There are problems in social science model building that most natural sciences do not face, and there are even some problems that are unique to social science models. We want to identify those problems so that we can be aware of their potential impact on the economic model we will study. From the broad social science perspective we will narrow our focus further to the field of economics. In order to do so we will distinguish economics from the other social sciences by identifying the basic issue that gives rise to economic questions: the "quandary of choice."

Having specified and explained the basic questions that economists seek to answer about society, we will begin our analysis in the context of the simplest of societies: a Robinson Crusoe society (i.e., a one-person society). In this context we will build a simple economic model. As we shall see, the model of this simple world is almost trival, but not quite so. It does, at least, give us a basic framework for the systematic analysis of our basic economic questions. This will prove useful when we turn our attention to a much more complicated context: a complex society.

A complex society is one in which there are a number of interdependent individuals. Our study of this society will begin with an examination of the forces that give rise to interdependence. Why, we will wonder, do individuals give up independence and accept the vulnerability that comes with interdependence? Our guide in answering this question will be Adam Smith, the man who, in 1776, wrote the first basic, full-scale work in economics, *The Wealth of Nations*. From him we will learn why simplicity gives way to complexity in a society and how markets can serve as a mechanism for coordinating individual choice decisions so that complexity does not become a road to chaos.

After this introduction to complexity by Adam Smith we will turn our attention to the model of individual behavior in a complex society (a "micro" model) presented by the father of modern NeoClassical microeconomic theory, Alfred Marshall (*Principles of Economics*, 1890). The microeconomic model that Marshall proposed is in its essentials the one NeoClassical theorists still use today. We will develop the basic model and apply it to some current issues in order to see it in action. We will find that the policy implications of the micro model depend on how well one believes the market system works and how coherently one believes policy can be organized.

When we complete our study of the microeconomic model we will look at the economy from a different perspective. Rather than looking through a microscope at the actions and interactions of individuals, we will examine the economy at the level of society as a whole. This latter perspective is called a "macro" view. We will develop a model of the macroeconomy. As we do so, we will pay special attention to the logical connections between the micro- and macroeconomic models. During our development of the macro model, we will refer to actual macroeconomic data and consider that information in light of our analyses. We will begin by studying the nation's macroeconomy in isolation, and then we will expand our model to include the impact of international trade.

When we have completed the macro model, we will examine its implications under varying assumptions about the microeconomic system. We will see that the basic macroeconomic model is consistent with different interpretations depending on the assumptions one makes about how well the microeconomic system works. These different interpretations are the basis for the debate at the cutting edge of current economic theory, and are fundamental to the different policy prescriptions that you are currently reading about in the newspaper or hearing espoused by various economists and political leaders on television.

We will see that there is a continuum of views within the NeoClassical mainstream, and that this continuum can be represented by identifying its two poles. The economists at one pole believe that the complex system is analogous to the simple Robinson Crusoe system. They view the system as self-correcting and believe, therefore, that there is no need for government intervention. The economists at the other pole contend that, unlike the simple system, the complex system does not always self-correct. As a result, they believe that there can be breakdowns in the aggregate economy (e.g., unemployment) that may make government intervention necessary.

Once we identify the microeconomic foundations of this macroeconomic policy debate over whether the government should intervene, we will turn our attention to how government does, by design or accident, influence the economy. The major influences we will examine are monetary policy (the supply of money the government generates), fiscal policy (the government's spending and taxation policy), and international trade policy. In each case we will identify the government institution(s) that exert(s) some control over these policies, and how that control is exercised. As each macroeconomic institution is introduced, we will present the opposing noninterventionist and interventionist views on what the policy of that institution should be.

Having examined the basis for the debate within the NeoClassical mainstream, we will review the evolution of that debate in the history of mainstream theory and the current state of that debate. We will find that prior to John Maynard Keynes, the traditional or Classical theorists generally held that, although the model of a complex society was more complicated than that for a simple society, the same basic principles applied whether the model was applied in a simple Robinson Crusoe society or a complex society. Keynes rejected this extrapolation from simple to complex, arguing instead that a complex society was by the very nature of its complexity fundamentally different in the aggregate. Keynes's book, *The General Theory of Employment, Interest and Money* (published in 1936), refocused attention on macroeconomic (aggregate) issues. Since *The General Theory* a large number of economists have turned their attention to macroeconomic theory. We will find that in more recent times there has been a resurgence of the traditional or Classical (as Keynes referred to it) view. This new view is referred to as the New Classical or the Rational

Expectations perspective. We will examine this new view and contrast it with its primary competitor—the Keynesian view.

Upon completion of our study of NeoClassical micro- and macro-economic theory, we will look at the problems of testing the model that make it possible for two opposing versions of mainstream theory to coexist, one unable to clearly prove its superiority over the other. Finally, we will conclude with some thoughts on why all this is so important for our future.

The Subject and Method of Economics

Economics is the science which studies human behaviour as a relationship between ends and scarce means which have alternative uses.

Lionel Robbins
An Essay on the Nature and Significance of Economic Science, 1932.

THIS BOOK presents the western, mainstream economic ideas, and the economic issues that arise when those ideas are applied to the real world.

Economists' ideas are based on the application of the scientific method to the study of economics. In this chapter we will examine that method in order to understand the framework within which economists think about our subject: economics. We will find that scientific analysis always begins with a clear definition of the terms to be used. Thus the best place to begin this book is with the most famous definition of economics—the one by Lionel Robbins given above.

A. THE SUBJECT MATTER OF ECONOMICS

What Is Economics About?

Economics is a science that studies the implications of the "quandary of choice." We all face this quandary because of one unavoidable fact of life:

Human beings have virtually limitless desires and yet are endowed with limited resources. This means that as individuals and as societies we are forced to make choices.

1

The "Quandary of Choice" or the "Science of Scarcity"

Surely you have been faced with the quandary of choice. Whenever you buy something, you spend that money and it is gone. Since you have limited funds, you cannot buy everything you might want. Therefore, whenever you spend money on one thing, you are giving up the opportunity to spend that limited resource, money, on something else. Economists call the best forgone opportunity the *opportunity cost* of the choice you have made. It is this cost of choosing—the fact that any choice you make in a world of limited resources has an opportunity cost—that gives rise to the "quandary of choice."

What if you had a zillion dollars? Would you still face the quandary of choice? It seems that a zillion dollars would be enough to buy anything your heart could possibly desire. Let us assume it is. Let us assume you have all the money you could ever need. Then you have escaped the quandary—right? Wrong! To enjoy all that you want requires not only money, it requires time. Even if you had all the money you could ever hope to spend, your time resources would still be limited. You are only 16, 20, 30, or 50 years old for a year. You cannot save up those years and use them later. Life, as time, goes by. You may be able to prolong your life with money, but by 80 or 90, or almost certainly by 100, your time resources will be exhausted, your life will be over. The lesson here is that time is a scarce resource for everyone, so all of us, from the richest to the poorest, face the quandary of choice as individuals.

Does society also face the quandary of choice? Yes. Society faces a problem that is just the opposite of that confronting the individual. For the individual, the natural resources of the earth are so great that relative to his or her wants, they are virtually infinite. Time is the individual resource that is inevitably scarce. A society, or at least humankind in general, could possibly go on forever, so for humankind time is not scarce. Humankind, however, includes lots of individuals. There are several billions of us now. Relative to the needs and desires of all these people, the resources of the earth are scarce. Since the earth's resources are not growing and the number of people is, humankind also faces the quandary of choice.

When economists examine the consequences of this quandary of choice at the level of the individual, they are studying what is called *microeconomics.* "Micro" comes from the Greek word *mikros,* meaning "little" or "small." As the name implies, microeconomics looks through a microscope at individuals and how they interact as they seek to resolve the quandary they face.

When economists inquire into the consequences of this quandary of choice at the level of a society, they are studying what is called macroeconomics. "Macro" comes from the Greek word *makros*, meaning "large." *Macroeconomics* is the study of how the quandary affects humankind in large groups—in other words, at the level of whole societies.

The quandary of choice raises a series of questions for individuals and societies, and it is these questions that define the subject of economics. The search for a single theory that will answer these questions is the work of economists.

Some Basic Economic Questions—Generally Stated

1. How are decisions on the use of our scarce resources determined? In other words, what goods and services are to be produced and in what quantities? (*Resource allocation*)

2. How do we determine the optimal (best) method for producing goods and services? In other words, by what methods are goods and services to be produced? (*Efficiency*)

3. How is the value (relative worth) of goods and services determined? (*Value determination*)

4. How is the division of the value produced by people determined—that is, who gets what share? (*Income distribution*)

5. What determines society's capacity to produce? What determines how much society is currently producing? (*National product*)

6. Why are society's available resources sometimes less than fully utilized? Or, to put it differently, why would some of society's available resources be idle? Under what circumstances would such a condition persist? (*Unemployment*)

7. What determines society's ability to expand productive capacity over time? (*Growth*)

8. What is money? Why do societies use money? If a society uses money, why does the purchasing power of money sometimes change over time? Under what circumstances would such a change continue? (*Inflation or deflation*)

Notice that the questions address two levels of activity.

As we said, microeconomics examines the economy through a microscope—it is the study of the behavior of individual actors in the context of finite initial endowments. The first four questions above are microeconomic questions.

Macroeconomics examines broader relationships—it is the study of economic aggregates, the ebb and flow of a society's economic behavior. The last four questions are macroeconomic questions.

B. HOW ECONOMISTS GO ABOUT ANSWERING THEIR QUESTIONS

The Economist's Use of Models

Economists attempt to answer their questions by designing theories. A *theory* is an abstract representation of how our world, or at least some part of it, works. The object of a theory is to explain and predict. If a theory can explain some part of the world around us, it gives us an appreciation for what forces are acting in that part and how those forces interact. For a theory to predict what will happen in some part of our world, it must be able, given a set of initial conditions, to describe how conditions will change when the balance of forces is changed.

Designing theories is not something that only economists do. All scientists design theories. Sir Isaac Newton explained a great deal of what we observe in our world by his theories of physics. His theories also allow us to predict fairly accurately the activity of masses. For instance, his gravitational law explains the attraction between masses and allows us to predict, all other conditions being constant, the velocity and acceleration at any moment of a ball released near the earth.

Similarly, in economics we have the law of demand. This law explains the relationship between the price of a good or service and the quantity of that good or service that people will choose to demand. The law predicts that, if all other conditions are held constant, as the price goes up, the quantity demanded will fall.

When the design of a theory is sufficiently well developed, a scientist is in a position to use that design as a blueprint for building a model. A *model* is the formal, concrete presentation of a theory. It may take the form of words or equations on paper, or it may be a three-dimensional structure. A scientist transforms theory into a model when she believes that her ideas are designed well enough so that the concrete presentation of those ideas—the constructed model—will withstand the tests to which she and other scientists will subject it. A test of a model is done in order to see if it is a useful representation of the world that warrants further consideration and work.

Before we begin examining an economic model in some detail, it will be useful to spend some time investigating how scientists, including economists, design theories and build models. By inquiring into the design and construction process, we will be in a much better position to carefully scrutinize the finished product we will be studying: an economic model. After all, if you know how something is designed and built, you are in a much better position to evaluate the quality of its construction.

Consider the following case. You find a beautiful old home that you would love to buy. It has the hardwood floors, the bookshelves, the fireplace, the porch, the yard—everything you have dreamed of having in a home. A structural engineer inspects it and advises you not to buy it. She says that it is going to collapse because of problems with the foundation. Sadly, but wisely, you decide not to buy.

Models are like houses in some respects. Some can be very elegant and/or comfortable in appearance, and therefore very attractive. But there is more to judging a model than surface appearances. A crucial question one must always ask is: How well is it built? To answer that you have to get behind the walls and under the floors to see how it was built. And to be able to judge what you see behind the walls and under the floors, you have to know how a home or a model *should* be built and where to look for problems.

In order to be informed evaluators of the economic model we will be examining, we turn our attention first to how theories are designed and models are built.

Model Building

• *The Basics* People build models because they want to understand how the world around them works and because they want to be able to predict changes in that world. We often wonder at what we observe, and for the sake of curiosity or comfort, we seek to understand the order that gives rise to what we see. To accomplish this we look behind what the eye can see. We look with the mind's eye for those "invisible chains which bind together all these disjointed objects" (Adam Smith, "History of Astronomy," in *Essays on Philosophical Subjects*). The better our model, the more effectively we can explain what we observe and the more likely we are to be able to predict what we will observe in the future. This power satisfies the curiosity. It also provides comfort because it allows us, where possible, to control events or, where control is impossible, to prepare for the inevitable.

We will call this process of model building the *scientific process*. Our objective here is to trace the steps in this scientific process in order to understand how a model is built. By doing so, we will be able to identify those crucial points that must be carefully scrutinized when judging the strength of a model.

The first step in the scientific process is the adoption of the most fundamental scientific assumption. An *assumption* is a specification of the conditions one is taking as given in all that follows. The condition all scientists must take as given as they begin the process of model building is that there is in fact some *order* to the world that can be recognized and represented by a model. If there were no order, there could be no theory to design or model to build, for all events would be random. There would be no connecting principles, no systematic relationships to report.

This assumption of an order comes to us very easily. We see the sun rise and set daily, the seasons come and go yearly, and lives begin and end with each new generation. The order of nature seems so obvious that we take it for granted, and yet it is so incredibly complex that we only understand its most rudimentary principles. In fact, we do not know that there is any perpetual underlying order. As a religious person, one takes it on faith; as a scientist, one assumes an order.

Having made the assumption that there is an order to be recognized, represented, and reported, the next step in the process is *observation*. A scientist observes two things. She observes the world around her, the events that her theory will be designed to connect. This is "looking out the window" to see how the world appears. She also observes the theories of others who have preceded her. These are the reported representations of the order that she can find in books or in classrooms. No one starts from scratch. All scientists learn from previous theories—from their strengths and weaknesses. By examining theories that are at the cutting edge of one's field (physics, economics, astronomy, etc.), and by studying the history of the development of the ideas in that field, a scientist sees how her predecessors extended the edge of the field. This knowledge, combined with one's own human experience—the facts, feelings, observations, and so on that one has assembled in one's mind—is the material from which the scientist draws as she forms her own vision of how the world works.

A *vision*, according to a famous economist named Joseph Schumpeter, is a "preanalytic cognitive act" (Joseph A. Schumpeter, *History of Economic Analysis*, 1954). It is, in other words, that rudimentary design one draws in one's mind's eye before the formal process of analysis begins. It is the synthesis of all the raw material one brings to the project of theory design that establishes the starting point for the project of theory design and model building.

If I told you to draw a blueprint of your ideal home, you would have to follow similar steps. First you would have to assemble the raw material in your mind's eye: views of places you have seen, places you have heard about, places you have dreamed about. Then you would scan all these images, picking and choosing elements from each. Finally, you would assemble all the elements into a coherent whole—a vision of your ideal home. Then, and only then, would you be in a position to pick up a pen and begin to represent that vision.

The process of theory design and model building begins the same way: with a vision. There is, however, a difference between representing our dream home and representing the order that surrounds us. There is no one correct version of a dream home. Whatever you choose to draw is correct. If as we assume, however, there is a unique order surrounding us that the scientist is attempting to represent, then there can be incorrect visions of that order.

Continuing to follow Schumpeter's description of the steps in the scientific process, the next one is the analytic effort. *Analysis* is that part of the scientific process in which the vision is formalized. It begins by drawing a theoretical design. Then the design is transformed into a concrete model. Quoting Schumpeter: "The first step [in analysis] is to verbalize the vision or to conceptualize it in such a way that its elements take their places with names attached to them that facilitate recognition and manipulation, in more or less orderly schema or picture." In other words, it is during this first stage of analysis that the scientist defines her terms and arranges them so that the relationships among terms become clear.

Schumpeter refers to this step as assembling a "box of tools." Defining terms clearly is absolutely necessary. If the designer's definitions are sloppy, then others who try to follow the analysis will give different meanings to the same terms and thereby totally misunderstand the structure of the design. If, for instance, an economic theory uses the term *utility* to mean something like "satisfaction," but an uninformed reader interprets utility to mean something like "an adequate substitute" (e.g., a utility infielder in baseball), then the reader will not be able to follow the logic of the design. A poor tool kit leads to poor construction.

For similar reasons the arrangement of terms must be done clearly. If terms are clearly defined but the arrangement is vague, or if there are inexplicable gaps in the arrangement, the reader will not be in a position to follow the logic of the design. Poor workmanship leads to poor construction.

As the model is framed, additional assumptions are made in order to simplify the problem of analysis. The world is an incredibly intricate web of connections. Since no scientist studies the whole order of the universe simultaneously, all scientists are required to isolate that piece of the web they want to study in detail. The traditional technique for accomplishing this is to assume a specific, fixed set of conditions that prevail in the surrounding environment. This tool of analysis, *assumption*, allows the scientist to abstract from changes in surrounding conditions that may in fact have an impact on the area or subject under scrutiny. Assumptions are necessary because otherwise scientists could only study the universe as a single whole. While this is the most realistic way to study the universe, it is also the most difficult—so difficult that it is virtually impossible. Thus, while assumptions may be unrealistic, they are made in order to simplify the problem. The structure of a model should make the order it is built to represent clear without being trite. To do so, scientists abstract from complication (by assumption), while at the same time trying to capture the essence of the order.

As the scientist works out the details of her design according to her original vision, it is inevitable that flaws will become obvious and adjustments will have to be made in definitions, arrangements, or the underlying vision. Initially, this adjustment process takes place entirely in the mind of the individual scientist. As the scientist becomes more confident, she will share her model with trusted colleagues, who will judge it on the basis of their experience and offer feedback. This feedback leads to further adjustments. Once the model is well developed, the scientist subjects it to formal empirical testing. In economics this often takes the form of a statistical technique known as *regression analysis*. If the empirical testing tends to support the model, the scientist reports her model and the supporting empirical evidence to others, generally scholars studying similar issues. This is done by publishing the information in a journal devoted to the topic she has investigated.

At this point the model and its supporting empirical evidence have entered the marketplace of ideas. If the marketplace is functioning in an unbiased manner, the scientist's model will be examined on its merits. Some scholars will trace the logic of the model's theoretical design for flaws. Others will examine the empirical analysis for any flaws in the technique applied. Still others will replicate the empirical analysis in order to ensure that the results are independent of the conditions not otherwise taken as given by the scientist who presented the model. This testing process leads to rejection, modification, or tentative acceptance of the model.

Now we will briefly review the scientific process with an eye out for points where flaws are most likely to occur and what the nature of those flaws might be.

• *Where to Look for Flaws* The first place to look for flaws is where the process begins: the scientist's vision. Schumpeter argues that all visions are flawed by what he refers to as "ideology." He says that "vision is ideological almost by definition." When our mind's eye reviews the reality we have taken in through our senses, it distorts what our eye sees. The shape of this distortion in our mind's eye is our ideology. As a result of this distortion, our mind sees reality through biased eyes.

Schumpeter believes that everyone has such a distortion, an ideology. He says, however, that this flaw does not automatically make everyone's theories totally flawed, and therefore all theories useless. His point is that as we review any theory, we must be wary of its ideological bias. He notes that in subjects where theories are easily and accurately tested, it is fairly easy to eliminate these biases. Unfortunately, economics is not such a subject, so we must be aware that biases may be embodied in theory. Still, we must not be so suspicious that we throw away valuable insights because we are too skeptical.

The next step in the process of theory design and model building is the beginning of analysis. At this point terms are defined and arranged, and assumptions are introduced. There are several potential flaws that may enter here. Vague definitions or leaps of faith can often be found in the structural foundation of a theory. Sloppy specification of assumptions is another flaw that is not uncommon. Often the presence of these flaws is not accidental. Malleable definitions or assumptions make it possible to adjust a theory to suit test results, and therefore make the theory difficult to refute. A theory built on such a movable foundation may have staying power, but it has very little value. Rather than finding that outcomes conform to the theory's prediction, we find that the theory's prediction conforms to the outcomes.

During the next step in the analytic effort, the theory is reviewed, tested, and critiqued by a successively wider audience. At the end of each cycle in this process, the theory is either rejected and discarded or it is adjusted to correct for flaws identified during the process. If the process were perfect, all error would eventually be eliminated from the theory. There is, however, a major limitation in the quality of this effort. Our methods for testing, especially in the social sciences, are far from perfect. The social sciences suffer from particularly difficult testing conditions because (1) it is difficult to study human beings without distorting the behavior of the subjects, (2) all but the most benign of controlled experimental settings are taboo, (3) the scientist is a member of the human population and therefore has a vested interest in the findings.

This leads to two problems. First of all, since the testing methods are imperfect, error may escape even the eye of a perfectly unbiased observer. Second, since there are no perfectly unbiased observers ("impartial spectators," as Adam Smith referred to them), error is determined in the biased eye of the beholder. As a result of competing interpretations of test results, it is possible for two competing theories, each with strong supporters, to coexist.

This is what one finds in economics, wherein the two dominant theories are NeoClassical theory and Marxist theory. Both theories have strong supporters. Both have spawned journals in which believers share their ideas. Neither theory has prevailed over the other because each presents evidence to support its point of view while attacking the evidence presented by the opponent as invalid because it is based on flawed testing.

As we said at the outset, in this book we will focus on NeoClassical theory. The choice is based on three facts: (1) covering both theories is beyond the expertise of the writer; (2) NeoClassical theory has many strengths that recommend it; (3) NeoClassical theory dominates Western economic thought, so those who live in that environment should be fluent in this theory and able to recognize its strengths and weaknesses.

Before we begin to examine NeoClassical microeconomic and macroeconomic theory, there is one last methodological question we should take up. It is a question one must ask if one is to make a choice between competing theories such as NeoClassical and Marxist.

• *What Makes Good Theory?* It is important to begin this discussion of what makes good theory with a disclaimer: All of the following rests, as does the whole exercise of theory design, on the assumption that there is, in fact, an order to the universe. This fundamental assumption is just that, an assumption—an assertion of a condition that for the sake of the argument is taken as given. What follows has no meaning if this assumption is not valid. The validity of this assumption is an endlessly debatable point. We avoid the debate by assumption. So it goes in theory design and model building.

Now we restate the question at hand: Assuming there is an order, what makes good theory? Or, stated in a slightly different way: By what criteria can we judge the quality of a theory?

The criterion that is currently the most widely accepted as an important measure of the quality of a theory is the theory's ability to predict accurately. By *predict* we mean that given the current balance of forces (a set of initial conditions), if one of those forces is altered, the theory should be able to describe the situation that will prevail when the new balance (the revised set of conditions) is achieved.

A second criterion is the ability of the theory to explain. By *explain* we mean that a theory describes what forces are acting and how those forces interact as they move the world from an initial condition to a new condition. Notice that to explain is a much trickier business than to predict. Prediction simply requires identifying the concluding condition given an initial stimulus. Explanation requires describing the whole intermediate process from initial stimulus to concluding condition.

Some scientists would argue that explanation is a fairy tale since more often than not we cannot directly observe the process of change. For example, when you explain that a ball drops because of gravity—what is this gravity stuff? Can you show it to me? No. These scientists argue that the story does not matter so long as the prediction is correct. Other scientists would argue that human curiosity compels us to try to explain as well as predict. They would say further that if two theories predict equally well, it is reasonable to prefer the one that presents a more plausible explanation. Finally, they would argue that explanation is a key to development of a theory's predictive power since explanation makes it possible to identify how the theory can be adjusted to different conditions.

This is not a matter we must resolve here. The point is that you recognize that these are some suggested criteria. If the issue at debate interests you, then you would probably enjoy reading more about the philosophy of science.

If we accept the view that explanation matters, there are several more criteria we can identify that relate to the quality of explanation. One of these is efficiency. The criterion of efficiency is often referred to as the standard of Occam's razor. This standard holds that, all else being equal, a simpler theory is preferred to a more complex one.

Closely related to the criterion of efficiency is that of scope. Again, all else being equal, a theory with a wider scope of explanation and prediction is preferred. Scope and efficiency are often a trade-off, however. A gain in one frequently implies a loss in the other.

Other criteria include internal consistency—a theory with a logical inconsistency built into it is less preferred; and completeness—theories that require leaps of faith are less preferred.

• **Choosing From Among Competing Theories** Given these criteria, how do we choose among competing theories? The easiest condition under which to make a choice is when all of the criteria but one are equal. In that case, the one unequal quality (e.g., the quality of prediction) determines choice. Unfortunately, this condition rarely, if ever, prevails. In lieu of such a clear choice, one must decide the quality of each theory by comparing theories with respect to each criterion and then determining how much weight to give each criterion. Only in this way is it possible to make a direct comparison between theories.

The Approach We Will Follow—Building an Economic Model

As we have seen, economic questions arise because of the quandary of choice and it is the job of economists to answer these questions. Doing so requires a model that explains and predicts choices and their consequences. One model that claims to do so is the NeoClassical model. It is this model that dominates the thinking of most Western economists, and this is the one that we will study.

We will develop the model as follows. First, we will assume a one-person world and examine the behavior of this isolated individual faced with the quandary of choice. We will refer to this case as the simple, Robinson Crusoe society. Studying this one-person society allows us to abstract from the complexity of human interaction and to concentrate on the analysis of individual decision making under scarcity.

Clearly, this is not a model of the real world. It is not meant to be. It abstracts from a lot of complications that are inherent in the interaction of individuals. This abstraction is accomplished by assumption. As noted above, we use assumptions to abstract from complexity and thereby to simplify the problem we are studying. This method is used in all sciences. In physics, for instance, one often finds that simple models describing the behavior of falling objects abstract from the effect of the earth's atmosphere by assuming a vacuum.

We will be using assumptions to simplify problems throughout the course of our study, so it is important that you keep your eye out for the assumptions embodied in a model. The assumptions determine the realism of the model. When assumptions abstract from a great deal, they are referred to as *strong assumptions*. If the degree of abstraction embodied in a set of strong assumptions is reduced, this is referred to as *relaxing the strong assumptions*. One strong assumption you will see often in economic models and elsewhere is called *ceteris paribus* (Latin for "other conditions being equal"). This assumption holds constant all forces except the one on which we are focusing. For instance, we will find that, *ceteris paribus*, as the price of a good rises, the quantity of that good demanded falls. The *ceteris paribus* assumption in that statement holds variables like income, tastes, and the price of other goods constant.

So what good is a model that is not realistic and does not even claim to be? It serves as a base of operations. Once we get this model set up and working, we can relax its strong (very unrealistic) assumptions in order to make it more realistic. As we do this, we can see how the model must be adjusted to each sucessive relaxation in an assumption. This allows us to understand how each new force we allow to enter our model affects the system. While this can be a frustratingly slow process, it is much more likely to be successful than trying to model all the complexity of the world immediately.

So this is the way we will develop our study of the NeoClassical model. We will start with a very abstract, unrealistic model, and by a progressive relaxing of assumptions, we will arrive at a less abstract, more realistic model. For example, when we have completed our model of individual decision making under the strong assumption of isolation, we will relax that strong assumption and introduce the complexity of human interaction.

The simplest NeoClassical model of what we will refer to as a complex society is the NeoClassical General Competitive Equilibrium model. In its most abstract form the NeoClassical General Competitive Equilibrium is a model of an economy in which no one is denied equal opportunity, everyone is created equal, and the only thing that determines how well you do in the economic race is how hard you try and random luck.

Again, this is not a model of the real world. It is not meant to be. It abstracts from a lot of distortions that actually exist in the world like sex or race discrimination. Again, this abstraction is accomplished by assumption. The General Competitive Equilibrium model assumes that social, political, and economic institutions are neutral—in other words, they do not distort the process. This is sometimes referred to as the *fair race assumption*. This, along with several other assumptions we will introduce, will make up a set of "nice" assumptions that are necessary for the General Competitive Equilibrium to exist.

When we have completed the NeoClassical General Competitive Equilibrium model, we will relax some of the nice assumptions that give rise to the general competitive equilibrium. Allowing for the existence of distortions that violate these assumptions will make it possible to examine the implications of the distortions. We will develop our model, making it more realistic, by relaxing assumptions. Unfortunately, the price of this process is, as you will see, increased complexity.

Upon completion of the steps outlined above, we will have completed our development of the NeoClassical microeconomic model. This model explains and predicts the behavior of individuals faced with the quandary of choice. We start with the micro model because it describes the foundation of the economic system. Once we have constructed this microeconomic foundation, we will build a macroeconomic model on it. We will find that there is a great deal of debate among NeoClassical economists about what the macroeconomic model predicts, and therefore what policy prescriptions it implies. We take a moment to note this here because you will only understand that macro debate if you understand the micro model. Underlying the macro debate is a basic disagreement about the micro model. The argument is not over the structure of the micro model. Rather, it is over how significant the distortions of our assumed "nice" conditions are and how quickly the adjustments, that the micro model explains and predicts, actually take place.

All this must wait, however, until we get the basic micro model built. In the following chapter we turn our attention to that task. We will follow the model-building process described above, beginning by assembling our tool kit, specifying some of the fundamental tools and assumptions, and then arranging them. This specification and arrangement process will be repeated again and again. As we proceed, you will see the model take shape. As it takes shape, we will apply it to the analysis of issues in our world.

An Analysis of a Simple Society and the Forces That Give Rise to Complexity

I cast my eyes to the stranded vessel, when the breach and froth of the sea being so big, I could hardly see it, it lay so far off, and considered, Lord! how was it possible I could get on shore?

After I had solaced my mind with the comfortable part of my condition, I began to look round me to see what kind of place I was in, and what was next to be done, and I soon found my comforts abate, and that in a word I had a dreadful deliverance: for I was wet, had no clothes to shift me, nor any thing either to eat or drink to comfort me, neither did I see any prospect before me, but that of perishing with hunger, or being devoured by wild beasts; and that which was particularly afflicting to me was that I had no weapon either to hunt and kill any creature for my sustenance, or to defend my self against any other creature that might desire to kill me for theirs. In a word, I had nothing about me but a knife, a tobacco-pipe, and a little tobacco in a box; this was all my provision, and this threw me into terrible agonies of mind, that for a while I run about like a mad-man. Night coming upon me, I began with a heavy heart to consider what would be my lot if there were any ravenous beasts in that country, seeing at night they always come abroad for their prey.

Daniel Defoe
The Life and Adventures of Robinson Crusoe, 1719.

THESE WERE Robinson Crusoe's thoughts as he contemplated the "condition" into which fate had thrust him. How was he to decide what to do? Indeed, how does any human being decide "what to do?" In this chapter we examine the economist's answer to this question.

This chapter is about how individuals make choices. We begin with Robinson Crusoe because it allows us to abstract from a complication we face in our own world: Crusoe is alone, we are not. His choices are entirely independent of any other human being, ours are not.—Once we understand independent choice we will be in a better position to understand the more complex reality of interdependent choice. Thus we begin this chapter with Crusoe, and by the end we will be leaving him behind.

15

A. ASSEMBLING OUR TOOL KIT

The Consumption Side

We begin by studying individual consumption behavior, and more specifically with a definition of the term *utility*. Utility is defined as satisfaction. To derive satisfaction from something is to receive utility from it.

We assume that households know what gives them utility and that they are able to rank items by the amount of utility they derive from them. In technical terms, this means the household must have a clearly defined preference ordering (i.e., that they can say for any two goods, A and B, that A is preferred, equal, or less preferred relative to B). In less technical terms, it means that the household must know its own tastes. Furthermore, we assume that the objective of all rational households is to maximize their utility. Therefore we define *rational behavior* as utility maximizing. Are you rational? Do you always act so as to maximize your utility?

A term closely related to utility is *consume*. Consumption is the act of deriving utility. Consumption is often associated with using things up, such as consuming a milkshake. In the sense in which we use it here, however, consumption does not invariably imply "using up." You can consume a work of art or Niagara Falls and it will still be there for the next person to consume.

Since we consume things that provide us with utility and since we like utility, we identify the things we consume with flattering names like *goods* or *services*. Both goods and services are things that provide utility when consumed. The distinction is that goods are tangible and can be stored (like food), while services are intangible and (like a haircut) cannot be stored. What goods have you consumed today? What services?

When economists discuss consumers it is common practice to refer to a household rather than an individual, so we will follow that practice. Technically, we define a *household* as a consumption unit. For example, a nuclear family that makes most of its big consumption decisions as a unit (e.g., where to live) is a household. Remember, however, a household can include one or more individuals, so when we talk about households, we are talking about you even if you live alone. How big is your household?

Now we should take a moment to collect and arrange the terms we have specified. The arrangement can take the form of a statement:

"Rational households consume goods and services in order to derive the maximum utility." This is not yet a model of behavior that can explain or predict. It is, however, a useful piece for model building because it identifies the relationship among several terms that will prove useful.

With one more assumption we will have a model with which we can identify a decision rule for household consumption behavior under very simple conditions. We assume that, *ceteris paribus* (other things being equal), the utility one derives from the consumption of a good or service diminishes with each successive unit consumed.

Consider the experience of someone who has been lost in the desert and suddenly finds an oasis. She begins to drink. The first gulp (we will consider the units of water by gulps) is literally a lifesaver. Its utility is almost infinite. The second gulp is almost as important, but not quite, so it brings slightly less utility. On and on the gulps go. If the utility of each successive gulp did not fall, she would not stop gulping, but she does—in fact, she must. Clearly the utility of gulps falls and she stops when the last gulp gives her no more (zero) utility.

This concept of "each successive unit" we have just used has a name. It is called the *margin*. In a succession of units the marginal unit is the last unit considered. In our "gulp" example the marginal unit is the last gulp considered. The woman was always making her decisions at the margin, considering: "Do I want one more gulp?" As long as all goods and services are divisible into units, we can make all our decisions at the margin. Clearly, big units of choice give us less decision flexibility than small units of choice. The smaller the units, the more finely tuned we can make our decision. We will assume, therefore, that all goods and services and inputs used in production are divisible into infinitesimally small units. (Is that a strong assumption?) This allows us to build a model based on marginal decision making. NeoClassical theory is, in fact, often referred to as marginal analysis.

Now let us return to our assumption that the utility one derives from the consumption of each successive unit of a good or service diminishes with each successive unit consumed. With our new term we can state this more efficiently as the assumption of *diminishing marginal utility*. Consider another example of this law. Celia really enjoys M&Ms but has not had any in a while. One day she finds a huge bag full of M&Ms with a sign on it saying "Free, take all you'd like." Happily she begins to consume. The schedule in Table 2–1 shows the number of utils she gets from each successive M&M consumed. In other words, it is a *marginal utility schedule*. (*Note:* A util is a unit of utility. Strictly speaking, these should be called Celia utils because

TABLE 2-1 Celia's Marginal Utility Schedule

M&Ms	Marginal Utility (in utils)
1st	50
2nd	49
3rd	48
4th	47
5th	46
6th	45
7th	44
8th	43
9th	42
10th	41

there is no way to compare utility across individuals. No one but Celia really knows how much satisfaction each successive M&M gives her.)

Notice that while the utility Celia derives from the consumption of each successive M&M is falling (i.e., the marginal utility is falling), the total utility she derives from consuming M&Ms is rising. This is true because each of the first ten M&Ms adds to her utility, albeit by successively smaller amounts. Her total utility is, after all, the sum of all the marginal utilities. Extending the schedule above to include total utility, we have Table 2-2. Graphically, we can represent marginal utility (MU) and total utility (TU) as shown in Figure 2-1.

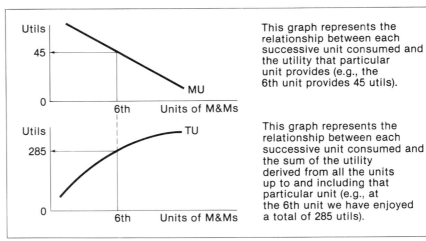

FIGURE 2-1 Graphical Representation of the Relationship Between Marginal and Total Utility Note that the scales on the vertical axes are different.

TABLE 2-2   Celia's Marginal and Total Utility Schedules

M&Ms	Marginal Utility	Total Utility (the sum of MUs)
1st	50	50
2nd	49	99
3rd	48	147
4th	47	194
5th	46	240
6th	45	285
7th	44	329
8th	43	372
9th	42	414
10th	41	455

If we extend the schedules, we find, as shown in Table 2–3, that her marginal utility becomes negative as Celia gets to her 52nd M&M and beyond. Notice that the 50th M&M gave her one additional unit of utility, the 51st M&M gave her no additional utility, the 52nd M&M reduced her utility by one unit, the 53rd M&M reduced her utility by two units, and so on. In other words, the marginal utility of M&Ms fell to zero and then became negative.

Now if Celia is making her decision to consume at the margin, at what point would she stop consuming M&Ms? She would eat the 50th because the 49th gave her utility and she would want more. She would eat the 51st because the 50th gave her utility and she would want more. She would not eat the 52nd because the 51st did not give her any additional utility, so why have more? If she was forced to eat

TABLE 2-3   Celia's Marginal and Total Utility Schedules, (Continued)

M&Ms	Marginal Utility	Total Utility (the sum of MUs)
45th	6	1,260
46th	5	1,265
47th	4	1,269
48th	3	1,272
49th	2	1,274
50th	1	1,275
51st	0	1,275
52nd	−1	1,274
53rd	−2	1,272
54th	−3	1,269
55th	−4	1,265

the 52nd M&M, she would wish she had not because it would actually lower her utility. Graphically, we can represent this additional information as shown in Figure 2–2.

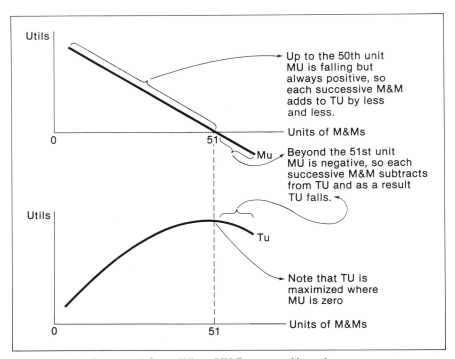

FIGURE 2–2   Graphical Case When MU Becomes Negative

Now we can pull together all of the consumption parts of our model and identify a decision rule for consumption behavior under the strong assumption that goods and services are free: A rational household will maximize utility by consuming all free goods or services up to the point at which the marginal utility derived from the consumption of each equals zero. In mathematical terms, the rule would appear as follows:

For all n goods and services set:

$$MU_1 = 0$$
$$\text{and } MU_2 = 0$$
$$\text{and } MU_3 = 0$$
$$\vdots$$
$$\text{and } MU_n = 0$$

OR

$$\text{Set } MU_1 = MU_2 = MU_3 = \ldots = MU_n = 0 \text{ for all } n \text{ goods and services.}$$

Is this a very realistic decision rule? No, because nobody faces choices under the condition that all goods and services are free. This rule abstracts from the obvious question: Where is all this stuff going to come from? Who's going to produce it?

So why do we bother to figure out such a decision rule? Because it provides a first approximation of reality. Now we know how people make choices under the very strong (unrealistic) assumption that everything is free. With a bit more preparation we will be in a position to relax that assumption and identify a more realistic rule. Remember, we are building a model. We must be patient if we are to build it logically and therefore sturdily.

The Production Side

At this point we shift our focus. So far we have been examining one side of the quandary of choice—the consumption side. We have defined the terms and made the assumptions necessary to identify a decision rule for consumption choice under the very strong assumption that all goods and services come like manna from heaven—free. Now we need to examine the other side of the issue. From where do the goods and services we desire actually come? We know they come from the production side, we must now examine how production decisions are made.

Remember, if we could produce more than we desire, there would be no quandary of choice. So there must be some constraint on production. There must be something about the production side that makes scarcity inevitable and therefore gives rise to the science of scarcity. What is it? It is the fact that our initial endowment is finite.

An *initial endowment* includes the natural and human resources from which all goods and services must be produced. The fact that these resources are finite and insufficient to meet all human desires is the ultimate reason for scarcity. Each society has an initial endowment. Society's endowment may expand through new resource discoveries or it may contract as resources are used up or ruined. It is, in other words, finite, but not fixed. The key thing to understand is that all of society's goods and services must be produced from this resource base, and since it is finite, there will be scarcity.

The transformation of inputs into outputs is called the *process of production*. The inputs that go into this production process are called *factors of production*. Two kinds of factors are the resources taken directly from the initial endowment. They are natural resources usually identified simply as land and labor. The other factor of production is not a gift of nature. It must itself be produced before it can be used in later stages of production. This produced means of production is called *capital*. The machines you see in factories are a kind of capital. There is another kind of capital you cannot see because it is intangible. Ironically, you probably own more of this kind than any other. It is called *human capital*. Much of the time and money you put into your health and education is being spent on accumulating human capital. (Recall our discussion of this concept in the Introduction.)

When a unit of a factor of production is put to use in a particular process of production, this is called an *allocation* of the factor. To allocate is to assign use. There is an array of ways in which the factors allocated to the production of a specific good or service can be combined in order to produce that good or service. Each of these methods is called a *technique of production,* and the whole set of available techniques is called the *technology.* Technology is like a book of blueprints in which every page is a technique.

Again, we should take a moment to collect and arrange terms. The arrangement can be described as follows: "Factors of production are allocated to and then combined in processes of production that apply techniques chosen from the available technology in order to produce goods and services."

Before we can determine a decision rule for production behavior, we need to make one more assumption. We assume that, *ceteris paribus* (holding technique and the quantity of all other factors constant), the output derived from the use of each successive (marginal) unit of a particular factor of production will eventually begin to diminish with each successive unit applied. We will call the output derived from the use of each successive unit of a particular factor the *marginal product* of that factor. Thus what we are assuming is that if we increase the use of one factor, holding technique and the quantity of all other factors constant, the marginal product (MP) of that factor will diminish.

Consider the following example: Martin lives in a rural area. He pumps his family's water from a well with a hand pump. Each push on the pump produces one gulp of water. If we divide his labor into minutes, his marginal product schedule as he proceeds to pump can be represented by Table 2–4. (All factors other than his labor—for instance, the capital he uses: the pump—are constant.)

Here we see that the marginal product of his labor rises at first, but then begins to fall. This is plausible. At first Martin is getting loose and into a rhythm, but inevitably he begins to tire. Eventually, after the 19th minute, he can pump no more. His arms are about to fall off.

TABLE 2–4 Martin's Marginal Product Schedule

Labor (min.)	Marginal Product (in gulps)
1st	6
2nd	8
3rd	10
4th	10
5th	9
6th	8
7th	7
:	:
18th	1
19th	.5
20th	0

In the schedule represented in Table 2–5 we see the relationship between the margin and the total product. Again, we see that as long as the margin is positive, it increases the total.

The *total product* refers to the combined output of all inputs during a given period of production. In our example the inputs were the land (the site of the pump), the capital (the pump), and the labor. We saw that as one input (labor) increased and all else remained constant, the total product (TP) increased. However, it increased by less and less as each successive unit of labor was added during this period of production. This is what we mean by *diminishing marginal product*.

In our example the lowest the marginal product can go is zero. More time applied does not make any of the total product disappear; that is, the marginal product never becomes negative. There are, however, cases in which the marginal product can become negative.

Consider the following example: You own a factory designed to produce widgets (the economist's term for generic output) on an assembly line that has 19 stations. Your only variable input is workers and you want to determine how many workers are necessary to maximize your factory's output. You experiment by adding one worker each day. On the first day the total product is very low because the one worker is spending most of her time running from station to station. On the second day the total product more than doubles (the MP of the second worker exceeds that of the first). As successive workers are added each day, the daily total product increases, but after the third worker the addition to the daily total contributed by each successive worker hired falls; that is, the marginal product falls. The 20th worker adds nothing because there is no empty station to cover. Her marginal product is zero. The addition of a 21st worker actually slows down the line because the card game of the two idle workers distracts those on

TABLE 2–5 Martin's Marginal and Total Product Schedules

Labor (min.)	Marginal Product (in gulps)	Total Product (in gulps)
1st	6	6
2nd	8	14
3rd	10	24
4th	10	34
5th	9	45
6th	8	53
7th	7	60
:	:	:
18th	1	98.5
19th	.5	99
20th	0	99

the line. The total product on the 21st day is lower than it was on the 20th—in other words, the 21st worker has a negative marginal product. Assuming perfectly divisible inputs, this case can be represented graphically as shown in Figure 2–3.

Now let us do another one of our abstraction exercises in order to see how the logic of a decision rule works. We will assume that there are four goods to be produced, and that the techniques and the quantities of land and capital for each production process are determined. We will also assume that the one variable factor, labor, is not scarce. Given these conditions, identify the decision rule for labor allocation that will produce as much of the four goods as possible.

You should be able to convince yourself that the appropriate decision rule would be to set:

$$MP_1 = 0$$
$$\text{and } MP_2 = 0$$
$$\text{and } MP_3 = 0$$
$$\text{and } MP_4 = 0$$

which we can rewrite more efficiently as:

$$MP_1 = MP_2 = MP_3 = MP_4 = 0$$

Once again, this may seem like a trivial decision rule. Who cares how a producer would behave under such clearly unrealistic conditions? If we were going to stop here, it would be trivial. But we are not. Again, this level of abstraction is just a stepping-stone. Remember our process: Use abstraction to make modeling easy, then relax the assumptions to make it more realistic. That is what we are doing, and it will serve us well because we are doing it systematically.

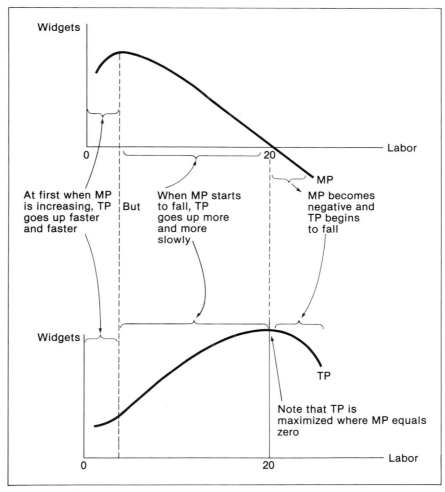

FIGURE 2–3   Graphical Representation of the Relationship Between Marginal and Total Product

B. A MODEL OF A SIMPLE ROBINSON CRUSOE SOCIETY

The Basic Decision Rules

We have looked at the consumption side in isolation(as if all goods and services were free) and the production side in isolation (as if our objective were to maximize productivity not utility). The next step is to connect these two pieces of our model. Remember, our objective as social scientists is to explain and predict aspects of human behavior. The particular aspect we are examining as economists is human behavior in response to the quandary of choice. Choice is a decision. So far we have built two parts of a model of choice—one part describing the decision rule one would follow as a consumer and the other part describing the decision rule one would follow as a producer. Unfortunately, each part abstracts from its connection to the other. Our consumer's decision rule takes production as given and our producer's decision rule ignores the role of the consumer. What is more, both decision rules ignore the issue of scarcity.

These pieces are not useless, but like any pieces, their real value is not apparent until we put them together. Doing so will give us the simplest form of our working model, a model of decision behavior by an individual whose only concern is current production and consumption—a "one-period time horizon," as it is called. Now we must connect the pieces.

In order to simplify the problem of pulling the pieces together, we will do so in the simplest of all societies: a Robinson Crusoe society or a society of one. Assuming that society has only one member allows us to abstract from a number of complications. The most important one is that we need not worry about how society's initial endowment is distributed among individuals. Since there is only one member in the society, Crusoe, his initial endowment is identical with that of the society.

Let us review the other assumptions we are making. First of all, we assume that Crusoe is rational (as we defined it above), knows his preference ordering, and experiences diminishing marginal utility. We also assume that his resources are finite (limited by what he brought ashore and finds on the island) and that he experiences diminishing marginal product. Finally, we assume, for the moment, that he is only concerned with current production and consumption —in other words, that he has a one-period time horizon.

Under these circumstances the choice Crusoe has to make is how to allocate resources in order to maximize his utility. To simplify the problem we assume that the problem Crusoe faces is how to allocate one resource: his labor. We know from the production side of our model that as he allocates his labor to its alternative uses (hunting, fishing, picking berries, pumping water), it will have diminishing marginal product in all these uses. Similarly, we know that the goods produced in each of these activities (meat, fish, berries, and water) will give him diminishing marginal utility. Our task is to connect the allocation of labor to the generation of utility. To make this connection we must identify the amount of utility Crusoe derives from each

TABLE 2-6   Crusoe's Marginal and Total Product Schedule(s)

Labor (hour)	Marginal Product (MP) (in deer)	Total Product (TP) (in deer)
1st	1	1
2nd	2	3
3rd	3	6
4th	2	8
5th	1	9
6th	0	9

successive unit of labor he allocates to a given activity. We will call this the *utility of the marginal product* (UMP) of labor.

To see how this UMP is calculated, let us consider the case of Crusoe as a hunter. This production schedule is represented in Table 2–6 (notice the diminishing MP).

And the schedule representing the marginal utility from consuming deer is shown in Table 2–7 (notice the diminishing MU).

We calculate the utility marginal product for each hour of hunting as follows: In the first hour of hunting Crusoe got his first deer, and the marginal utility of the first deer is 100, so the utility of the marginal product of that first hour is 100. In the second hour he got his second and third deer, and the marginal utilities of these are 90 and 80, respectively, so the UMP of that second hour is 170. In the third hour he got his fourth, fifth, and sixth deer, and the marginal utilities of these, respectively, are 70, 60, and 50, so the UMP of the third hour is 180. In the fourth hour he got his seventh and eighth deer, and the MUs of these are 40 and 30, respectively, so the UMP of the fourth hour is 70. In the fifth hour he got his ninth deer, and the MU of this deer is 20, so the UMP of the fifth hour is 20. In the sixth hour Crusoe was exhausted and all the slow deer near his hut were dead, so he got nothing. Thus the UMP of the sixth hour is zero.

The amount of utility derived from each successive unit of labor

TABLE 2-7   Crusoe's Marginal Utility Schedule

Deer	Marginal Utility (utils)
1st	100
2nd	90
3rd	80
4th	70
5th	60
6th	50
7th	40
8th	30
9th	20

TABLE 2–8   Calculating Utility Marginal Product

Labor (hour)	Deer and MU of Each		UMP	Total Utility
1st	1st @ 100	=	100	100
2nd	2nd @ 90 + 3rd @ 80	=	170	270
3rd	4th @ 70 + 5th @ 60 + 6th @ 50	=	180	450
4th	7th @ 40 + 8th @ 30	=	70	520
5th	9th @ 20	=	20	540
6th	0	=	0	540

spent hunting (or the utility of the marginal product) is calculated as shown in Table 2–8.

The first thing to notice about the table is that as Crusoe allocates more and more labor to hunting, the UMP eventually begins to fall. This is inevitable because the UMP is determined by the MP, which may increase briefly but inevitably begins to fall, and by the MU of the successive units produced, which falls from the very first unit. What is more, since for any possible allocation of units of labor the MP will eventually fall and the MU of the product will fall from the first unit produced (remember we have assumed diminishing MP and MU), the UMP for all possible allocations of his labor will fall. If Crusoe knew the MP for each possible allocation of his labor (e,g., hunt, fish, pick berries, pump water) and the MU derived from the units of output, at the outset of each day he could calculate the UMP schedule for each feasible allocation of his labor. With this information he could then determine the optimal allocation of his labor. "Optimal" means "best." Since Crusoe is rational, the optimal allocation of his labor is the one that generates the maximum utility.

Suppose he wakes up in the morning, makes these calculations, and finds the results represented in Table 2–9. (Total utilities are noted in parenthesis.)

Assuming these are only ways Crusoe can use his labor, Table 2–9 represents his set of opportunities for labor allocation. He also knows that he faces a time constraint. All of these activities must be done during the 13 hours of daylight, because at night the bears come out. His problem then is: How does he allocate 13 hours of labor among these competing uses in order to maximize his utility? In other words, what decision rule should he follow?

Notice that he cannot get all the possible utility available. To do so would mean doing each activity until UMP = 0 for all activities. Following that decision rule would require 6 hours of hunting, 7 hours of fishing, 6 hours of berry picking, and 4 hours of pumping (confirm from Table 2–9). That is 23 hours total, and since he has only 13 hours to "spend," it is not feasible. Should he choose to do each activity until he gets to the maximum UMP per hour? That would mean doing

TABLE 2-9 Crusoe's Utility Marginal Product and (TU) Schedule(s)

Labor (hrs.)	UMP (hunt)	UMP (fish)	UMP (pick berries)	UMP (pump water)
1st	100(100)	50(50)	50(50)	180(180)
2nd	170(270)	60(110)	70(120)	70(250)
3rd	180(450)	180(290)	40(160)	5(255)
4th	70(520)	170(460)	10(170)	0(255)
5th	20(540)	70(530)	5(175)	0(255)
6th	0(540)	5(535)	0(175)	0(255)
7th	0(540)	0(535)	0(175)	0(255)
8th	0(540)	0(535)	0(175)	0(255)

3 hours of hunting, 3 hours of fishing, 2 hours of picking berries, and 1 hour of pumping (confirm from Table 2–9). That adds up to 9 hours. Following this decision rule would mean wasting 4 hours—4 hours when he could have been generating more total utility but was not. So what decision rule should Crusoe follow? How should he make his choice of labor allocation so as to maximize his utility? This is his "quandary of choice."

Clearly, part of the decision rule is that he should allocate all the available hours to utility-generating activities. As the expression goes, "You gotta make hay (in this case, meat, fish, berries, and water) while the sun shines." Given that all 13 hours are going to be used, how should they be allocated? Here we can call upon a concept we met at the outset of this process: opportunity cost. Remember, opportunity cost refers to the value of the best alternative you forgo by using a resource (e.g., time) one way rather than another. In this case, Crusoe is allocating hours of labor, and the opportunity cost of an hour allocated to one activity is the UMP lost in the alternative uses. Clearly, each successive hour should be allocated to the activity with the highest available UMP.

If Crusoe always chooses the best available opportunity for each successive hour he allocates, he will allocate the first hour to pumping water. Doing so generates 180 units of utility, and the best available alternative (the first hour of hunting) only generates 100 units. Having used up the first hour, he will allocate the second hour to hunting. This is his first hour at hunting, so that allocation generates 100 units of utility and the best available option, a second hour of pumping water, only offers 70. His third hour will also go to hunting because another (a second) hour of hunting offers 170 units of utility and the best option, a second hour of pumping, only offers 70. If he continues to follow this logic—choosing the best available option for each successive hour allocated—Crusoe would allocate his 13 hours as shown in Table 2–10.

TABLE 2-10   Optimal Allocation of Time

Activity	Hours Allocated	Total Utility from That Activity
Hunt	4	520
Fish	5	530
Pick	2	120
Pump	2	250

The overall total utility he would generate by the allocation shown in Table 2–10 would be 1,420 units of utility. No other allocation of 13 hours would generate as much utility. (Try it and see.) Notice that for Crusoe's optimal allocation the utility marginal products of the last hour allocated to each activity are equal, as shown in Table 2–11.

There is no way that a further reallocation of hours could increase his utility, because one hour reallocated to any other activity would produce less than the 70 utils it currently generates. We know this because we know that UMP falls as the number of hours increases.

We have identified the decision rule Crusoe would follow if he is rational. All available hours must be allocated and the allocation must be such that for any set number of alternative activities (n) the UMPs across all activities must be equalized. (In the Crusoe example, $n = 4$.)

$$UMP_1 = UMP_2 = \ldots = UMP_n$$

In our example, Crusoe is limited to allocating his time by the hour. If, in fact, no hour allocation across activities satisfied our decision rule, then Crusoe would have to break down his allocation of time into smaller units (e.g., minutes) in order to realize the optimum allocation of time. Since time is perfectly divisable, he can always fine-tune his allocation of time in order to set

$$UMP_1 = UMP_2 = \ldots = UMP_n$$

and thereby maximize his utility. Remember, this decision rule is based on the assumption of perfect divisibility.

We can demonstrate the general validity of the decision rule with an example from your own experience. Suppose you have four options for allocating your time between now and midnight: (1) eating, (2) sleeping, (3) studying, and (4) playing. Once you consider your evening you plan your time allocation such that (here the unit of allocation is minutes):

$$UMP_1 = UMP_2 = UMP_3 = UMP_4 = 100$$

TABLE 2–11 UMPs at Optimal Allocation

Activity	Hours	UMP from Last Hour Allocated
Hunt	4	70
Fish	5	70
Pick	2	70
Pump	2	70

Is there any way to reallocate your time in order to generate more utility? Suppose you take a minute away from studying. What is the opportunity cost? It would be 100 units of utility because the UMP_3, the utility generated by the last minute of study, is currently 100 and that is what you would give up by taking that minute away from studying. Now if you reallocate that minute from studying to eating, sleeping, or playing, how much utility would you gain? Considering that UMP_1, UMP_2, and UMP_4 all currently equal 100 (i.e., the last minute currently allocated to those activities in generating 100 units of utility) and considering that UMP is falling (because MP and MU, the components for UMP, are falling), the utility you would gain from one more minute of eating, sleeping, or playing would be less than 100 units. Thus we see that because UMPs fall, any reallocation of time would lower your total utility. The flip side of this argument is that whenever inputs are continuously divisible and UMPs across allocations are not equal, there is utility to be gained by reallocating the input until its UMPs are equal across all allocations. In other words, setting the UMPs equal is the only way to maximize utility. This rule is generally true because the fact that UMPs fall is generally true.

Now consider the following question: Will Crusoe's behavior change in the winter when the days are shorter (assume he can only be out seven hours) and there are no berries to pick (assume that the MP and MU schedules for the other goods remain the same)? Here we have a case wherein the structure of incentives and the constraints he faces have changed. He has no opportunity to pick berries and he has less time to do his labor. So, will his behavior change? Yes. How will he allocate his time now? You should be able to convince yourself that he will allocate three hours to hunting, three hours to fishing, and one hour to pumping.

Consider your own time allocation. There are some external constraints (like the bears for Crusoe), but of the time you can allocate freely, do you follow this rule? Do you consciously or unconsciously allocate your time so that the utility derived from that time is maximized? If so, you must be allocating each successive moment to the best use (highest UMP), and when you are done, the UMPs of all allocations must be equal (remember we are assuming perfectly divisible activities.) Do you behave that way? Are you rational? If you think about it, you will probably find that this is a pretty good description of your time allocation.

Adding a Time Dimension

At this point we should add another dimension to our model, time. Thus far we have spoken of resources, production, and consumption as if we live for one cycle of production, then die. We have assumed a one-period time horizon. That may be the way of the world for some insects, but not for humans. Most of us plan on being around for a while. Now we will relax the assumption of a one-period time horizon, but in order to do so we need to define a few more terms that describe the behavior we see in people with long time horizons. The terms are save and invest.

To *save* is to forgo the use of current resources for the generation of current utility. To *invest* is to use current resources (saved) in order to increase future productivity and thereby future utility. Obviously, no one would save or invest if there was no future.

We assume that people have a bias toward current consumption. Thus we can say that, *ceteris paribus,* 100 units of utility today is worth more than the expectation of 100 units of utility 365 days from now. In other words, *ceteris paribus,* we prefer immediate to delayed satisfaction.

Suppose someone offered to give you $100 right now or $100 in 365 days, and that person demanded that you spend it when you get it and that you decide immediately which you want. If, *ceteris paribus,* you are indifferent between the two options, then you do not have a time preference in consumption. If, *ceteris paribus,* you prefer the $100 next year, then you have a bias toward future consumption. All else being equal, you prefer your utility in the future rather than the present. The economist would say that you *discount* (diminish) the value of the present relative to the future. If, *ceteris paribus,* you prefer the $100 now, you have a bias toward current consumption. Such a bias means that, all else being equal, you discount the value of the future relative to the present. Our assumption is that people discount the future.

When you look forward to consuming something in the future (e.g., a good meal at home), then we say that the utility you expect to enjoy in the future has a *present value*. In other words, it gives you a certain amount of utility now as you look forward to enjoying it. Economists define the rate (the amount per unit of time) at which an individual diminishes the present value of utility as its realization moves further into the future as that individual's *discount rate*. In order to clarify this concept, consider the following example.

Suppose I ask to borrow $100 from you today and I promise (and you believe me) that I will pay you back the $100 in 365 days. (we will assume the dollar itself will lose no value during the year.) If you discount the future at all, you will reject my proposal because $100 next year is not worth as much to you as $100 today. In the face of your rejection, I adjust my proposal.

How about $101 in 365 days for $100 today? You say no.
How about $102 in 365 days for $100 today? You say no.
How about $103 in 365 days for $100 today? You say no.
How about $104 in 365 days for $100 today? You say no.
How about $105 in 365 days for $100 today? You say yes!

What happened?

At $101, $102, $103, and $104 you say no because $100 today is worth more to you, given your discount rate, than any of those amounts next year. In economic terms we say that the present value of those future sums (i.e., how much they are worth to you now, given your discount rate) is less than $100. In this example it takes 5 percent extra next year ($5 extra) to make the future value equivalent to the present value ($100). Thus you must be discounting the future at a 5 percent per year discount rate.

Note that not everyone discounts the future at the same rate. If I went to someone else for the loan (e.g., Rupert), my offer might have to be different. Assuming Rupert trusted me but discounted the future at 10 percent per year, I would have to promise him at least $110 next year in order to get a $100 loan from him today.

Our discount rates are a fundamental part of our decision making process. All of our decisions are made in the present, but we face a multiperiod time horizon. Most of the options from which we must choose generate a stream of utilities across time. For example, if you consider buying a new car, you expect it to generate utility for years to come. In effect, each option represents a package of utility spread over time. In order to make a choice, we must be able to compare all of the available packages and we must make that comparison now—in the present—because we must make our choice now.

We do this by determining the present value of each package. Using our discount rate, we can calculate the present value of all the utility in each package even though the utility in each package is spread out over time. Once we have calculated the present value of each package, we can compare packages directly and make our choices.

Returning to our simple society example, let us assume that in each new period Crusoe's initial endowment will be the same as in the current period. Under this condition, *ceteris paribus,* he would not want to save if whatever he set aside was simply going to lie idle. Since he discounts future consumption, it would give him more utility to consume something today than to wait to consume it. What if, however, he could invest what he saved and thereby expand his future consumption of goods by making himself more productive? Under what conditions would he choose to do this? As we demonstrated, he would do so whenever the discounted value of utility gained from the expanded future consumption (the present value of that increased future consumption) more than offsets the current utility loss from having to wait to consume. In order to make this choice, he must be able to compare the present value (utility) of consuming the item now to the present discounted value (the future utilities discounted to the present) of the returns (the future consumption increase) from the investment.

For instance, Crusoe could spend all of his time picking berries, hunting, and pumping water for current consumption. If, as we have assumed, his initial endowment is the same in each successive period (the berries, animals, and water are always replenished), then his level of consumption will be constant across time, as shown in Figure 2–4.

FIGURE 2–4 Graphical Level of Consumption

Crusoe may choose, however, to take some time out from the pursuit of goods for current consumption in order to make a bow and some arrows. How would he decide if this is a worthwhile allocation of his time? Clearly, making a bow and arrows would lower his current consumption because some time from berry picking, hunting, or pumping would have to be reallocated to investing in this capital (a produced means of production), the bow and arrows. This loss of current consumption means a loss of current utility.

What is the potential benefit of this reallocation of time? Crusoe expects that with a bow and arrow his hunting time will be more productive in the future. This would increase his future level of consumption for all periods after the capital is completed, which, in turn, would increase his level of utility in all future periods or at least as long as the capital lasts, as shown in Figure 2–5.

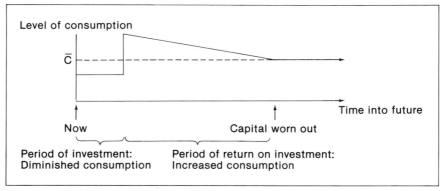

FIGURE 2–5   An Alternative to Constant c̄: Investment and Return

We have assumed, however, that a util next year is not equal to a util today because Crusoe discounts the value of things in the future. So how does he decide whether the benefit of reallocating the time to investing in capital is worth the opportunity cost—the current utility lost? He has to make the future utility gains directly comparable to the current utility loss. To do this he uses the discount rate to calculate the present value of the future utility gain. If the present value of the future utility gain is greater than the current utility he will have to forgo (the opportunity cost), then the investment is worth making. This case is shown in Figure 2–6.

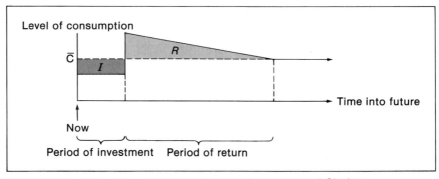

FIGURE 2–6   The Role of Present Value in Intertemporal Choice
If the present value of the cost of the investment is less than the present value of the return on the investment, then, *ceteris paribus*, he will make the investment.

Now consider the following cases, based on Figure 2–6. (Assume area *R* is larger than area *I*):

1. Crusoe's discount rate is zero (i.e., he doesn't discount the future at all). Would he make the investment?—Yes. The size of the benefits *R* is greater than the size of the costs *I*, and since there is no discounting, the present value of the benefits must also be greater than the present value of the costs.

2. Crusoe's discount rate is infinite because he believes the world will end tomorrow. Would he make the investment?—No. The benefits might be greater than the costs, but since he won't live to enjoy them, he discounts their value completely (i.e., their present value equals zero), and therefore he won't make the investment today.

3. There is some discount rate, $\overline{D}$, between zero and infinity at which the present value of the costs is exactly equal to the present value of the benefits. At discount rate $\overline{D}$ Crusoe is indifferent about the investment—it doesn't hurt, but it doesn't help. *Ceteris paribus*, if his discount rate is less than $\underline{D}$, he will make the investment. If his discount rate is greater than $\overline{D}$, he won't make the investment.

This is what saving and investing is all about. Saving and investing only becomes attractive when the discounted value of the utility it generates in the future (the present value of that utility) is greater than the opportunity cost—the utility one could have enjoyed by using that resource for current consumption. We saw this principle in action in the Introduction when the logic of choosing college was explored. Now we have a more detailed model for the analysis of that choice. The option of choosing college offers a utility package that includes present utility (college as a consumption activity) and a stream of future utilities due to better salary, more enjoyment of ideas, and so on (college as an investment activity). If you choose to be in college, then you reveal that, given your preferences, the present value of the college package is at least as good as the present value of the other options available to you.

Almost all options for resource and capital allocation have an intertemporal element, so our decision rule must reflect the intertemporal nature of our choice. This decision-making process can be represented by a slight modification of our one-period time horizon decision rule.

We found before that if the time horizon for decisions is only one period, then to maximize the utility derived from a resource's use we should set the UMP for all (n) alternative uses of the resource equal:

$$UMP_1 = UMP_2 = \ldots = UMP_n$$

Now we can modify this slightly to account for the fact that some resources will be used now in processes that will not produce utility until some future time period. This modified decision rule would be to set the present value (*PV*) of the UMP from all (*n*) alternative uses of the resource equal:

$$PVUMP_1 = PVUMP_2 = \ldots = PVUMP_n$$

Note that if the utility is generated in the present period, then *PVUMP = UMP*, because there is no discounting. Thus our first version of the rule that had all UMPs equal is just a special case in which all production is for current-period consumption only.

Relaxing our assumption about a replenished initial endowment in each new period, if Crusoe's initial endowment were not replenished in each successive period, he would clearly have the incentive to save because he would eventually starve otherwise. Just as surely he would have the incentive to invest in productive activities so that he could maintain his existence as long as possible. In this case, the same decision rule would hold.

A Note on Risk and Uncertainty

So far we have discussed decision making as if to decide is to accomplish. We know, however, that deciding to do something does not necessarily mean that one will accomplish what one set out to do. If Crusoe decides to fish, that does not mean he will catch anything. If he decides to build a house, that does not mean he will have a house to show for his efforts. We are assuming that decisions are real commitments, not simply lip service, so the source of failure is not lack of commitment to the activity. Failure, occurs, rather, because of circumstances beyond one's control.

Economists refer to the existence of these counterproductive circumstances beyond our control as risks or uncertainties. A *risk* is beyond our control, but we can assign a probability to its occurrence. For instance, if you decide to drive a car in order to visit friends, a probability can be assigned to the chance that you will get killed in an accident on the way. The chance of an accident is a risk. *Uncertainty* is also beyond our control, and we do not know the probability of its occurrence.

Risk and uncertainty have different effects on our planning. Since we know the probability associated with risk, we can factor it into our plans and even insure against it. Uncertainty, on the other hand, is not something we can plan on. We could worry about what might happen, but if we do not know the probability of its occurrence, we have no basis for knowing the degree of concern it warrants with respect to one choice as opposed to another. As a result, we have no basis for adjusting our plans to compensate for uncertainty.

Because of risk and uncertainty, all of the utilities we look forward to when we make choices should be referred to as *expected utilities*. Based on a particular choice, given the risks and ignoring what we cannot account for—the uncertainties—we expect a certain amount of utility to result. This is noted here because risks and uncertainties are an unavoidable part of life. Given this reality, our decision rule for allocating a resource or capital in order to maximize our utility becomes, set:

$$EPVUMP_1 = EPVUMP_2 = \ldots = EPVUMP_n \text{ for all } n \text{ potential}$$
$$\text{allocations}$$

where E is the adjustment for risk (it stands for "expected")
          PV is the adjustment for the time dimension in returns
          UMP embodies our marginal productivity (MP) and marginal utility (MU)

Concluding Our Analysis of a Simple Society

Clearly, in making all of his decisions, Crusoe is in a unique position. He does not have to depend on anyone except himself. When he decides to produce, it is automatically, by definition, a decision to consume: obviously, there would be no point in producing something unless he plans on consuming it. Similarly, if he decides to invest time in building a bow and some arrows or in planting seeds, it is automatically, by definition, a decision to save time or seeds for those investments. In other words, Crusoe's decisions to save and invest or to produce and consume are always perfectly coordinated because they are made simultaneously and inseparately in his own mind. We will see when we get to the model of a complex society that when separate people are making interdependent decisions to save and invest or to produce and consume, the coordination of these decisions can become a problem, and that lack of coordination can have disastrous economic effects.

Keep in mind, we are not arguing that Crusoe's decisions always lead to results he desires. He might decide to save corn for seed and find it wasted because no rain comes. He might build a tool that proves to be useless. Being alone does not make Crusoe immune from the problems of risk and uncertainty. Just because his production and consumption or savings and investment intentions are consistent, that does not mean they will work out as intended.

In sum, Crusoe's initial endowment is finite, his preferences are immediately discernible to himself, he is aware of available technology, and he need not coordinate his actions with anyone else. Since he is entirely independent, he has a view of the whole process from initial endowment allocation to the consumption of goods and services, and his problem becomes a technical exercise. For every allocation choice he has to make, he must consider the ultimate effect on his utility. The cost of any given choice is the utility he would have received from the best alternative usage. We have called this the opportunity cost because the cost of choosing to use a resource in one way is the missed opportunity of using it in the best alternative way.

We have seen this in more concrete terms by looking at the way Crusoe allocates one of his resources, his time. Crusoe spends his day making time allocation choices minute by minute, often without even thinking about the process consciously. So do you. Think about it. Whenever you spend a minute here, it is one less minute you can spend there. Whenever you spend a minute doing this, it is one less minute you can spend doing that. Even in the case where it seems as if no decision is made, you have made a choice. If you cannot decide between a movie and a party and you end up sitting at home, your decision is effectively a decision to stay at home. The time is spent at home and you will never have that time back again. We make these choices every minute of our lives because with every minute we have to make a choice as to how to use it. It is so for Crusoe, and so it is for you. We all face the quandary of choice.

C. THE EMERGENCE OF A COMPLEX SOCIETY

Introducing the Complex Society

In Robinson Crusoe's simple society we found that since he was the only member, the entire societal initial endowment belonged to him. Further, because he was the only participant, all decisions to produce and consume or to save and invest were make simultaneously in his head and were therefore perfectly coordinated. Finally, given that he knew his resources, his technology, and his preferences, as a rational being he would always choose the most efficient technique of production available.

A complex society is exactly the same as a simple society with respect to all of our assumptions about initial endowment, technology, diminishing marginal utility, diminishing marginal product, and rationality, as well as with respect to the utility maximization decision rule that we follow as individuals. However, the complex society is an entirely different situation in some important respects. In a complex society, such as the one in which we live, we are not independent actors like Crusoe. For example, in our society people produce and people consume, but individuals do not generally produce only for their own consumption nor do they consume only what they have individually produced. Instead, goods and services are exchanged. Also people save and people invest, but the savings of one individual may be passed through many hands before it reaches the individual who will use it for a real investment. This means that in a complex society decisions to produce and consume or to save and invest are not, as in Crusoe's world, simultaneously determined in one person's mind and thus perfectly coordinated by definition. The complex society requires a system that will coordinate all these separate individual decisions. There are three ways in which this coordination can be accomplished: a traditional, a centralized, or a decentralized coordination system. Each of these cases has strengths and weaknesses, and features of each may coexist within a given society. Let us consider each in turn.

A *traditional coordination system* has the virtue of continuity. Patterns of saving and investing and of producing and consuming were determined generations ago, and current patterns follow the tradition passed down from those past generations. This continuity gives a great deal of internal stability to the system. The problem with such a system is that it is not very flexible, so it is very fragile and may break down easily when external conditions change.

A totally *centralized coordination system* would be directed by a dictator. Such a dictator could determine what is produced and consumed and what is saved and invested by command. Thus we call this case a *command economy*. In such an economy the decisions to produce and consume and to save and invest are perfectly coordinated because, as in the Robinson Crusoe case, they are all determined in the head of one person. If we assume that the dictator is benevolent, these decisions would reflect the dictator's view of what is best for the people, and if we assume that benevolence includes justice, the result would be in some sense just or fair.

There are two problems with this centralized coordination system. First of all, while the dictator may be benevolent, she is not omniscient. Her decisions must be made according to her own impressions of what the people desire, not on the basis of their actual preferences.

Thus while her decisions may be internally consistent, they will probably not be efficient if by efficient we mean getting the most utility out of the resources and capital available. The second problem is that benevolent dictators are very rare (if they exist at all), and there is little chance that their successors will be so enlightened.

A *decentralized coordination system* is a *market system*. This is the kind or coordination system we will examine in this text. In a market system all individuals make their decisions autonomously. Producers supply goods and services and consumers demand these goods and services. In a perfect market the decisions of both will be coordinated such that the quantity supplied and the quantity demanded will be equalized. There will be no surplus or shortage. Similarly, savers and investors interacting in a perfect market will make independent decisions that are perfectly coordinated. Adam Smith, the father of modern economic thought, wrote that the market coordinates as if it were guided by an "invisible hand." We will see as we study the market system that if the system is perfect, it does coordinate as if all the decisions were being made by and for one individual—or in other words, as if the complex world is analogous to the simple world of Robinson Crusoe. We will also see, however, that markets are not perfect in the real world. We will identify some sources of imperfection as we examine the microeconomy. When we turn our attention to the macroeconomy, we will see how these imperfections can diminish the wealth and welfare of our nation.

Before we begin our analysis of microeconomics in a complex society, it will be useful to examine the factors that give rise to complexity, and consequently to the use of money in complex economies.

Factors That Give Rise to Complexity, Including the Division of Labor and the Gains from Trade

Is it inevitable that simple economies give rise to complex economies? There are animals that live Robinson Crusoe–type existences even though they are not isolated from others of their species. Why do humans choose to live in complex societies rather than in isolation, and why is it that human society becomes progressively more complex over time? Why would anyone give up the security of total independence for vulnerability of interdependence? We can suggest several reasons.

First of all, there is the possibility that we are instinctively social animals. Adam Smith wrote in his book on ethics (*The Theory of Moral Sentiments*, first published in 1759) that humans "can only subsist in society," and therefore "all members of human society stand in need of each other's assistance, and are likewise exposed to mutual injuries." According to this view, we are interdependent by nature.

Another view of our interdependence is that it is inevitable. Since there are many of us and the resources of the earth are finite, we inevitably find ourselves seeking to live off the same set of resources. Even Crusoe did not have the island to himself forever. In economic terms, this means that we share a finite initial endowment. This inevitably leads to issues of interdependence, questions of social choice. How will we share this initial endowment? Shall we share it, and the fruits of our labor on it, as a community with no separation of property? Do we define property rights, divide up the social initial endowment among individuals, and then let each use her own share as she sees fit? If the latter method is chosen, it raises another set of social choice questions. How will we define property rights? How will the division of the social initial endowment among individuals be determined? How will property rights be protected? Clearly, it is through the process of answering these social choice questions that we determine the nature of the social, political, and economic institutions in our society.

As these institutions evolve, they create a structure of control that regulates out interaction in this interdependent world. In doing so, these institutions determine, in large part, the set of opportunities available to each individual in society. It is within these institutional constraints that we make our personal choices. As the institutional structure of control changes, our set of opportunities changes, therefore, our choices change. The evolving position of minorities and women vis-à-vis the institutional structure of control in the United States is an example of this.

An economic institution that exists in all societies is the market system. In some societies this structure plays a very small role, while in other societies its role is very significant. Wherever it functions, it acts as a choice-coordination system. Our purpose here is to see how the market system works and how it interacts with other institutions, social and political, to determine the conditions in society. These are important issues, for if we are to live in a complex society and if we have some ethical vision of a "good" society that we seek to achieve, we must know how the condition of society is determined. If interdependence is inevitable, we must inevitably deal with the issues it gives rise to.

Whether or not interdependence is natural or inevitable, it is encouraged by the increased productivity it makes possible. Adam Smith offers a valuable insight into this aspect of the evolving complexity of human society. Because he recognized the importance of this connection between complexity and social productivity, he began his famous work on economics, *The Wealth of Nations,* with the following words:

> The greatest improvement in the productive powers of labour, and the greater part of the skill, dexterity, and judgment with which it is any where directed, or applied, seem to have been the effects of the division of labour.

What Smith is referring to here is individuals dividing up the labor across trades as well as within trades; the former is often referred to as *specialization.* In his classic example of the increased productivity that comes from the division of labor within a trade, Smith cites pin making. He writes that there are "eighteen distinct operations" involved in making a pin. According to his estimates, if one person tried to do them all she would be lucky to produce twenty pins in a day. If, however, the operations were divided among ten persons, they could "make among them upwards of forty-eight thousand pins in a day." As for the productivity benefits of the division of labor across trades, he cites the advantages of dividing labor so that some people specialize in farming while others specialize in manufacturing.

Smith proposes three reasons for the increased productivity from the division of labor. First, there is what he refers to as "the increase of dexterity in every particular workman." By this Smith means that when one concentrates one's attention on a particular task, one gets better at it. This is Smith's version of the old adage: "Practice makes perfect." Second, Smith notes that the division of labor saves "time which is commonly lost in passing from one species of work to another." He points out that aside from the simple time loss of switching processes, there is the time loss due to regearing your brain. Surely you have had the experience when studying that a switch in subject matter is often the opportune time for a phone call or a trip to the refrigerator. While he did not know of phones or refrigerators, Smith knew the basic feeling. Finally, Smith writes that when one specializes, one gets to know the operation she is concentrating on very well. This, he argues, gives rise to inventions designed to "facilitate and abridge labour." It is for these reasons that the division of labor increases productivity.

The division of labor implies that any given individual will produce only one good or only a part of a good. Thus, while the pin makers are extremely productive at the process of pin making, at the end of the process they have only pins and none of the other goods and services their welfare requires (e.g., food, clothes, water). Their holdings in pins is, in fact, far in excess of their need. This excess is called *surplus.* Since all people in this world find themselves in a similar position— with a surplus of one good and a desire for many others—there is a

TABLE 2–12   What One Hour of Time Can Produce

	Wheat (bushels)	Cloth (yards)
Me	10	7
You	6	10

need for exchange. It is through exchange that the benefits of the division of labor are realized.

We can see the benefits of such a system with a simple example of the *gains from trade*. Assume that I am better at producing wheat and you are better at producing cloth. If we both worked one hour at wheat production and one hour at cloth production, then we see from Table 2–12 that I would produce 10 bushels of wheat and 7 yards of cloth, while you would produce 6 bushels of wheat and 10 yards of cloth. Between the two of us, we produce 16 bushels of wheat and 17 yards of cloth.

If we could divide up the labor, specializing in the productive activity at which we have our respective advantages, I could spend two hours producing 20 bushels of wheat and you could spend two hours producing 20 yards of cloth. Notice that, as shown in Table 2–13, between us we have increased our net wheat production by 4 bushels and our net cloth production by 3 yards. Now, I am holding all the wheat and you are holding all the cloth, so we trade. The exact outcome of the trade is not clear. What is clear is that so long as we both benefit from some of the net gains, we would be willing to continue this mutually advantageous division of labor. The division of labor will continue as long as the gains from the trade of the surpluses it generates are beneficial to the parties involved.

E E2-6   P 259

How can this exchange process be accomplished? How does one know how much of a particular good or service she will be able to exchange? In other words, how does one determine what quality of surpluses should be supplied so that resources will not be wasted on producing goods or services in excess of the quantity others will demand? The fact of the matter is that without some kind of coordinating mechanism, one does not know. The market provides that coordinating mechanism for the exchange of surpluses, and the quality of the market system determines how quickly and effectively these economic decisions are coordinated.

Smith points out that a limitation on the division of labor is, in fact, the extent of the market. After all, one cannot specialize if there is not enough of a demand to warrant the specialty. For instance, in New York City you will find people who make their living as taxi drivers, as couriers, and as professional baseball players, but none of these pro-

TABLE 2–13 Change That Would Occur If Each of Us Transferred One Hour of Time Toward Her Advantage

	Wheat (bushels)	Cloth (yards)
Me	+10	− 7
You	− 6	+10
Net gain	+ 4	+ 3

fessions could be justified in a village of 600 people in upstate New York or in the bayou country of Louisiana.

This division of labor brings tremendous benefits in the form of increased productivity and the greater quantity of goods and services increased productivity represents. It is not without costs, however. Adam Smith, who extolled the virtues of the division of labor, expressed concern that it would focus people's minds so narrowly that it would make them dull and stupid. The division of labor also increases the complexity of society. As this complexity grows we are progressively more interdependent and this complex interdependence makes us vulnerable. Robinson Crusoe's fate depended on luck, nature, and his own decisions. In a complex society our fate depends on these three factors, but it also depends on the decisions of others and on the quality of the coordinating system—the markets. The greater the complexity, the more dependent we are on one another and on the health of the market system.

It is precisely this interdependence and the role of markets as the coordinators that makes the subject matter of economics so interesting, so important, and so complex. We do not have a perfect understanding of this economic system; in fact, our understanding is very rudimentary. We do, however, have theories and models that are our best efforts to represent it.

Next we will introduce the role of money in this complex society. Then we will develop the NeoClassical model of this complex economic system, beginning with an analysis of how markets coordinate.

Role of Money in a Complex Society

As simplicity gives way to complexity with the division of labor, exchange begins. Initially, exchange is through barter. *Barter* is the exchange of equivalents: my good or service for your good or service. The barter system is full of problems, however. First of all, it requires matching. If I have surplus wheat and desire cloth, I must find someone who has surplus cloth and desires wheat. Failing this, I must go through the very tricky business of arranging a multiperson trade; for instance: wheat for meat, then meat for cloth. A related problem is that in a barter system signaling trading intentions can be very inefficient. If I have excess wheat and I would accept an array of possible goods in exchange, I would have to publish a menu of acceptable trades. Alternatively, if my surplus was in wheat and I only wanted cloth in exchange I would have to make numerous inquires in order to find a successful match.

The inefficiency in barter (the exchange of equivalents) gives rise to the identification of a *general equivalent*—one good that is generally accepted in barter for any other good. Gold is a good that historically took on such a role. As gold became accepted as a general equivalent, units of gold became an acceptable measure of the exchange value— in other words, the price of any good or service. A coat, for instance, was worth a certain number of units (grains) of the general equivalent, gold. Since gold does not deteriorate, it also became a useful way to store value between exchanges.

Thus gold became a multipurpose good. It was always valued for its ornamental beauty, but it also took on the roles of a unit of account (it allowed one to measure the value of one's holdings), a medium of exchange (others accepted gold for any good or service), and a store of value (one could hold value in the form of gold). We define any item that serves these three roles as *money*.

Gold has many characteristics that made it an attractive candidate for the role of money . It is, except for periods of plunder or discovery, fairly fixed in supply. (Anything that grows on trees would not make very useful money. Why?) It is portable, which is handy, since money is used in trade. (Land would not make good money.) It is continuously divisible, so that fractional payment is easy. (Cows are portable but do not make good money because half a dairy cow is not half as valuable as a whole dairy cow.) It will not spoil, so it does not inherently lose value.

Gold and other goods that have been used for money are called *commodity money*. Commodity money, a form of money that has uses other than as money (e.g., gold as jewelry), has generally been replaced by what is called *fiat money*. Fiat money has no use except as money, and its usefulness as money depends entirely on the willingness of people to accept it as such. In the United States the cash we use is called Federal Reserve notes and on each one it states: "This note is legal tender for all debts, public and private." Thus the government decrees its acceptability, and as long as people accept this decree and as long as it serves well as a unit of account, medium of exchange, and store of value, the fiat money serves the purpose of money effectively.

The NeoClassical General Competitive Equilibrium Model of a Complex Society —Exchange Under Perfect Competition

Human society, when we contemplate it in a certain abstract and philosophical light, appears like a great, an immense machine, whose regular and harmonious movements produce a thousand agreeable effects.

Adam Smith
The Theory of Moral Sentiments, 1759.

IN THIS CHAPTER we will examine society under just such an "abstract and philosophical light" and we will identify the source of "regular and harmonious movements [that] produce a thousand agreeable effects."

A. REVIEWING OUR ASSUMPTIONS

There are several assumptions we will maintain as we move from an analysis of a simple society to that of a complex society. We continue to assume that all individuals are rational actors and that these actors know their preference ordering. We also maintain the assumptions of diminishing marginal utility, diminishing marginal product, and perfect divisibility of all factors, goods, and services.

In addition to these assumptions, we need a new assumption that sets one of the conditions necessary for the NeoClassical perfectly competitive environment. We will call this new assumption the "fair race" or "no market power" assumption. A fair race requires that all social, political, and economic institutions in society be neutral. This institutional neutrality assumption is analogous to the assumption that for a foot race or a softball game or a basketball game to be fair, the judges, umpires, or referees must be neutral. In other words, the institutional milieu in which the race takes place must not skew the outcome if the race is to be considered fair.

47

This fair race assumption implies that all participants have equal mobility and equal access to information. By equal motility, we mean simply that everyone has equal access to all markets—in other words, that all participants enjoy the same set of opportunities. In terms of our race analogy, the individual can choose the event in which she wants to participate and all individuals face the same obstacles in a given race. Clearly, it is not a fair race if one person faces 100 yards of clear track, while a competitor faces 100 yards with many hurdles along the way. Equal information access ensures that all participants have equal opportunity to determine the options available to them so that each person can choose the best available opportunity. At the track it would clearly be unfair to deny some people the opportunity to participate in a given event by denying them access to information about the event's time and place.

The fair race assumption is not necessary in the simple Robinson Crusoe society because there is no competition and therefore no incentive for, or even meaning to, the concept of an unfair race. In the complex society, however, there is competition. It can be healthy and mutually beneficial, spurring all participants on to greater efforts; or it can degenerate into mutually destructive and wasteful allocations of time and resources to gaining advantages over one another (e.g., spending energy trying to trip your opponent rather than trying to outrun her). By assuming the conditions necessary for a fair race, we assume the positive productive environment of *constructive competition*. Once we have examined this special case, we will relax this assumption in order to investigate the economic consequences of a less than fair environment and the *destructive competition* it engenders.

Another assumption we will make has to do with the nature of the markets we will examine. We will assume that there is no market failure. This assumption implies that the market structure is complete and that the markets are functioning smoothly. By complete market structure we mean that for every product there is a market formed to coordinate exchange. By markets functioning smoothly we mean that markets do their coordinating quickly and effectively. Later we will relax this no market failure assumption in order to examine the implications of an incomplete market structure and of slow or unsuccessful market coordination.

These two assumptions—no market power (a fair race) and no market failure—will be called our *"nice" NeoClassical assumptions*. They are called "nice" assumptions because, as we will see, they give rise to a nice condition in a complex exchange economy: efficiency. These assumptions, combined with the more basic ones reviewed above, are those necessary for a NeoClassical perfectly competitive environment to exist.

Before we begin, we need one more assumption that was not necessary in the Robinson Crusoe simple society. In that case, the societal initial endowment was identical to Crusoe's endowment because he was the only member of society. In a complex society the societal initial endowment can be distributed among the multitude of individuals in an infinite number of ways or it may be held in trust by some societal institution that we have assumed is neutral. How the societal initial endowment is distributed among individuals has a tremendous impact on the outcome of a perfectly competitive economic system, just as the distribution of genetic endowments has a tremendous impact on a fair race at a track. For the time being, we will assume that the distribution of initial endowments is given (i.e., that it has been determined and is fixed) so that we can concentrate our attention on the analysis of the race, the perfectly competitive market system itself. When we conclude our analysis, we will relax this assumption and examine the implications of treating the distribution of initial endowments as variable.

B. HOW MARKETS COORDINATE THE DECISIONS OF INDIVIDUALS IN A PERFECTLY COMPETITIVE ENVIRONMENT

An Overview

As we learned from Adam Smith, the division of labor makes us more productive as a society, but it requires a system for the exchange of the surpluses generated by this specialization. With the evolution of the division of labor and exchange, individuals can enjoy the combination of goods and services they desire in greater quantity and quality than anyone could produce in isolation. As we have seen, one kind of exchange system that makes the division of labor possible is a market system. Markets can provide the coordinating mechanism for decentralized decisions in a complex society. The effectiveness of market coordination will determine the quality of the exchange process, and therefore the success with which the benefits of the division of labor in society (the gains from trade) are realized. The fact that such a system for coordinating decentralized decisions could work at all is amazing. As two famous economists, Kenneth Arrow (winner of the 1972 Nobel Prize in Economics) and Frank Hahn, have written in *General Competitive Analysis* (San Francisco: Holden-Day, 1971 pps. vi-vii):

There is by now a long and fairly imposing line of economists from Adam Smith to the present who have sought to show that a decentralized economy motivated by self-interest and guided by price signals would be compatible with a coherent disposition of economic resources that could be regarded, in a well-defined sense, as superior to a large class of possible alternative dispositions. Moreover, the price signals would operate in a way to establish a degree of coherence. It is important to understand how surprising this claim must be to anyone not exposed to this tradition. The immediate "common sense" answer to the question "What will an economy motivated by individual greed and controlled by a very large number of different agents look like?" is probably: There will be chaos. That quite a different answer has long been claimed true and has indeed permeated the economic thinking of a large number of people who are in no way economists is itself sufficient grounds for investigating it seriously. The proposition having been put forward and very seriously entertained, it is important to know not only whether it *is* true, but also whether it *could be* true. A good deal of what follows is concerned with this last question.

That question is indeed our question. We have made all the necessary assumptions for markets to act as undistorted, effective, and quick coordinators. Now we turn our attention to these perfectly competitive markets in order to see how they could carry out this coordinating role.

We will identify two players in this basic version of a complex economy. They are the households and the firms.

The *households* are the holders of shares in the society's initial endowment of resources and capital. In other words, all factors of production are held by households. Households are also the ultimate consumer of all the finished products (goods and services) in society. Thus households are the source of all inputs and the destination of all final outputs of production. The objective of households is, as we have assumed all along, to maximize utility.

Firms are the catalyst for production. Firms determine the goods or services they will produce, choose techniques from the technology of production, buy the factors of production from households, and combine the factors in a process of production to make the goods or services that they will sell to households. The objective of firms is to maximize profits. Profits are the net revenue above and beyond costs of production. Since firms are owned and managed by members of households, this profit-maximization objective of firms is derived from the ultimate utility-maximization objective of households. Greater profits means greater incomes, which, in turn, means greater utility. (Consider: Could there be a conflict of interest between firms' owners and managers?)

The firms and households interact in two kinds of markets. In the *factor market* firms demand factors of production and households supply them. The cash the firms spend in order to demand factors is the firms' costs, and the cash the households receive in return for supplying factors is the households' incomes. The households take their income and use it in the *product market* to demand goods and services. These goods and services are supplied by the firms that have used the factors they purchased to produce them. In return for supplying the goods and services, the firms receive revenues that will be used to cover the costs of production. Notice that the system is circular (see Figure 3-1). Each step is necessary for the next, yet there is no beginning and no end.

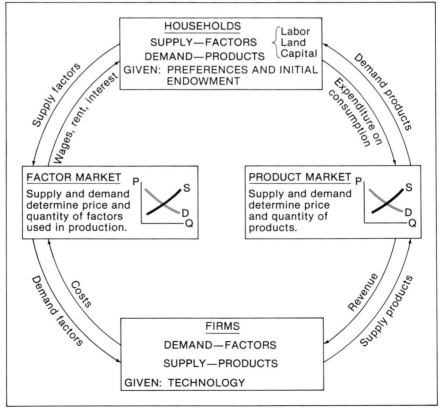

FIGURE 3-1   Market Economy Circular Flow   There are two decision makers: households and firms. There are two kinds of markets: product and factor.

Each market brings together suppliers and demanders of an item. The item may be a factor of production (like labor) or a product (a good or service). The suppliers come to the market with some notion as to what quantity of the item they are willing to supply at any given price. Similarly, the demanders have a notion as to what quantity they are willing to demand at any given price. Notice that both the quantity supplied and the quantity demanded depend on price. Price is measured in terms of our general equivalent, money. We will refer to price in dollars.

Unlike the Robinson Crusoe society wherein the supplier and demander were one and the same person, in this complex society the suppliers' and demanders' decisions on quantity to supply and quantity to demand must be coordinated. Similarly, unlike the barter economy wherein exchange can only take place if each party holds a good the other values enough to warrant the exchange, in this fiat-money society all parties offer and accept cash for the quantities exchanged. In this case, money facilitates much more complex exchanges by serving in its role as a medium of exchange.

In order to see how an actual market works, we will focus our attention on the product market, in particular, the market for candy bars. We will assume for the moment that conditions in all factor markets and all other product markets are fixed.

The Demand Curve

The intentions of the candy bar demanders in the candy bar market are represented by a demand curve. A demand curve is a graphical representation of a demand schedule that shows the quantity of candy bars the household is willing to demand at any given price. The demand schedule can be represented as in Table 3-1; or it can be represented as a demand curve, as in Figure 3-2.

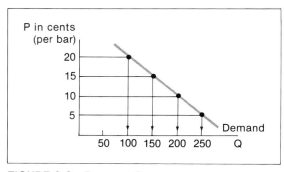

FIGURE 3-2   Demand Curve

TABLE 3-1   A Demand Schedule

Price (P) (per bar)	Quantity (Q) of bars
$.05	250
$.10	200
$.15	150
$.20	100

The demand curve in Figure 3-2 shows that at $.05 per bar the quantity demand will be 250, at $.10 per bar the quantity demanded will be 200, at $.15 per bar the quantity demanded will be 150, and at $.20 per bar the quantity demanded will be 100.

Note the distinction between *demand* and *quantity demand*. The entire demand curve (or schedule) represents the level of demand— the general attitude of the household under given conditions: "As the price per unit changes, this is how the quantity I'm willing to demand changes." Quantity demanded, on the other hand, is a specific number. It is the amount the household would desire at a specific price under given demand conditions. A change in price when demand conditions remain constant will move the household along its demand curve or schedule to a new quantity demanded, but it will not affect the level of demand. The curve or schedule remains unchanged. But change in the conditions of demand will change the whole level of demand. In terms of the demand schedule, this means that there will be a new quantity demanded at each price. In terms of the demand curve, this means that the entire curve shifts. We will see in a moment what conditions affect the level of demand and how they do so.

The Supply Curve

The intentions of the candy bar suppliers are represented by a supply curve. A supply curve is a graphical representation of a supply schedule that shows the quantity of candy bars the firm is willing to supply at any given price. The supply schedule can be represented as a schedule, as in Table 3-2; or it can be represented by a supply curve, as in Figure 3-3.

Table 3-2   A Supply Schedule

Price (per bar)	Quantity of Bars
$.05	50
$.10	100
$.15	150
$.20	200

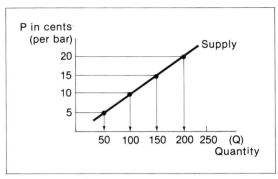

FIGURE 3-3 Supply Curve

The supply curve in Figure 3-3 shows that at $.05 per bar the quantity supplied will be 50, at $.10 per bar the quantity supplied will be 100, at $.15 per bar the quantity supplied will be 150, and at $.20 per bar the quantity supplied will be 200.

Note the distinction between the *supply* and *quantity supplied*. The entire supply curve or schedule represents the level of supply—the general attitude of the firm under given conditions: "As the price per unit changes, this is how the quantity I'm willing to supply changes." Quantity supplied, on the other hand, is a specific number. It is the amount the firm would offer at a specific price under given supply conditions. A change in price when supply conditions remain constant will move the firm along its supply curve or schedule to a new quantity supplied, but it will not affect the level of supply. The curve or schedule remains unchanged. But change in the conditions of supply will change the whole level of supply. In terms of the supply schedule, this means that there will be a new quantity supplied at each price. In terms of the supply curve, this means that the entire curve shifts. We will see below what conditions affect the level of supply and how they do so.

Combining Supply and Demand

Combining the supply and demand curves together on one graph, we can represent the candy bar market as shown in Figure 3-4.

The first point to emphasize is that the people who determine the supply of candy bars are distinct from those who determine the demand. Not only are the people distinct, but the basis on which suppliers and demanders make their respective supply and demand decisions are also entirely distinct. In short, supply and demand are totally separate —determined by different people concerned about different things. It

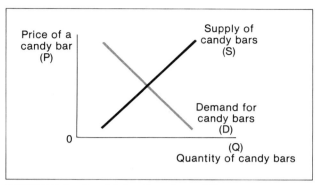

FIGURE 3-4   Combining Supply and Demand

is precisely this point that distinguishes the complex society from the
Robinson Crusoe society. It is for precisely this reason that the complex society benefits from a system of markets to coordinate quantity
supply and quantity demand decisions. As we will see, under our nice
assumptions, a market system can be a very efficient coordinator.

How do markets coordinate? The best way to see how the market
works is to look at how it responds under various circumstances. In
our candy bar market we will assume that the current price is P_1, and
that at that price the quantity supplied is greater that the quantity
demanded. This case is shown in Figure 3-5.

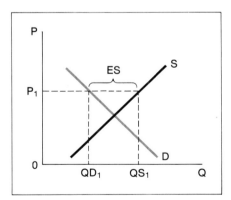

FIGURE 3-5   Excess Supply

Under this circumstance we see that firms responding to this price
will offer a quantity supplied (QS_1) and households will desire a quantity demanded (QD_1). In this case, QS is greater than QD. In other
words, at this price there will be an excess supply (ES) equal to QS
minus QD ($ES=QS-QD$). What do you expect will occur?

The firms will recognize very quickly that their inventories (unsold product) are going to grow if they keep producing QS. Since they are in business to make a living and not to accumulate inventories, they will cut back on production and lower their price to reduce inventories. As the price falls, households' QD will increase. Thus as price falls, QD will begin to expand and QS will begin to contract; therefore the excess supply will shrink, as demonstrated in Figure 3-6.

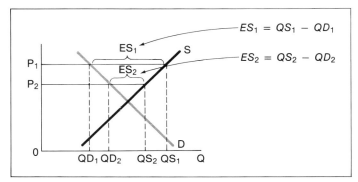

FIGURE 3-6   Adjustment Process   As P falls from P_1 to P_2, ES shrinks from ES_1 to ES_2.

Suppose the firm made a drastic price cut from P_2 to P_3 and that at P_3 the quantity demanded is greater than the quantity supplied. This case is shown in Figure 3-7.

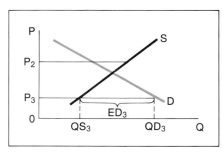

FIGURE 3-7   Excess Demand

At this relatively low price the quantity demanded is greater than the quantity supplied ($QD_3 > QS_3$); therefore, instead of an excess supply, the market is experiencing an excess demand; ED_3 ($ED_3 = QD_3 - QS_3$). How will the participants respond to this circumstance?

The firms find that they can sell more than they are producing. Inventories dwindle and finally disappear. When inventories are gone, consumers are standing in line waiting for the next shipment. Given inadequate supplies, consumers begin to bid up the price in order to get some of the good. As price rises, the firms expand QS and the households contract QD. Thus, as the price rises, the excess demand will begin to shrink.

We see that at any price that results in an excess supply or excess demand, forces will be set in motion that reduce the excess. The amazing thing about the process is that no one is in charge. There is not one central person or agency playing the role of coordinator. The process is decentralized. All firms and households are acting in their own interests. The coordination is accomplished because they are all observing the same *signal* emitted by the market: the price. Their individual decisions are in response to this common signal. If the current signal (price) results in individual decisions that are inconsistent (i.e., an excess supply or demand results), the signal (price) adjusts automatically in a way that brings the decisions into consistency. Only at that price which sets quantity demanded equal to quantity supplied will the price stop adjusting. At that point, as shown in Figure 3-8, the market is said to have reached an *equilibrium* (a maintainable position, *ceteris paribus*). The price is at the *equilibrium price* because it sets the quantity demanded equal to the quantity supplied. We call this amount the *equilibrium quantity exchanged*.

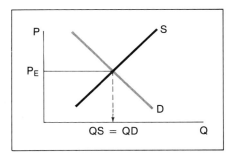

FIGURE 3-8 Equilibrium

The equilibrium shown in Figure 3-8 will be disturbed if for any reason the level of supply and/or demand changes. Given our nice assumptions, the market will quickly respond to such changes by moving to a new equilibrium. In order to see how this works, we will examine how the market responds to each of the following cases: (1) a fall in supply, (2) a rise in supply, (3) a rise in demand, (4) a fall in demand. For each case, we will assume that initially the market supply and demand are S_0 and D_0, that the market equilibrium point is at e_0, and that the equilibrium price and quantity exchanged are P_0 and Q_0. The initial·position is shown in Figure 3-9.

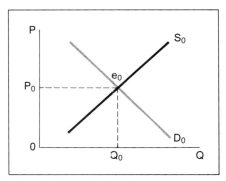

FIGURE 3-9   Equilibrium

Case 1 (see Figure 3-10). Suppose supply falls from S_0 to S_1. At price P_0 there is now an excess demand, so P_0 is no longer an equilibrium price. The excess demand at initial price P_0 will cause a price adjustment upward. The price will continue to adjust until a new equilibrium is established at price P_1. At the new equilibrium point, e_1, the price is higher and quantity exchanged is lower.

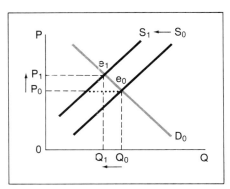

FIGURE 3-10   Adjustment After Supply Shift (S Decreases)   The dotted line (...) shows the size of excess demand after the supply shift but before the price adjustment.

An example of this would be a bad grain crop. *Ceteris paribus,* the consequence. as Figure 3-10 shows, would be a fall in quantity exchanged and a rise in price.

Case 2 (see Figure 3-11). Suppose supply rises from S_0 to S_2. At price P_0 there is now an excess supply, so P_0 is no longer an equilibrium price. The excess supply at initial price P_0 will cause a price adjustment downward. The price will continue to adjust until a new equilibrium is established at price P_2. At the new equilibrium point, e_2, the price is lower and the quantity exchanged is higher.

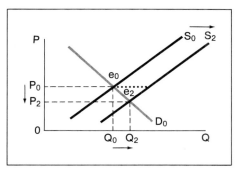

FIGURE 3-11   Adjustment After Supply Shift (S Increases)   The dotted line (...) shows the size of excess supply after the supply shift but before the price adjustment.

An example of this would be a bumper grain crop. *Ceteris paribus,* the consequence, as Figure 3-11 shows, would be a rise in the quantity exchanged and a fall in price.

Case 3 (see Figure 3-12). Suppose demand rises from D_0 to D_3. At price P_0 there is now an excess demand, so P_0 is no longer an equilibrium price. The excess demand at initial price P_0 will cause a price adjustment upward. The price will continue to adjust until a new equi-

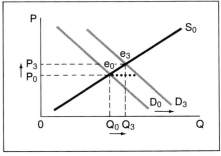

FIGURE 3-12   Adjustment After Demand Shift (D Increases)   The dotted line (...) shows the size of excess demand after the demand shift but before the price adjustment.

librium is established at price P_3. At the new equilibrium point, e_3, the price is higher and the quantity exchanged is higher.

An example of this would be a rock group that gets hot. *Ceteris paribus*, the consequence, as Figure 3-12 shows, would be a rise in quantity exchanged (of tickets or records) and a rise in price.

Case 4 (see Figure 3-13). Suppose demand falls from D_0 to D_4. At price P_0 there is now an excess supply, so P_0 is no longer an equilibrium price. The excess supply at initial price P_0 will cause a price adjustment downward. The price will continue to adjust until a new equilibrium is established at price P_4. At the new equilibrium point, e_4, the price is lower and the quantity exchanged is lower.

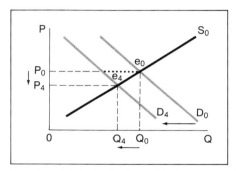

FIGURE 3-13   Adjustment After Demand Shift (*D* Decreases)   The dotted line (...) shows the size of excess supply after the demand shift but before the price adjustment.

An example of this would be a rock group that falls out of fashion. *Ceteris paribus*, the consequence, as Figure 3-13 shows, would be a fall in quantity exchanged (of tickets or records) and a fall in price.

Again it must be emphasized, the market system is a self-adjusting mechanism based on price signals. In a complex society in which our nice assumptions hold, the markets automatically provide the necessary information (in the form of price signals) for all individual decisions to be coordinated perfectly. Such a complex society would, therefore, be perfectly analogous to a simple Robinson Crusoe society. Every resource would be employed in the most efficient way in order to produce maximum utility for the resource holder.

In order to gain a deeper understanding of a market system, we need to look at the concepts of demand and supply more carefully. Next, therefore, we narrow our focus and examine each of these pieces of our model in more detail.

C. CONDITIONS THAT DETERMINE THE EQUILIBRIUM IN THE PRODUCT MARKET

Conditions That Determine Demand

• *The Downward Slope of the Demand Curve* Given the assumption of diminishing marginal utility, one characteristic that all demand curves share is that they slope down to the right. This can be demonstrated by building on the individual utility maximization decision rule we identified while examining the simple Robinson Crusoe society.

Abstracting from risk and the time dimension, we found that in order to maximize utility Crusoe allocated his scarce resource, time, so that the last unit in every use would give equal marginal utility. In other words, for all n uses of his time he set:

$$\frac{MU_1}{\text{minute}} = \frac{MU_2}{\text{minute}} = \ldots = \frac{MU_n}{\text{minute}}$$

A household faces a similar problem when deciding how to spend its income. Dollar income is a scarce resource that the household wants to spend on n alternative goods and services so as to maximize its utility. The solution to the household's money-budgeting problem is perfectly analogous to Crusoe's time-budgeting solution. The household must spend its income so that the last dollar spent on every good or service gives equal marginal utility. If all goods and services cost $1 per unit, the solution could be written as:

$$\frac{MU_1}{\$1} = \frac{MU_2}{\$1} = \ldots = \frac{MU_n}{\$1}$$

Since, however, each good or service has a different price, in order to calculate the marginal utility per dollar from the last unit of the good or service purchased, we must divide each of these marginal utilities by the price of the relevant good or service. Therefore the utility maximization decision rule must be written:

$$\frac{MU_1}{P_1} = \frac{MU_2}{P_2} = \ldots = \frac{MU_n}{P_n}$$

With this decision rule we can demonstrate that the price of a good or service and its quantity demanded are inversely related—in other words, demand curves slope down.

Let us assume that you initially maximize your utility at a given set of prices and then one price, P_1, rises. The rise in P_1 confronts you with a new structure of incentives. Relative to other goods and services, item 1 is now more expensive. How will you respond to this relative price change?

If you do not change your pattern of consumption when relative prices change, you will no longer be following the utility maximization decision rule. Instead, you will be setting

$$\frac{MU_1}{P_1} < \frac{MU_2}{P_2} = \ldots = \frac{MU_n}{P_n}$$

because P_1 rose but MU_1 has not changed. In order to return to the utility maximization condition, MU_1/P_1 must rise to again equal the marginal utility per dollar generated by the other uses of your income. Since market forces that are beyond your control determine prices, the only thing you have the power to change is MU_1. You must increase MU_1 in order to satisfy the utility maximization rule. How can you do this?

We know that given the assumption of diminishing marginal utility, as you decrease the quantity of a good consumed, the marginal utility you receive from the last unit of that good consumed increases. Thus when the price of good 1 (P_1) rises, causing:

$$\frac{MU_1}{P_1} < \frac{MU_2}{P_2} = \ldots = \frac{MU_n}{P_n}$$

which violates the utility maximization decision rule, you must reduce your consumption of good 1 (the quantity of good 1 you demand) until the marginal utility from good 1 rises proportionately to the price rise for good 1, thus restoring the equality:

$$\frac{MU_1}{P_1} = \frac{MU_2}{P_2} = \ldots = \frac{MU_n}{P_n}$$

and thereby ensuring that utility is again maximized.

Beginning with the utility maximization decision rule and the assumption of diminishing marginal utility, we have shown that a rise in the price of good 1 will result in a fall in its quantity demanded. Similarly, it could be shown that a fall in the price of good 1 will result in a rise in the quantity demanded. This result confirms that the demand curve for good 1 must slope down to the right. Since a change in the price of any good or service will give a similar result, we can generalize and assert that all demand curves slope down to the right.

• *The Responsiveness of a Good or Service's Quantity Demanded to a Change in Its Own Price—Own Price Elasticity* We have just demonstrated that demand curves slope down to the right, or, that as the price rises, the quantity of that good demanded falls. Now we want to examine how sensitive quantity demanded is to a change in price. As price rises, does quantity demanded go down rapidly or slowly? This responsiveness of the quantity demanded of a good to a change in the good's own price is referred to as the *own price elasticity of demand*.

Clearly, some goods or services are not very responsive to a change in their own price. Consider addictive drugs. Once you're addicted to a drug, you *need* it–no ifs, ands, or buts—and price is no object. This last phrase is the one that relates to elasticity. When "price is no object" it means, in effect, that you want the stuff no matter what it costs. In economist's terms, your demand is very (totally) unresponsive to price—in other words, your demand is very (totally or perfectly) inelastic.

Conversely, some goods or services are very responsive to a change in their own price. For example, if one farmer at a farmer's market yells that she's going to charge less than the going rate for apples, that farmer's stall will probably attract a lot of customers.

Think about it. Would K Mart choose a good with an inelastic demand when it announces: "Attention K Mart shoppers, there's a Blue Light Special in aisle three"? Putting a good with a very inelastic demand on sale doesn't stimulate any increase in the quantity demanded. What kind of good would you choose for a Blue Light Special if you were a manager at K Mart?

What makes the demand for one good or service more or less elastic than that for another? We can identify four conditions that affect the own price elasticity of demand for a particular good or service. No one of them determines price elasticity; they interact—sometimes exerting influences in opposite directions.

One condition is the *number and quality of the substitutes* a good has. More and better substitutes tend to make demand more price-elastic because it is easy to switch to another good as price rises. Another condition is the *size of the price relative to one's income*. If the price is small relative to income (e.g., bubble gum), a large percentage change in price (a 100 percent change from $.01 to $.02) will probably not cause a significant percentage change in quantity demanded. Thus the smaller the price relative to income, the more likely the demand will be inelastic. A third condition is whether the good is viewed as a *luxury or a necessity*. Necessities by their nature have a less price-elastic demand than luxuries. We can do without luxuries as their price rises, but we cannot give up necessities. The final condition is the *time horizon* involved. More time generally means more potential options can be identified, so a good that has a fairly inelastic demand over a short time horizon may have a fairly elastic demand over a longer time horizon.

Mathematically we define elasticity as follows:

$$\text{Elasticity of demand} = \frac{\text{percentage change in quantity demanded}}{\text{percentage change in price}}$$

When quantity demanded is changing by a greater percentage than price, we say that demand is responsive and we call this the case of *elastic demand*. Mathematically, we define elastic demand as the case in which elasticity is greater than 1. When quantity demanded is changing by a smaller percentage than price, we say that demand is unresponsive and we call this the case of *inelastic demand*. Mathematically, we define this as the case in which elasticity is less than 1. The special case in which quantity demanded is changing by the same percentage as price is called *unitary elasticity* because mathematically it is the case in which elasticity equals 1.

The elasticity equation uses percentage change rather than absolute change because the former reflects the degree of change more accurately than the latter. For example, a change in price from $1 to $2 is the same in absolute terms as a change in price from $1,000,001 to $1,000,002. Clearly, however, the change $1 to $2 is a much larger degree of change (100 percent) than the change from $1,000,001 to $1,000,002 (a fraction of 1%). Since percentage changes reflect the degree of change more truly, and since elasticity is a measure of responsiveness, the elasticity equation uses percentage rather than absolute changes.

Own price elasticity reveals some fascinating and valuable information. Consider the following facts: As price rises, quantity demanded falls. When elasticity is less than 1, as price rises, the quantity demanded falls by a smaller percentage than the price rises. When elasticity is greater than 1, as price rises, the quantity demanded falls by a greater percentage than the price rises. Now consider the following question: If you were the owner of a firm and you decided to raise the price of your product, would you pray that, *ceteris paribus*, your demand is elastic or inelastic? Does it make a difference? Yes! It makes a big difference.

The total amount that an individual will spend on your product, and therefore your total revenue from that individual, is:

$$Total\ expenditure = Total\ revenue = Price \times Quantity$$
OR
$$TE = TR = P \times Q$$

If as you raise your price the quantity demanded falls by a smaller percentage than the price rises, your total revenue will rise. All else being equal, this will make you very happy. If, on the other hand, as you raise your price the quantity demanded falls by a larger percentage than the price rises, your total revenue will fall and, all else being equal, woe is you for that decision. In the first case, demand was inelastic—and that's the case you would pray for, *ceteris paribus*.

Many large firms resort to economists rather than prayer. They hire economists to estimate the elasticity of the demand for their product so they can evaluate the consequences of a price change. If the economist's calculations of elasticity are correct, the firm can avoid pricing mistakes.

To see this relationship between the demand curve for a good and the household's expenditure, consider Figure 3-14, which shows the demand curve and the amount spent for various quantities demanded:

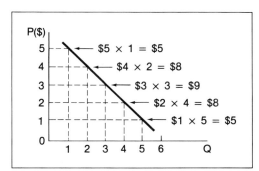

FIGURE 3-14 Demand and Total Expenditure   Price × quantity = household's total expenditure.

Starting at a price of $1, as the price rises, the household's expenditure goes up, levels off at the $3 price, and then falls as the price rises to $5. From this evidence we can say that the demand curve is most inelastic at the bottom right (as P goes from $1 to $2 [a 100 percent change], *Q* goes from 5 to 4 [a 20% change]), gets less inelastic up to the $3 price, and then becomes more and more elastic as the price rises above $3 (as *P* goes from $4 to $5 [a 25% change], *Q* goes from 2 to 1 [a 50% change]). Three dollars is where the demand curve switches from inelastic to elastic. At the $3 point the curve is unitary-elastic.

Thus we see that the relationship between elasticity along a demand curve and the household's total expenditures (TE) can be represented by the two graphs in Figure 3-15.

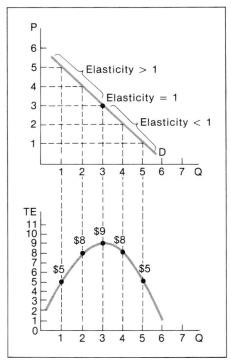

FIGURE 3-15 Demand, Elasticity, and Total Expenditure   The numbers at each dot are P × Q derived from demand curve above. Remember, P×Q = TE.

It is often useful to compare two demand curves in terms of their elasticity. The common convention for doing so can be understood as follows. We saw in our example above that for a demand curve a slope of minus one (−1) that passes through the point (3,3), the own price elasticity equals 1 at point (3,3), as shown in Figure 3-16.

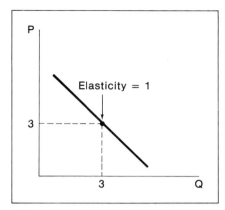

FIGURE 3-16 Elasticity

Now if we rotate the demand curve around the (3,3) point so as to make it more vertical, the elasticity = 1 point moves up and to the left, as shown in Figure 3-17.

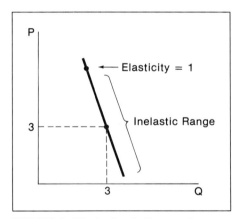

FIGURE 3-17 Inelastic Demand

As a consequence, the price at which the demand curve leaves the inelastic range becomes higher and higher and the quantity at which it leaves the inelastic range becomes smaller and smaller. (Compare Figure 3-16 and Figure 3-17.) Since fewer and fewer elastic points along the curve are in the relevant price/quantity range (the range in which we would actually expect the market to function), the convention in this case is to say that the demand curve is becoming more and more inelastic. At the extreme, when the demand curve is exactly vertical, a change in price has no effect on quantity demanded. In this case, own price elasticity equals zero for all points along the curve because any percentage change in price results in a percentage change in quantity that is always zero. We call this extreme case, shown in Figure 3-18, a perfectly inelastic demand curve.

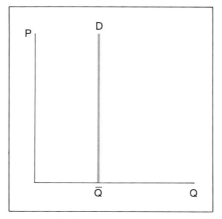

FIGURE 3-18 A Perfectly Inelastic Demand Curve

Conversely, if we rotate the demand curve around the (3,3) point so as to make it more horizontal, the elasticity = 1 point moves down and to the right, as shown in Figure 3-19.

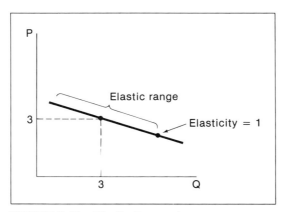

FIGURE 3-19 Elastic Demand

As a consequence, the price at which the demand curve leaves the elastic range becomes lower and lower and the quantity at which it leaves the elastic range becomes greater and greater. (Compare Figure 3-16 and Figure 3-19.) Since fewer and fewer inelastic points along the curve are in the relevant price/quantity range (the range in which we would actually expect the market to function), the convention in this case is to say that the demand curve is becoming more and more elastic. At the extreme, when the demand curve is exactly horizontal, the change in price is always zero because demand only occurs at one price. In this case, price elasticity equals infinity (or is undefined) for all points along the demand curve because percentage change in price (the denominator in our elasticity equation) is always zero. We call this extreme case, shown in Figure 3-20, a perfectly elastic demand curve.

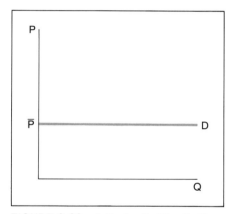

FIGURE 3-20   A Perfectly Elastic Demand Curve

We can represent the relationship between these cases as shown in Figure 3-21.

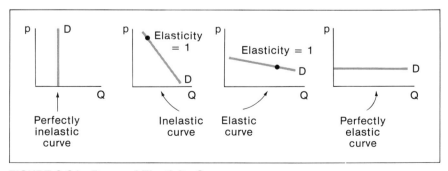

FIGURE 3-21   Demand Elasticity Cases

A heart pacemaker might be an example of a good for which the demand is perfectly inelastic. If you need one, you can't live without it; within the bounds of your income and wealth "price is no object." Addictive drugs also represent a very inelastic demand. As the price of this good(?) goes up, consumers cannot, and therefore will not, reduce quantity demanded very much.

An example of a good that exhibits an elastic demand would be Penney's plain pocket jeans. If Penney's raises its price significantly, it can expect that a large number of its potential customers will buy one of the many other available brands. The same reasoning applies to soft drinks, fast food, and so on. When the products of the various suppliers are virtually interchangeable, the demand faced by any one supplier is very elastic because lots of good substitutes are available. One way in which individual suppliers try to escape this intense competition from apparent substitutes is to advertise their product as somehow unique. Thus we learn that if you want to be young, you should join the Pepsi generation, but only Coke is the real thing; that a great place for a break is McDonald's, but it's Burger King that does it your way; and, that if you're confused about your future, the Army is a great place to start.

These advertising campaigns are designed to create product awareness and brand loyalty so that consumers will not see the alternatives as perfect substitutes. To the degree that the ads work, they make the demand for the goods involved somewhat less price-sensitive and therefore slightly less elastic.

If, in fact, the goods of various suppliers are considered perfect substitutes, then the demand facing any individual supplier will be perfectly elastic. This is the case of the apple seller at the farmer's market. Assuming all the available apples are essentially the same in quality and that there are a lot of apple sellers at the market, the competition among the sellers will push the going rate for apples (the "market price") down to the lowest price the sellers can accept and still stay in business. At that point, no one will try to lower her price and anyone who tries to raise the price will lose all her customers. Under those circumstances, buyers can't find a lower price and won't pay a higher price than the "going rate," so the demand facing each seller is perfectly elastic at the market price. (Why do you think Chiquita started putting little labels on their bananas?)

- ***The Responsiveness of a Good or Service's Demand and Quantity Demanded to a Change in Income or in the Price of a Related Good or Service—Income and Cross-Price Elasticities*** Now that we have examined the characteristics of a given demand curve, we turn our attention to the conditions of demand that determine the overall level of demand or where the demand curve is on the graph. These conditions are the prices of related goods, income, and taste. In order to see how these conditions affect the position of the demand curve, we will examine each in turn. Before we do so, however, we should define some terms that describe shifting demand curves. If D identifies the demand curve's initial position, then we can define demand shifts as shown in Figure 3-22.

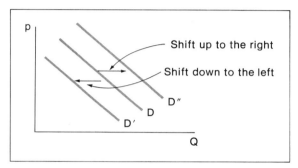

FIGURE 3-22   Demand Shifts—Defining Terms

A shift to the left (down) is represented by the new demand curve D'. This shift represents a fall in quantity demanded at all prices (pick some prices and show yourself that this is so). A shift to the right (up) is represented by the new demand curve D''. This shift represents a rise in quantity demanded at any given price (again, convince yourself).

Now consider the effect of a change in *tastes*. If, *ceteris paribus*, a number of people suddenly feel a much weaker or stronger desire for a good or service, then we say that their preferences or tastes have changed. Tastes in clothes, tastes in music, tastes in food—tastes are constantly changing, and as a result, demand curves are constantly shifting. An increase in a person's taste for an item implies that at any given price the person will buy more of that item. This, in turn, implies an increase in the level of demand or a shift of that individual's demand curve to the right. A decline in an individual's taste for an item results in a shift of that individual's demand curve to the left.

The second demand condition we will consider is *income*. We want to know what the response of demand will be to a change in income. The responsiveness of demand to a change in income is called the *income elasticity of demand*. If income goes up and households respond by buying more of the good at the given price, the demand curve shifts to the right. In this case, where an income rise causes quantity demanded at any given price to rise, we say that the good has a *positive income elasticity*. Since for most goods it is normal for households to buy more as their incomes go up, goods with positive income elasticity are called *normal goods*. For some goods demand shifts to the left as income goes up, so at the given price, quantity demanded falls and we say that the income elasticity of these goods is *negative*. These are goods we prefer not to use as we get wealthier, so goods with a negative income elasticity are called *inferior goods*. Can you think of an example of an inferior good?

The third demand condition we will look at is the *price of related goods*. Lots of goods are related: peanut butter and jelly, wine and beer, hamburgers and french fries, hamburgers and pizza. Surely, you can think of many more. When the price of one in a pair of related goods changes, it has an effect on the demand for the other good. The direction of this effect depends on whether the goods are substitutes or complements. *Substitutes* are goods that generally represent an either/or choice, like hamburgers and pizza. *Complements* are goods that are typically consumed together, such as hamburgers and french fries. The responsiveness of the demand for one good to a change in the price of another is called the *cross-price elasticity of demand*.

If the price of one good goes up and as a consequence the demand for another related good goes down (to the left), the price of good 1 and the demand for good 2 are moving in opposite directions. We refer to this as a *negative cross-price elasticity*. When goods have a negative cross-price elasticity they are complements. Take the hamburger and french fries example. As the price of hamburgers rises, the quantity of hamburgers demanded falls. When we consume fewer hamburgers, the demand for french fries will fall and so, too, *ceteris paribus*, the quantity demanded. Thus a rise in the price of good 1, hamburgers, results in a fall in the quantity demanded of good 2, french fries. We define this as a negative cross-price elasticity case and we see that this is the case of complements. We demonstrate the interaction between markets for complements in Figure 3-23.

Obviously, the *positive cross-price elasticity* case is one of substitutes. If the price of hamburgers rises, people will begin to substitute pizza for hamburger, shifting out the demand for pizza and consequently increasing the quantity demanded. Thus a rise in the price of good 1, hamburgers, results in a rise in the quantity demanded of good 2, pizza. We define this as the positive cross price elasticity case and we see that this is the case of substitutes. Draw the graphs of two substitute goods and demonstrate for yourself this interdependence when the price of one of the goods rises because of a shift in supply, *ceteris paribus*.

This cross-price elasticity information is very important to "real

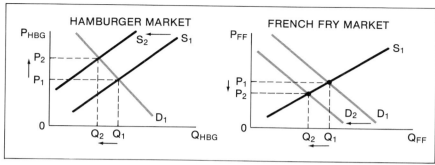

FIGURE 3-23 Market Interaction Suppose that for some reason the supply of hamburgers fell. _Ceteris parabus_, at the new equilibrium the price would be higher and the quantity demanded would be lower. Since hamburgers and french fries are compliments (i.e., consumed together), this reduction in the quantity demanded of hamburgers results in a fall in demand for french fries. The new equilibrium in the french fry market would exhibit a lower quantity demanded and a lower price.

world" marketing people. If you are the executive who sets prices at Burger King, you need to know the size of cross-price elasticity between items. If the positive cross-price elasticity is very high between your burgers and McDonald's, and if the negative cross-price elasticity is very high between your burgers and your fries, an increase in burger prices could send your customers scurrying off to McDonald's and could kill your fries business.

• _**Individual vs. Market Demand.**_ Finally, we must identify the relationship between the demand of an individual household and the total market demand. The sum of all households' demands for a given good or service is the market demand for that good or service. In other words, at any given price, the market quantity demanded is the sum of the individual households' quantities demanded at that price.

We see in Figure 3-24 that in a world of three households the market demand is the sum of the three individuals' demands; therefore, at any given price, the market quantity demanded is the sum of the three households' quantities demanded at that price. In this example, at a $1 price for candy bars, we find that household 1 has a quantity demanded of 3 bars; household 2 has a quantity demanded of 4 bars; and household 3, has a quantity demanded of 5 bars. Summing these up, we see that the market quantity demanded at a $1 price is 12 candy bars (3+4+5=12). At a $5 price, households 1, 2, and 3 have as quantities demanded 1, 2, and 1 bar, respectively. Therefore the market quantity demanded for candy bars at a $5 price is 4 bars. By

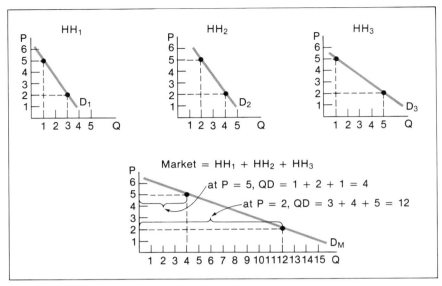

FIGURE 3-24   Market Demand

repeating this calculation over all prices we derive the market demand curve.

Since the market demand curve is simply the sum of the individual households' demands, shifts in an individual household demand caused by a change in tastes, income, or prices of related goods will cause a shift in the market demand curve. The net effect on the market demand curve will be the sum of all the individual households' demand shifts.

There is one additional condition that will shift the market demand curve: the entry or exit of households from the market in question. Market analysts follow demographics because they know that as the size of age groups in the population changes, so does the demand for goods and services that are used primarily by particular age groups.

A classic case in point is the impact of the baby boom on demand for diapers in the late 1940s and early 1950s, for primary and secondary education in the early 1960s, and for college education in the late 1960s and early 1970s (recall the discussion in the Introduction). You can bet that there will be a surge in demand for Polygrip, medical care for the elderly, nursing homes when the "boomers" reach their 70s and 80s.

In Figures 3-25 and 3-26 we can see the effect of market demand shifts on the market price when supply is constant. Figure 3-25 represents a fall in market demand (shift to the left).

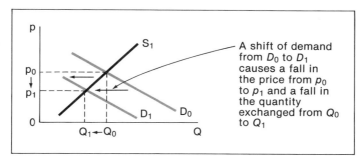

FIGURE 3-25   Adjustment to a Decrease in Demand

Figure 3-26 represents an increase in market demand (shift to the right).

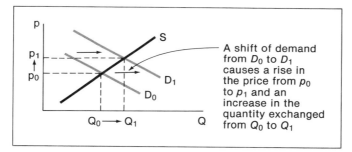

FIGURE 3-26   Adjustment to an Increase in Demand

This, then, is the story of market demand. It originates in the behavior of individual households with limited incomes following the utility maximization decision rule. We examined the characteristics of a given level of demand (what it represents and its responsiveness) and the conditions that determine the level of demand (tastes, income, and price of related goods). We saw how all these individual household demands constitute the foundation of market demand. Now to complete our analysis of the market picture we turn to an analysis of supply.

Conditions That Determine Supply

When firms make supply decisions for the current period, some of the inputs they use are fixed in quantity (e.g., factory size). Given this fact and the assumption of diminishing marginal returns, the firm's supply curve will slope up to the right. This is so because as the marginal product falls with successive applications of units of an input, the marginal cost of successive units of output will rise. Consider the candy bar maker. As the marginal product of successive additional workers falls because of diminishing returns, the marginal cost of producing candy bars is going to rise. If, for instance, the marginal product of adding a 300th hour of labor in the candy factory is 50 bars of candy and the labor cost is $20/hour, then the marginal cost of those last 50 bars is $.40/bar. If yet another hour of labor (a 301st hour) is added and its marginal product is 40 bars (reflecting diminishing marginal returns), then the marginal cost of producing those additional 40 bars is $.50/bar. Clearly, the manufacturer will only increase output if price rises enough to cover the increasing marginal costs she faces as a consequence of diminishing marginal returns in production. We see, then, that as marginal cost rises, supply price must also rise to cover the supplier's costs. In other words, under our nice assumptions, supply price and marginal cost move together as quantity supplied increases—in short, the marginal cost curve is the firm's supply curve. The positive slope of the supply curve reflects this: quantity supplied increases as price rises.

As with the demand curve, the supply curve has the characteristic of elasticity or responsiveness. For a given set of axes (i.e., holding scales constant), the steeper the supply curve, the more inelastic it is (the less responsive quantity is to a change in price); and the closer to horizontal the supply curve is, the more elastic it is (the more responsive quantity is to a change in price.).

The conditions of supply determine the overall level of supply, that is, where the supply curve is on the graph. These conditions include the prices of factor inputs, the technique used, and the circumstance under which production takes place (e.g., weather). The more favorable the conditions (the lower the factor prices, the better the technique, the better the circumstances), the farther down to the right the supply curve will be. This is so because better conditions mean a greater marginal productivity, greater marginal productivity means lower marginal cost, and lower marginal cost means a lower supply curve.

When conditions change, the supply curve will shift from its initial position. As the previous paragraph suggests, improved conditions (a fall in input price, an improvement in technique, an improvement in circumstance) shift the supply curve to the right (down). This shift represents the fact that improved conditions make it possible for the firm to charge a lower price at any particular quantity supplied (pick a Q and show yourself that this is the case). A deterioration of conditions (opposite cases) shifts the supply curve to the left (up). This shift represents the fact that deteriorated conditions force the firm to charge a higher price at any particular quantity supplied (again, convince yourself). Graphically, these shifts appear as shown in Figure 3-27.

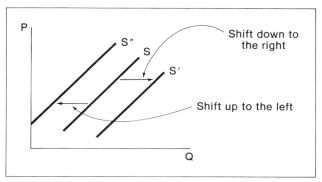

FIGURE 3-27   Supply Shifts—Defining Terms

At this point we must identify the relationship between the supply by an individual firm and the total market supply. The sum of all firms' supplies of a good or service is the market supply of that good or service. In other words, at any given price, the market quantity supplied is the sum of the individual firms' quantities supplied at that price.

We see in Figure 3-28 that in a world of three firms the market supply is the sum of the three individual firms' supplies; therefore, at any given price, the market quantity supplied is the sum of the three firms' quantities supplied at that price. In this example, at a $1 price, we find that firm 1 has a quantity supplied of 1 bar, firm 2 has a quantity supplied of 1 bar, and firm 3 has a quantity supplied of 1 bar. Summing these up, we see that the market quantity supplied at price of $1 is 3 bars (1+1+1=3). Similarly, at a $5 price, firms 1, 2, and 3 have as quantity supplied 4, 4, and 4 candy bars, respectively. Therefore the market quantity supplied for candy bars at a $5 price is 12 bars. By repeating this calculation over all prices, we derive the market supply curve.

Since that market supply curve is simply the sum of the individual firms' supplies, shifts in the firms' supplies caused by a change in technique, prices of factor inputs, or circumstances of supply will cause a shift in the market supply curve. The net effect on the market supply curve will be the sum of all individual firms' supply shifts. There is one additional condition that will shift the market supply curve, and that is the entry or exit of firms into or out of the market in question.

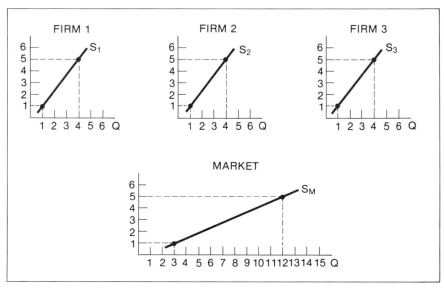

FIGURE 3-28   Market Supply

Ceteris paribus, entry will shift market supply to the right because there will be more production at any given price. Conversely, exit will shift market supply to the left.

In Figures 3-29 and 3-30 we can see the effect of market supply shifts on the market price when demand is constant. Figure 3-29 represents a fall in market supply (shift to the left) due, for instance, to exits.

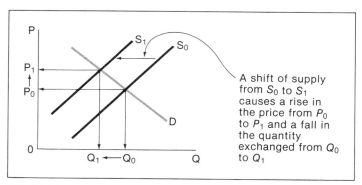

FIGURE 3-29   Adjustment to a Decrease in Supply

Figure 3-30 represents an increase in market supply (shift to the right) due, for example, to entries.

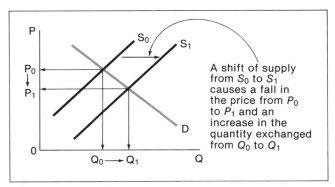

P
S_0
S_1
P_0
P_1
D

A shift of supply
from S_0 to S_1
causes a fall in
the price from P_0
to P_1 and an
increase in the
quantity exchanged
from Q_0 to Q_1

0
$Q_0 \longrightarrow Q_1$
Q

FIGURE 3-30   Adjustment to an Increase in Supply

There are several points we can make about the market supply curve that are true only under our assumed perfectly competitive conditions. As we have seen, factor costs, technique, and the circumstances under which supply takes place are the conditions that determine the costs of supply.

It is important to note here that included in the costs of supply is the firm owner's opportunity cost of investing her labor and capital in her own business rather than working for and loaning the capital to someone else. In order to make the business worthwhile, the owner must be able to pay herself at least as much as she could earn from the best alternative use of her labor and capital. We say, therefore, that built into the costs that must be covered in order for the firm to stay in business is an implicit wage and interest return to the owner. Covering these costs is necessary and sufficient for the continued existence of a firm, but the owners of firms seek to do better. They would like to realize a return above and beyond costs—an excess return we will call *profit*.

Under our nice assumptions, profit is a powerful, yet ephemeral, magnet. It attracts resources in pursuit of it, and yet it disappears in the process. Since firms are profit maximizers, they would like to set the price high enough to cover costs and make a profit. However, under the fair race assumption (equal access to information and equal access to markets), profits attract competitors. Each new competitor will enter the market and set her price above costs but below the old firms' price. The new competitor attracts customers by accepting a lower profit margin. This forces all the old firms to lower price accordingly. As long as profits exist this process will continue. Ultimately the price will be forced down to the point where only costs are covered and profit disappears.

As we noted earlier, this does not mean that the owners of the firms earn nothing. Given equal access to markets and information, people with labor and capital to invest in firms will always shift their labor and capital to the best available opportunity. Such shifting will continue until all the advantages (profits) are eliminated. This does not mean that the returns paid to the owner's capital and labor are eliminated. These returns—interest and wages, respectively—are absolutely necessary for the activity to be maintained. Without an interest and wage return on her capital and labor, there would be no incentive for the owner to keep a firm in business. These returns are built into the costs that determine the shape of the supply curve. In sum, under perfectly competitive conditions, firms seek profit, but end up earning an interest and wage return on their investments and labor, called *normal returns*, but not a profit. Ironically, it is in pursuit of profit that perfect competitors eliminate one another's profits. We will see when we relax the perfectly competitive assumptions that it is possible, if distortions exist (e.g., unequal market access), for a firm to maintain a return above and beyond the normal return—that is, a profit.

The final point to be made about the supply curve under perfect competition is that it is always based on the most efficient technique of production and therefore the lowest possible costs. Perfect competition eliminates profits and it also eliminates inefficiency. If the existing firms are producing inefficiently and a new firm enters the market using a more efficient method of production, the supply curve will shift down to the right because the new firm is able to offer lower prices for any given quantity. Unless the older firms adopt the more efficient techniques, they will be driven out of business.

The Power of the Invisible Hand Under Our Nice Assumptions

We have seen that unencumbered markets self-adjust in response to price signals in a manner that coordinates the decisions of suppliers and demanders perfectly. As a result, excess supplies or excess demands will disappear and resources will be used most efficiently in order to supply the given demand. The market is guided to this equilibrium as if by an invisible hand. In fact, under our nice assumptions, *all* power rests in the invisible hand. The participants—the individual households and individual firms—have no market power.

Consider Figure 3-31, which shows graphs of the market conditions and the conditions facing one firm and one household in the candy bar market.

Market forces (the sum of all individual households' demands and firms' supplies) determine that the equilibrium price is P^*. Once the

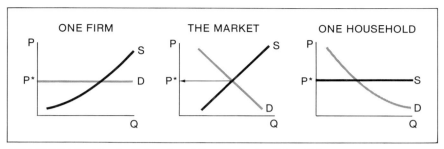

FIGURE 3-31   The Individual and the Market—Price Takers

market determines this equilibrium price, the household faces a perfectly elastic supply at P^*. This is so for the following reasons: The firm cannot lower the price in order to attract business because, as we saw above, perfectly competitive conditions have already driven the market price down to a level that just covers the firms costs, including a normal return. Thus lowering the price would make it impossible for the firm to cover costs. The firm cannot raise the price because other firms would be happy to supply its customers at the price P^*. In short, the firm must accept P^* as its supply price because it has no power to control the market. Similarly, the firm faces a perfectly elastic demand. This is so because the household has no desire to pay above P^* and has no option to pay less than P^*. The household must accept P^* as its demand price because it has no power to control the market.

When the fair race assumptions hold, the invisible hand has all the power and the players in the market, the firms and households, have none. We say that under these conditions the players are *price takers*. In other words, the firms and households must take the price the market sets—like it or leave it.

D. CONDITIONS THAT DETERMINE EQUILIBRIUM IN THE FACTOR MARKET GIVEN OUR NICE ASSUMPTIONS

All of our analysis thus far has focused on the product market. We have seen that in the product market the forces of supply and demand establish the price and quantity exchanged of all goods and services. In the factor market the forces of supply and demand establish the price and quantity exchanged of all factors. Recall from the circular flow diagram (Figure 3-1 on page 51) that in the factor market firms are the demanders and households are the suppliers. In return for supplying factors of production, the households receive the money that is their income. The size of this income determines the amount of goods and services the household can purchase. Thus it is in the factor market that the division of the value produced in society is actually made. Households receive income and therefore shares of the distribution for supplying labor, capital, and/or natural resources (e.g., land).

Graphically, a factor market will look like any other (see Figure 3-32).

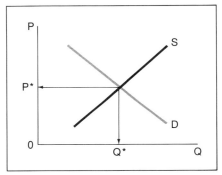

FIGURE 3-32   A Factor Market

It will move to an equilibrium that will establish the return to the factor, P^*, and the quantity of the factor employed, Q^*.

As in the product market, the decisions of suppliers and demanders in the factor market are independently determined but are coordinated by the market adjusting on a price signal. We will consider the conditions that determine factor supply and demand in turn, beginning with the supply curve.

The first point to be made about the factor supply relationship is that at any level of supply the price of the factor and its quantity supplied are positively related. In graphical terms this means that the supply curve slopes up to the right. This is true because of the relationship between quantity of a factor supplied and opportunity cost. As the quantity of factor supplied increases, the opportunity cost associated with each successive unit supplied increases. As a result, it requires a higher and higher price to bring each successive unit of the factor to the market. The upward-sloping factor supply curve reflects this.

Take the market for nurses. When a nurse is determining how much time he would be willing to work at any given wage, he must calculate the opportunity cost of the time at work (he could be at the beach or working at another kind of job). The individual supply curve slopes up because the opportunity costs rise. Think about it: As you give up alternative opportunities, you would obviously give up the least desirable alternative first, the second least desirable second, and so on. The more opportunities you forgo (the longer hours you work), the higher the opportunity cost will be, and therefore the higher the wage you would require to induce you to work for each extra hour. Thus the wage is compensation for current opportunities forgone, a return for labor.

The level of factor supply (the position of an individual's factor supply curve on the graph) is determined by income and preferences. A change in one of these can change the level of supply (shift the factor supply curve). A dramatic increase in income may cause you to choose to work less at any given wage (the price of labor). In this case, your supply of labor will shift to the left. A drastic income decrease may have the opposite effect. Similarly, a change in preferences can cause such shifts in factor supply. If you suddenly decided that leisure time with your family is much more important than it ever seemed before (maybe you had a brush with death and realized how much you value that sharing), then your labor supply curve would shift left.

As with product supply, the factor market supply curve is the sum of the individual supply curves. Thus any shift in an individual factor supply curve will shift the market supply curve. The market supply curve will also shift in response to entry and exit. In order to understand the forces that determine entry and exit, let us consider the labor market.

If we consider the labor market in a generic sense, "entry and exit" simply means that people choose to begin or to stop selling their labor. The reason for such a decision may relate to income, preferences, or alternative uses of that labor. As regards the first two, it is possible that a radical increase in income (a big lottery win) or change in preferences would cause someone to leave the labor market. As for alternative uses, one might choose to stop selling labor in the market if there is suddenly a more valuable way to use that labor at home. For example, upon the birth of a child, a man or woman may choose to leave the labor market in order to do labor at home in the form of child care. Such a decision depends on the relative returns of the two options. The higher one's market wage, the greater the opportunity cost of leaving the market—this would suggest that high-wage people hire a baby nurse and low-wage people quit paid work to take care of their own child. However, there is also an income issue. Those with a good income source that is independent of their market work (e.g., investments or a spouse's income) have a lower opportunity cost of quitting work than someone with no nonwage income. This

84 — Chapter Three

suggests that poorer people are less likely to quit their jobs in order to stay home with a child. The decision of any given individual to enter or leave the labor force will depend on the interaction of these income and relative return (market wage versus value of home production) issues.

When the labor market is considered less generically, entry and exit (and therefore shifts in supply) seem more volatile. By "less generically," we mean that instead of looking at "the market for labor," we consider the market for a *particular* form of labor. Here again, any individual's actual decision will depend on that person's income and preferences and on the nature of the alternatives, but in this case the alternatives include not only market versus nonmarket activity, but also alternative kinds of market activity.

Consider the market for nurses. If there is to be a steady entry of new people, the pay rate for nurses must include not only a wage but also an interest component. The investment in human capital necessary to become a nurse will only be made if the expected interest returns have an expected present value that is greater than the opportunity cost of the investment: current consumption or alternative investments. Thus, if the new people are to be enticed into the nursing profession, the pay rate the potential nurse expects to receive must include not only a wage element to compensate him for current effort, but also an interest element to compensate him for the human capital investment he must make. If the pay in the nursing profession is so high that such an investment in human capital seems advantageous, then, given our nice assumptions, there will be plenty of new entrants. This will continue, shifting supply out, until the pay falls and all advantage is gone.

Exits from the nursing market occur because of death, retirement, or the discovery of better alternatives. People who have already made the human capital investment necessary to become a nurse cannot get back the time and money they spent on that training—those costs are sunk. The choice current nurses face is whether to use their skill to work in nursing or to go into some alternative occupation or activity. They may choose an alternative if their expectations about nursing turn out to be wrong and the actual pay rate falls to a very low level. Even if their expectations about nursing are realized, they may leave the field if an unexpected preferred alternative becomes available.

If nurses' pay is low relative to that for comparable occupations, then, given our nice assumptions, we should find individuals seeking opportunities in those alternative occupations. This flow of labor out of nursing and into the other occupations would decrease the supply of nurses and increase the supply in those other occupations. These supply shifts would, *ceteris paribus*, cause the pay of nurses to rise and the pay in comparable occupations to fall. The adjustment would cease when the pay levels for the comparable occupations and for nursing are equalized. At that point there would be no further advantage to changing jobs. (Demonstrate this graphically for yourself.) If we find, as some economists argue, that comparable jobs are not receiving equal pay, that is *prima facie* evidence that our nice assumptions have been violated. We will explore the kinds of violations that could occur shortly.

On the factor demand side, the firm finds that, as we have demonstrated for any factor, the marginal product falls (eventually, if not immediately) because of diminishing returns. Given our nice assumptions, the firm is a price taker: the price of its product is set by the market. Since the price per unit of product is constant but the product of each successive unit of a factor used is falling, the value of the marginal product of the factor (output price × factor marginal product) is falling. Clearly, if the value of the product from each successive unit of a factor input falls, the firm will only hire more units of that factor if the price of the factor goes down. Therefore the demand curve for the factor will slope down.

The conditions that determine the level of demand for a factor are the price of the product the factor is producing, the technology available, and the relative price of other factors.

If an increase in demand for a product causes the price of that product to go up, we know that, *ceteris paribus*, the quantity supplied will also increase. The result will be a rise in demand for the factors used in the production process. Because the demand for factors used in production depends on the demand for the output that those factors are used to produce, economists refer to factor demand as a *derived demand*.

Usually several different techniques are available in our technology to produce a particular product. Since the firm has a choice among these techniques, it will choose the one that minimizes the cost for the level of production it intends. If labor is very expensive and capital is relatively cheap, the choice will be a technique that economizes on labor. This is called a *capital-intensive technique*. If the labor is cheap and the capital is expensive, the choice will be a technique that economizes on capital, a *labor-intensive technique*. If technology allows for the possibility of input substitution, the demand for any particular factor will be affected by the price of other factors. For instance, if the price of labor rises and capital substitution is possible, then this substitution will be made. Thus the increase in the price of labor would result in an increased demand for capital. The responsiveness of capital and labor substitution as relative prices change is measured by the *elasticity of input substitution*: the more elastic, the more responsive.

E. CONCLUSION ON THE GENERAL COMPETITIVE EQUILIBRIUM MODEL

Overview

Now that we have seen how individual markets function, we will examine how these markets are connected to one another so that decisions are coordinated not only within markets but also across all markets. It is this general coordination process within the market system that allows us to speak not simply of market equilibrium but also of a general equilibrium in which all individual markets have adjusted together to a simultaneous equilibrium.

The two basic types of markets and the connections among markets are represented graphically in Figure 3-33.

If we join these markets, then given our nice assumptions, we have a simple, fully developed model for the NeoClassical General Competitive Equilibrium analysis of a market economy. We have seen that, given our nice assumptions, each market is a perfect coordinator of the intentions of suppliers and demanders. All markets automatically adjust on price signals to an efficient equilibrium. The amazing thing is that this whole adjustment process, encompassing millions of individual factor and product markets, adjusts to a General Competitive Equilibrium without anyone taking charge. The process is guided as if by an invisible hand.

It is particularly important to understand that there is no starting point or ending point within the economic system. For the entire system to be in a General Competitive Equilibrium, each individual market must be in equilibrium. Conversely, if any individual market is still adjusting toward equilibrium, then all markets must still be adjusting. The system has millions of parts, and because they are interconnected, so long as anything is changing, everything must be changing. In terms an economist might use: All markets adjust simultaneously and a General Competitive Equilibrium is reached when all markets simultaneously reach equilibrium. Once this General Competitive Equilibrium is reached, the allocation of resources, the value (relative prices) of all goods and services, and the distribution of income (relative prices of all factors) in society are determined.

The actual characteristics of the General Competitive Equilibrium an economy would reach depend on several conditions that are determined at least in part, outside this whole market system adjustment process. These conditions include:

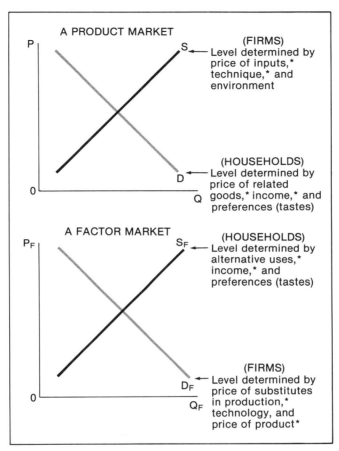

A PRODUCT MARKET

(FIRMS)
— Level determined by price of inputs,* technique,* and environment

(HOUSEHOLDS)
— Level determined by price of related goods,* income,* and preferences (tastes)

A FACTOR MARKET

(HOUSEHOLDS)
— Level determined by alternative uses,* income,* and preferences (tastes)

(FIRMS)
— Level determined by price of substitutes in production,* technology, and price of product*

FIGURE 3-33 A Review of Markets Everything marked with an asterisk is wholly or partly determined by conditions in other markets. Thus we see that any one market is connected to other markets. These lines of connection link all markets directly or indirectly.

1. The distribution of society's initial endowment among individuals
2. Tastes/preferences
3. Technology

Given these initial conditions and our nice assumptions, the market adjustment process will proceed until a General Competitive Equilibrium is reached. The outcome may vary somewhat because the actual path to the General Competitive Equilibrium can vary. If one of these externally determined conditions is changed (e.g., the distribution of initial endowments), the outcome of the market process will definitely change.

Efficiency and Equity

We need to define *efficiency* and *equity* because these concepts represent the standards by which we measure the quality of economic outcomes. By defining them here we will be able to apply them in judging the quality of the outcome of the market process under our nice assumptions, a General Competitive Equilibrium. Then, when we relax our nice assumptions in Chapter IV, we will be able to use these terms to contrast the quality of that perfectly competitive environment with the market outcome in a world with less than a fair race (market power) and with market failures.

Efficiency relates to resource use. Clearly, if a change in technique or in resource allocation makes it possible to improve the lot (increase the utility) of one individual without harming the condition (decreasing the utility) of anyone else, then the change is an improvement in efficiency because more utility is being extracted from the same given initial endowment and technology. We say that a system is efficient if there is no possible change in techniques of production or allocations of resources that would make any one person better off without making anyone else worse off. If there were a way to make someone better off without making anyone else worse off, that implies that society's resources could be used more effectively. If no such alternative exists, this implies that society must be using its resources most effectively. This optimal efficiency condition was first defined by an Italian economist named Vilfredo Pareto (1848–1923) and is called a Pareto optimum after him. *Pareto optimality* is the standard (norm) by which economists measure the efficiency of any general equilibrium condition.

Equity relates to the distribution of the fruits of human labor. It is measured by an essentially subjective, ethical criterion: Is the distribution "just"? Thus, in order to determine the equity of economic outcomes, we must first answer for ourselves the question: What is just? Equity is not an issue on which economists or the public in general have any scientific basis for setting a standard, but there are at least four popular concepts of equity one finds in the general literature: equal-share distribution to all, share distribution on the basis of contribution to production, share distribution on the basis of effort and sacrifice, and share distribution on the basis of need.

With standards of efficiency and equity, we can make judgments about the quality of the market process under our nice assumptions, a General Competitive Equilibrium.

When measured by the efficiency standard, the General Competitive Equilibrium is the best possible case. It achieves a Pareto optimum because under our nice assumptions resources are free to flow to their optimum use and the forces of competition will drive firms to adopt the optimum technique.

As we have noted, equity relates to the distribution of the fruits of human labor. Is the distribution just or not? This is a subjective question. Thus we cannot say that one General Competitive Equilibrium is more just than another until we define what we consider to be just or equitable. We can say, however, that given our nice assumptions, the distributive outcome of the market process (who gets how much) will directly reflect the distribution of society's initial endowments among individuals.

A Pareto optimal outcome of a General Competitive Equilibrium ensures that each participant in the market system will get as much utility as possible out of the share of the initial endowment with which she started—no more, no less. Under our nice assumptions, if one person starts with a very large share of that endowment and all others start with a very small share, then the one will enjoy a much larger share of the fruits of the market system than the many, but all will have used their share of the endowment most efficiently. The nice assumptions ensure a Pareto optimal General Competitive Equilibrium, not equity. So, however we define equity, in order to have an equitable outcome, perfect competition is not enough. Achieving equity requires that the process _begin_ with a just distribution of society's initial endowment among individuals.

Kenneth Arrow eloquently summarized the nature of a General Competitive Equilibrium in his Nobel Lecture _"General Competitive Equilibrium: Purpose, Analytical Techniques, Collective Choice,"_ (_American Economic Review,_ June 1974, p. 269):

General Competitive Equilibrium above all teaches the extent to which a social allocation of resources can be achieved by independent private decisions coordinated through the market. We are assured indeed that not only can an allocation be achieved, but the result will be Pareto efficient. But, as has been stressed, there is nothing in the process which guarantees that the distribution be just. Indeed, the theory teaches us that the final allocation will depend on the distribution of initial supplies and of ownership of firms. If we want to rely on the virtues of the market but also to achieve a more just distribution, the theory suggests the strategy of changing the initial endowments rather than interfering with the allocation process at some later stage.

Thus, even under assumptions most favorable to decentralization of decision making [our nice assumptions], there is an irreducible need for a social or collective choice on distribution.

This need for social choice raises a fundamental set of questions for society. What social decision-making structures should be used? Who should have a voice in decisions? What weight should be given to the various voices? What institutional structure is appropriate to meet the objectives agreed on? These questions have been debated since simple society gave way to complexity. Not only do the answers continue to elude us, but there may not be a first best answer that allows society to achieve a harmonious, stable equilibrium. Clearly, a look at our world (a look "out the window") suggests that such an achievement is not on the horizon.

Answering the Basic Microeconomic Questions Given Our Nice Assumptions

Let us recall the four basic microeconomic questions we set forth at the outset of our inquiry into NeoClassical theory. They were:

1. What goods and services are to be produced and in what quantities?
2. By what methods are goods and services to be produced?
3. How is the value (relative worth) of goods and services determined?
4. How is the value produced by people divided among them?

We are now in a position to answer these questions under the assumed nice conditions:

1. *What goods and services are to be produced and in what quantities?* The model predicts that, given our nice assumptions, the combination of goods and services produced will be determined by the distribution of society's initial endowment among individuals (i.e., individual resources), individual preferences, and the state of technology. These conditions are the starting point from which the market system (the invisible hand) coordinates activity. The specifics of these conditions will determine the specifics of supply and demand, and therefore what and how much is produced. Our model also allows us to predict how a change in these conditions will affect what and how much is produced.
2. *By what methods are goods and services to be produced?* The model predicts that, given our nice assumptions, the most efficient technique of production will always be chosen from the available technology. The model also allows us to predict how a change in technology will alter the choice of techniques.
3. *How is the value (relative worth) of goods and services determined?* In the model the unit of account for value (relative worth) is

money and the measure of a good or a service's value is its money price. The model predicts that prices will be determined by the forces of supply and demand as the economy reaches a General Competitive Equilibrium, and will be observed in the product markets. Further, the model allows us to predict how a change in initial endowments, tastes, or technology will affect price and therefore value.

4. *How is the value produced by people divided among them?* The model predicts that income will be determined by the forces of supply and demand as the economy reaches a General Competitive Equilibrium and will be observed in the factor market. Further, the model allows us to predict how a change in initial endowments, tastes, or technology will affect the distribution.

Relaxing Our Nice Assumptions—General Equilibrium Analysis

As in any other beautiful and noble machine that was the production of human art, whatever tended to render its movements more smooth and easy, would derive beauty from this effect; and, on the contrary, whatever tended to obstruct them would displease on that account. . .

Adam Smith
The Theory of Moral Sentiments, 1759.

IN THE LAST chapter we examined society under Smith's "abstract and philosophical light" and identified the "regular and harmonious movements [that] produce a thousand agreeable effects." In this chapter we will relax the nice assumptions which underlie these "regular and harmonious movements," and we will see the world in a less abstract light that exposes "that vile rust, which makes them ["the wheels of society"] jar and grate." Smith, *The Theory of Moral Sentiments*, 1759.

A General Competitive Equilibrium is a special case of general equilibrium that can only occur when our nice assumptions hold. If we relax our nice assumptions and allow for the possibility of market power (a violation of our nice assumptions that competition is a fair race) and/or market failure (a violation of our nice assumption that markets exist when needed and work well), then the market process becomes much more complex and the possible kinds of outcomes expand dramatically. In what follows we will examine the implications of market power and market failure in turn, noting in each case how market outcomes under these conditions differ from the outcomes under our nice assumptions.

92

A. MARKET POWER

Introduction to Market Power

Adam Smith wrote in the *Wealth of Nations*:

> The whole of the advantages and disadvantages of the different employments of labour and stock must, in the same neighbourhood, be either perfectly equal or continually tending to equality. If in the same neighbourhood, there was any employment evidently either more or less advantageous than the rest, so many people would crowd into it in the one case, and so many would desert it in the other, that its advantages would soon return to the level of other employments. This at least would be the case in a society where things were left to follow their natural course, where there was perfect liberty, and where every man was perfectly free both to chuse what occupation he thought proper, and to change it as often as he thought proper. Every man's interest would prompt him to seek the advantageous, and to shun the disadvantageous employment.

This "perfect liberty" Smith speaks of is what we have referred to as our fair race assumption. He expresses very succinctly the point that given this assumption, freedom of activity will ensure that all advantages and disadvantages will be eliminated. Now we will see that where market power exists and the fair race assumption does *not* hold, advantages can persist.

Power, as we use the term here, is the product of control. Control can be acquired directly or through human institutions. Social, political, and economic institutions determine the distribution of many opportunities in society, including use of society's initial endowment. Thus to exert control in these institutions is to have power over the distribution of a society's opportunities among its members. In our analysis thus far we have assumed a fair race. This condition requires that power be exercised so as to be neutral, that it not skew the process. For this to happen, either power must be in the hands of a benevolent dictator (like a referee in a basketball game) or be distributed equally among participants (as in an idealized democratic process) so that no power advantages are possible. Our nice assumption that the race is fair has allowed us to abstract from these power advantages thus far. Now we want to relax that assumption in order to examine how the exploitation of control, or in other words power advantages, affect economic efficiency and equity.

Naturally Occurring Market Power

First we will relax our assumption by allowing for the possibility of naturally occurring advantages that can be exploited at the market. For a firm, this might mean that the production process it uses displays continually increasing *economies of scale.*

Increasing scale of production means that all inputs are being increased simultaneously in equal proportions. Increasing economies of scale means that as the scale of production increases, the cost per unit of output falls. If these economics occur up to a very large scale, then the first firm into the business can, merely by virtue of its head start, always underprice new firms and thereby kill off competitors. Thus increasing returns give rise to what is called a *natural monopoly.* A *monopoly* is a supplier that has no competition.

An individual household may also enjoy the position of a natural monopoly if it is endowed with a unique genetic gift. Superstar athletes or performers hold just such monopolies.

For the firm, the monopoly is in the product market; for the household, the monopoly is in the factor market. While the markets differ, the implications are the same. In both cases, those who enjoy the power escape the inflexible position of price taker. Since they are the only sellers, they face the entire market demand, not the perfectly elastic demand of a price taker. Thus they can choose any price/quantity combination the demanders will accept. In other words, the sellers can choose any point on the market demand curve as the price/quantity combination at which they will supply. Their only constraint in choosing is considerations of costs.

This market power means that it is possible to extract and maintain a return above and beyond the normal return that would occur under perfectly competitive conditions. These excess returns are called either *profits* or *rents*. Profits and rents are alike in that both are excess returns derived from the exploitation of power advantages. The distinction between the two is that a profit is a return equal to the opportunity cost of using power in other ways, while a rent is a return above and beyond the opportunity cost. For instance, the eye-hand coordination that makes someone a tennis or basketball superstar could also be used to her advantage in other careers. The excess return this eye-hand coordination would generate in the best alternative career is the opportunity cost of choosing to be an athlete, and this determines the amount of profit. All the excess return above and beyond profit is a rent. For our purposes, the important point is that both rent and profit are returns one derives from a power advantage. From here on we will ignore the distinction and refer to all such returns as rents.

The efficiency implication of exploiting market power derived from natural advantage is clear. If a firm faces less than perfect competition, it is is not forced to be as efficient as it would be if it faced perfect competition. This is true because in the absence of competition some inefficiency does not automatically imply elimination from the market. Similarly, a tennis or basketball superstar facing less than perfect competition can sometimes get away with sloppy play and still win. Because of such inefficiencies, the general equilibrium that is reached in a world with market power will not be a Pareto optimum.

The equity implications will not be clear until we determine a norm for equity. What is clear is that exploiting market power does alter the distribution of income to the benefit of those who enjoy the power and does therefore have an impact on equity. The nature of the impact depends on the norm we choose.

Artificially Created Market Power

In the examples above, market power was derived from naturally occurring advantages in production (increasing economies of scale) or in endowment (genetic gifts). Market power can also be artificially derived from advantages that are the product of human contrivance. Remember that under our fair race assumption all social, political, and economic institutions are neutral—no institution distorts the race to the advantage of some and the disadvantage of others. In order to understand the economic implications of the skewed advantages produced by human contrivance, we must now relax that neutrality assumption.

Institutions exert a great deal of influence over individuals in society. It is institutions that at some point in time determined how the social initial endowment (land and natural resources) would be distributed among the individuals in society. (Recall the Arrow quotation above where he cites the "irreducible need for a social or collective choice.") It is institutions that define and protect property rights over individuals' shares of the social initial endowment and over the shares of the social product as distributed. It is institutions that largely determine the set of opportunities anyone may choose from when she is deciding how to allocate the resources in her share of the initial endowment. If institutions are neutral, then the distribution of social initial endowment will not be skewed, the definition and protection of property rights will be unbiased, and the set of opportunities open to any one individual will be equally accessible to all.

Let us look at two specific examples in which assumptions necessary for a fair race are relaxed and consider the implications.

- *Mobility—All persons or commodities must have equal access to all markets* The necessity of this assumption is straightforward. The price is a signal of the opportunity each market affords. People and commodities flow to the market affording the greatest advantage. Free flow assures that all relative advantages will be eliminated and therefore that resources will be used most efficiently. If people and/or commodities were not allowed equal access to all markets, this would stifle the adjustment mechanism based on price signals.

An example of an institutional constraint on the mobility of individuals is unions. One tactic a union might use is to limit access to an employment market. Then instead of a perfectly elastic supply at a market determined wage, employers face (in the extreme case) a perfectly inelastic supply. If the union is effective, it can push the price of labor to the firm above the level of the normal wage. Does that mean that unions are unequivocally bad? Not necessarily. Unions may exist to offset the redistributive force of some other source of market power such as collusion among employers. But those who would argue for the existence of unions must do so on an equity basis, because they clearly distort markets and cause inefficiency.

Another example of an institutional constraint on mobility is collusion among businesses in hiring practices. For example, for many years professional baseball teams had by mutual agreement exclusive rights to the players they signed. Players could be traded but could not be enticed away. It is clear that this limitation on player mobility kept salaries down, because when it was lifted, salaries shot up dramatically. It is precisely this kind of market power on the part of firms that encourages workers to unionize in an effort to counter with their own market power.

- *Information—All persons must have equal access to information* Information is the basis of judgment. If people are going to make the best possible decision, they need as much information as it is cost-efficient to acquire. Anyone who does not have equal access to information is at a disadvantage relative to those who have superior access. Therefore that informationally starved individual will make less efficient decisions. (*Note:* This does not imply that information is a free good. It simply means everyone must have equal access to information *acquisition* if the market is to be perfectly competitive.)

One example of a violation of this assumption is insider trading at the stock market. People who work within an institution whose stock is being traded have access to information that outsiders do not have. By exploiting this access, it is possible to beat the rest of the market, which can only respond later when the information becomes public.

Another example of an institutional constraint on equal access to information is discrimination in education. If some members of society attend inferior schools, they enter the economic race in a disadvantageous position because their skills are less developed. More to the immediate point, if they are weak in reading, writing, or math skills, they are not able to evaluate or to transmit information as effectively as those with whom they compete. As a result of such discrimination those with poor skills are forced to compete with one another for low-skilled jobs. People who had the opportunity to acquire superior skills are able to compete for society's high-skilled jobs, and what is more, they face reduced competition because those who were discriminated against are not able to join in competition. So what are the economic consequences? Because some individuals who would choose to compete in the high-skill job market are forced into the low-skill market, supply in the low-skill market is artificially expanded and supply in the high-skill market is artificially contracted. Given demand conditions, the consequences are that wages for low-skill jobs are artificially depressed and wages for high-skill jobs artificially increased.

We can better comprehend these consequences by returning to our race analogy. Skewed distribution of society's initial endowment is analogous to a race in which competitors arrive at the track meet having had unequal coaching and training facilities and carrying equipment of unequal quality. Skewed opportunity set is analogous to a track meet at which some competitors are denied access to some events or at which competitors in a given event face unequal obstacles. One competitor may face 100 yards of clear track and another face 100 yards with hurdles along the way. Both at the track and in the larger competition of the race to do well in life, those who enjoy institutionally created advantages will have a better chance to get ahead.

A newspaper article entitled *Found Baby's Future Dictated by Apartheid* (Syracuse: *Post Standard*, July 16, 1983) captures the essence of the implications of exploiting non-neutral control over institutions. It reads in part:

JOHANNESBURG, South Africa (AP)—Lize Venter is 4 weeks old and nobody knows who her parents are. In a society where the races are separated by law, that means the government will decide if she's black, white, or of mixed race—and set the course of her life. . .

The decision on her race will determine who can adopt her, where she goes to school, what neighborhood she may live in, who she can marry, whether she can vote, where she can eat—what she can hope for in life.

This decreed by the Population Registration Act of 1950, adopted by the governing National Party two years after it took control of the white minority government.

Lize Venter's share of society's initial endowment, her opportunity set, and therefore her future share in the distribution of society's product were all determined by where she was placed in the social and political pecking order. For most children the decision is clear at birth—determined by sex, race, and other indices. While it is not impossible to overcome disadvantage or to waste advantage, on average the relative advantages participants bring to a competition determine the outcome.

The efficiency implications of artificially created market power are the same as those for the natural case. Lack of competition eliminates the punishment for inefficiency: losing the race. Thus market power allows inefficiency. The equity implications of artificial market power are, also as for the natural case, a matter of ethics. It may appear immediately obvious that by any standard the equity implications are negative, but that is not necessarily so. Some people argue that while advantages created by institutions are apparently unfair, there are cases in which artificially created advantages are necessary for the sake of equity, in order to offset the effects of current disadvantages or the persisting effects of past disadvantages. This is the logic of affirmative action. Under affirmative action, special efforts are made to identify and hire those from groups that suffer from the effects of current or past discrimination. People who oppose affirmative action argue that, as with any institutionally decreed advantage, it creates inefficiency. Those in favor argue back that while affirmative action may create short-run inefficiency, it encourages more efficiency in the long run because it breaks down old barriers.

The case for awarding patents rests on the same type of reasoning. Patents protect inventors from competition for a period of time. The argument in favor of granting patents is that the extra distributive share—the rent—derived from the patentor's market power is an incentive for invention. Thus patents, while apparently a distortion, serve society in the long run.

Economists as economists have no basis for making a judgment on the equity question related to market power because this judgment depends not on the criteria of science, but rather on the criteria of ethics. Nonetheless, economists' tools are very valuable in analyzing the distribution within a given society and in understanding how an individual or coalition might seek to change that distribution.

Note that even when the market itself appears to be competitive, market power, and therefore distributive shares derived from advantage can exist. This is analogous to the fact that even when conditions at the track are fair, biased prerace conditions like unequal training facilities and equipment can skew the outcome at the track. Power can be derived from premarket institutional conditions (like unequal schooling) that are invisible when one focuses on the market alone.

Seeking Market Power

We have seen that market power can be generated by natural causes (genetic endowments) or by human contrivance (institutional control). We have also introduced some issues of equity and efficiency related to the exercise of market power. There is, however, one efficiency issue related to market power that we have neglected.

Consider the following facts: Many institutions can exert the market power necessary to generate rents (e.g., monopoly rents). The people who control these institutions are in a position to enjoy those rents. Control over institutions is subject to change. The consequence of a change in institutional control would be a redistribution of income from the people who lost control to those who won control.

These facts have important implications for understanding human behavior. A rational individual would seek control of institutions in order to increase her share of the distribution of goods and services. The only limiting factor on such behavior is the costs encountered in seeking control. If, as in other pursuits, costs are rising and benefits are falling at the margin, a rational person will continue to seek control of relevant institutions until the marginal benefit is equal to the marginal cost.

The term in the economics literature for such activity is *rent seeking*. Rent-seeking is the pursuit of an extra distributive share (a rent) by striving to gain a power advantage. The rent-seeking concept helps us understand the competition for institutional control. For instance, the large political action committee (PAC) contributions from organized interests may in part reflect rent-seeking behavior. If an interest group wants Congress to pass a tariff that protects its products from foreign competition, it may find more access to a more sympathetic ear if it donates significantly to a successful congressional campaign.

The primary focus of most of the literature on rent-seeking is on its inefficiency. The point made is that potentially productive resources are being used in an unproductive manner: the pursuit or protection of advantages and the resulting rents. Here again, the private pursuit of market power has social costs.

The race analogy can also shed light on this concept. In the economic race, as in a foot race, rewards are distributed on the basis of competition and each competitor desires to win the greatest possible reward. In contrast to a foot race, at which the rewards are determined in advance, the size of the rewards in an economic race depends on the degree of ability and productive exertion of *all* the competitors. In the economic system the race is the period of production and the award ceremony is the period of distribution. As with any other kind of race, if the event is fair, the outcome (distribution) will be determined by the relative exertions of the competitors. Thus rational competitors will waste no energy and will exert themselves to the fullest in order to win. This creates just the incentive necessary to produce the greatest possible wealth for the nation, because the better everyone performs, the more will be produced. So under our fair race assumption, competition is constructive.

But races are not always fair. It is not unknown for one competitor to seek an advantage by expending effort on hindering the progress of a fellow competitor. While such behavior may provide the individual with an advantage, it is socially wasteful because it diverts both competitors' energies from getting down the track as swiftly (productively) as possible. Such competition is destructive. This is the essence of the inefficiency argument made in the rent-seeking literature. Seeking rents is a wasteful use of productive resources. The cost to society is referred to in the literature as a *social welfare loss*.

Conclusion

By relaxing our fair race assumptions and examining the implications of market power, we have made our model much more realistic. The world is not a fair race, so the model should not be limited to the fair race case. We have bought realism at the price of increased complexity, but the complexity should not overwhelm us since we built the fair race version solidly and have relaxed the assumptions gradually.

We have also found that the distortions of the fair race arise in large measure from forces generated by social and political institutions. This recognition leads us to a very important point. Economic analysis is not designed to explain the world. Society is an incredibly complex weave of social, political, and economic forces. Thus the patterns we see cannot be fully understood by analyzing only the forces exerted by the economic threads as they wind their way through the social fabric. The economic forces weave through the patterns we observe, but there is more to the patterns than these forces. So while the tools of the economist are very powerful, they are only part of a complete social science tool kit. In order to gain a full understanding of society, one needs the tools of the sociologist and the political scientist as well as the economist. For foundational work, one must also consult psychology; for perspective, anthropology; for connections to the natural environment, geography; and for a fourth dimension (time), history.

This is not to argue that we should abandon the specialized study of economics for some transcendent theory of social science. The division of labor in the study of society is necessary because of complexity of the subject. The point here is that economic tools are necessary but not sufficient to understand society and its problems, because the problems are created by the entire structure of social, political, and economic institutions. Solutions must begin with a social choice as to what is the optimal condition. Then, using a complete tool kit to understand how the world works, we can build that better world.

B. MARKET FAILURE

There is another problem with markets that would cause a micro-economy to give results different from those found under our nice assumptions. It is that under some circumstances markets will not act as coordinators because they will fail to form. Economists call this condition *market failure*. An example is the externality case.

Externalities

As we have seen, a market system begins with a distribution of initial endowments and ends with the distribution of the social product. It is a constant cycle of production and consumption, with savings and investment included to expand the capital of the initial endowment and therefore the size of the social product.

This process assumes that property rights are assigned and that they are enforceable. A failure to assign or an inability to enforce property rights can lead to a market failure called an *externality*. To understand why, consider the following case.

In the absence of assignment or enforcement of a property right to a resource, all individuals have equal right to use that resource. Often, however, use is interdependent. For example, if you smoke in class, you use the air as a disposal space for your smoke. I, on the other hand, may want to use the air to refresh my lungs. In the absence of the assignment and enforcement of property rights to the air, we have an equal right to use, yet your use costs me the opportunity to use the air as I would like. Furthermore, if I am unable to transfer some of those costs back to you, you have no incentive to take the costs you impose on me into account when you decide how much to smoke. This problem could be solved in one of two ways:

1. If I was assigned and could enforce a property right to the air, then I could send you a signal that I don't like smoke in my air: I could charge you a price for polluting my air. If you were willing to pay a high enough price, I might let you smoke a bit because your money would compensate my opportunity cost—clean air.

2. If you were assigned and could enforce a property right to the air, then I could still send you a signal that I don't like smoke in the air: I could offer to pay a price to have you reduce or stop your smoking. The higher price I am willing to pay, the more you'd reduce your smoking.

Both of these solutions work because the assignment and enforcement of property rights makes it possible for a market to form. When it does, the market price provides a signal between us that brings our interdependent choice into equilibrium. Unfortunately, as with air, property rights are not always assigned, and where they are, they are not always easily enforced.

In such cases there is no market formed. Therefore the individual whose use intrudes on others (e.g., the polluter) receives no signal in the form of a price that would motivate her to take the intrusion into account when making choices. Thus the intrusion is outside of, or external to, that individual's choice mechanism. We call such an unpriced external effect an externality.

The case of smoking is called a *negative externality* because the activity imposes an external cost that smokers don't take into account when determining the level of their activity. It is also possible for a *positive externality* to occur. For example, if I keep bees in order to harvest their honey, I'll determine the size of my apiary by my costs relative to the demand for honey. What I will not take into account is any benefit my bees provide to nearby homes and farms by the pollinating they do.

So when individual households or firms act in a way that maximizes their own *private* benefit, they may generate effects that benefit or cost others. If, because property rights are not defined, it is impossible for those who generate positive effects to charge for the benefits others receive, or for those who incur the costs of negative effects to charge those who generate them, then no market will form for these positive or negative effects.

Without a market, there is no equilibrating mechanism, no price signal, that could ensure an optimal level of production of these external effects. In the absence of a market price the emitter simply ignores her external effects. Negative external effects are overproduced because the producer pays no price for doing so. Positive external effects are underproduced because the producer receives no price for doing so. The consequence of market failure is that individuals' activities in pursuit of their private self-interest may be privately optimal but not socially optimal.

Sometimes property rights are assigned but cannot be enforced, because while the emitter of certain externalities can be excluded from your property, the emission cannot. An example is acid rain.

Figure 4-1 assumes that each region has property rights over its air. Because the airflow is beyond its control however, the Northeast cannot enforce its right to keep midwestern pollution out. If the Northeast could enforce its property right the Midwest would have to compensate the Northeast for dumping waste in its lakes. The price that would result would keep northeastern lakes as acid-free as the price of pollution would dictate. Can you identify some positive or negative externalities you encounter?

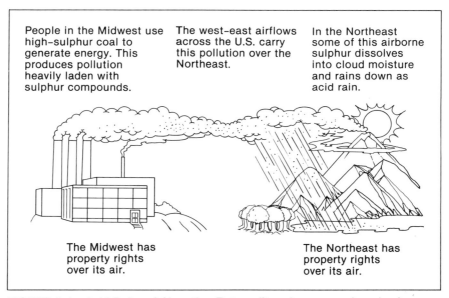

People in the Midwest use high–sulphur coal to generate energy. This produces pollution heavily laden with sulphur compounds.

The west–east airflows across the U.S. carry this pollution over the Northeast.

In the Northeast some of this airborne sulphur dissolves into cloud moisture and rains down as acid rain.

The Midwest has property rights over its air.

The Northeast has property rights over its air.

FIGURE 4-1   Acid Rain—A Negative Externality   Assume each region has property rights over its air. Because the airflow is beyond its control the Northeast cannot enforce its right to keep midwestern pollution out of its air. If there were a market, the Middle West would have to compensate the Northeast for the right to dump waste in northeastern lakes. The price that would result would keep northeastern lakes as acid-free as the price of pollution would dictate.

In technical terms, a positive externality exists when the social benefits of an activity (that is, the benefits to all people, not just the one doing the activity) are *greater than* the private benefit (the benefit to the one doing the activity). That difference is the size of the positive externality. In mathematical terms (we use marginal terms since our choices are made at the margin):

Marginal social benefits = Marginal private benefits + Marginal external benefits

or

$$MPB + MEB = MSB$$

Rearranging, we see that:

Marginal external benefits = Marginal social benefits − Marginal private benefits

OR

$$MEB = MSB - MPB$$

Note that if there is no externality, the marginal external benefit is zero and therefore the marginal private benefits equal the marginal social benefits.

If $MEB = 0$, then $MPB = MSB$

Similarly, a negative externality exists when the social cost of an activity is *greater than* the private cost to the one doing the activity. That difference is the size of the negative externality. In mathematical terms:

$$MPC + MEC = MSC$$

Rearranging, we get:

$$MEC = MSC - MPC$$

Again, if there is no externality, the marginal external cost is zero and therefore the marginal private costs equal the marginal social costs:

If $MEC = 0$, then $MPC = MSC$

Since society as a whole must consider all costs and benefits when determining an optimal choice, the social decision rule would be:

Social optimization condition: set $MSB = MSC$

Rational individuals only take into account their private costs and benefits when determining an optimal choice, so the private decision rule would be:

Private optimization condition: set $MPB = MPC$

Note that if no externalities exist ($MEB = 0$ and $MEC = 0$), then setting $MPB = MPC$ implies $MSB = MSC$. So under that condition, private optimization implies social optimization.

If, as we've assumed, marginal costs rise and marginal benefits (utility) fall with increased levels of activity, we can represent the negative externality case $MEC > 0$ (let $MEB = 0$) graphically as shown in Figure 4-2.

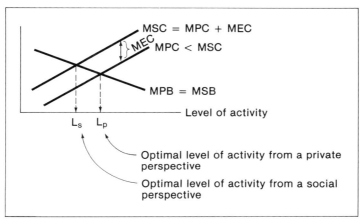

FIGURE 4-2   Representing a Negative Externality Graphically   The individual (firm or household) carries on a level of activity greater than that which is socially optimal because the individual does not have to take into account the external costs generated.

The positive externality case $MEB > 0$ (let $MEC = 0$) is represented in Figure 4-3.

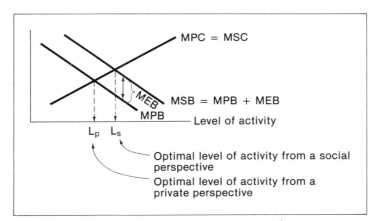

FIGURE 4-3   Representing a Positive Externality Graphically   The individual (firm or household) carries on a level of activity less than that which is socially optimal because the individual does not have to take into account the external benefits generated.

Public Goods

Another example of market failure occurs in the case of a public good. A *public good* is one that cannot be provided exclusively. Once a public good is provided, everyone can enjoy its use, even those who did not pay for it. For the nation as a whole, national defense is a public good. The army protects everyone, not just those who pay for defense. Your neighborhood street lights are a public good because they contribute to everyone's safety.

The problem this kind of market failure presents is that it gives an incentive to individuals to be *free riders*. If you believe that the public good will be provided even if you do not contribute toward its provision, you will be tempted to enjoy the benefit without contributing. A literal example of the free ride is a Portland (Oregon) experiment with an honor system for paying bus fares. The system had to be abandoned because too many people cheated—they took the free rides.

Conclusion of Our Analysis of the Microeconomic Model

> [T]he organization of economic activity through voluntary exchange presumes that we have provided, through government, for the maintenance of law and order to prevent coercion of one individual by another, the enforcement of contracts voluntarily entered into, the definition of the meaning of property rights, the interpretation and enforcement of such rights, and the provision of a monetary framework. . . . We may also want to do through government some things that might conceivably be done through the market but that technical or similar conditions render it difficult to do in that way. These all reduce to cases in which strictly voluntary exchange is either exceedingly costly or practically impossible. There are two general classes of such cases: monopoly and similar market imperfections, and neighborhood effects.
>
> **Milton Friedman**
> *Capitalism and Freedom*, 1962.

WE HAVE assumed, as Friedman does in the first paragraph above, that at least a minimal government exists. In this chapter, we examine the issue Friedman identifies in the second paragraph: given market power and market failure, is there a broader role for government?

A. THE ROLE OF GOVERNMENT IN THE MICROECONOMY: POLICY DEBATE

So far we have abstracted from the role of one of the major players in the microeconomy, the government. Now that we have introduced some of the problems a microeconomic market system can encounter, we should take some time to examine the role of government in the microeconomy and whether it can contribute to the solution of the problems we have identified.

The government plays a role in the economy through the policies it adopts. Every government has an economic policy, whether it is a

107

conscious choice or not, for every government taxes, spends, and regulates to some degree and these activities affect the economy.

Recall that when a general equilibrium is reached, the relative prices of all goods and services (and therefore their values) and the relative prices of all factors (and therefore the distribution of income) are determined. If at that point the government steps in and by taxing, spending, or regulating changes the relative prices, then the economy will no longer be in general equilibrium. In response to this government-directed change in relative prices, the system will begin adjusting again until a new general equilibrium is reached. Thus we see that government policy will affect the microeconomy. Whether the policy is coherently designed to achieve some well-defined economic objective is another matter.

We will assume that the government does have well-defined microeconomic policy objectives, and that these are Pareto optimality and equity. What policy should the government pursue to achieve these objectives? The answer to this question depends on two things: one's perception of how closely the microeconomy actually approximates our nice assumptions, and the degree to which one believes government policy can be effectively and efficiently accomplished. First we will examine the policy necessary to achieve efficiency.

Recall that if the nice assumptions actually hold, the self-adjusting market system realizes Pareto optimality automatically. In this case the market system works well and realizes the efficiency objective, so no government intervention is necessary. Those who believe that the market system does in fact work this way advocate a noninterventionist policy that is often called *laissez-faire*. This term was coined by an eighteenth-century French economist, Gournet, who was arguing for a dismantling of government obstacles to free trade. In effect, laissez-faire, means "let the market work its magic."

There are those, however, who believe that while in many areas of the economy the market coordinates very well, in many other areas, because of market failure or market power, the coordination mechanism is distorted. As we have seen, these distortions lead to inefficiencies. Many believe that these distortions and the accompanying inefficiencies are the rule rather than the exception. Given this belief they advocate government intervention to eliminate, or at least regulate, the degree of distortions.

Take a market failure example, a negative externality created by a firm generating air pollution. As Figure 5-1 demonstrates, the private level of production in this case is greater than socially optimal.

If the government decided to intervene, it could do so in several ways. It could assign air property rights to the people living around the plant. If these rights were enforced by the government, this would

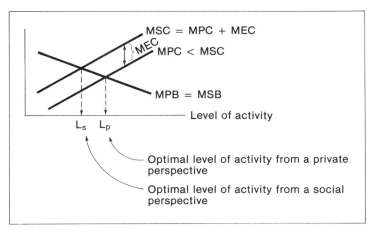

FIGURE 5-1 A Negative Externality

mean the plant would have to pay for the right to pollute. In effect, the market failure that occurred because of an unassigned air property right would be resolved by assigning the property right and thereby creating an "air" market. Alternatively, the government could put a tax on the producer equal to the marginal external costs (MEC), thereby raising private costs to the level of social costs. This would bring the private optimal level of activity down to L_s. Or the government could try various kinds of regulation. It could require the firm to produce no more than L_s, or it could require the firm to install scrubbers that eliminate the externality. (Can you identify any other possible solutions?)

Unfortunately, all of the solutions identified above have problems. If the government tries to create a market solution to the problem by assigning air property rights, this presents several new problems. First, how will these rights be enforced? Second, how do we know the market solution will be efficient? After all, before the government intervened, the firm was acting as if it had property rights—it was polluting. So why didn't a market form then? Homeowners could have paid the firm to lower the pollution level, with the price adjusting to an equilibrium, but this did not happen. Why? The reason is that clean air is a public good: if anyone provides it, everyone gets to enjoy it. As we saw earlier, provision of public goods encourages free riders. In this case, if some homeowners formed a coalition to negotiate with the firm to reduce pollution, other homeowners might choose to enjoy the benefits of the coalition's effort without contributing to its cost. It is unlikely that a successful homeowner coalition could be created—so the market would fail to materialize.

What if the government assigned property rights to the homeowners and enforced those rights? This would create a different set of problems. Now the firm would either have to pay for pollution rights or move. If the firm had less to lose than the homeowners did from such a move (e.g., if the homeowners work at the firm), the firm would have market power: it could threaten to move. Using this blackmail, it could maintain artificially low charges for the right to pollute. On the other hand, if the homeowners had less to lose than the firm, the homeowners could exploit that advantage in order to charge artificially high prices for the right to pollute.

What if the government chose a nonmarket solution like taxing or regulating, or an artificial market solution in which it sold rights to pollute to the highest bidder? There are problems here, too. The government would have to have some indication as to the severity of the externality (the size of MEC) in order to correctly set the tax or the regulation or the amount of pollution rights to be sold. Since the size of the MEC depends on the feelings, the preferences, of those who endure the externality, the government would have to determine the true preferences of those people. We know that when there is no cost for expressing distaste for an externality, there is no incentive for people to reveal their true preferences—in fact, they have an incentive to overstate the degree of the externality. So how can the government determine the actual MEC and therefore set the tax or regulate L_p correctly or decide the optimal degree of scrubbing? It has to rely on an educated guess.

These are some of the potential problems with government intervention. So we see that even if one believes the market system is flawed, the question remains: Is government intervention a contribution to the solution or will it exacerbate the problem? This question pertains both to market failure and to market power. Many government agencies have been created to regulate the behavior of powerful economic players such as monopolies. Some economists argue, however, that because the individuals in these agencies develop close working relationships with those they regulate, they tend to act as agents of the powerful players. Regulations become rules for the protection of a powerful interest rather than rules for the protection of the social welfare. This problem is particularly likely to occur where regulators look forward to high-paying future employment with the firms they are presently regulating. Clearly the incentive the powerful economic player has in securing this kind of "protective regulation" is rent-seeking (acquiring new rents) or rent-protection (protecting old rents). Even if we assume that the regulators are genuinely trying to serve the public interest, they face a very difficult task because the primary source of their information is the very firms they are trying to regulate.

It should be clear that the government policy our model implies with respect to efficiency depends first and foremost on how realistic one believes our nice assumptions are. Those who think they are a reasonable approximation of reality argue that markets work very nicely, and therefore the appropriate policy to realize efficiency is laissez-faire. Those who believe that the nice assumptions are unrealistic argue that the market has many distortions, and therefore efficiency could be improved by appropriate intervention. Those who hold this latter view are then confronted with the question: Will government intervention be appropriate? The different beliefs people hold about the quality of markets and the quality of government lie at the heart of the debate over government intervention.

The debate about the role of government in the microeconomy is further complicated if we add to the efficiency objective an equity objective. Clearly the government can, by taxing and spending, redistribute income in society. It can do so by simply transferring wealth—taxing one group and giving the money to another—or by taxing one group and spending on programs that benefit another. Redistribution can also be accomplished by regulating the behavior of one group to the benefit of another. For instance, rent controls limit how much landlords can charge and, in effect, redistribute income from landlords to renters.

There are several problems with government intervention in the name of equity. The most fundamental problem is determining a definition of equity. If society simply defines the current state of affairs as equitable, those who are doing well will be happy, but those who are poor will cry foul. If some other definition of equity is chosen and we assume the size of the economic pie is constant, the realization of equity would require a redistribution. Obviously, people who would lose by this process, being rational, would resist such a definition. If we assume that the pie can expand, then the question becomes: How can the expansion be accomplished equitably? The method of expansion will determine who benefits, and people will argue for the method that benefits them the most—they will all define the equitable choice differently. Thus the choice of a definition acceptable to all is very difficult, if not impossible.

This lack of consensus creates serious problems for government. It may have to ignore, or even expend resources suppressing, the claims of some segments of the population. Alternatively, it may try to satisfy the claims of all segments of the population. This may be possible for a short period, but it is doomed to failure in the longer term since, as we have learned, demands can be limitless and resources are finite. Even the government cannot escape the inescapable: the quandry of choice.

Even assuming that a *generally* acceptable definition of equity is agreed upon, the government faces the problem of implementing a policy that will realize that goal. Government policy on behalf of equity has efficiency implications. Anytime the government taxes, spends, or regulates, it is distorting the market system from its natural, unencumbered course.

Take the rent control example we cited earlier. The graph in Figure 5-2 represents the market for apartments when rent controls are imposed that put a ceiling on rents at R_c. The effect is an excess demand for apartments.

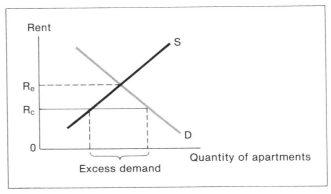

FIGURE 5-2   Representing Rent Control Graphically

Since rent controls are the law, the automatic market adjustment mechanism—adjusting prices to bring quantity supplied and quantity demanded to an equilibrium—is not able to eliminate the shortage. The shortage becomes a long-term problem. If controls were lifted, rents would rise to R_e. As rents rise, the quantity supplied would rise (new apartments would be built) and the quantity demanded would fall (fewer people could afford the price of housing). Here we have an efficiency/equity trade-off. In order to get the efficiencies of the apartment market, poorer people would be priced out of the market for apartments.

If we could agree on some standard of equity, the question of government intervention becomes: How do we realize the equity standard at the lowest possible cost in terms of efficiency? In theoretical terms, the answer is straightforward. As we read in a quotation from Kenneth Arrow cited in Chapter IV: "Indeed, the theory teaches us that the final allocation will depend on the distribution of initial supplies and of the ownership of firms. If we want to rely on the virtues of the market but also to achieve a more just distribution, the theory suggests the strategy of changing the initial endowments rather than interfering with the allocation process at some later stage."

This solution returns us, however, to our initial quandary. How do we get individuals to agree on a definition of equity when someone will lose based on any definition other than the status quo and many reject the status quo? What we find is that there is no grand solution to this question of social choice. In practice government intervention for equity purposes is often, when it is done at all, an ad hoc (case-by-case) process with all the attendant efficiency problems that implies.

Does all this mean that laissez-faire is the clear winner in the debate over microeconomic government policy? No. The debate continues because there continues to be disagreement among economists and within the general public over how well the market economy works, how well the government works, and how fair the status quo is. This debate plays itself out in the form of social and political competition. Those who take varying positions in the debate compete for control of society's institutions so that they can shape the future to conform to their vision of an ideal society. This competition can be peaceful, as it is in most American political campaigns; or it can be violent, as it is in Northern Ireland, Lebanon, and South Africa; or it can be played out in both ways simultaneously, as it was in the civil rights movement during the 1950s and 1960s.

As we will see, these very fundamental disagreements also underlie the debate at that other level of economic analysis, discussion, and policy: macroeconomics.

B. AN EXAMPLE OF THE COMPLEXITY OF APPLIED MICROECONOMIC ANALYSIS: DRUG POLICY

We have seen that an analysis of individual behavior and the interaction of individuals in a complex economy begins with a specification of initial endowments, preferences, and technology. Through a system of markets these individuals, responding to price signals, adjust their behavior until all interdependent choices are consistent. The result is a general equilibrium, and if our nice assumptions hold, it will be the special case of a Pareto optimal General Competitive Equilibrium.

The coordinator of the system is the adjustment of relative prices. The power of prices derives from the fact that households and firms respond to relative prices. Thus the set of relative prices represents the structure of incentives in society. This is a valuable insight. It implies that by changing relative prices, the structure of incentives and therefore the behavior of firms and/or households can be manipulated.

What is more, if we know how responsive households and firms are to a change in price (i.e., the own and cross-price elasticities), we can predict to what degree behavior will change when the structure of incentives, relative prices, is changed. All of this can be very useful at an applied level.

As we mentioned earlier in the text, large firms often hire economists to determine the elasticities of their products. It is obviously important to know how consumers are going to respond to a price change. Trial and error will answer the question, but if professional analysis can reduce the likelihood of a serious error, the advice will more than pay for itself.

The government also uses the services of economists in order to predict the effects of a contemplated policy. Suppose, for instance, the government is convinced that a major source of crime is heroin junkies who steal in order to pay for their habit. That might immediately suggest to drug enforcement officials that less heroin would mean less crime. Following this logic, officials might crack down on the importation of heroin, only to find, contrary to their expectations, that the number of heroin-related crimes has gone up. To an economist this is not a surprising result.

Since heroin use is an addiction, the drug is an absolute necessity. An absolute necessity has a *very* inelastic demand. People want such things no matter what the price. Given such a demand, as supply is cut back, the result will be a percentage increase in price that is greater than the percentage fall in quantity demanded. This is, after all, what we mean by inelastic demand. Thus, the consequence of the government's action is to decrease the quantity of heroin used, but it also increases the total expenditure on it. Since buying this smaller amount of heroin requires more money, ironically it causes more crime.

This does not mean that the policy is necessarily a bad idea. In the long run, the high price of heroin might discourage kids from trying it. If no new users came along, then demand would begin to fall over time. If over the same time supply could be continually reduced, the heroin problem might be reduced.

The problem with this scenario is that it ignores a crucial economic incentive on the supply side. As the street price of heroin rises, the incentive to smuggle it into the country or to identify marketable substitutes rises. Thus, if the government successfully slows down smuggling, thereby causing the price of heroin to rise, it automatically creates greater incentives for drug entrepreneurs to use more cleverness and violence to get the stuff into the country or to identify marketable substitutes (e.g., crack).

Some alternative changes in incentives that have been proposed are: increase the likelihood of apprehension and/or severity of sentences for drug traffickers, give the drugs away free, change the preferences of kids by educating them about the dangers of drugs. How would an economist analyze each of these alternatives, and what would be the advantages and disadvantages of each?

This example demonstrates both the power and the complexity of applied microeconomic analysis.

C. CONCLUSION

We began the development of a microeconomic model by defining and arranging terms and specifying some assumptions. With that foundation we built a microeconomic model for a simple Robinson Crusoe society. We identified how a lone individual with limited resources would solve the quandary of choice, then we successively relaxed assumptions in order to build the issues of a multiperiod time horizon and of risk and uncertainty into the decision rule.

Next we examined the forces that give rise to complexity. We found that the benefit of the division of labor—increased social product—makes everyone better off as long as there is a mechanism for coordinating the exchange of the surpluses produced by all the participants. The market, adjusting on a price signal, provides such a mechanism. If it works perfectly, it ensures that all individual decisions to produce and consume or save and invest are coordinated.

We analyzed the concepts of supply and demand, the role of price as the signal on which coordination is based, and the concept of a market equilibrium. We found that under our strong nice assumptions a market system outcome in a complex society is analogous to that in a Robinson Crusoe society: coordination of decisions to supply and demand and to save and invest is perfect; all productive resources offered for use are put to use in the most efficient technique of production available; for every good or service, the quantity supplied will be equal to the quantity demanded; and all individuals will derive the maximum utility from their initial endowment.

Having examined this case, we began to relax our assumptions. First we relaxed the fair race assumption and analyzed the impact of a distortion—market power—on the efficiency and equity of the system. We found that distribution, and therefore equity, was affected by this distortion but noted that the question as to the desirability of the change is not an economic question, it is an ethical question. We found that efficiency was diminished.

Then we noted that many market power distortions are generated by social and political institutions that skew the distribution of society's opportunities to the advantage of some members of society and to the disadvantage of others. It is this point that connects the study of economics to the study of other social sciences. This connection makes it clear that while the tools of the economist are indispensable for a complete analysis of social forces, only when those tools are used in conjunction with the tools of sister social sciences can an analysis of society be complete.

Another distortion of the market system that we identified is the failure of markets to develop under some conditions. In cases such as externalities or public goods, there is then no mechanism for coordinating individual decisions and a socially suboptimal condition results.

Finally, we turned our attention to the role of government in the process and problems of a microeconomic market system. We identified two basic positions on this issue: noninterventionist and interventionist. Those who believe that the market system works well advocate a noninterventionist, laissez-faire policy. Those who believe that government can be a constructive force and that the problems of market power and market failure are very serious, advocate government intervention to correct them. In fact, while many economists lean toward one view or the other, most do not adopt either position consistently. Rather, they treat each policy proposal as a separate case.

We have seen that the market system has one great virtue. When it is working well and is unencumbered, it is the most efficient system for allocating society's resources and thus for generating the greatest wealth for the nation. But the market system does lack another great virtue that many people mistakenly ascribe to it. The system is not inherently fair. Actually, the market system is amoral. It is simply a coordinating mechanism for exchange that self-adjusts on price signals. Under our nice conditions, the fairness of the outcome depends entirely on the fairness of the distribution of society's initial endowment and opportunities among individuals. As we have seen, the system can be distorted in ways that allow some individuals to exploit others.

This completes our analysis of the microeconomy of a complex society such as ours. Now we turn our attention to another perspective on the economic system—the macroeconomic perspective.

6 Introduction to Macroeconomics

THIS PICTURE reflects the relationship between micro and macroeconomics. They are different perspectives on the same subject. Micro focuses on the pieces while macro looks at the whole. Micro focuses on disaggregated (individual) variables. Macro focuses on aggregate (summed) variables. At such, macroeconomics is the study of the sum of microeconomic events. Yet, as the picture suggests, macroeconomics is more than the sum of its parts. In this chapter we introduce macroeconomics.

A. OVERVIEW

To this point we have been studying microeconomics, focusing on disaggregated (individual) variables like the allocation of resources, the values of goods and services, and the distribution of society's product among individuals. Now we shift our focus. Instead of analyzing the actions and interactions of individual players within the economy, we will be analyzing the overall state of society's economy. Studying the economy at this level is called *macroeconomic analysis*.

117

Macroeconomics focuses on questions about aggregated (summed) variables such as:

1. What determines society's capacity to produce? What determines how much society is currently producing? (National product)

2. Why are society's available resources sometimes less than fully utilized, or to put it differently, why would some of society's available resources lie idle? Under what circumstances would such a condition persist? (Unemployment)

3. What determines society's ability to expand productive capacity over time? (Growth)

4. Why does the purchasing power of the money society uses as a medium of exchange sometimes change over time? Under what circumstances would such a change continue? (Inflation or deflation)

Macroeconomics is to microeconomics as the study of a forest is to the study of its trees. When we study those relationships between individual people or individual trees that determine, the growth of individual peoples' incomes or individual trees' sizes, we are doing analysis at a micro (in former case Microeconomic) level. When we study the economic system or ecosystem as a whole unit, we are doing analysis at a macro (in the former case Macroeconomic) level.

A forest is made up of trees but it is more than the sum of its trees. There are characteristics of the forest, such as size, maturity, and growth rate, that transcend any particular tree. Yet because these characteristics have implications for the strength and stability of the forest in the face of environmental disturbances, they have a bearing on the well-being of every tree in the forest. The same can be said about the relationship between the micro- and the macroeconomy. There are characteristics of any whole economy, such as size, maturity, and growth rate, that transcend any individual. Yet because these characteristics have real implications for the strength and stability of the economy in the face of outside disturbances, they have a bearing on the well-being of every individual in the economy. We study micro- and macroeconomic topics separately because the nature of the issues at each level is different. We do not study them separately because they are independent of one another. To consider them so would be as absurd as considering the forest independent of its trees.

The key point here is that micro- and macroeconomics are different perspectives on the same subject. The former focuses on the pieces while the latter looks at the whole. While the whole is in some sense greater than its parts, the microeconomic system is the foundation on which the macroeconomic system is built. This relationship should become clear as we build the macroeconomic model. We will find that if we make our nice microeconomic assumptions, the macroeconomy will reflect the efficiency that these conditions generate in the microeconomy: the macroeconomy will produce the greatest feasible wealth for the nation and there will be no unemployed resources. We will also find that when these assumptions are relaxed, the resulting inefficiency we found in the microeconomy will be reflected in the form of less-than-full-capacity production and the presence of unemployed resources in the macroeconomy.

Our study of the macroeconomic model will follow the same approach we used in studying the microeconomic model. We will begin by defining the terms necessary to build the model. With this "tool kit" we will proceed to assemble the model. Once the model is constructed, we will examine the explanations and predictions it implies.

As with the micro model, we will examine the implications of the macroeconomic model under two different sets of assumptions. First we will assume that our nice microeconomic assumptions hold, and then we will relax those assumptions. We will find that the implications of the macro model are different depending on which micro assumptions one makes. Identifying and understanding this connection between microeconomic assumptions and the macroeconomic model's implications is a key objective of our study.

Once we have developed the macroeconomic model under both sets of microeconomic assumptions, (that our "nice" conditions do *versus* do not hold), we will turn our attention to the policy implications of the model. We will find that these implications also depend on the micro assumptions one makes. Those who believe that the nice assumptions are relatively realistic support a policy of government nonintervention (noninterference). They argue that the micro adjustment system (the invisible hand) works just fine, and therefore that government interference at the macro level is not only unnecessary, but may be counterproductive. Those who believe that the microeconomic system is full of distortions and does not work well argue that government must intervene at the macro level to correct for the effects of these distortions. These are the polar cases, with most economists arrayed in between.

Having established the theoretical basis for the policy debate, we will introduce the tools of macroeconomic policy so that we can examine the debate at the level of policy implementation. We will see how each side believes these tools should be handled. Examining these policy tools will also allow us to explore the difficulties inherent in manipulating the macroeconomic policy tools.

Finally, we will step back from the theory and briefly examine the actual course of the policy debate from the early nineteenth century to the present. Doing so will allow us to see how the current state of the debate has evolved. It will also allow us to analyze in more detail the fundamental problem we briefly introduced early in our study: the fact that empirical problems make it possible for competing theoretical views to coexist.

B. DEFINING TERMS

Introduction

At the outset of our study the point was made that sturdy model building is possible only if the terms used are clearly and consistently defined. It is important, therefore, that we begin our development of the macroeconomic model, as we did the microeconomic model, by carefully defining the terms we will use.

National Product

One of the macroeconomic questions we want to explore is: What determines society's capacity to produce and how much is society currently producing? In order to examine this question, we need a term that defines what is included in the national product. The broadest measure of the national product is the *gross national product* (hereafter GNP). We will define GNP as the value of all the final goods and services produced in the economy during a given year. Keep in mind that this is our theoretical definition. The government's technical definition is, as we will see, much more complicated.

GNP is a valuable concept because we need a measure of current production in the economy. Such a measure allows us to determine if the output of the economy is growing or falling over time. What is more, if we can determine the full, sustainable capacity GNP for the economy, then by comparing this to current measures of actual GNP, we can gauge the productive health of the economy. If actual GNP is close to or at full, sustainable capacity GNP, the economy is productively healthy. If, on the other hand, actual GNP is well below full, sustainable capacity GNP, that is strong evidence that productive resources are either lying idle, being used inefficiently, or both. Indicative of this role of GNP as an indicator of the productive health of the economy, the economy is called healthy when GNP is growing, but we are in a *recession* if the economy experiences one half year (two consecutive quarters) of falling GNP, and a *depression* if there is a prolonged depressed level of GNP.

GNP is often treated as a measure of social welfare: more GNP means a better society. Before we go on, we should examine this proposition. The first question one should ask is: Better for whom? If, as GNP expands, a few rich people are getting richer and a lot of poor people are getting poorer, then it may not be "better." The point is that the level of GNP does not tell us much about the general standard of living in a country until we know how the GNP is distributed.

Another problem with GNP as a measure of welfare is the assumption that welfare is always improved by human production. Whether we invariably improve our world as we produce is a debatable point. If we "harvested" all the trees in the world, GNP would reflect that "productive" activity, and yet we might be worse off for having done so. If we burned all those harvested trees, we might need to produce air purifiers to protect our lungs from the soot produced. In that case, GNP would go up from the harvesting and burning as well as from the production of goods that protect us from the externalities of our own production. Does an increase in GNP that reflects expenditures to protect ourselves from the negative externalities of our production represent a welfare gain? It would seem not. The point here is *not* that GNP is a useless tool for measuring social welfare, only that it is not a sufficient one and we should not treat it as such.

Labor-Related Terms

Another macroeconomic question we want to explore is: Why are society's available resources sometimes less than fully utilized, or, why would some of society's available resources be idle? Society's most precious resource is its people. In order to determine how well this resource, labor, is being utilized, we need terms that define the quantity available for use, the quantity being used, and the quantity lying idle. The first of these terms is *labor force*. The labor force includes all those persons who are participating or are making themselves available for participation in the economy's productive process. It makes sense that people who do not want a job are not counted in the labor force. We refer to this group as *voluntarily unemployed*. (If you won the lottery, you might choose to be voluntarily unemployed.) From here on, when we use the term unemployed, it will *not* include the voluntarily unemployed.

Those within the labor force fall into two categories: *employed* and *unemployed*. There are three kinds of unemployment, each distinguished by its cause. *Frictional unemployment* includes those people who are between jobs but for whom the right job exists. They are out of a job because they are looking for the right job but have not yet found it. The job search process takes time. One collects information and adjusts expectations. One would not accept a job until, at the margin, the rising costs of further search (resumés, gasoline, stamps, ulcers, wages lost, risk of losing an available offer, etc.) equal the falling expected benefit of further search (the chance of getting a better offer). Because a job search takes time, there will be some frictional unemployment even in the best of economic times. The quicker the search process can be completed, the lower the frictional unemployment will be.

Another kind of unemployment is *structural unemployment*. This means that there are jobs for people but the jobs and the people are mismatched. The mismatch may be on the basis of skill, geography, or some other reason. Structural unemployment occurs because the economy is constantly going through technological transformations and geographic relocations. For instance, when the economy went from carriages to cars, there were plenty of buggy whip makers who, without some training, could not take the new mechanics' jobs that became available. A more recent instance of structural unemployment resulted when heavy industrial jobs in the Midwest were being lost and high-tech jobs in other areas were expanding. Structural unemployment rises with an increased rate of change in the economy, but it can be reduced by more speedily adjusting the skills and location of workers.

Since frictional and structural unemployment are naturally occurring characteristics of a healthy economy, the sum of the two is called the *natural rate of unemployment*. The natural rate is a key macroeconomic concept. When economists speak of *full employment*, they do not mean zero unemployment, because even in the best of times there will be some frictional and structural unemployment. Full employment denotes the situation when the only unemployment is the natural rate.

There is one other kind of unemployment. It is generally referred to as *demand-deficient unemployment*. Recall that for both frictional and structural unemployment there were enough jobs for everyone who wanted one; the problem was one of searching or matching. Demand-deficient unemployment occurs when there are not enough jobs for everyone who wants one. In other words, the aggregate quantity of labor supplied to the economy is greater than the aggregate quantity demanded; *ergo* the term *demand-deficient* unemployment.

Persistently high levels of any kind of unemployment are a problem for the macroeconomy because productive resources are not being put to use. What is more, for all those individuals who are actually unemployed, life is difficult at best and tragic at worst. Thus the costs of unemployment are the social product lost and the individual suffering incurred when people who desire work cannot find a job. The unemployment rate is measured as follows:

$$\text{Unemployment rate} = \frac{\text{Number unemployed}}{\text{Number in the labor force}} \times 100\%$$

Historically, the natural rate of unemployment has not been very high. As late as the 1970s, most economists put it at around 4 percent. In recent years some economists have argued that the rapidly changing economy has raised it as high as 7 percent. Whether this has actually occurred is a subject of current debate.

The major unemployment problem that has plagued advanced market economies has been demand-deficient unemployment. From 1929 to 1933 the United States unemployment rate (the percentage of the labor force that is unemployed) soared from 3.2 to 25 percent (*Source: Historical Statistics of the United States*, Department of Commerce, Series D86). This was the most tragic manifestation of that period called the Great Depression. Clearly, this dramatic rise in the unemployment rate was not due to frictional or structural problems as we have defined them. There were simply no jobs for millions of people who were ready, willing, and able to work.

The Great Depression set the agenda for post–World War II economic thought until the 1960s. The primary policy objective of the generation of economists who came of age during the Depression was to avoid its repetition. That generation is passing from the scene and new issues dominate the current agenda, but any economic theory must still be judged by the standard: What does it tell us about the Depression experience? As we will see, each of the competing versions of "mainstream" macroeconomic theory has an explanation for the Depression, and the debate over what really happened during the 1930s still goes on. Our purpose here is to understand the model and the sides in the debate, not to resolve the issue.

Price Level: Inflation and Deflation

Another macroeconomic question we want to explore is: Why does the purchasing power of money used in society sometimes change over time? Since the value of money always moves inversely to the price level (as prices rise, money buys less), we must define *price level* and terms for changes in the price level before we can examine the question posed. The price level is, as the name implies, the general position of prices in the economy at any point in time.

Inflation is a rise in the price level and therefore a fall in the value of money. *Deflation* is a fall in the price level and therefore a rise in the value of money. We can distinguish two kinds of inflation: *One-shot* or *temporary* inflation, in which the price level rises and then stops; and *sustained* inflation, an ongoing rise in the level of prices.

Before we go on, we must emphasize the distinction between the macroeconomic concept of a rise in the level of prices (inflation) and the microeconomic concept of a relative price change. A *relative price change* occurs when the relative value of goods or services changes because of shifts in an individual market's supply or demand conditions. A *rise in the price level* is in the broadest case a rise of all prices. It is possible for the price level to rise without affecting relative prices. If all prices doubled, the price level would double, but relative prices would remain the same. If, in fact, all prices rose by the same proportion, the only thing that would lose value in the economy is money. If prices doubled, money's value would fall by a half.

It is this undermining of the value of money that constitutes the major cost of inflation. Recall that money evolves in a market economy because it allows for more efficient exchange than a barter system. Money takes on three roles: a medium of exchange, a store of value, and a unit of account. When high inflation is sustained, people hold less money because it is losing its value quickly. Thus inflation undermines money's role as a store of value. When sustained inflation gets very high, people abandon the use of money altogether, because holding it for even a short period can mean a loss of almost all value. This kind of inflation is called *hyperinflation*. When it occurs, money is useless as a store of value, a medium of exchange, or a unit of account because its value is falling so fast. The loss of these roles is called the *efficiency cost of inflation* because the efficiency benefits money brings to an exchange economy are eroded by inflation.

As noted above, inflation does not cause microeconomic changes so long as all prices, including factor prices, are rising at the same rate. However, it is possible for the general level of prices to rise, and thus for inflation to occur, even as some individual prices are constant or falling. If, as most prices rise, some prices such as the price of labor (wages) or the price of capital (interest) are locked at a certain dollar level by long-term contract, the recipients of the payment (wage earners and creditors) lose real value. This is so because they are paid in progressively less valuable dollars. Thus we see that inflation can also have a redistributional effect. One way individuals protect their income from inflation is to peg contractual returns to the price level. This is called *indexing*, because people peg payments to a government index (measure) of the price level. An indexed payment is one for which dollar values are constantly adjusted to changes in a specified price index so that the real value of the payment remains constant.

A *price index* is a number that represents the current level of prices for a group of products relative to the level of prices for those products in a specified base year. The base-year level is always set at 100. The "group of products" may be as large as all final products in the economy or as small as only items related to medical care. The former price index would be called a GNP price index, while the latter would be called a medical price index. Price indexes may also vary by the geographical area they cover. One could, for example, calculate a price index that covered the entire nation or one that covered only a state or a city. Thus we see that the kinds of items and the geographical area included in a price index can vary.

The price index you have probably heard and read most about is a national version of a price index called the consumer price index or CPI. The CPI is supposed to measure the level of prices for the group of products consumers buy (i.e., it would include milk but not missiles).

In order to see how a price index can be constructed, we will consider the CPI. To determine the CPI the government begins by identifying the items it would expect to find in the market basket of a "normal" household. Let us assume that the government (the Bureau of Labor Statistics) defines a normal market basket and identifies the unit prices over time as shown in Table 6-1.

The CPI is calculated as follows:

$$\text{Given-year CPI} = \frac{\text{Price of the market basket in the given year}}{\text{Price of the market basket in the base year}} \times 100$$

TABLE 6-1: Data Base for Consumer Price Index

Items in Basket	Unit Prices in Dollars			
	Dec '97	Dec '98	Dec '99	Dec '00
10 jars of peanut butter (chunky)	2	5	1	6
10 jars of jelly (raspberry)	1	2	2	2.5
100 loaves of bread (whole wheat)	1	2	4	1
10 gallons of milk (low-fat)	2	3	2	4

Note that when the given year (the year in which we are interested) is the base year, the CPI = 100. For example, if we choose 1997 as the base year:

$$CPI_{97} = \frac{10\times2 + 10\times1 + 100\times1 + 10\times2}{10\times2 + 10\times1 + 100+1 + 10\times2} \times 100 = \frac{150}{150} \times 100 = 100$$

Using 1997 as a base year and calculating the CPIs for 1998, 1999, 2000, we find:

$$CPI_{98} = \frac{10\times5 + 10\times2 + 100\times2 + 10\times3}{10\times2 + 10\times1 + 100\times1 + 10\times2} \times 100 = \frac{300}{150} \times 100 = 200$$

$$CPI_{99} = \frac{10\times1 + 10\times2 + 100\times4 + 10\times2}{10\times2 + 10\times1 + 100\times1 + 10\times2} \times 100 = \frac{450}{150} \times 100 = 300$$

$$CPI_{00} = \frac{10\times6 + 10\times2.5 + 100\times1 + 10\times4}{10\times2 + 10\times1 + 100\times1 + 10\times2} \times 100 = \frac{225}{150} \times 100 = 150$$

To measure inflation from one point in time to another, we calculate the percentage change in a particular price index over that period. For example, to measure inflation in consumer prices, we use the CPI. Given the numbers above, we see that inflation between 1998 and 1999 will be:

Inflation

$$\text{'98 to '99} = \frac{CPI_{99} - CPI_{98}}{CPI_{98}} \times 100\% = \frac{300 - 200}{200} \times 100\% = 50\%$$

Since the government calculates price indexes for various groups of items and/or geographical areas, it is possible to compare things like the inflation rate for medical items with that for food items or the cost of living in Sullivan, Missouri, with that in New York City.

Consider: If the cost of living in New York is twice as high as it is in Sullivan, in which city would a $30,000 salary buy more? Clearly in Sullivan, because if the overall price level there is only one-half what it is in New York, $30,000 in Sullivan will go twice as far. This reality is the basis for an important distinction between what economists refer to as *nominal* and *real values*. If you are paid $30,000 whether you live in Sullivan or New York, then in nominal terms (in other words, at face value) your salary is the same in both places. However, because of the dramatic difference in the cost of living, the real value of your salary is twice as much in Sullivan as it is in New York.

Real versus Nominal

You may have heard the expression "the dollar is not what it used to be." That's true. While a dollar looks essentially the same as it did in 1960 (except for the signatures on the front), it does not buy as much. This is so because a dollar is still a dollar but the dollar price of virtually everything—in economic terms, the price level—has gone up. As the price level goes up, the real amount of goods and services a dollar will buy—the value of a dollar—goes down. Because of this inflation (or deflation) there is a problem with using the dollar as a measurement of value over time.

For example, if I told you that I earned $7,000 in 1973 and $28,000 in 1988, it would seem that my salary went way up during that period —and in nominal terms it did. But did it really go up? Is the real value of $28,000 in 1988 greater than the real value of $7,000 in 1973? In other words: Can $28,000 in 1988 buy more than $7,000 could in 1973? The answer to that question depends on what happened to the price level. My salary quadrupled, so if the price level less than quadrupled, I'm better of in real terms; but if it more than quadrupled, I'm worse off in real terms. Thus we see that for any economic variable measured in dollars (e.g., salaries, GNP, interest rates, tax levels), information about changes in their face value (nominal changes) is not adequate to determine how they have changed in real terms.

Consider GNP. Nominal GNP is not a good measure to use when comparing the value of GNP in two different years because changes from year to year in nominal GNP may reflect changes in real production (the actual physical output), the price level, or both. An increase in real production increases nominal GNP. An increase in the price level increases nominal GNP. The problem with comparing nominal GNP from year to year is that if the nominal value changes, we cannot identify whether the change represents a real change in society's production, a change in the price level, or both.

Consider the following fictitious data:

Nominal GNP in Jamestown, Virginia:
1607 $GNP = \$100$
1608 $GNP = \$198$

What do these data tell us about the change in *real* production in Jamestown from 1607 to 1608? That it almost doubled? That it stayed the same? That it fell? Any one of these outcomes is possible, depending on what was happening to the price level. If the price level was constant from 1607 to 1608, then real production almost doubled. As long as the price level is constant, nominal changes are equivalent to real changes.

What if the price level doubled from 1607 to 1608? If this happened, then the value of a dollar in 1608 (a dollar in 1608?) would be half what it was in 1607. How can we adjust the nominal values so that direct comparison of real values is possible? This requires eliminating the effect of the change in price level so that we can isolate and compare the effect of real changes. In this simple case, we know that the 1608 dollars are worth half as much as the 1607 dollars, so we can simply scale down the nominal 1608 GNP by half to eliminate the effect of the price rise. We call this adjusted value of the 1608 GNP the *real* 1608 *GNP*. Since 1607 was the dollar we used as our standard, the 1607 *nominal GNP* does not have to be adjusted. It is equal to real 1607 GNP because 1607 dollars are our standard or base-year dollars.

The statistics presented in Table 6-2 (United States data) should convince you that changes in nominal GNP may not reflect the real change in GNP. From the third quarter of 1981 to the third quarter of 1982, real GNP fell every quarter except one, while nominal GNP only fell from the fourth quarter of 1981 to the first quarter of 1982. During this whole period the price level was rising, but only once did the effect of falling real GNP offset the effect of the rising price level enough to cause nominal GNP to fall. During this period the country was in a severe recession but you would never know that from looking at the changing value of nominal GNP. Only real GNP gives the real facts about output.

This distinction between nominal and real values is emphasized for two reasons. We will use it during the development of the macroeconomic model, so it is important that you understand the distinction as we build the model. Moreover, you must understand the distinction if you are to be an informed reader of current or historical macroeconomic data and/or an informed observer at the debate over macroeconomic policy. Any macroeconomic variable that is measured in

TABLE 6-2:

Year (by quarters)	Nominal GNP	Real GNP (1972 base year)
1981 (3)	3004.9	1525.8
1981 (4)	3032.2	1506.9
1982 (1)	3021.4	1485.8
1982 (2)	3070.2	1489.3
1982 (3)	3090.7	1485.7
1982 (4)	3109.6	1480.7

Source: Economic Report to the President, February 1984, Tables B1-2.

dollars or in dollars per something else (like time) has a nominal and a real value. When you read or hear such variables used, you must know if the values being cited are in nominal or real terms if they are to correctly convey information. Real variables are immediately useful for comparisons over time. Nominal terms are not useful for such comparisons unless they are accompanied by information about changes in price level that allow you to convert them into real terms.

As noted above, the reason comparing nominal values does not reflect the underlying relative real values is because the yardstick used to measure, money, changes its value.

To see this problem more clearly and to see how it is solved, consider the following "Parable of the Foot":

Imagine that you are doing research in medieval history and you want to determine how changes in nutrition affected health. You have data that show that the quality of an average person's diet improved between 1300 and 1400. Your proxy for health is height. Your hypothesis is that better nutrition makes people grow taller, and therefore your prediction is that because of improved nutrition between 1300 and 1400, the average height of individuals increased. Happily you also have three record books listing individual heights. The first book covers the reign of Queen Celia from 1300 to 1333, the second book covers the reign of King John from 1334 to 1366, and the third book covers the reign of King Martin from 1367 to 1400.

In order to get an early impression as to whether your hypothesis is supported by the data, you calculate the average for each book. Much to your chagrin, you find the following results:

1300–1333 average height was 11 feet
1334–1366 average height was 5 feet 7 inches
1367–1400 average height was 7 feet 8 inches

Obviously, this makes no sense. Consultation with a historian of weights and measures clarifies the problem. You learn that during the fourteenth century the standard measure "foot" always referred to the foot length of the ruling monarch. The standard of measure was not constant over time.

Happily, the historian also has a book that contains reproductions of ancient L. L. Bean boot order forms for the royal family with the required foot outlines sketched on them. You choose King John's foot as a "base foot." Since Celia's foot is half and Martin's foot is three-fourths as long as John's foot, you now have all the information to normalize or adjust all values to the common base foot. Celia's values are scaled down by one-half and Martin's by one-fourth. Adjusted accordingly, the data show:

1300–1333 average height was 5 feet 6 inches
1334–1366 average height was 5 feet 7 inches
1367–1400 average height was 5 feet 8 inches

So the adjusted data support your hypothesis.

TABLE 6-3:

Year	Nominal GNP	GNP Price Index
1836	500	100
1850	1200	200
1880	2500	250

Remember, the problem for macroeconomic variables measured in dollars is that the value of the yardstick, money, changes as the price level changes. In the parable there were pictures to show how the size of the ruler's foot changed. In macroeconomics we need something analogous, an indicator of how the price level and therefore the value of money is changing. The indicator the government uses to measure the price level is the price index we introduced above.

As a measure of the price level, the price index is precisely the tool necessary to transform nominal into real values. Dividing any nominal value by the relevant price index and multiplying by 100 transforms the nominal value into a real value measured in base year dollars. For instance, if 1836 was our base year and the numbers shown in Table 6-3 were true, then the real GNP for 1850 in 1836 dollars would be:

$$\text{Real GNP}_{1850} = \frac{\text{Nominal GNP}_{1850}}{\text{GNP Price Index }_{1850}} \times 100 = \frac{1200}{200} \times 100 = 600$$

Similarly, the real GNP for 1880 in 1836 dollars would be:

$$\text{Real GNP}_{1380} = \frac{\text{Nominal GNP}_{1880}}{\text{GNP Price Index}_{1880}} \times 100 = \frac{2500}{250} \times 100 = 1000$$

Building the Basic Macroeconomic Model

Analytic effort starts when we have conceived our vision of the set of phenomena that caught our interest. . .The first task is to verbalize the vision or to conceptualize it in such a way that the elements take their places with names attached to them that facilitate recognition and manipulation, in a more or less orderly schema or picture.

Joseph Schumpeter
History of Economic Analysis, 1954.

IN MICRO we followed this process and constructed a complex model of a market economy that allowed us to understand how value, distribution, and efficiency are determined. In macro we repeat the process in order to understand the forces that move the macroeconomy to higher or lower, unemployment and inflation. In this chapter we construct that macro model.

A. THE BIG PICTURE—AGGREGATE DEMAND/AGGREGATE SUPPLY

When we studied the microeconomy we identified a single picture that enabled us to analyze the activity in every kind of microeconomic market. It was the supply and demand picture shown in Figure 7-1. Given supply and demand conditions, we are able to determine the equilibrium price and quantity exchanged in every market.

Now we want to analyze the economy from a different perspective—a macroeconomic (aggregate) point of view. This view encompasses the sum of the activity in literally millions of microeconomic markets. We would like to identify a picture that will capture the macroeconomic perspective as clearly and efficiently as our simple supply and demand picture did the microeconomic perspective. But how do we sum up so much in a single picture? It is not as difficult as

131

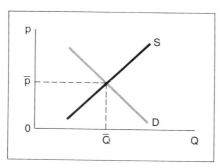

FIGURE 7-1 Microeconomic Supply and Demand

it might seem. A little picture can capture the essence of a big scene if the details can be summed up and conveyed in simple terms.

The details of the microeconomy are millions of individuals, inter-acting in millions of markets, exchanging millions of items, each at a price. The key economic variables that this market activity deter-mines are quantities of final goods exchanged and prices. We have defined terms that allow us to aggregate the millions of values of these two micro variables. The quantities exchanged in the millions of micro markets are summed up by the macro concept of real GNP. The prices determined by these millions of micro markets are represented by the macro concept of the price level.

Clearly, this aggregation obscures details and therefore our macro variables obscure micro events. Real GNP is an aggregate measure of the quantity of final goods and services exchanged, but changes in real GNP do not necessarily reflect conditions in any particular micro market, or vice versa. As real GNP grows, it means the aggregate pro-duction of final goods and services in the economy is increasing, but it does not mean that production of all individual goods and services is increasing. Real GNP grew in the early twentieth century even as the production of horse-drawn carriages declined. The reverse is also true: A fall in real GNP does not imply that the production of all items counted within the GNP is falling. Similarly, the price level is a repre-sentation of the general position of prices and therefore the value (buying power) of a dollar. A rise in the price level does not imply, however, that all individual prices are rising; it only means that, in general, prices are going up. In the 1970s as the general price level was rising, the cost of pocket calculators was going down. The reverse is also true: A fall in the price level does not necessarily imply a fall in all prices.

The point here is that the aggregate terms we use in our macro-economic analysis should not be confused with the individual values they summarize. The question remains: How do we draw a macro picture that will do for our macro analysis what the supply and demand picture did for our micro analysis?

Recall that in the micro analysis we had two relationships between price and quantity: supply and demand. Both suppliers and demanders had to be satisfied with the market condition for that market condition to be stable (in equilibrium). In other words, both had to be on their "willingness" (to sell and to buy, respectively) curves simultaneously for the market to be in equilibrium. That condition is met at only one point on the graph—where supply and demand intersect. That equilibrium point determines the equilibrium price (p) and the equilibrium quantity exchanged (Q), as shown in Figure 7-2.

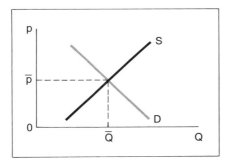

FIGURE 7-2 Microeconomic Equilibrium

Macro conditions can be represented with equal efficiency. On the macroeconomic level at any point in time there is a particular real GNP (Y) and a particular price level (P) prevailing in the economy. We can identify two macroeconomic relationships that together identify the unique price level/real GNP (P,Y) combination that exists at any point in time. By analyzing the conditions that shape and shift each of these relationships we can shed light on the forces that determine macroeconomic outcomes.

These two relationships are called aggregate demand (AD) and aggregate supply (AS). The aggregate demand curve (AD) traces the relationship between the price level (P) and the real GNP (Y) demanded. The aggregate supply curve (AS) traces the relationship between the price level (P) and the real GNP (Y) supplied.

We have seen that it is microeconomic forces that bring the economy to a general equilibrium. Clearly, however, when there is a general equilibrium at the microeconomic level, there must be a particular price level prevailing at the macroeconomic level. Furthermore, since at a general equilibrium there is an equilibrium quantity exchanged in all output markets, in the aggregate the real GNP supplied equals the real GNP demanded at the given price level. These macroeconomic conditions can be represented graphically as shown in Figure 7-3.

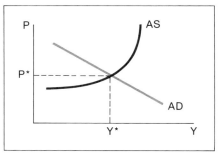

FIGURE 7-3   Representing Macroeconomic Conditions Graphically—Aggregate Supply/Aggregate Demand

The P^* and Y^* in Figure 7-3 represent the price level and the real GNP prevailing in the economy: the macroeconomic conditions. By examining the AD and AS relationships in detail, we will be able to justify their shape as we have drawn them and to determine what conditions shift the curves. Once we understand the relationship that each curve represents, we will be in a position to analyze how the forces that shift each curve affect the macroeconomic conditions. This will equip us to answer the basic macroeconomic questions we have identified. It will also enable us to understand the debate over macroeconomic policy and its roots in microeconomics.

The next step in our study is, therefore, an examination of the AD and AS relationships. We begin with the AD relationship, at its roots.

B. AGGREGATE DEMAND

Aggregate Expenditure and Real Income—the Roots of Aggregate Demand

Aggregate expenditure (hereafter AE) is the total amount of money spent on all final products in the economy during a given year. It is measured in current dollars, so it is a nominal measure. Since AE measures the total current dollars spent on all final products in the economy during a given year, and since spending is the way in which desires for products are translated into effective demands, AE is also a measure of the nominal GNP demanded.

Now consider the fact that in our simple model one person's spending is another person's income. With this in mind, we can see that AE is also equal to the nominal aggregate income earned. If, for instance, the aggregate expenditure on final products in 1967 was $800, then $800 was earned in 1967 by those providing those products. In sum, AE is equal to nominal GNP demanded and nominal aggregate income.

As we have already seen, to transform nominal values into real values we must divide the nominal values by the price level (as measured by the price index). Therefore, if AE is equal to nominal aggregate income, P is a measure of the price level, and Y_I is a measure of real aggregate income, we have:

$$\frac{AE}{P} = Y_I \qquad\qquad \textbf{(Equation 1)}$$

Recall that AE divided by the price level is also a measure of real GNP demanded. Thus, Y_I measures both real income and real GNP demanded.

Deriving the Aggregate Demand Relationship

The aggregate demand curve is a graphical representation of the relationship between the price level and the real GNP demanded. It is shown in Figure 7-4.

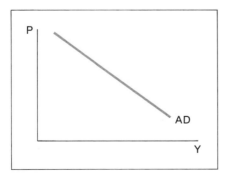

FIGURE 7-4 Aggregate Demand Note that we use a _Y_ on the horizontal axis to measure real GNP. Keep in mind that along the _AD_ curve we are measuring real GNP demanded.

Now we want to justify that representation of AD and identify the conditions that can cause shifts in AD. We begin with equation (1) from above:

$$\frac{AE}{P} = Y_I$$

which (multiplying both sides by P) can also be written:

$$AE = PY_I \qquad \textbf{(Equation 2)}$$

This equation contains both of the variables, price level (P) and real GNP demanded (Y_I), that are included in the aggregate demand relationship. We can, therefore, use it as our basis for analyzing that relationship. In order to do so, however, we must first identify the kinds of expenditures that make up AE.

There are six major components of AE. *Consumption* (hereafter C) is the nominal aggregate expenditure households make on domestic goods and services such as clothes, homes, and haircuts. *Investment* (hereafter I) is the nominal aggregate expenditures private firms make for items such as plants, equipment, and inventories. The *net government budget position* (hereafter (G-T)) is the nominal net effect of the government's budget on AE. The G represents the nominal amount the government spends; the T represents the nominal amount the government takes out of the hands of households and firms in the form of taxes. (Note: Generally AE is calculated on a pretax basis, but in order to introduce taxes in a simple fashion we will calculate AE on an aftertax basis.) Every dollar the government spends increases nominal aggregate expenditure. Every dollar it taxes reduces nominal aggregate expenditure, because it reduces the amount that firms and households have to spend. The combined effect of G and T is, therefore, the net government budget position (G-T). If ($G>T$), then the government is adding to aggregate expenditures; if ($G=T$), then the government is not affecting aggregate expenditures; and if ($G<T$), then the government is subtracting from aggregate expenditures. *Trade balance* (hereafter (X-M)) is the combined effect of exports and imports on AE. The X (exports) represents the nominal aggregate expenditure of foreigners for our products. It is an addition to the AE on our products. The M (imports) represents the nominal aggregate expenditure we make on the products of other nations. It is a subtraction from the AE on our products because it represents domestic expenditures (those parts of C, I, and G) that are being channeled to foreign producers. Thus the combined effect of exports and imports (X-M) is the trade balance.

In sum:

$$AE = C + I + (G - T) + (X - M) \qquad \textbf{(Equation 3)}$$

and given equation **(2)**:

$$AE = PY_I$$

we can write:

$$PY_I = C + I + (G - T) + (X - M) \qquad \textbf{(Equation 4)}$$

This basic equation becomes much more complicated if we account for the fact that C, I, G, T, X, and M are all affected by each other, the level of real aggregate income (Y_I), and other variables. In order to simplify the analysis, we will assume that C, I, G, T, X, and M are all independent of one another and that only C is affected by Y_I.

We will call I, G, T, X, and M *autonomous variables*. We will see how the level of private investment (I), the net government budget position (G-T), and trade balance (X-M) are determined as we develop the model. The level of consumption is partly autonomously determined and partly dependent on PY_I. Specifically:

$$C = a + b\,(PY_I) \qquad \textbf{(Equation 5)}$$

where

PY_I = nominal aggregate income or nominal aggregate demand

b = the portion of nominal aggregate income used for consumption called the *marginal propensity to consume* (MPC)

a = the aggregate *autonomous consumption*, the amount independent of Y_I

The a represents the nominal amount households spend on consumption out of wealth (accumulated saving). There are always some households in society that are spending more than they are earning in income. These households are spending out of the wealth they have built up by accumulating savings. In some cases, such as with retired people, this is a household's preferred choice, but many times it occurs because jobs are lost or household members are unable to work because of illness. Most households have some wealth to fall back on, but often it is not enough to see them through the crisis. In any case, our model represents the aggregate amount of all such spending by the a variable.

The $b(PY_l)$ represents the nominal amount that households spend on consumption out of current aggregate nominal income. Most households in our society are earning enough income so that they do not have to spend out of wealth in order to maintain their consumption. These families earn enough income to both pay for their consumption and to save. In other words, a portion of their income goes to consumption and the rest goes to saving (to put in the bank or pay taxes). When we sum up the behavior of all these households, we can calculate the portion of aggregate nominal income that goes to consumption. That portion is $b(PY_l)$ where b is the fraction of aggregate nominal income used for consumption. The b is called the marginal propensity to consume.

Notice that if a is aggregate spending out of wealth, then $-a$ represents the amount of aggregate "dissaving." Further, if $b(PY_l)$ is the amount of nominal aggregate income used for consumption, then the rest of nominal income, $(1\text{-}b)\,(PY_l)$, must be going to savings. Thus if:

$$C = a + b(PY_l)$$

is the *consumption function* reflecting how much households consume, then:

$$S = -a + (1 - b)\,(PY_l) \qquad \textbf{(Equation 6)}$$

is a *savings function* reflecting how much households save. Net nominal savings depends on the size of $-a$ and $(1\text{-}b)PY_l$. If $-a$ is larger than $(1\text{-}b)PY_l$, then net savings will be negative and wealth will fall. If $-a$ is smaller than $(1\text{-}b)PY_l$, the opposite will be true.

Returning to our aggregate expenditure equation **(4)**:

$$PY_l = C + I + (G - T) + (X - M)$$

and plugging in equation **(5)**:

$$C = a + b(PY_l)$$

we have:

$$PY_l = a + b(PY_l) + I + (G - T) + (X - M)$$

Collecting the PY_l terms on the left side, we have:

$$PY_l - b(PY_l) = a + I + (G - T) + (X - M)$$

Factoring the left side, we have:

$$(1 - b)PY_I = a + I + (G - T) + (X - M)$$

Dividing both sides by (1-b), we have:

$$PY_I = \frac{1}{1 - b}[a + I + (G - T) + (X - M)]$$

Dividing both sides by P, we have:

$$Y_I = \frac{1}{1 - b}\left[\frac{a}{P} + \frac{I}{P} + \frac{G - T}{P} + \frac{X - M}{P}\right] \qquad \textbf{(Equation 7)}$$

Dividing a, I, $(G\text{-}T)$, and $(X\text{-}M)$ by P adjusts these nominal values for the price level. Thus $\frac{a}{P}, \frac{I}{P}, \frac{G - T}{P}$ and $\frac{X - M}{P}$ are real values of autonomous consumption, private investment, the net government budget position, and net exports, respectively. As these real values change, real GNP demanded (Y_I) changes by a factor $\frac{1}{1\text{-}b}$ as much.

Note, however, that if P rises and a, I, G, T, X, and M all remain constant, then the real values $\frac{a}{P}, \frac{I}{P}, \frac{G - T}{P}$, and $\frac{X - M}{P}$ will all fall and, as a consequence, so will Y_I. This inverse relationship between the price level, P, and the level of real GNP demanded, Y_I, is consistent with the way we have drawn the AD curve.

To make this relationship intuitively clear let us consider the effect of a rise in P on autonomous consumption (a). Since some or all of the wealth that is the source of this autonomous consumption is held as cash, a rise in P diminishes the real value of that wealth. Thus, while a may remain constant in nominal terms, as P rises, the real

amount of demand based on wealth, $\frac{a}{P}$, falls. Similarly, if the government decides on nominal level of $(G\text{-}T)$ and P rises, the real values of the government's part of the aggregate demand will fall. Thus we see that as P rises, the real value of all the parts of the aggregate demand falls, and therefore so does total real aggregate demand. The AD curve traces this inverse relationship between the price level, P, and the real GNP demanded, Y_I.

Note the similarity between the macroeconomic AD curve and the microeconomic demand curve. In the latter case, the curve represented, _ceteris paribus_, the relationship between the price of a good and its quantity demanded. Any given point on the demand curve reflected, _ceteris paribus_, a unique price/quantity combination, and multiplying that quantity and price together equaled the total expenditure that point represented. The AD curve represents, *ceteris paribus*, the relationship between price level and the quantity of real GNP demanded. Any given point on the AD curve reflects, *ceteris paribus*, a unique price level/real GNP demanded combination. Multiplying the price level (measured by the price index) times the real GNP demanded gives the value of the nominal GNP demanded or the aggregate expenditure (AE). Yet, similarities are superficial.

It is also extremely important to note the distinction between aggregate demand (AD), the macroeconomic concept, and demand (D), the microeconomic concept. Demand traces the relationship between the quantity demanded of a particular good or service and its own price. Changes in prices of related goods and/or incomes have an effect on demand. Aggregate demand traces the relationship between real GNP demanded and the price level. If one person's income rise is offset by another's income loss, then real aggregate income, and therefore real GNP demanded, will not change. If one price rise is offset by another price fall, then the price level will be unaffected. In either of these cases, the relative changes, which have microeconomic consequences, have no macroeconomic consequences because there is no change in the aggregate. In sum, it is *relative* changes that shift *micro* demand, but it is *aggregate* changes that shift *macro* aggregate demand.

The next question we want to explore is: What aggregate changes shift AD and how do they do so?

Aggregate Demand Shocks

As we have seen, the relationship between real GNP demand, Y_I, and the price level, P, can be derived from the aggregate expenditure equation. From:

$$AE = C + I + (G - T) + (X - M)$$

we derived by a process of substitution and algebraic manipulation:

$$Y_I = \frac{1}{1-b}\left[\frac{a}{P} + \frac{I}{P} + \frac{G-T}{P} + \frac{X-M}{P}\right] \qquad \textbf{(Equation 8)}$$

Applying the distributive law, we have:

$$Y_I = \frac{1}{1-b}\frac{a}{P} + \frac{1}{1-b}\frac{I}{P} + \frac{1}{1-b}\frac{G-T}{P} + \frac{1}{1-b}\frac{X-M}{P}$$

This form allows us to see the source of shifts in AD very clearly. Recall that I, G, T, X, and M are assumed to be autonomous variables. We see from this equation that the relationship between Y_I and P depends on the values of I, G, T, X and M, and yet the values of these variables are determined independently of the relationship between P and Y_I represented by the AD function (equation 8). Such variables that are important to a relationship and yet are determined outside of that particular relationship are referred to as *exogenous* variables. While they are independent of the relationship, the relationship is not independent of them. A change in an exogenous variable will shift the entire relationship. A change in an exogenous variable is called an *exogenous shock* to the relationship.

In order to better comprehend the concept of an exogenous variable, consider the following example. A marriage is a relationship. There are some things that can occur which are entirely independent of the marriage relationship, but which have a significant impact on the relationship. For example, if one partner gets seriously ill from causes that have nothing to do with the relationship, it will nevertheless have a dramatic impact on the relationship. Health is generally an autonomous variable with respect to a romantic relationship, but a dramatic change in one partner's health status (for better or worse) will have a tremendous (shock) effect on the relationship. Thus health is an exogenous variable with respect to that relationship.

Consider another example. If you know you are going to be tested on this material, you will probably prepare for the exam. If, however, just before the exam but for reasons unrelated to the exam you get sick, it will presumably affect your ability to perform on the exam. In this case, your health is an exogenous variable with respect to the course that can cause an exogenous shock to your grade.

The variables I, G, T, X, and M are exogenous variables with respect to the relationship between P and Y_I represented by the aggregate demand function. Changes in these exogenous variables will cause exogenous shocks to the macroeconomic aggregate demand and therefore to the macroeconomy. We will call this kind of exogenous shock an *aggregate demand shock*.

How do changes in I, G, T, X, and/or M affect aggregate demand?

Increases in I, G, or X are aggregate demand shocks that shift AD to the right. To see this, recall that I, G, and X are expenditures on domestic production measured in nominal terms. If the nominal value of these expenditures rises, then at any given price level the real value of GNP demanded also rises. This is so because a nominal change represents a real change if price level is held constant. A look at the AD function (equation 8) above should make this clear. If P is constant and I, G, or X rises, then, *ceteris paribus*, Y_I will also rise.

Take, for instance, a nominal increase in government spending from G to G'. This can be represented graphically as shown in Figure 7-5.

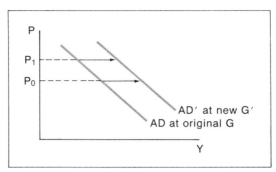

FIGURE 7-5 An Increase in Aggregate Demand At any given price level P_0 or P_1 the *AD* curve will shift out by the increase in G.

An increase in I or X has a similar effect on AD. A decrease in G, I, or X has the opposite effect on AD.

Increases in T or M are aggregate demand shocks that shift AD to the left. This is true because a rise in T diminishes the amount of money households or firms have to spend, and a rise in M means that more of the money households and firms are spending is going for foreign rather than domestic purchases. A decrease in T or M has the opposite effect on AD. By leaving more money in the hands of households and firms or by transferring spending from foreign items to domestic, it increases AD.

C. AGGREGATE SUPPLY

The aggregate supply curve represents the relationship between the price level and the real GNP supplied.

We can distinguish two different aggregate supply curves. One represents the long-run aggregate supply conditions. We define the *long run* as the period necessary to complete all microeconomic adjustments under our nice assumptions. We saw in our study of the microeconomy that, under our nice assumptions, when *and if* all microeconomic market adjustments are completed, all factors will be used most efficiently and there will be no available factors lying idle. In other words, in the long run (as defined here) all capital, natural resources, and labor will be fully and efficiently employed. (Note that for labor this means unemployment will be at the natural rate.)

Given this fact, we can represent the long-run aggregate supply curve (LAS) graphically as shown in Figure 7-6.

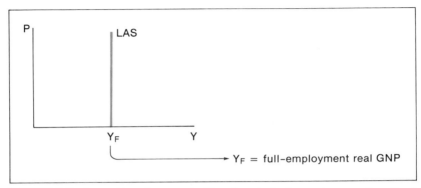

FIGURE 7-6   Long-Run Aggregate Supply   As before, we use a *Y* on the horizontal axis to measure real GNP. Keep in mind that along the *LAS* and the *AS* (which we will introduce shortly) we are measuring real GNP supplied.

Figure 7-6 reflects the fact that in the long run the level of real GNP will always reach the full-employment real GNP (Y_F), regardless of the price level.

What determines Y_F? Since Y_F is the real GNP produced when all available factors (natural resources, labor, and capital) are fully and efficiently employed, it reflects the *maximum sustainable productive capacity* of the economy. This capacity is determined by the bounty of society's natural endowment, the size of the labor force, the quantity and quality of society's capital, and the degree of the division of labor in society. These last two conditions represent the technological advancement of a society and determine the productivity of the first two.

If we define the *very long run* as the period necessary for change in these basic economic conditions, then in the very long run these conditions may change, thereby changing Y_F and thus shifting the LAS. Increases in the natural endowment, the size of the labor force, and the quantity and/or quality of capital (human or physical) will shift LAS to the right. Such a shift means that the sustainable productive capacity of the economy has grown, and can be represented graphically as shown in Figure 7-7.

Notice that in this process of building our model we have answered two of the questions about macroeconomics that we set out to answer. We had asked: What determines society's capacity to pro-

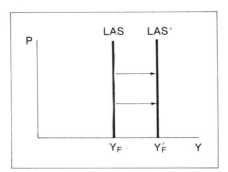

FIGURE 7-7   An Increase in Long-Run Aggregate Supply

duce? We find that the sustainable productive capacity of society is determined by the bounty of society's natural endowment, the size of and degree of division of labor in its labor force, and the quantity and quality of its capital. We had also asked: What determines society's ability to expand productive capacity over time? We find that capacity grows with increases in natural endowment, the quantity and/or quality of capital, and the quantity and the degree of division of labor in society.

The other kind of aggregate supply curve we will use is a short-run aggregate supply curve. We will identify it with the letters AS. The *short run* is a period in which some microeconomic market adjustments have *not* been completed. Specifically, we will assume that in the short run the factor markets have not adjusted. Thus, along a given short-run aggregate supply curve, the factor prices (e.g., the wage), having not adjusted, remain constant.

Graphically, the short-run aggregate supply curve can be represented as shown in Figure 7-8.

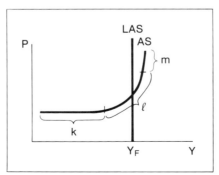

FIGURE 7-8   Short-Run Aggregate Supply   Note that we include the *LAS* as a reference line to show where we reach long-run sustainable capacity.

Along the AS curve in Figure 7-8 three segments are identified. Along the k segment of the curve the real GNP supplied is significantly below full-employment real GNP; therefore there are large quantities of idle factors (i.e., unemployment is high). Under these circumstances, real production can be expanded by hiring the idle factors. This kind of expansion puts no pressure on the production system, so with factor prices constant, the cost of producing (and therefore the prices of products) remains constant. Thus along the k segment, as real GNP supplied increases, the product price level, P, remains constant.

Along the l segment real GNP supplied approaches, reaches, and then surpasses the sustainable, full-employment real GNP. As this happens, resources are stretched beyond normal use. Labor works overtime, factories put on extra shifts, and inferior resources are brought into use. Production bottlenecks begin to occur as the pressure on the production process increases. All of these pressures drive up the short-run costs of production (e.g., workers are being paid overtime), even though basic factor prices remain constant. As this occurs, the product price level (P) associated with higher and higher levels of real GNP supplied begins to rise, and then rises progressively more quickly. The greater the pressure, the faster the costs—and therefore the product prices—rise. Segment l of the AS curve reflects this relationship between building production pressure and the price level increasing.

Finally, along segment m the economy has reached the limits of its short-run capacity. This capacity exceeds the long-run, sustainable capacity because people and machines are being worked harder than they can sustain in the long run. Notice that any further pressure on production generates virtually no more output; all it does is raise product prices. For instance, people who are already working 60 hours a week (40 at regular pay and 20 at double pay) must be paid triple pay to get them to work 10 more hours a week, and those last 10 hours put in by exhausted workers would produce hardly anything.

These three segments together make up the short-run aggregate supply curve, AS. The AS curve represents the positive relationship between the produce price level, P, and real GNP supplied, when basic factor prices are constant. (Remember: We have defined the short run as the period prior to adjustments in factor markets.) The relationship is positive, because as production pressure grows (as output approaches and surpasses Y_F in the short run), the cost of production and therefore the prices that must be charged for outputs rise.

While factor prices are constant along a given AS curve, the AS relationship between price level and real GNP supplied does depend on these factor prices. Factor prices are, in fact, the exogenous variables in the AS relationship. As we found in the AD case, a change in exogenous variables will shift the relationship. In this case, an increase in exogenous factor prices (e.g., a wage-level increase or an increase in the price of oil) will cause the cost of producing any given level of real GNP to rise. This, in turn, will mean that higher product prices must be charged to cover the costs of production. Thus an increase in factor prices increases the cost of producing any given level of real GNP supplied and as a result of these increasing costs, the price level will rise.

Graphically, a rise in factor prices causes a shift up in the AS curve, as shown in Figure 7-9.

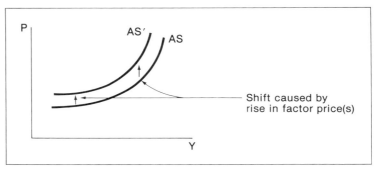

FIGURE 7-9   A Shift Up in Short-Run Aggregate Supply

A fall in factor prices would cause AS to shift down, as shown in Figure 7-10.

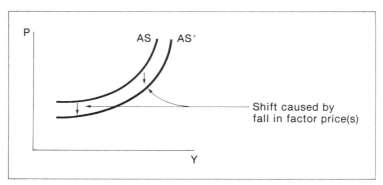

FIGURE 7-10   A Shift Down in Short-Run Aggregate Supply

We refer to these kinds of exogenous shocks on the aggregate supply curve as *aggregate supply shocks*.

D. COMBINING AGGREGATE DEMAND, AGGREGATE SUPPLY, AND LONG-RUN AGGREGATE SUPPLY

To review: Aggregate demand, AD, represents the relationship between the price level and real GNP demanded. Aggregate supply, AS, represents the short-run (as defined above) relationship between the price level and the real GNP supplied. Long-run aggregate supply, LAS, represents the long-run (as defined above) relationship between the price level and the real GNP supplied.

The short-run conditions in the macroeconomy are represented by the intersection of the AD and AS curves. Combining AD and AS we get a shapshot of current macroeconomic conditions. As it is shown in Figure 7-11, currently the macroeconomy is at price level $= P^*$ and real GNP $= Y^*$.

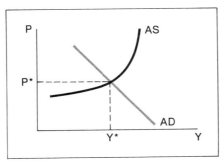

FIGURE 7-11 Representing Macroeconomic Conditions with Aggregate Supply and Aggregate Demand

We can use our macroeconomic AD/AS graph to represent the case in which the short-run condition is consistent with long-run full employment, as in Figure 7-12. In that case, AD, AS, and LAS all intersect at the same point and actual real GNP, Y^*, is equal to full-employment real GNP, Y_F (i.e., unemployment is at its natural rate).

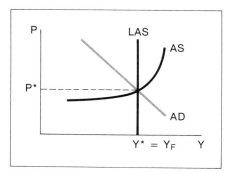

FIGURE 7-12   Full-Employment Macroeconomic Condition

It is perfectly possible, however, for the short-run conditions to be different from the full-employment condition that would be achieved in the long run (full adjustment under our nice assumptions). For example, we can use our macroeconomic AD/AS graph to represent the case of less than full employment as in Figure 7-13.

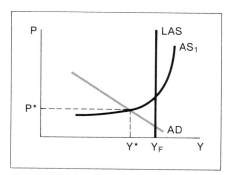

FIGURE 7-13   Less Than Full-Employment Macroeconomic Condition

There we see that the short-run condition is a price level of P^* and a real GNP of Y^* that is not consistent with the long-run real GNP, which we know by definition is equal to Y_F. In this case, we find that the actual real GNP, Y^*, is less than the full-employment real GNP, Y_F. Clearly, this difference implies that there is some demand-deficient unemployment in the economy.

At the beginning of our study of macroeconomics in Chapter VI, we set out to answer these questions:

• What determines society's capacity to produce? What determines how much society is currently producing? (National income)

- Why are society's available resources sometimes less than fully utilized—to put it differently, why would some of society's available resources lie idle? Under what circumstances would such a condition persist? (Unemployment)
- What determines society's ability to expand production capacity over time? (Growth)
- Why does the purchasing power of the money society uses as a medium of exchange sometimes change over time? Under what circumstances would such a change continue? (Inflation or deflation)

So far we have answered the first part of the first question and the third question. As it stands, our model enables us to represent the level of unemployment and the price level. Furthermore, by shifting around the AD and AS curves, we can represent changes in these levels. Consider, for example, the following cases:

(A) Figure 7-14: Increasing AD due to a rise in I, G, or X or a fall in T or M.

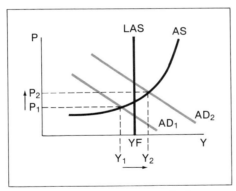

FIGURE 7-14 Macroeconomic Consequences of Increasing Aggregate Demand

Here increasing AD (from AD_1 to AD_2) raises the price level in the economy from P_1 to P_2 (i.e., causes inflation), but it takes the economy from less-than-full-employment real GNP (Y_1) to more-than-full-employment real GNP (Y_2). (*Note*: It is possible in the short run for the economy to have unemployment below the natural rate—but this is not a sustainable condition because it puts great pressure on the productive capacity of the economy. It is precisely that pressure that causes the associated inflation.)

(B) Figure 7-15: Decreasing AD due to a fall in *I*, *G*, or *X* or a rise in *T* or *M*.

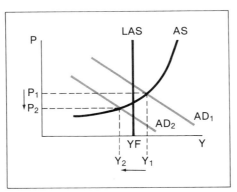

FIGURE 7-15   Macroeconomic Consequences of Decreasing Aggregate Demand

Here the decreasing AD (from AD_1 to AD_2) takes pressure off the economy and even results in demand-deficient unemployment (since $Y_2 < Y_F$), but this reduction of pressure also allows the price level to decline.

(C) Figure 7-16: Shift up in AS due to rise in factor prices.

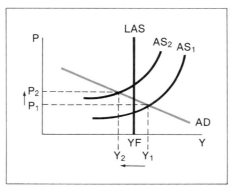

FIGURE 7-16   Macroeconomic Consequences of a Shift Up in Aggregate Supply

Here a shift up in AS (from AS_1 to AS_2) causes the price level to rise and the real GNP to fall, thus increasing unemployment.

(D) Figure 7-17: Shift down in AS due to a fall in factor prices.

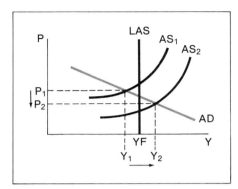

FIGURE 7-17   Macroeconomic Consequences of a Shift Down in Aggregate Supply

Here a shift down in AS (from AS_1 to AS_2) causes the price level to fall and the real GNP to rise, thus decreasing unemployment.

Now we have a model that allows us to represent any macroeconomic case. However, the model offers us no basis for analyzing these cases because while we have identified the forces that actually move AD and AS, we have not analyzed the sources of these forces. In order for the model to come alive as a powerful analytical tool, we must examine the sources of these exogenous demand and supply shocks that move the macroeconomy. In the next chapter we will look at the sources of exogenous supply and demand shocks in detail. Once we have done so, we will have a complete model with which we can do a complete analysis.

Putting the Basic Macroeconomic Model to Work: Analyzing Macroeconomic Shocks and Macroeconomic Adjustments

It appears to me that one great cause of our difference in opinion on the subjects which we have so often discussed is that. . .[p]erhaps you estimate these temporary effects too highly. . .

David Ricardo
Letter to Robert Malthus, Jan. 24, 1817.

I really think that the progress of society consists of irregular movements, and that to omit consideration of causes [of such movements]. . .is to omit the causes of the wealth and poverty of nations—the grand object of all enquiries in Political Economy.

Robert Malthus
Letter to David Ricardo, Jan. 26, 1817.

DAVID RICARDO believed that after a shock the macroeconomy would always return to full employment. Robert Malthus believed that "general gluts," periods of extended high unemployment, could persist. While the model we use is very different from the ones Ricardo and Malthus had in mind, the debate between these two great economists still goes on among economists who subscribe to the NeoClassical theory we are studying. In this chapter we will examine that debate and the micro foundations of each of these points of view.

A. SOURCES OF EXOGENOUS AGGREGATE DEMAND SHOCKS

We have seen that along any given aggregate demand curve (AD) the levels of *I*, *G*, *T*, *X*, and *M* are fixed. It is changes in the values of these variables, exogenous demand shocks, that shift the AD curve. Thus, in order to identify the source of exogenous demand shocks, we must identify the forces that determine the levels of *I*, *G*, *T*, *X*, and *M*. In this

152

section we will examine investment (*I*), trade balance (*X-M*), and the government budget position (*G-T*) in turn.

How the Investment Level Is Determined

The level of investment (here we are concerned with real investments; e.g., in plants and equipment) is determined in a macroeconomic market called the *loanable funds market*. (*Note*: To simplify, we are abstracting from business investment out of retained earnings.) The supply of loanable funds comes from saving. Recall that saving implies forgoing current consumption and that we have assumed a time preference biased toward the present when it comes to consumption (i.e., *ceteris paribus*, we prefer to consume now). This means, as we saw earlier, that saving will only occur if it is rewarded with a positive return—a positive interest rate, to be exact. The interest rate is the price savers are paid for their funds. *Ceteris Paribus*, the higher the interest rate, the greater the aggregate savings will be. Thus, as shown in Figure 8-1, when the interest rate rises, the supply of loanable funds goes up.

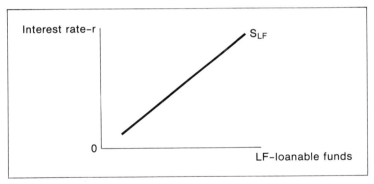

FIGURE 8-1 Supply of Loanable Funds

A primary source of demand for loanable funds comes from those who desire funds in order to make real investments. (*Note*: There is another significant source of demand for loanable funds that will be introduced later.) The interest rate is the price borrowers, the demanders, pay for loanable funds. There is an array of investments potential borrowers have in mind. In their minds they order this array according to the rate of return they expect to make on the investments. The best investments, those with the highest rate of return, are

_____

put first in line and the rest are placed in order of declining rates of return. Clearly the potential borrowers, the investors, will only borrow as long as the price of the borrowed money, the interest rate, is less than the expected rate of return. Thus, as shown in Figure 8-2, the higher the interest rate, the less investments are worthwhile, and therefore the less loanable funds will be demanded.

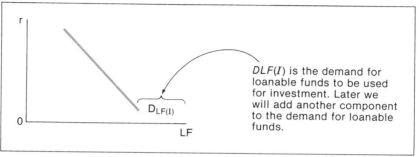

FIGURE 8-2 Demand for Loanable Funds

When we combine the supply and demand for loanable funds (where the only demand is for investment), we see that the interest rate and the level of investment are determined when the loanable funds market reaches equilibrium (Figure 8-3).

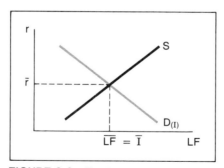

FIGURE 8-3 Equilibrium in the Loanable Funds Market

• *The Effect of Expectations on Investment—An Example* One force that determines the level of investment is the expectations in the economy. Recall that the demand for loanable funds for investment is determined by the array of returns investors expect to receive on potential investments. The more positive investors' expectations are, the more investments will look good at any given interest rate. This implies that increased positive expectations will shift the demand for loanable funds curve (D_I) to the right. As a result, the level of investment and the interest rate will rise, as shown in Figure 8-4.

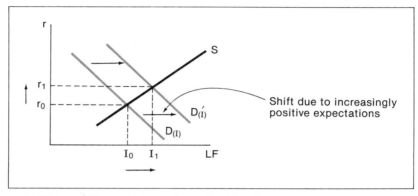

FIGURE 8-4   Effect of Increasingly Positive Expectations on the Loanable Funds Market

Conversely, a depression of expectations would cause D_I to shift left. As a result, the level of investment and the interest rate will fall, as shown in Figure 8-5.

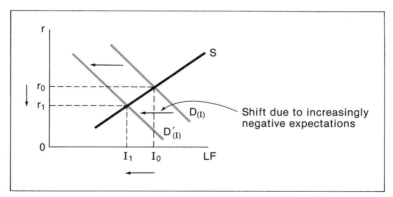

FIGURE 8-5   Effect of a Depression of Expectations on the Loanable Funds Market

As Table 8-1 suggests, this second case is, at least in part, responsible for the depth of the Great Depression.

TABLE 8-1: Investment, GNP, and Unemployment; 1929–1932

Year	Investment ($ billions)	GNP	Unemployment Rate
1929	40.4	203.6	3.2
1930	27.4	183.5	8.7
1931	16.8	169.3	15.9
1932	4.7	144.2	23.6

Source: Historical Statistics of the United States, Department of Commerce, Series D86, F47,F52.

The data in the table are consistent with the view that a decline in expectations reduced *I*, contributing to a fall in AD, which in turn led to a fall in real GNP and a rise in the unemployment rate. This case is represented graphically in Figure 8-6.

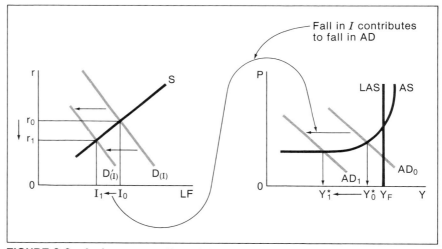

FIGURE 8-6 An Investment-Based Aggregate Demand Shock

While there was clearly a lot more going on, this depression of expectations at the outset of the Great Depression contributed to the depth of the downturn.

How the Trade Balance Is Determined

International trade exists for the very same reason that domestic trade exists. There are, as we have seen, benefits from trade when individual people or nations specialize and then exchange surpluses. Markets form in order to coordinate the exchange of these surpluses.

From the United States perspective, there are markets for our exports and markets for our imports. Clearly, one of the determinants of our trade balance is the conditions in the export and import markets. As conditions in those markets change, the level of our exports and imports—and, consequently, our trade balance $(X-M)$—will also change. However, for reasons we are about to examine, the conditions within the export and import markets, per se, are not the only determinants of the trade balance.

Given our nice assumptions, trade between nations can be analyzed with the same tools we applied to trade within nations, but for one significant complication: each country uses a different kind of fiat money. For example, the United States uses dollars ($s) and Britain uses pounds (£s). In order for us to buy British goods, we must first buy pounds; and in order for the British to buy our products, they must first buy dollars.

"But wait," you say, "I've purchased British wools, French wines, Italian shoes, Sudanese sandals, Indian cottons, Chinese paintings, Japanese cars, and Mexican art—and in every case I bought them in the United States with dollars." That may be so, but somewhere up the line of exchanges that led to your final purchase the dollars had to be exchanged for pounds, francs, and so forth. The people in Britain, France, Italy, Sudan, India, China, Japan, and Mexico who produced these goods do not get paid in dollars. They get paid in their domestic currency.

If you take a trip to another country, at some point you will have to exchange your currency so that you can pay for things with a currency acceptable in the country you are visiting. This exchange of currencies, be it for tourism or for importation of goods or services, takes place in a foreign exchange market.

There is a foreign exchange market for the exchange of any two currencies. For example, a market exists for the exchange of dollars and pounds. For simplicity, we will assume a two-nation world in which this is the only foreign exchange market.

Each country has its own perspective on the market in which its currency is exchanged. From the perspective of a United States citizen who wants to buy pounds, the price of pounds is in dollars (i.e., how many dollars will one have to pay for a pound). At any given price of pounds (dollars per pound), there will be a quantity of pounds people desiring pounds would be willing to buy (a quantity demanded) and a quantity of pounds those holding pounds would be willing to sell (a quantity supplied). In short, there would be a supply and demand for pounds priced in dollars.

In other words, from the United States perspective, $s are our fiat money and £s are a commodity that we must buy in the market for £s if we are going to import British goods. Thus the foreign exchange market from our perspective looks as shown in Figure 8-7.

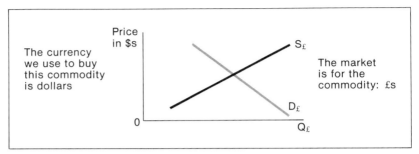

FIGURE 8-7   Foreign Exchange Market—U.S. Perspective

From the British perspective, it looks just the opposite because £s are their fiat money and $s are the commodity they must buy in the foreign exchange market in order to purchase our exports. Thus the foreign exchange market from their perspective looks as shown in Figure 8-8.

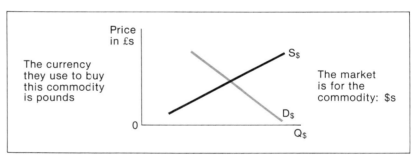

FIGURE 8-8   Foreign Exchange Market—British Perspective

Now notice something important: The demand for pounds is the source of the supply of dollars to the British. Every dollar we want to exchange for a pound is a dollar we are willing to supply to the British. Thus as the demand for pounds increases, by definition the supply of dollars also increases, and vice versa. Similarly, British citizens supply pounds in order to exchange them for dollars.

Notice the symmetry again. The source of the supply of pounds is one and the same as the source of the demand for dollars. Thus, as shown in Figure 8-9, when the supply of pounds increases, the demand for dollars increases, and vice versa.

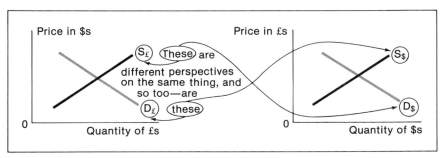

FIGURE 8-9   Connecting Perspectives on the Foreign Exchange Market

We see then that, though we can view the exchange of dollars and pounds from two perspectives, these are two views of exactly the same market.

Notice something else about these two perspectives on the pound/ dollar market. Using the United States perspective, we identify the price of the British pound in dollars and cite the number of dollars it takes to buy one pound (or $s/£). Using the British perspective, we identify the price of the United States dollar in pounds and cite the number of pounds it takes to buy one dollar (or £s/$). These two prices are mirror images of one another. If the dollars per pound is $2 for 1£, then the pounds per dollar is .5£ for $1; the ratio remains the same. This exchange ratio between currencies is called the *exchange rate*.

What happens if the $D_£$ (demand for pounds) increases? The $D_£$ shifts to the right (more £s demanded at any given price), and since $D_£$ is the $S_\$$, the $S_\$$ also shifts to the right (more $s supplied at any given price), as shown in Figure 8-10.

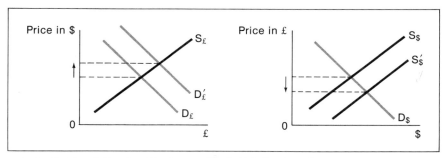

FIGURE 8-10   A Foreign Exchange Market Adjustment

We see that the dollar price of the pound goes up and the pound price of the dollar goes down. If the dollar price of the pound went from

$2/£ to $4/£, what must have happened to the pound price of the dollar? It went from .5£$ to .25£/$. When this occurs, we say that the pound is getting stronger because it buys more dollars and the dollar is getting weaker because it buys less pounds.

Another very important thing to note about the foreign exchange market is that the exchange rate for any currency will adjust such that the quantity of the currency supplied is always equal to the quantity of the currency demanded. In other words, for the United States currency, the actual number of dollars sold during any given period must equal the actual number of dollars purchased during that period. Clearly, that must be the case by definition. Every dollar sold must be purchased by someone, and vice versa. In the jargon of economics, the *balance of payments* must always be in balance. It is the adjustment of the exchange rate that maintains this balance.

The account by which we keep track of currency (e.g., dollar) flow through the foreign exchange market is called the *balance of payments account*. In order to see how the balance of payments account works, consider the following example. Let us assume that in our two-nation world (United States and Britain) the only reason currencies are exchanged is for private trade in goods and services. We supply dollars to the foreign exchange market in order to demand pounds with which we can import British goods and services. The British demand our dollars (by supplying pounds) in order to buy our exports of goods and services. In such a case, the balance of payments account might look as shown in Table 8-2.

Here we see that the dollars demanded in the foreign exchange market equal the dollars supplied; in other words, the balance of payments is in balance. As we saw above, exchange rate adjustments ensure that it could not be otherwise. In Table 8-2 the trade balance is also in balance. This is so because given our assumption that the only reason for exchanging currencies is for export and import, and given that the balance of payments *must* be in balance, the trade balance here is also in balance.

TABLE 8-2: Balance of Payments Accounts—Case 1

Balance of Payments Accounts		
Exports	+ 90	Notice that the trade
Imports	− 90	balance $(X - M)$ is in
Balance of		balance: $X = M$ or
payments =	0	$X - M = 0$

Note: "+" is quantity of dollar demand (e.g., to buy U.S. exports, the British must demand dollars in the foreign exchange market). "−" is quantity of dollar supply (e.g., to buy British imports, we must supply dollars to the foreign exchange market).

Any familiarity with current events tells you that the balance of trade is not always, or even often, in balance. How can this be if the balance of payments is always in balance? There must be some other activities that require currency exchange and that together with trade-based exchanges bring the balance of payment accounts into balance. One such activity is *capital flows*.

Foreign investors often want to invest in the United States economy. They may want to invest in plants and equipment, stocks, or government debt paper such as United States Treasury bills or bonds. All of these items are bought and sold in United States dollars, so in order to buy these things foreigners must exchange their currency for dollars (e.g., demand dollars with pounds). Money that flows through the foreign exchange market for such investment purposes is called an *international capital flow* into the United States. Such a capital flow would occur if foreigners' confidence in the United States economy became more positive and/or if interest rates in the United States rose relative to those in other countries. Either event would make the United States a more attractive place to send money and thus would cause a capital flow into the United States.

Conversely, if confidence in the United States economy declined and/or if United States interest rates fell relative to those in other countries, the United States would become a less attractive place to invest. As a result, foreign capital would leave the country and some United States investors might send their capital out of the United States to more attractive foreign investments. This would be a capital flow out of the United States. Capital flows across international boundaries would continue until all relative advantages of investing in one country rather than another were eliminated. If and when a new advantage occurred, new capital flows would be generated. Given our nice microeconomic assumptions, this process would ensure the most efficient international use of capital, given initial endowments (remember, efficiency does not ensure equity). However, if our nice assumptions do not hold, international capital flows may not be efficient.

When we include capital flows along with the trade flows in the balance of payments accounts, we refer to the former as the *capital account* and the latter as the *current account*. Such an expanded balance of payments accounts might look as shown in Table 8-3.

Here we see that while individual accounts, current or capital, may be out of balance, the overall balance of payments is, as it must be, in balance.

In order to complete our accounting exchange, we must include one more source of currency supply and demand: governments. Governments hold a portfolio (an array) of foreign currencies and gold, and they buy and sell these for reasons we will explore shortly. Thus a

TABLE 8-3:   Balance of Payments Accounts—Case 2

Balance of Payments Accounts

Current account activity		
Exports	+ 90	Notice that the trade balance $(X - M)$ is
Imports	− 120	negative (trade deficit) offset by a positive
Capital account activity		capital flow into the country
Capital flow in	+ 40	
Capital flow out	− 10	
Balance of payments =	0	(Quantity of dollars demanded equals quantity of dollars supplied)

full accounting of the United States balance of payments might look as shown in Table 8-4.

As we learned above, the adjustment of the foreign exchange rates will keep the balance of payments in balance. Note, also, that a change in activity within one account must be offset by an equal and opposite change in the sum of all other accounts because the sum of the accounts, the balance of payments, must always equal zero. Understanding this allows us to analyze the sources and the effects of changes in the balance of trade $(X - M)$.

Consider the following example. Suppose that the United States government has been spending more than it has been taking in through taxes $(G - T < 0)$, and in order to cover its growing debt it offers to borrow money at very attractive interest rates. Suppose further that these high rates attract British capital (we are still assuming a two-nation world). This British capital will flow through the foreign exchange market and into the United States. Pounds are supplied in order to demand dollars, so the demand for dollars and the supply of pounds shift out, as shown in Figure 8-11.

TABLE 8-4:   Balance of Payments Accounts—Case 3

Balance of Payments Accounts

Current account activity		
Exports	+ 85	
Imports	− 120	Trade deficit
Capital account activity		
Capital flow in	+ 35	
Capital flow out	− 10	Net flow in
Government account activity	+ 10	Government is buying dollars
Balance of payments =	0	(Quantity of dollars demanded equals quantity of dollars supplied)

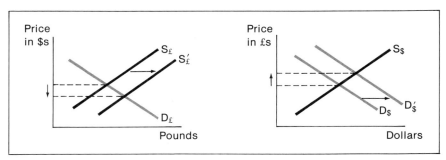

FIGURE 8-11 Exchange Rate Adjustments

Because of this, the dollar price of pounds to Americans falls (left graph) and the pound price of dollars to the British rises (right graph).

What will be the effect on United States trade with Britain? The fall in the pound (pounds cost less now in dollars) means that British goods are cheaper for Americans (e.g., a 50£ wool sweater now costs less dollars) and United States goods are now more expensive for the British (e.g., a $20 book now costs more in pounds). Given what we know about demand, this means that Americans will buy more British goods and the British will buy less United States goods. From the United States perspective, this implies a rise in imports and a fall in exports.

Assuming that government activity does not change, the exchange rate will automatically adjust so that the change in the capital account will be exactly offset by the change in the current account. In other words, owing to exchange rate adjustments, the increased purchase of dollars by the British in order to invest in the United States will be exactly offset by the increased sale of dollars for pounds by United States citizens looking for bargains in British goods and services. We know that, barring any government activity, the exchange rate must adjust this way because the balance of payments must be balanced. These adjustments are reflected in Table 8-5, where we see that exchange rates automatically adjust to balance the balance of payments.

We know that this capital flow into the United States causes an aggregate demand shock through its effect on the balance of trade $(X - M)$. Recall our AD relationship (equation 7):

$$Y_1 = \frac{1}{1-b} \left[\frac{a}{P} + \frac{I}{P} + \frac{G-T}{P} + \frac{X-M}{P} \right]$$

We demonstrated above that a change in I, $(G - T)$, or $(X - M)$ would cause an exogenous shock to the AD relationship, shifting the AD curve. In our example, $(G - T) < 0$ is not a change, since these deficits have been occurring for a while. Furthermore, we will assume that I

TABLE 8-5: Balance of Payments Adjustments

Balance of Payments Accounts	Before	After	Change by Account
Current account activity			
Exports	+ 85	+ 80	− 10
Imports	− 120	− 125	
Capital account activity			
Capital in	+ 35	+ 45	+ 10
Capital out	− 10	− 10	
Government account activity	+ 10	+ 10	0
Balance of payments	0	0	

does not change because the capital flow into the country is not going to real investment, but rather to finance the government's debt. Thus the only effect of the capital flow in is to change the exchange rate (strengthen the dollar), reducing the balance of trade, and thereby causing an exogenous AD shock. Graphically (if AD_1 is the initial position), this shift can be represented as shown in Figure 8-12.

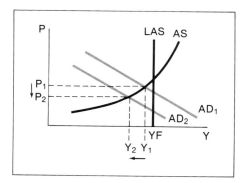

FIGURE 8-12   A Trade-Based Aggregate Demand Shock

There we see that the shock reduces real GNP, increases unemployment, and lowers the price level.

This demonstrates that one of the determinants of the trade balance, and so of AD and therefore the national macroeconomic condition, is activity in the capital account (international flows of capital). Similarly, activity in the government account could have an effect on the trade balance.

Of course, the trade balance is also sensitive to changes in the actual markets for the goods and services being exported or imported. As in any domestic market, the key factor that determines how many of our goods foreigners will buy (exports) and how many foreign goods (imports) we will buy is individual market supply and demand curves. The classic example of this was the OPEC decision to restrict the supply of oil in the 1970s. Since in the short-run United States demand for oil was very inelastic, as the price of oil shot up, so did our total expenditures on oil imports. (Recall our discussion of the relationship between elasticity and total expenditures on page 66.) Such an increase in imports could cause an aggregate demand shock to the domestic economy. In the OPEC case, the effect on exchange rates was less dramatic because the oil countries accepted payment in dollars rather than requiring an exchange of currency. Many of these dollars then returned to the United States as capital inflows for investment. As we will see, this large holding of United States dollars by foreigners is a problem for policymakers who try to control the number of dollars in the United States economy because these foreign dollars can flow in and out of the economy at the discretion of foreign holders.

In sum, there are two sets of factors that determine the level of trade balance: the underlying supply and demand for goods and services and the conditions in the foreign exchange market. Dramatic shifts in market supply or demand for an important export or import will cause a direct and significant change in trade balance and therefore an aggregate demand shock. Similarly, any event that dramatically affects the exchange rate will cause a significant change in trade balance and therefore an aggregate demand shock.

Another example of a balance of trade–based shock to aggregate demand can be found in the coming of World War II. As we have seen, during the Depression the unemployment rate hit 23.6 percent in 1932. The lowest it got between 1932 and 1939 was 14.3 percent in 1937. In 1938 it stood at 19 percent. Then the war began in Europe. We increased our shipments of materials to those nations we supported. This increase in exports was an exogenous demand shock that contributed to a fall in unemployment. By 1940 unemployment had fallen to 14.6 percent.

Then in 1941 Japan attacked Pearl Harbor and the United States entered the war. This set off another exogenous demand shock to the economy, which took unemployment from 14.6 percent in 1940 down to 1.2 percent in 1944. This time the shock came from a dramatic change in the government budget position. (*Source: Historical Statistics of the United States*, Department of Commerce, Series D86.)

How the Government's Budget Position Is Determined

The government's budget position is determined by the Congress and the president through the budget process. In theory, the current budget process works as represented in Flow Diagram 8-1.

How the Budget Process Works—in Theory

Late January or early February: President sends his budget to Congress.

February through early March: Senate and House Budget Committees hold hearings on the budget.

March 15: Other committees make recommendations to the budget committees on spending for areas in their jurisdictions.

March through early April: Budget committees draw up plan to set overall spending totals and ceilings for 21 functions of government. Plan calls for "reconciliation," in which other committees are required to modify existing laws to cut spending or increase revenue.

April 15: Budget committees send proposed budget resolutions to the House and Senate.

April 15 to May 15: House and Senate pass separate versions of budget resolutions. Differences are ironed out in a conference committee.

May 15: Congress passes first budget resolution. No Presidential signature required.

May through September: Funds for specific departments, agencies, and programs are approved first by the House and Senate appropriations subcommittees, then by the full committee, and then by the House and Senate. Differences are ironed out in conference committees and final appropriations bills are passed and signed by the President. (By September 15, Congress is supposed to pass a second budget resolution revising spending limits and making them binding. This step has been omitted in recent years and the April resolution made binding.)

October 1: Federal fiscal year begins. For agencies whose appropriations bills have not been passed, Congress passes a "continuing resolution," which allows them to continue operating, usually at previous year's spending levels.

Article 8-1   Flow Diagram

Source:*The Chronicle of Higher Education*, 23 Oct 85.

The actual government position can be affected by international events beyond the government's control: for example, the 1941 attack on Pearl Harbor. As we have seen, Japan's attack was an exogenous shock to the United States security that set off an exogenous demand shock to the United States economy. The government geared up for war very quickly. This meant a rapid, huge increase in government spending. As demonstrated in Table 8-6, the government budget position went from a slight deficit in 1940 to a huge deficit in 1944. Graphically, this is represented by the dramatic shift in AD shown in Figure 8-13.

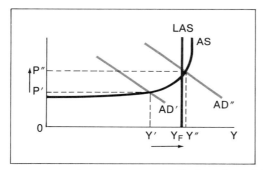

FIGURE 8-13   A Government Budget Based Aggregate Demand Shock

We would expect this shift in AD to be accompanied, as Figure 8-13 suggests, by a dramatic fall in the level of unemployment and a rise in prices. In fact, we find that during this period the unemployment rate fell dramatically to a level below what could reasonably be considered the natural rate and prices rose just as dramatically, until the government's program of price controls put a lid on that momentum. (See Table 8-7).

TABLE 8-6:   Expanding Government Budget Position, 1940–1944

Year	G	T	(G − T)
	($ billions)		
1940	9.6	6.9	2.7
1941	14.0	9.2	4.8
1942	34.5	15.1	19.4
1943	78.9	25.1	53.8
1944	94.0	47.8	46.1

Source: Historical Statistics of the United States, Department of Commerce, Series Y 339–341.

TABLE 8-7: **Macroeconomic Effects of Expanding Government Budget Position, 1940–1944**

Year	Unemployment Rate	$ Change in Price Level (Based on CPI, 1967 base year)
1940	14.6	1.0
1941	9.9	5.0
1942	4.7	10.2
1943	1.9	6.1
1944	1.2	1.7

Source: Historical Statistics of the United States, Department of Commerce, Series D86, E135.

Summary on Aggregate Demand Shocks

Our aggregate demand curve (AD) is a graphical representation of the aggregate demand relationship represented mathematically by equation 7:

$$Y_I = \frac{1}{1-b} \left[\frac{a}{P} + \frac{I}{P} + \frac{G-T}{P} + \frac{X-M}{P} \right]$$

We saw earlier that the exogenous variables of this relationship—in particular, I, G, T, X, and M—affect the relationship even though the values of these variables are determined outside of the relationship. That is, a change in one of these variables causes an exogenous shock to the relationship. Graphically, this is represented by a shift in the AD curve. Given our macro picture (the *AD*, *AS*, *LAS* graph), we can demonstrate the effect of changes in the level of investment (I), the trade balance ($X - M$), and/or the government budget position ($G - T$) on the macroeconomic conditions.

In this section of the chapter we identified the sources of the forces that determine the levels of I, G, T, X, and M, and thus the ultimate sources of the AD shocks that can move the macroeconomy from one condition to another.

Keep in mind that our model is simplified by a number of assumptions, one of the key ones being that I, G, T, X, and M are independent of one another. They are not, and a more complex model would reflect this. We will see some of this interaction when we examine government policy.

Now we turn our attention to other forces that can move the macroeconomy. These forces exert themselves not through their effect on aggregate demand, but rather through their effect on aggregate supply (AS).

B. SOURCES OF EXOGENOUS SHORT-RUN AGGREGATE SUPPLY SHOCKS

Recall that along a given short-run aggregate supply curve (AS) the prices of factors are fixed. It is changes in factor prices that shift AS. Thus an aggregate supply shock is the result of an exogenously determined change in the price of a factor of production. Such shocks may be gradual, as when wages are continually rising, or they may be sudden and dramatic.

The classic case of a dramatic supply shock to the United States economy was the oil price rises dictated by OPEC during the 1970s. (*Note:* The same event can affect both AS and AD.) In this case, the price of oil was, to a significant degree, exogenously determined by the members of OPEC. They decided to raise the price of oil, and up the price went. This exogenous supply shock caused the AS curve to shift up, as shown in Figure 8-14.

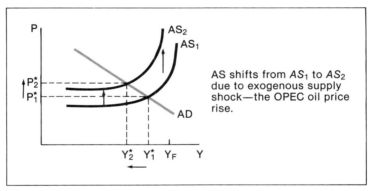

FIGURE 8-14   Macroeconomic Consequences of an Aggregate Supply Shock —the OPEC Oil Price Increase

We see from Figure 8-14 that the consequence of such a supply shock would be, *ceteris paribus,* a rise in the price level (inflation), a fall in the level of real GNP, and therefore a rise in the level of unemployment. In fact, we find that after each OPEC-induced supply shock (1973 and 1979), there was a period of rising prices and rising unemployment. The OPEC supply shocks were not the only shocks to the aggregate economy during these periods, but it seems clear that they were significant and contributed to the observed conditions.

Foreign nations are not the only source of supply shocks. Terrible weather might increase the cost of producing agricultural goods; a drastic change in the minimum wage or the power of workers vis-à-vis employers would alter the wage level and therefore the costs of production. Anything that dramatically affects the prices of factors of production would be the source of a supply shock.

C. THE WORKING MODEL—A SUMMARY

Now we not only have a model that allows us to represent various macroeconomic conditions such as unemployment and inflation, but we also have identified the forces that move the model. With this solid analytical framework in hand we can answer one of our basic macroeconomic questions: Why are society's available resources sometimes less than fully utilized, or why would some of society's available resources lie idle? In more common terms: Why is there unemployment?

Our model makes the answer to that question straightforward. If the economy is initially at full employment, any exogenous supply shock that shifts AS up (such as the OPEC oil price rise) or any exogenous demand shock that shifts AD down (such as a fall in investment) will cause actual real GNP to fall below full-employment real GNP (Y_F). If this happens, the unemployment rate will be above the natural rate; there will be demand-deficient unemployment.

This satisfies the first part of our basic question on unemployment but we have still to answer: Under what circumstances would such a condition persist? The answer to this question lies in the microeconomic foundation of the macroeconomy. In what follows we will see that under our nice microeconomic assumptions unemployment will not persist because the perfectly adjusting micro markets will eliminate unemployment in all factor markets and therefore in the whole macroeconomy. We will find, however, that if the nice assumptions do not represent reality, then in the real world of slowly adjusting markets, market power, and market failure, it is possible for unemployment to persist indefinitely.

It is in these next few pages that the connection between the micro and the macro worlds of the economy should become clear. Recognizing this connection is crucial if one is to fully understand the workings of a complex economy and the debate in NeoClassical economics over macroeconomic policy. Now let us examine those connections by contrasting the working of the macroeconomy with and without the nice microeconomic assumptions.

D. MACROECONOMIC ADJUSTMENTS TO EXOGENOUS SHOCKS—THE MICRO/MACRO CONNECTION

Macroeconomic Adjustment Under the Nice Microeconomic Assumptions

Recall the nice microeconomic assumptions that gave the Pareto optimal General Competitive Equilibrium at the micro level. We assumed:

1. No market failure—markets exist where needed and they adjust smoothly and quickly.
2. No market power—a fair race.

We will find that when these microeconomic conditions exist, the macro economy responds to an exogenous shock by adjusting to a position consistent with microeconomic Pareto optimality: when adjustments are complete (i.e., in the long run), the microeconomic condition of full, efficient use of all available factors implies that the macro system will be at full employment. Furthermore, these conditions also assure that the adjustment to the long-run full-employment condition occurs quickly because markets do work and they work quickly. How, then, does the adjustment occur?

To answer this question we will examine two suboptimal conditions in which the macroeconomy is not at the natural rate of full employment ($Y_* = Y_F$). Those suboptimal macroeconomic conditions are a GNP gap ($Y_* < Y_F$) and an inflationary gap ($Y_* > Y_F$). Recall that for the macroeconomy to be at an optimal condition—the natural rate of unemployment—the microeconomy must have adjusted to a Pareto optimal General Competitive Equilibrium. If a macroeconomic GNP or inflationary gap does exist, it means that the microeconomy must not have adjusted to a General Competitive Equilibrium. Therefore for both suboptimal macroeconomic conditions, the GNP and inflationary gaps, we must see what suboptimal microeconomic condition underlies each kind of gap.

Having established this micro/macro connection, we will then demonstrate that given our nice assumptions, microeconomic adjustments will occur that eliminate the suboptimal microeconomic condition and as a result, simultaneously, the suboptimal macroeconomic condition. Recall that it must be so since it is microeconomic adjustments that move the economy and any macroeconomic changes are just the sum of the microeconomic adjustments. To demonstrate this point further, in the next section we will show that if the nice microeconomic assumptions do not hold and therefore no micro adjustments occur, then the suboptimal macro condition will persist indefinitely.

• *CONDITION 1: A GNP GAP* Consider the AD/AS graph presented in Figure 8-15 in which the macroeconomy is in a short-run condition of less than full employment.

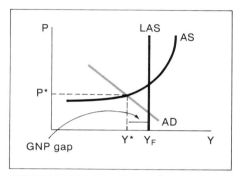

FIGURE 8-15   The Macro Condition: A GNP Gap

In this short-run condition the real GNP, Y_*, is less than full-employment GNP, Y_F. We call this circumstance a *GNP gap*. The existence of a GNP gap means there are unemployed factors in the economy (e.g., labor). We also know that by the definition of the short run, this circumstance represents conditions prior to adjustments in the factor markets. In other words, along AS, the factor prices are constant (e.g., the wage is constant).

As we learned earlier, this macroeconomic condition is just an aggregation of the conditions in millions of individual microeconomic markets. Thus if the macroeconomy is experiencing demand-deficient unemployment (a GNP gap), there must be conditions in micro markets—specifically, the micro factor markets—that add up to unemployment. What must those conditions be? There must be individual factor markets that are experiencing an excess supply (in other words, a deficient demand).

Consider an individual labor market (e.g., the market for brick-layers, or nurses, or MBAs). An excess supply would appear graphically as shown in Figure 8-16.

We see in the figure that as long as the wage remains at W_1, there will be an excess supply of, or a deficiency of demand for, this kind of labor. If this condition is prevalent in micro factor markets through-

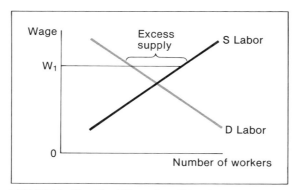

FIGURE 8-16   The Micro Condition Underlying a Macro GNP Gap

out the economy, in the aggregate it adds up to a macro condition of a GNP gap $(Y_*<Y_F)$—in other words, demand-deficient unemployment.

Now consider the adjustments that would occur at the microeconomic level if our nice assumptions are realistic. Initially, there is an excess supply of the unemployed factors—in our example, labor. As a result, the unemployed workers will begin bidding for employment. How do they do so? They offer to work for lower than the going wage. As we learned, the microeconomic markets adjust on a price signal. In this case, the price involved is the price of labor, the wage. We learned that the signal will adjust to clear the market. In this case, represented by Figure 8-17, the wage will fall in order to eliminate the excess supply (unemployed) labor.

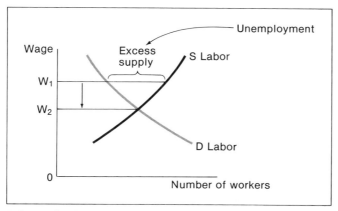

FIGURE 8-17   Microeconomic Adjustment to Market Excess Supply Under Nice Assumptions W_1 is the wage prior to adjustment. At that wage unemployment exists. W_2 is the wage after adjustment. The adjustment eliminates the unemployment.

How does this microeconomic adjustment process show up on the graph representing the macroeconomic model? Recall that as factor prices change, the AS curve shifts. A fall in factor prices shifts the AS curve downward. Thus the unemployment present when short-run AS is at AS_1 (see Figure 8-18) will set off microeconomic adjustments that clear the individual labor markets. These microeconomic adjustments include a fall in the price of labor (wages), which causes the macroeconomic AS curve to begin shifting downward. The microeconomic adjustments will continue until the labor markets are cleared (i.e., the economy is at full employment). At the macroeconomic level, this means that AS_1 will shift to AS_2, at which point the economy is in a short- and long-run full-employment condition (shown in Figure 8-18).

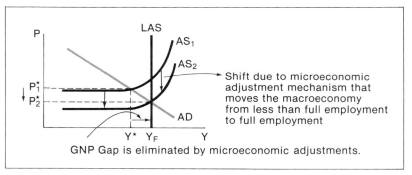

FIGURE 8-18 Macroeconomic Consequences of Microeconomic Markets Adjusting Under Nice Assumptions

Note also that the microeconomic adjustments necessary to eliminate the excess supply of (unemployed) factors lowered the costs of factors, which lowered the costs of production. This, in turn, lowered product prices (recall that in the fair race case as production costs go down, competition forces product prices down), and therefore, as shown in Figure 8-18, the price level fell.

This demonstration of the relationship between microeconomic adjustments and macroeconomic adjustments is very, very important because it sheds light on the direct connection between the micro and macro levels of the economy. The macroeconomic adjustment just shown is the aggregate consequence of millions of microeconomic market adjustments. If our nice assumptions are realistic, macroeconomic unemployment will be automatically eliminated by the workings of millions of markets for various kinds of factors. As each of these microeconomic factor markets does its self-adjusting, the unemployed factors of that individual market (e.g., bricklayers, teachers, mechanics, pasture, metal stamping machines) will be put back to work. As this happens throughout the microeconomy, the evidence will be seen at the macroeconomic level in lower unemployment rates and higher utilization rates for plant and equipment.

We see, therefore, that the nice assumptions that gave efficient microeconomic results are the very assumptions that are consistent with efficient macroeconomic results. This should not be surprising. As has been emphasized all along, micro and macro analysis are different perspectives on the same economy. If the economy is working efficiently at the micro level, this will be reflected at the macro level.

What we have just demonstrated is that microeconomic efficiency means that from a macroeconomic perspective society has a bigger pie. We must always remind ourselves, however, that efficiency does not imply equity. Equity has to do with how the pie is divided among the individuals in society. It is easy to become mesmerized by the elegance and power of the invisible hand. Nevertheless, we must not lose sight of the fact that while efficiency is desirable, it does not ensure justice. You should keep this in mind as we examine the efficiency conditions of the macroeconomy.

• _CONDITION 2: AN INFLATIONARY GAP_ Now let us examine an adjustment process from the opposite direction. Consider the case shown in Figure 8-19, in which AD is very high (above the AS/LAS intersection), thereby causing actual GNP, Y_*, to be greater than full-employment GNP, Y_F.

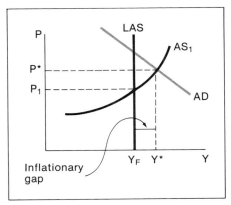

FIGURE 8-19   The Macroeconomic Condition: An Inflationary Gap

In this short-run circumstance the resources of society are being used to a degree that is not sustainable in the long run at the given state of technology. The initial short-run condition represents, therefore, an excess demand for factors. This case is called an *inflationary gap* because excess demand causes the price level to be higher than necessary for full employment. (Notice in Figure 8-19 that P_* is greater than P_1.) In analyzing the adjustment process we will focus, as before, on the labor market.

The pressure on the productive capacity of the economy is reflected at the microeconomic level as an excess demand for the available factors of production. For any given factor market such an excess demand would appear graphically as shown in Figure 8-20.

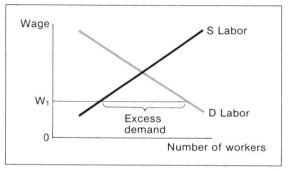

FIGURE 8-20   The Micro Condition Underlying a Macro Inflationary Gap

As time passes, the ability of labor to maintain the long hours necessary to maintain Y_* output wanes. When this occurs, firms must bid against one another for the labor necessary to maintain Y_*. As we saw in our study of microeconomic markets, when there is an excess demand, the price signal will adjust upward to clear the market. In this case, the wage level in millions of microeconomic labor markets (e.g., bricklayers, teachers, mechanics) will rise until quantity supplied and quantity demanded in every individual market are equalized. This microeconomic adjustment is represented in Figure 8-21.

How does this microeconomic adjustment process show up in a graph representing the macroeconomic model? Recall that as factor prices change, the AS curve shifts. A rise in factor prices shifts the AS curve upward. Thus the excess demand present when the short-run AS is at AS_1 (in Figure 8-22) will set off microeconomic adjustments that clear the individual labor markets. These adjustments include a rise in the price of labor (wages), which causes the AS curve to begin shifting upward. The microeconomic adjustments will continue until

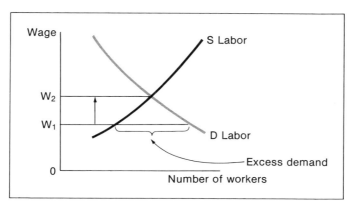

FIGURE 8-21 Microeconomic Adjustment to Market Excess Demand Under Nice Assumptions W_1 is the wage prior to adjustment. At that wage excess demand exists. W_2 is the wage after adjustment. The adjustment eliminates the excess demand.

the labor markets are cleared (i.e., the economy is at a sustainable full employment). At the macroeconomic level, this means that AS_1 will shift to AS_2, at which point the economy is in a short- and long-run full-employment condition, as shown in Figure 8-22.

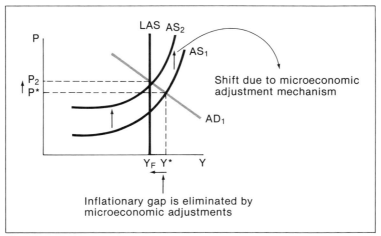

FIGURE 8-22 Macroeconomic Consequences of Microeconomic Markets Adjusting Under Nice Assumptions

Note that the microeconomic adjustments necessary to eliminate the excess demand for factors raised the costs of factors and therefore the costs of production. This, in turn, raised product prices and the price level.

Again we see the direct connection between the microeconomic and macroeconomic levels in the economy. As we examine the macroeconomy, we are studying the aggregate consequences of literally millions of adjustments in microeconomic markets. The degree to which these microeconomic markets are not distorted by market power or market failure determines the degree to which they automatically adjust quickly and fully. It should be clear at this point that the degree to which our nice microeconomic assumptions are realized is what determines the degree to which the macroeconomy will quickly reach a long-run full-employment condition.

Macroeconomic Adjustment in the Absence of the Nice Assumptions

Our nice assumptions give the NeoClassical general competitive conditions with the associated Pareto optimality as well as macroeconomic full employment. Now we want to examine the macroeconomic consequences when we relax those assumptions. Specifically: What are the macroeconomic consequences if there are significant microeconomic distortions owing to market power, market failure, or markets adjusting very slowly or not at all?

The answer is straightforward. The quick adjustments of markets and the absence of market failure and market power are the conditions necessary for the microeconomy to reach a Pareto optimum, and therefore for the macroeconomy to reach full employment. If these conditions do not hold, then the microeconomic system will *not* automatically adjust to a Pareto optimal General Competitive Equilibrium and the macroeconomic system will *not* necessarily reach a long-run full-employment condition. So if the nice assumptions do not hold in reality, the exogenous shocks that cause macroeconomic unemployment will not be automatically offset by the workings of the microeconomic adjustment process. This implies that unemployment can persist, and would appear graphically as shown in Figure 8-23.

In the figure we see that a GNP gap exists ($Y_* < Y_F$), which implies that there are available factors lying idle: unused capital or land or unemployed workers. Under our nice assumptions, of course, this condition sets off a microeconomic adjustment mechanism that eliminates the underlying microeconomic problem and is reflected at the macroeconomic level by the shifting of AS downward until the economy is at full employment. But when the microeconomic adjustments are very slow or (owing to market power or market failure) nonexistent, the micro adjustments do not occur and the macroeconomy does not move to full employment.

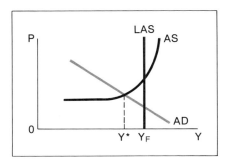

FIGURE 8-23   Absence of Macroeconomic Movement When Microeconomic Nice Assumptions Do Not Hold: Persistent Unemployment

In other words, without the automatic microeconomic adjustments, nothing is going to automatically change at the macroeconomic level. If the invisible hand is sprained, broken, or handcuffed, it cannot do its work.

Conclusion on the Micro/Macro Connection

The connection between micro and macroeconomics should now be clear: The quality of the microeconomic market adjustment system determines the quality of the macroeconomic system's ability to respond to shocks.

This fact has signficant implications for the role of government in the macroeconomy. Those who believe that the micro market system is very healthy and works very well maintain that the macroeconomy will heal itself when it is hit by shocks. On the other hand, those who believe that the micro market system is significantly flawed advocate government intervention to help the macroeconomy overcome adverse shocks. The issue is government macroeconomic policy: What should it be?

In the next chapter we will first take a brief look at the promise of the macroeconomy—the ideal for which a nation strives—and the problems of the macroeconomy—the actual less-than-ideal circumstances a nation often faces. These cases will be represented using our model. Then we will turn to an analysis of policy. The basic questions we want to examine are: What influence can the government exert over the macroeconomy? Should government use its macroeconomic influence? Is government intervention in the macroeconomy part of the solution or part of the problem?

Macroeconomic Policy— The Tools and The Debate

We the people of the United States, in Order to form a more perfect Union, establish Justice, insure domestic Tranquility, provide for the common defence, promote the general Welfare, and secure the Blessings of Liberty to ourselves and our Posterity, do ordain and establish this CONSTITUTION for the United States of America.

Preamble, 1787.

THE "PREAMBLE" to the United States Constitution defines the purpose of the government as envisioned by those who wrote that constitution. The Constitution defines the structure of the government, the responsibilities of each branch within that structure, and the boundaries of federal government power. Since 1787, amendments have changed and Supreme Court decisions have interpreted the words of the Constitution. Since 1787, however, the "Preamble" has remained the same—always defining the common purpose. All this raises a practical question: given the structure of government, what should the role of government be in order to fulfill its purpose? In this chapter we examine the government structures that control United States macroeconomic policy and we examine the debate, among economists with different philosophical perspectives, about how macroeconomic policy should be managed in order to realize the purposes of government as laid out in the "Preamble."

A. BACKGROUND TO MACROECONOMIC POLICY

The Promise and the Problems

Now that we have a fully developed macroeconomic model at our disposal, we are in a position to represent various economic problems an economy might face.

180

In order to do so, however, we must be able to identify the ideal case. Problems, after all, imply a failure to achieve some ideal. Most economists would agree that the long-run ideal for a macroeconomy is to have full employment (the natural rate of unemployment) and a stable price level. (*Note:* In the very long run growth is also considered desirable.) In this ideal case no available resources are idle and money is utilized to its full potential. Keep in mind, as always, that while this ensures the largest feasible pie, it does not ensure a just distribution of the pieces among individuals.

The ideal case can be represented as shown in Figure 9–1.

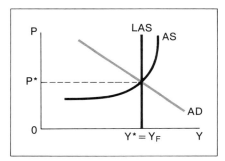

FIGURE 9–1   Full Employment at a Stable Price Level

If no shocks hit the economy, the price level will remain at P^* and the real GNP, Y^*, will be at a level that sustains full employment.

The problem we face is that in the real world shocks do hit the economy and they lead to serious macroeconomic problems. In this section of the chapter we will describe the nature of some of the most difficult macroeconomic problems we have faced in recent years. After the problems are presented, we will turn our attention in the next section to national government policy and attempt to answer the question: Should the government intervene to fix these problems, or is the government intervention itself in fact a source of the problems?

Now, with our ideal case as an analytical norm, we examine cases that do not realize this norm. Whenever one of these cases actually exists in the economy, we can say that the macroeconomy has a problem. They are:

1. Demand-deficient unemployment at a stable price level.
2. Full employment with inflation.
3. A wage/price inflationary spiral at full employment.
4. A wage/price inflationary spiral with demand-deficient unemployment. (This case is called *stagflation*.)

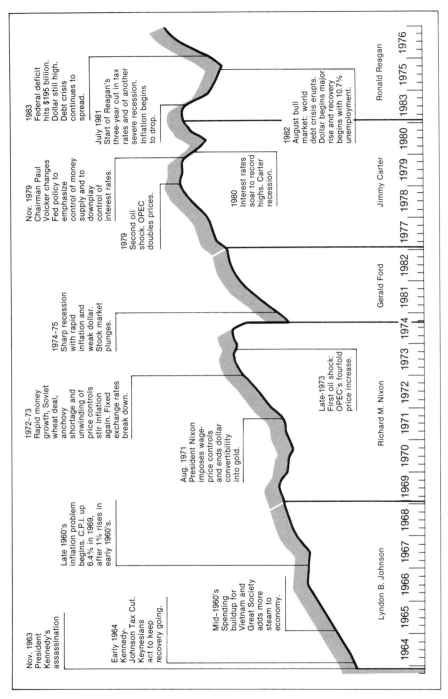

ARTICLE 9-1 Recovering From the Era of Shocks

Two Decades: The American Economic Experience

U.S. Industrial production index (1967–100)

Source: *The New York Times*, 8, Jan. 1984.

The first two cases can be understood as follows:

If the AS curve is stable, the macroeconomy may experience either unemployment without inflation, if AD is falling, (shown in Figure 9–2), *or* full employment with inflation, if AD is rising (shown in Figure 9–3).

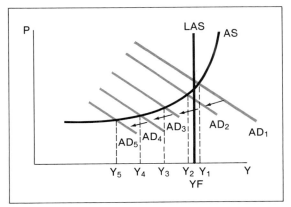

FIGURE 9–2 Unemployment Without Inflation *Note:* Arrows reflect continuous downward shift in AD.

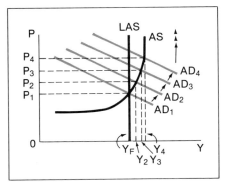

FIGURE 9–3 Full Employment With Inflation *Note:* Arrows reflect continuous upward shift in AD.

Thus we see that if AS is stable, there is a trade-off between unemployment and inflation: the macroeconomy can experience one or the other but not both. Until the 1970s, in fact, it was the view of most NeoClassical economists that government faced a policy trade-off: the price of lower unemployment was inflation, and the price of lower inflation was unemployment. This trade-off is represented graphically by a picture called the *Phillips Curve* (Figure 9–4).

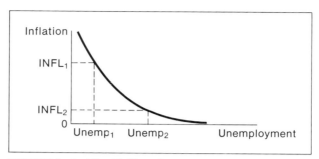

FIGURE 9–4 The Phillips Curve *Note the Inverse Relationship:* If inflation is high (e.g., *INFL₁*), unemployment is low (*UNEMP₁*). If inflation is low (e.g., *INFL₂*), unemployment is high (*UNEMP₂*).

This "trade-off" view of the economic problems of inflation and unemployment was held so long because it seemed to be consistent with actual experience. But in the late 1960s a sustained inflationary period began. Government spending on domestic programs such as Medicare and Medicaid expanded in an effort to realize President Lyndon Johnson's Great Society. Spending on the Vietnam War also increased dramatically after 1965. This spending splurge was not off-set by major tax increases. Thus we find that during this period AD shifted out and as a result unemployment fell from 6.7 percent in 1961 to 3.5 percent in 1969, while the inflation rate rose from 1.0 percent in 1961 to 5.4 percent in 1969. (*Source: Historical Statistics of the United States*, Department of Commerce, Series D86, E135.)

This condition of rising prices at full employment set off a phenomenon known as the *wage-price spiral* (our third case). Recall that as the price level rises, the value of anything measured in nominal terms falls. Wages are always measured in nominal terms because today's wages are paid with today's money. Thus, with inflation the real value of a fixed nominal wage falls.

It doesn't take long for workers to figure this out. Eventually they see that rising prices are reducing the value of their nominal wage. Their response is obvious. They begin to demand wage increases that maintain their real standard of living. This is particularly easy to do when aggregate demand is very high and unemployment therefore very low.

At first these demands are made contract by contract: each new contract negotiated includes a wage catch-up. However, as inflation continues, it becomes built into the expectations of the wage earners. When you expect inflation, you seek to avert its effects by building automatic inflation adjustments directly into your wage contract. This is accomplished by tying the nominal wage agreed to in a contract to a price index (e.g., the CPI). Thus, as the price level rises, the nominal wage will rise along with it, thereby keeping the real wage constant. This is called *wage indexing*.

Recall that increases in nominal wage levels shift the aggregate supply curve upward. When this wage-price spiral sets in, the case looks graphically as shown in Figure 9–5.

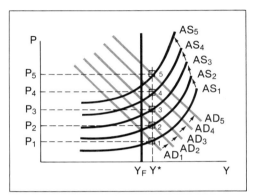

FIGURE 9–5   Wage-Price Spiral Inflation

We see in the figure that the inflation set off by expanding AD sets off a wage response, and therefore an AS response, which generates AD/AS conditions at points 1, 2, 3, 4, and 5. At each new condition there is no greater output in response to the increase in AD. The real GNP remains constant at Y^*. However, at each new condition the price has increased—the inflation continues, which reaffirms the expectations, which in turn feeds the inflation, and so on.

These inflationary expectations are what underlie our last case, unemployment with inflation (often called *stagflation*). It is possible to have a situation in which there is demand-deficient unemployment and yet those who remain employed are still fighting to maintain the real value of their wages. Graphically, the case can be represented as shown in Figure 9–6. Here again, conditions 1–5 in the figure map straight up, so real GNP, Y^*, is constant and all that is changing is the price level, P. In this case, however, $Y^* < Y_F$, so it is inflation with demand-deficient unemployment, or stagflation.

When Jimmy Carter ran for president against Gerald Ford in 1976, he cited the 1975 statistics that reflected economic stagflation: the

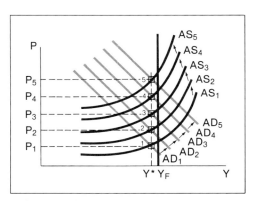

FIGURE 9–6   Stagflation

unemployment rate was 8.5 percent and the inflation rate was 9.1 percent. Mr. Carter added these two values together and called it a "misery index." The misery index was 17.6 percent that year and Carter won the election.

This concept came back to haunt Mr. Carter, however. When he ran against Ronald Reagan for reelection in 1980, Reagan pointed to 1979 figures showing the unemployment rate to be 5.8 percent and the inflation rate to be 11.3 percent, for a misery index of 17.1 percent. Mr. Reagan won that election. (*Source: Economic Report of the President*, February 1984, Tables B-33 and B-55.)

Clearly, in the opinion of American voters, Mr. Ford and Mr. Carter did not solve the country's macroeconomic problems. It is not clear that they could have. Traditionally, economists had considered unemployment and inflation an either/or issue. As we have seen, conventional logic held that if the economy became overheated with demand, it would set off inflation, and that if demand pressure was reduced, unemployment would replace the inflation. But Mr. Ford and Mr. Carter faced a new malady—the worst of both worlds, stagflation. An expectationally fueled inflation seemed to survive even in the face of increased unemployment. To make matters worse for both men, each saw their efforts to reduce inflation offset by dramatic increases in oil prices by OPEC, which hit the economy with an aggregate supply shock.

Mr. Reagan's eight years in office are over. During his term the misery index was reduced, but many economists argue that his success at reducing the misery index was purchased at the price of the country's long-term economic health. They note the unevenness of the "success," with some sections of the country doing well, while others were in recession or near-depression. (One problem with looking at aggregate data for the entire United States is that it obscures such localized differences.) Many economists also point to record budget and trade deficits as evidence that Mr. Reagan's success is being paid for on credit and that eventually this huge bill will come due. President Bush has inherited the bill. As we move into our analysis of policy, you should apply what you learn to current events: How are the current policymakers, the President and others, coping with the problems they've inherited and the new challenges that are arising?

In order to understand the past and current policies of our presidents and the current debate over policy, we will now examine the macroeconomic policy tools at the government's disposal. Once we have identified these tools and how they work, we can examine the logic of policies past and of those currently proposed for our nation's future.

The Government's Role—Introducing the Debate

We have seen that the levels of I, G, T, X, and M influence the level of aggregate demand in the economy. All of these variables are influenced directly or indirectly by the government. Government spending (G) and taxation (T) are entirely determined by the government. Investments (I), exports (X), and imports (M) can, as we shall see, be dramatically influenced by the government.

We have also described several macroeconomic problems that the economy can encounter and, in fact, has encountered in the past. These are unemployment (recession or depression), inflation, and stagflation.

The next question we must address is: If the macroeconomy faces problems and the government can exert influence directly or indirectly on the aggregate economy, should the government use its influence to solve the problems? The answer to this question may seem obvious. Surely, if there is a problem and the government has influence, it should use its influence to solve the problem. Right?

Right! Government must intervene! During the Great Depression the changing currents of economic events wiped out the livelihoods and savings of literally millions of people. If it had not been for the government, the Depression would have engulfed all Americans. There would have been social upheaval—a revolution in response to the endless tragedy. The United States government was established, according to the Preamble to the Constitution, to "promote the general welfare." Thus the government has a duty to intervene whenever times are bad. Right?

Wrong! Government is not the solution, it is a major part of the problem. If the government had not interfered, what became the Great Depression would have been a short recession. The economy would have adjusted and corrected itself. The government must always give the economy the freedom to do that. The writers of the Constitution state in the Preamble that the government is being established to "secure the blessings of liberty to ourselves and our posterity." Liberty and prosperity go hand in hand. Less government intervention means more liberty and more prosperity.

There are a large number of very famous NeoClassical economists who hold the first position: "Right! Government should intervene." There are also a large number of very famous NeoClassical economists who hold the second position: "Wrong! Government should not intervene." The greatest number of NeoClassical economists, including many famous ones, would probably come down firmly on the side of: "Maybe, it depends on the situation."

The first question about policy thus becomes: Why this range of opinion? How does each side (the two extremes) justify its position?

Choosing to avoid influencing the economy is called a *noninterventionist* or a *laissez-faire policy*. (*Laissez-faire* is French for "to let to do"—in other words, let it work itself out on its own.) The alternative choice open to government is to use its influence to manipulate macroeconomic conditions. This is called an *interventionist policy*.

At the heart of this spirited macroeconomic debate is a fundamental difference of opinion about the effectiveness of the microeconomic adjustment mechanism and the likelihood that government will exert constructive influence in the macroeconomy.

The various tools of policy will be presented in the balance of this chapter. Each tool will be examined in detail. Our examination will include: Who determines how the tool is used? How do noninterventionists believe the tool should be handled? How do interventionists believe the tool should be handled? How does each group justify its rejection of the other approach?

As we present the debate, always keep in mind that at its heart lie different beliefs about the effectiveness of the microeconomic adjustment mechanism, the market structure. The advocates of government intervention argue that the microeconomy is seriously flawed, and therefore the macroeconomy requires attention and artificial adjustment through policy. The noninterventionist laissez-faire advocates believe that reality approximates the nice assumptions, and therefore the micro- and, in turn, the macroeconomy work fairly well when left alone.

B. MONETARY POLICY

Introduction

One of the primary policy tools of the government is monetary policy. *Monetary policy* refers to government manipulation of the supply of money. Recall that as an economy becomes increasingly complex (the division of labor becomes finer and finer), it becomes increasingly dependent on the exchange of surpluses through trade in markets. As the market structure becomes more complex, barter gives way to a money system of exchange. Initially, this money is commodity money such as gold, but almost invariably commodity money gives way to fiat money printed by the government. One reason the government takes on the role of money printer is that it gives the government the power to manipulate the supply of money. In most countries the central bank has the job of supplying money to the economy. In some countries the central bank acts as a fairly independent agency, while in others it is required to follow the dictates of some higher authority.

In this section we will first examine how the monetary authority of the United States, the Federal Reserve Board, actually carries out these duties. Then we will see how the manipulation of the money supply can affect the economy. Finally, we will present the debate between the noninterventionists and the interventionists over how the Federal Reserve Board should behave.

How the Fed Influences the Money Supply

• ***Open Market Operations and the Discount Rate*** The monetary policy of the United States is determined by the Federal Reserve Board, commonly called the Fed. The seven members of the board serve 14-year terms. They are appointed by the president and must be approved by the Senate. This board governs the Federal Reserve System.

The Federal Reserve System is divided into 12 districts, each served by a Federal Reserve Bank. Private banks must buy stock in their district banks if they wish to be members of the Federal Reserve System. Most major banks do so because this gives their depositors confidence and them access to Fed services (such as being able to borrow money from the Fed). While member banks nominally own the Fed, real decision-making power rests with the Fed's board of governors and with a larger body called the Federal Open Market Committee or FOMC. The FOMC is composed of the seven board members plus the presidents of five of the district Federal Reserve Banks. The FOMC, under direction of the Fed chairperson, decides the nation's monetary policy.

The fiat money that serves as legal tender in the United States is issued by the Fed and is called Federal Reserve notes (look at the front top of a United States bill to see this). On each bill it states that it is "legal tender for all debts, public and private."

New bills are constantly being printed to replace old ones that are wearing out from use. This one-for-one replacement does not change the money supply. In order to change the money supply, the Fed must change the number of its bills in circulation: that is, it must take money out of its vaults and put it into the economy without taking an equivalent amount of money out of the economy at the same time. In order to decrease the money supply, the Fed must take money out of the economy without replacing it. The Fed can accomplish this manipulation of the money supply in two ways.

First, it can buy or sell government debt paper (United States Treasury IOUs) in the open market. This debt paper is generated by the United States Treasury Department.

It's important to keep in mind that the Treasury Department and the Fed are entirely separate government agencies. The Fed is an independent agency, while the Treasury Department is a department in the executive branch under the President. It is the Treasury Department that must collect the taxes and pay the government's bills. If the government does not collect the money necessary to pay its bills (i.e., if it has a deficit), the Treasury must borrow money. It does so by selling debt paper (IOUs that come due months or years later) in the open market to private citizens or to the Fed. Since there is an open and active market for this debt paper, it can be resold: anyone can buy and sell it. There is plenty of it because over the last few decades the government has been running deficits (spending more than it collects) almost every year. What is more, during the 1980s these deficits increased dramatically. As deficits continue, the government gets deeper and deeper in debt.

So one way the Fed can manipulate the money supply is by participating in this open market for government debt paper. If the Fed wants to expand the money supply, it can do so by buying this debt paper with money that it was holding in its vaults. The money ends up in the economy and the debt paper ends up in the Fed's vaults. That gets the money into circulation. If the Fed wants to contract the money supply, it can do so by selling debt paper it had been holding and then taking the money it receives in return out of circulation.

This method of manipulating the money supply is called *open market operations.*

The Fed's alternative means of influencing the money supply comes through its role as the bankers' bank for members of the Federal Reserve System. If one of these banks wants to borrow money, one place to which it can turn is the Fed. Like any other bank, the Fed charges for the money it loans. This charge is called the *discount rate.* When the Fed makes loans to banks this way, it is taking money that was previously in its vaults and adding that money to the economy, thereby increasing the money supply. Since banks borrow more when the discount rate is low, the Fed can expand the money supply by lowering the discount rate. If the Fed wants to contract the money supply, it can reduce the amount of loans it makes by raising the discount rate.

As the Fed expands or contracts the amount of money it is providing to the economic system, the effect on the money supply is actually a multiple of the amount of dollars the Fed injects or withdraws. In order to see why this is so, we must examine the characteristics of the kind of banking system we have in the United States, a fractional reserve system.

• *On Banks and Reserves* In order to understand the role of reserves in the banking system, we must begin by defining some terms. An *asset* is anything one holds that has value (e.g., property, cash, a good name). A *liability* is a claim someone else has on your valuables.

When you open a checking account at a bank (e.g., $100), you instantly create both an asset and a liability for the bank. The asset is the money ($100) you deposited in order to open the account. The liability is the fact that you can demand that the bank deliver that amount of cash ($100) to whomever you designate on a check. That is why economists refer to checking accounts as *demand deposits.*

Note that the asset and liability created are of equivalent value. Abstracting from all other accounts at the bank, the bank's *portfolio*— its asset and liability position—can be represented by a simple *T-account.* For your bank (Bank A) the T-account would appear as shown in Figure 9–7.

Bank A	
Assets: $100 Cash	Liabilities: $100 Demand deposit

FIGURE 9–7   T-Account

In order for the bank's books to be in balance the assets must equal the liabilities.

Now we need to introduce another term: *liquidity*. Liquidity is the speed with which an asset can be exchanged without sacrificing value. Some assets can generally be exchanged almost instantaneously without sacrificing value. For example, money as a general equivalent has a very high degree of liquidity. On the other hand, for some kinds of assets one must either be lucky or be willing to wait patiently for the right offer if the asset is going to be exchanged without sacrificing value. Such assets have a very low degree of liquidity or are said to be illiquid. Generally, a family home is considered a fairly illiquid asset. The liquidity of assets falls on a continuum between very high and very low liquidity. As our example stands, Bank A is holding its assets in a very liquid form: cash.

Now we introduce the last term we need in order to understand a fractional reserve banking system: *reserves*. Reserves are very liquid assets held by banks to cover the actual exercise of claims against the bank's assets. For instance, a bank has to hold reserves because people are constantly writing checks on their demand deposits and the bank must honor these checks on demand.

As our example stands, Bank A is holding all its assets in cash, so it has reserves equal to the entire amount of its liabilities. If Bank A did this with all deposits, depositors could rest assured that Bank A was rock solid: all the money necessary to pay off all its liabilities would be right there when needed. When all the banks do this, we say that the banking system is a *full reserve system*.

• *The Fractional Reserve System and the Multiplier Effect* Is it necessary for banks to hold full reserves? No. Except for a very rare circumstance that we will describe shortly, banks never need to have the cash to cover all of their liabilities at once. Based on experience, banks can predict fairly accurately what the flow of cash through their tellers' windows will be. Holding reserves above and beyond the amount necessary to cover this normal cash flow with a bit of safety margin is called holding *excess reserves*.

Is there any disincentive for banks to hold excess reserves? Yes. Banks make most of their money by putting depositors' money to work. If a bank can attract depositors at one interest rate and borrowers at a higher interest rate, the bank makes money on the difference. In effect, the bank makes its money by serving as a *financial intermediary* between borrowers and savers (banks are only one kind of financial intermediary, savings and loans are another). Financial intermediaries are the clearinghouse of the loanable funds market and they make a return for rendering that service. If they facilitate the coordination of borrowing and saving without themselves distorting the market (e.g., by discriminating in making loans), then they provide a valuable service to the economy.

We see, therefore, that there is a real incentive for banks to hold less than full reserves. We call a system in which banks hold less than full reserves a *fractional reserve system*.

Note that a fractional reserve system does pose a potential threat to the economy. Some banks may abuse the opportunity to make money on assets by holding inadequate reserves. If at some point the depositors' demands exhaust the bank's reserves, the bank will fail because it will not be able to put its hands on enough cash to pay off its liabilities. This kind of problem often creates a snowballing effect. If one bank fails, that makes depositors at other banks nervous; they fear that their life savings for college, a home, or retirement will vanish. These nervous depositors go to banks to withdraw funds. Others see them doing so and join in for fear that all the funds will be gone if they don't get there soon enough. This can cause banks that are holding normally adequate reserves to have cash flow problems and even fail. As more banks fail, people get more and more nervous. Concern turns into panic. A rising rate of withdrawal becomes a *run on the banks*. Under a fractional system, even the most conservative of banks is in danger when confronted with a run on its resources. Because all banks hold only fractional reserves, a collapse of confidence and expectations of further bank failures can be self-fulfilling.

One of the reasons the Fed was created in 1913 was to keep an eye on the management of major Unites States banks. Banks that belong to the Federal Reserve System (as we noted earlier, all major banks do) are required to keep a certain percentage of their assets as reserves (i.e., in a liquid form). This percentage, determined by the Fed, is called the *reserve requirement*. This requirement was supposed to reduce the problem of bank failures. Nevertheless, at the beginning of the Great Depression there was a run on the banks and many of them failed. That traumatic national experience gave rise to the Federal Deposit Insurance Corporation (FDIC), which insures individuals' deposits up to a certain amount. The FDIC was supplemented by the FSLIC when savings and loans became a popular place for individuals to save. The logic of these plans should be clear. They are intended to allay the fears of depositors and thereby reduce the likelihood of a run on the banks. Such plans are not perfect, however. In 1984 a statewide version of the FDIC failed to prevent a run on some state-insured Ohio banks. The problem in this case was that a serious run exhausted the resources of the state insurance system. If a run became serious enough on the national level, the FDIC and FSLIC would face the same problem.

While a fractional reserve system does pose this danger, it also has benefits. First and foremost, it makes it possible for financial intermediaries to earn a living while furnishing a service to the economy—providing a link in the loanable funds market, indirectly bringing savers and investors together. The system also creates a multiplier on the central bank's manipulation of the money supply. To see this you must understand how a fractional reserve system can "create money." Consider Table 9-1.

TABLE 9-1: **Money Creation** A simple T-account can be represented as follows:

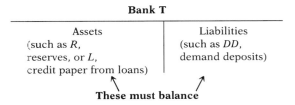

Bank T

Assets	Liabilities
(such as R,	(such as DD,
reserves, or L,	demand deposits)
credit paper from loans)	

These must balance

Assume (reserve requirement) $rr = 10\%$.

Suppose you discover a $100 bill in your attic and deposit it in your bank—Bank A. Bank A can hold the $100 as reserves, and in return you get a $100 demand deposit.

Period 1:

Bank A

$R = 100$	$DD_1 = 100$

But! Bank A can loan out $90 of this (remember, $rr = 10\%$) at interest, and it does so to person 2, who banks at Bank B. When person 2 makes her deposit, we have:

Period 2:

Bank A

$R = 10$	$DD_1 = 100$
$L_2 = 90$	

Bank B

$R = 90$	$DD_2 = 90$

Now Bank B is holding reserves above the required level. It puts the excess reserves ($81) to work by loaning the money to person 3, who banks at Bank C. When person 3 makes her deposit, we have:

Period 3:

Bank A

$R = 10$	$DD_1 = 100$
$L_2 = 90$	

Bank B

$R = 9$	$DD_2 = 90$
$L_3 = 81$	

Bank C

$R = 81$	$DD_3 = 81$

Well, C isn't stupid, so:

Period 4:

Bank A	
$R = 10$	$DD_1 = 100$
$L_2 = 90$	

Bank B	
$R = 9$	$DD_2 = 90$
$L_3 = 81$	

Bank C	
$R = 8$	$DD_3 = 81$
$L_4 = 73$	

Bank D	
$R = 73$	$DD_4 = 73$

And so on . . . If we carried it out, we'd find that the sum of the demand deposits (ΣDD) equals the sum of the reserves held (ΣR) multiplied by 1 over the reserve requirement $\left(\frac{1}{rr}\right)$. Mathematically:

$$\Sigma DD = \Sigma R \cdot \frac{1}{rr}$$

$$\Sigma DD = 100 \times \frac{1}{.10} = 1000$$

Notice that for the first three banks (A, B, and C) we see

$$100 + 90 + 81 \approx (10 + 9 + 8) \cdot \left(\frac{1}{.10}\right)$$

$$271 \approx 27 \cdot \left(\frac{1}{.10}\right) \qquad \text{(error due to rounding)}$$

By the time the injected \$100 works its way through the entire process, the actual increase in the money supply will be \$1,000.

Since demand deposits are effectively money, we see that a fractional reserve system sustains a money supply, the size of which is determined by:

1. the amount of reserves in the system (R)
2. the reserve requirement (rr)

where $DD = R \cdot \left(\frac{1}{rr}\right)$

i.e., DD moves directly with R and inversely to rr.

From this we see that every new dollar that enters the system can be used by the banks as reserves, and that for every new dollar of reserve, the actual money supply will increase by a factor of $\left(\dfrac{1}{rr}\right)$. If the reserve requirement is 10 percent, every new dollar entering the system will expand the money supply by ten times:

if $DD = TR \cdot \dfrac{1}{rr}$ where TR is total reserves

then $\Delta DD = \Delta TR \cdot \dfrac{1}{rr}$ where Δ stands for "change in"

$\Delta DD = 1 \cdot \dfrac{1}{.1}$

$\Delta DD = 1 \cdot 10 = 10$

Thus the flow of dollars in or out of the Fed is multiplied in its effect on the money supply. The Fed takes this into account in determining its policy. It can, in fact, change the size of the multiplier effect since it dictates the size of the reserve requirement that banks must hold.

The Fed does not exert absolute control over the money supply for several reasons. For one thing, financiers are always creating new financial instruments that serve a role as "near money." To the degree that this new-money creation is out of the Fed's control, the Fed does not control the money supply. Another reason the Fed's control is limited is that there is another exogenous source of dollars for the loanable funds market: the foreign-held dollars that flow into and out of the United States economy.

From Monetary Policy to Macroeconomy Results—the Transmission Mechanism

Manipulation of the money supply can exert influence on the macroeconomy. The effect of changes in the money supply is transmitted to the macroeconomy through the impact of these changes on the interest rate and the level of investment. This transmission process occurs in the loanable funds market. A change in the money supply will alter the supply of loanable funds made available at any given interest rate. In other words, a change in the money supply will shift the loanable funds supply curve. An expansion of the money supply will increase the supply of loanable funds (shifting the supply curve to the right) and a contraction of the money supply will decrease the supply of loanable funds (shifting the supply curve to the left).

In order to understand this relationship between the Fed's manipulation of the money supply and the loanable funds market, recall how the Fed carries out this manipulation. It does so by open market operations or by changing the discount rate. Consider the case in which the Fed increases the money supply. If it buys debt paper on the open market, the seller of the debt paper (e.g., a bank) ends up with cash that it can loan out, and thus the supply of loanable funds available to the market is expanded. Similarly, if the Fed lowers the discount rate and banks borrow more cash from the Fed, the result is that more money is available for banks to loan. Again, the supply of loanable funds in the market is expanded. The opposite Fed policy would have the opposite effect. As we have seen, the Fed's manipulation of the money supply is multiplied in its effect on the loanable funds market because of our fractional reserve system.

Figure 9–8 shows how an increase in the money supply shifts out the supply of loanable funds and causes, *ceretis paribus*, a decline in the interest rate and an increase in the level of investment. (*Note:* We continue to assume that loanable funds are only demanded for investment. We will relax this assumption shortly.)

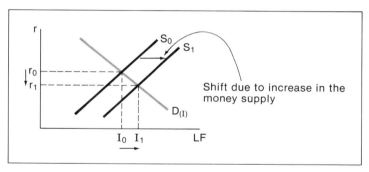

FIGURE 9–8   Effect of Increase in Money Supply on Loanable Funds Market

This rise in investment, the size of which depends on the elasticity of D_I, causes a aggregate demand shock. It shifts AD to the right, as shown in Figure 9–9.

Clearly, a fall in the money supply, often called a *contraction of the money supply*, has the reverse effect. Such a contraction reduces the supply of loanable funds, which, in turn, increases interest rates and reduces investment, as shown in Figure 9–10.

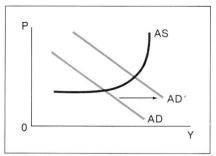

FIGURE 9-9   Aggregate Demand Shock as Consequence of Increase in Money Supply

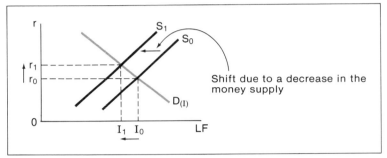

FIGURE 9-10   Effect of Decrease in Money Supply on Loanable Funds Market

This fall in investment causes an aggregate demand shock. It shifts AD to the left, as shown in Figure 9–11.

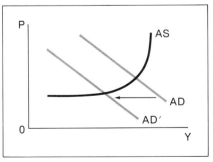

FIGURE 9-11   Aggregate Demand Shock as Consequence of Decrease in Money Supply

This relationship between the money supply and GNP can also be represented by the equation:

$$MV = PY$$

Here PY is the nominal GNP, M is the money supply, and V is the *velocity of money*. Money cycles through the economy from firms to households to firms to households to firms. . . (recall our circular flow diagram on page 51). The velocity of money measures how fast money makes this cycle: the faster, the higher the velocity; and the higher the velocity, the more purchases a given amount of money can make. Thus the amount of money times the number of times it makes a purchasing cycle, MV, measures the nominal value of the purchases the current amount of money in the economy is making—in other words, how much that money is buying. PY measures the nominal value of current sales, or how much is being bought. Obviously, MV must be the same as PY. If we assume that V is relatively constant, as M changes, PY must change the same way (e.g., if M doubles, PY must also double). Thus if V is constant, the equation shows how much a change in M affects PY. It does not, however, tell us how the effect of a change in M will be distributed between the price level, P, and the real GNP, Y. This distribution of effect depends, as we will see, on whether or not the microeconomic system is working as if our nice assumptions are realistic.

The point is that a change in the money supply can, through the transmission mechanism, cause an aggregate demand shock. The government institution that exerts influence over the money supply is the Fed. Recall, however, that the Fed's control is not perfect because the creation of new forms of money and the flows of foreign-held dollars into and out of the economy also influence the money supply.

The latter influence makes the United States economy vulnerable to decisions by large foreign holders of dollars. An influx of these foreign-owned dollars would increase the supply of loanable funds, thereby expanding investment and causing an AD shock. Aggregate demand would shift right, increasing real GNP and/or prices. A sudden withdrawal of these foreign-owned dollars from the economy would have the opposite effect. As long as the *net flow* or foreign-owned dollars is only slightly positive or negative, it has a minimal effect on our economy. If, however, the net flow is very large (either positive or negative), it can have a dramatic effect. When our relations with Iran broke down in 1979 because of the hostage crisis, President Carter froze Iranian assets held in United States financial institutions. This was done, at least in part, because it was recognized that a quick withdrawal of this large amount of foreign-owned dollars would have a disruptive impact on United States financial (loanable fund) markets, and, in turn, on the whole economy.

Conclusion on Monetary Policy

Earlier in the text we saw that aggregate demand shocks can occur through exogenously determined changes in the level of investment. Now we see that the changes in the money supply can affect the conditions in loanable funds market, and thus the level of investment and, in turn, the level of aggregate demand. Since the Fed has significant influence over the money supply, it is in a position to manipulate aggregate demand. The question remains: How should the Fed use its influence? In other words: What should Fed policy be?

The answer to this question depends on one's beliefs about the effectiveness of the microeconomic market adjustment system. Someone who believes that the real world closely approximates our nice microeconomic assumptions, and therefore that the economic system adjusts fairly quickly to long-run full-employment real GNP (Y_F), would urge that the Fed leave well enough alone—that is, follow a laissez-faire policy. On the other hand, someone who believes that the micro adjustment system is very slow or nonexistent would argue that the Fed has an active role to play.

Let's take the case of unemployment ($Y_1 < Y_F$) as an initial condition, represented graphically as shown in Figure 9–12.

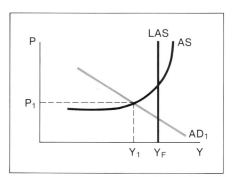

FIGURE 9–12   Unemployment

If those who advocate laissez-faire are correct, unemployment will cause wages to begin falling, which, in turn, will cause AS to start shifting down. This micro adjustment in wages will continue until all unemployment is eliminated. At the macro level, this means that, as

Figure 9–13 shows, AS will shift to AS', at which point the economy will be at full employment, *YF*.

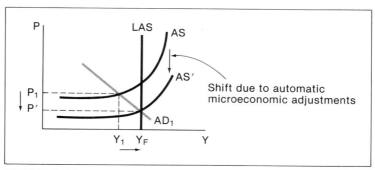

FIGURE 9–13 Macroeconomic Shifts Given Nice Microeconomic Assumptions

Not only does *Y* increase to full employment, but the price level, *P* falls as well.

But what if the noninterventionists are wrong? What if the micro adjustments do not work as if the nice assumptions hold? Then the level of unemployment would remain above the natural rate indefinitely. Those who fear that this would happen advocate government intervention. The interventionists argue that in order to eliminate unemployment, the Fed should expand the money supply. This would, through the transmission mechanism (lowering interest rates and increasing investment), expand AD. If the policy were gauged correctly, the effect would be to move the economy to full employment, as illustrated in Figure 9–14.

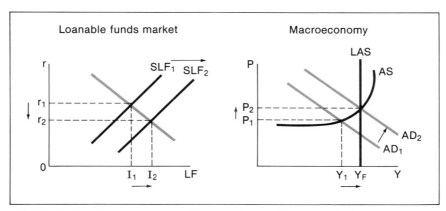

FIGURE 9–14 Consequences of Expansionary Monetary Policy

The figure shows that the price we pay for this intervention to achieve full employment is a one-time price rise from P_1 to P_2. The interventionists would argue that this price is cheap: elimination of long-term unemployment at the expense of one shot of inflation.

But what if the advocates of intervention are wrong? The laissez-faire advocates paint a grim picture of mistaken intervention. If the Fed intervened to eliminate unemployment when the micro adjustments would have done so naturally, the interventionist policy would have no real effect on unemployment. Rather, the macroeconomy would have achieved full employment in any case. The only effect of an expansion of the money supply would be inflation. According to the laissez-faire advocates, instead of going from initial condition A (see Figure 9–15) by micro adjustment to condition B, interventionist expansion of the money supply would take the economy from A to C. Both B and C are full-employment conditions, but C achieves this objective at a much higher price level.

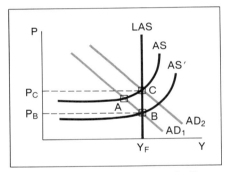

FIGURE 9–15   Macroeconomic Cases

Laissez-faire advocates are particularly adamant in opposing money supply expansion as a policy tool because they believe that the problems it creates may be even worse than the one-shot inflation just shown. They argue that the rise in price level (to P_c in Figure 9–15) would cause workers to demand higher nominal wages in order to maintain their real incomes. If workers were successful, the AS curve would shift up. This would create a new GNP gap, representing a return of unemployment. If the Fed then responded with another expansion of the money supply, AD would shift up, eliminating the GNP gap but again causing the price level to rise. Thus the cycle would begin again.

Graphically, the process would appear as shown in Figure 9–16 (starting at equilibrium C shown in Figure 9–15).

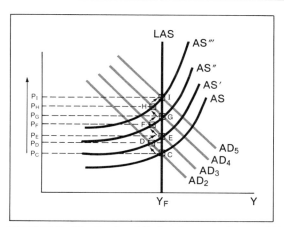

FIGURE 9-16   Cycle of Policy Intervention and Public Response

The result would be a vicious cycle leading to a continuous rise in prices: sustained inflation. Furthermore, once expectations get built into the process, the AD/AS adjustments occur almost simultaneously, and that leads to the expectationally based inflationary spiral shown in Figure 9-17.

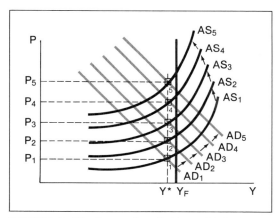

FIGURE 9-17   Expectionally Based Inflationary Spiral

Thus, according to the laissez-faire advocates, Federal Reserve expansionary monetary policies, rather than solving anything, are in fact the source of a major macroeconomic problem: sustained inflation.

Almost all economists would agree that sustained inflation is at root a monetary phenomenon. We can see why by considering the equation:

$$MV = PY$$

If velocity (V) is fairly constant while the money supply (M) remains constant, it's clear from the equation that the only condition under which the price level (P) could rise continuously (sustained inflation) would be if the real GNP (Y) fell continuously. In other words, if MV is constant and P is rising, then Y must fall in order to maintain the equality $MV = PY$. In terms of the AD/AS analysis, this implies a rising AS curve. In this case, inflation would be sustained by increasing unemployment. However, it would have to be self-extinguishing inflation, because as unemployment rose, there would be no basis for the forces pushing up factor prices (e.g., wage demands would subside in the face of increasing unemployment), and thus the AS curve would stop shifting up when unemployment became very severe. (Draw this case to convince yourself.) The only reasonable scenario for a sustained inflation (a sustained increase in P) is when the money supply (M) rises continuously.

Most historical cases of runaway or hyperinflation were, in fact, accompanied by huge increases in the money supply. In the 1920s the German Weimar Republic faced the burden of high reparation payments required by the Treaty of Versailles at the end of World War I. In order to make these payments, the government printed large sums of money.

Thomas Sargent describes this period as follows: "Between January 1922 and August 1923, wholesale prices increased by a factor of 25,723 while Reichsbank notes circulating increased by a factor of 5,748." He goes on to note that "the fact that prices increased proportionally many times more than did the Reichsbank note circulation is symptomatic of the efforts of Germans to economize on their holding of rapidly depreciating German marks." (*Source*: Thomas Sargent, "The End of Four Big Inflations," in Robert Hall, ed., *Inflation: Causes and Effects*, University of Chicago Press, Chicago, 1982.)

The German government's expansion of the money supply was so dramatic that it contributed to a rapid increase in the price level. This made people anxious to avoid holding money, which, in turn, increased the velocity of the money in the economy. The expansion of the money supply (M), along with the increase in velocity (V) in an environment of stagnant real production (Y), caused a hyperinflation of the price level (P).

Advocates of intervention respond that such cases are not arguments against interventionist monetary policy as such. Rather, they assert that such examples are arguments against *irresponsible* interventionist monetary policy. The interventionists believe that the market system is a complicated and imperfect mechanism. Left alone, it will produce undesirable results and irresponsible manipulation will do the same. They recognize that intervention is a tricky business, but they also believe that *responsible* intervention is sometimes necessary to improve the economy. Those who argue against this view say that intervention is unnecessary, is too tricky, and is not likely to be responsible, so the policy should be laissez-faire.

C. FISCAL POLICY

The other major policy tool the government has at its disposal is fiscal policy. Fiscal policy is the government's policy with respect to its budget position. As we have seen, a major source of aggregate demand shocks is a change in the government budget position (*G-T*). Such shocks can be caused by a change in government expenditures (*G*), government taxation (*T*), or both.

When we examined exogenous demand shocks in detail, we demonstrated that an increase in the government budget position increases aggregate demand and shifts AD to the right. For this reason, such a change in *G-T* is called an *expansionary policy*. Conversely, a decrease in the government budget position shifts AD to the left and is called a *contractionary policy*. Increasing government spending while not simultaneously increasing taxes is expansionary; decreasing government spending while not simultaneously decreasing taxes is contractionary. Similarly, decreasing taxes and not spending is expansionary, and increasing taxes and not spending is contractionary. (Under what circumstances is fiscal policy expansionary/contractionary if both *G* and *T* are changing?)

The government budget position, and therefore its fiscal policy, is determined by a process that involves both the President and the Congress. Since fiscal policy can influence the macroeconomy, the question is: How should the President and Congress use this influence? In other words: What should fiscal policy be?

Again, the answer to the question depends on one's beliefs about the effectiveness of the microeconomic market adjustment system. Those who think that the real world closely approximates our nice microeconomic assumptions, and therefore that the economic system adjusts fairly quickly to long-run full-employment real GNP (Y_F), believe the appropriate fiscal policy is to leave well enough alone—that is, to follow a laissez-faire policy. This would imply keeping G and T as low as possible and keeping G-T=0 (i.e., the government's budget in balance). Those who think that the micro adjustment system is very slow or nonexistent believe that fiscal policy has a role to play in solving macroeconomic problems.

Once again, we will use the case of unemployment as an initial condition, represented graphically as shown in Figure 9–18.

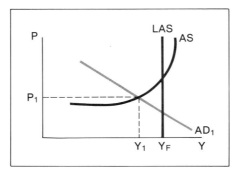

FIGURE 9–18   Unemployment

If those who argue for laissez-faire are correct, the existence of unemployment will cause wages to begin falling, which, in turn, will cause AS to start shifting down. This micro adjustment in wages will continue until all unemployment is eliminated. At the macro level, this means AS will shift to AS', at which point the economy will be at full employment, Y_F, as shown in Figure 9–19.

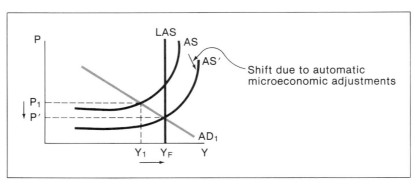

FIGURE 9–19   Macroeconomic Shifts Given Nice Microeconomic Assumptions

Not only does Y increase to full employment, but the price level, P, falls as well.

What if the laissez-faire advocates are wrong and micro adjustments do not work as if the nice assumptions hold? In the absence of intervention, the level of unemployment would remain above the natural rate indefinitely. Those who fear this result advocate intervention, arguing that in order to eliminate unemployment the government should implement an expansionary fiscal policy. This would expand AD. If the policy were gauged correctly, the effect would be to move the economy to full employment, as shown in Figure 9–20.

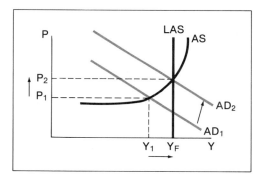

FIGURE 9–20   Consequences of Expansionist Fiscal Policy

The figure demonstrates that the price we pay for this intervention to achieve full employment is a one-time price rise from P_1 to P_2. Again, intervention advocates would argue that this is cheap: elimination of long-term unemployment at the price of one shot of inflation.

But suppose the advocates of intervention are wrong. The laissez-faire advocates paint a grim picture of mistaken intervention. If an expansionary fiscal policy is implemented to eliminate unemployment when the micro adjustments would have done so naturally, the interventionist policy would have no real benefit. The macroeconomy would have achieved full employment in any case, and, if the laissez-faire advocates are correct, the only effect of the expansionary fiscal policy would be inflation. According to the laissez-faire advocates, instead of going from initial condition A (see Figure 9–21) by micro adjustment to condition B, interventionist expansionary fiscal policy would take the economy from A to C. Both B and C are full-employment conditions, but C is at a much higher price level.

The laissez-faire advocates' rejection of fiscal interventionist policy is also based on their belief that such a policy will have harmful side effects. They argue that an unbalanced government budget distorts

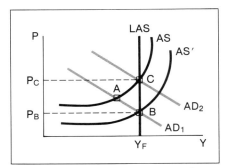

FIGURE 9-21 Macroeconomic Cases

the loanable funds market, and consequently has a detrimental effect on the level of investment.

If the government spends more than it has taken in during any given year, we call this a government *deficit*. If the government spends less than it has taken in, this is called a *surplus*. Government deficits over the years add up to more than the government surpluses, so the government is currently in debt. Since recent experience has been (and the foreseeable future promises to be) dominated by deficits, we will examine the impact of deficits on the loanable funds market in some detail.

Whenever the government has a deficit, it has to make up the difference between G and T ($G>T$) by borrowing. The source for the money the government needs is the loanable funds market. The government must enter the market and compete with other borrowers for the available loanable funds. The demand for loanable funds increases by the addition of the government's demand, but the supply remains the same.

If demand increases and supply remains constant, the interest rate rises and the total amount of loanable funds exchanged goes up. However, because of the higher interest rate, the amount of this total that would go to private investment falls. In order to see this, recall that the amount of private investment is inversely related to the interest rate. In Figure 9-22 we see that prior to the government's entry into the loanable funds market, the interest rate was r_0 and the total loanable funds, all of which went to private investment, was TLF_0. After the government enters the market in search of funds, private investors' demand for loanable funds (D_I) is augmented by the government's demand (D_G). At this new level of total demand the interest rate rises to r_1 and the total amount of loanable funds exchanged increases to TLF_1.

Notice, however, that at the new interest rate r_1 private investors, whose demand has not changed (it is still D_I), only want I_1 of the funds for investment. This is because the higher interest rate makes fewer investments worthwhile. Thus while the total amount of loanable funds exchanged has increased, the share going to investment has decreased. This decline in the amount of investment caused by the entry (or increase) of government demand for available loanable funds is called the *crowding-out effect*.

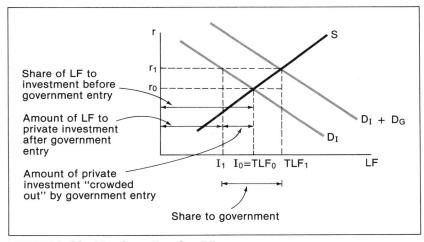

FIGURE 9–22   The Crowding-Out Effect

The size of the crowding-out effect depends on the responsiveness of the supply of loanable funds to changes in the interest rate. In other words, it depends on the elasticity of the supply of loanable funds. If the supply of loanable funds is not very responsive to the interest rate (i.e., it is inelastic), then the government's entry will increase interest rates dramatically but the total quantity of loanable funds supplied will not go up very much. Thus, in order for the government to get the quantity of loanable funds it needs, it must crowd out a lot of private investment (see Figure 9–23).

If, on the other hand, the supply of loanable funds is very elastic (i.e., very responsive to the interest rate), the government's entry will be met by a rapid expansion of the quantity of loanable funds supplied. The effect on interest rates will be small and the crowding-out effect will also be small (see Figure 9–24).

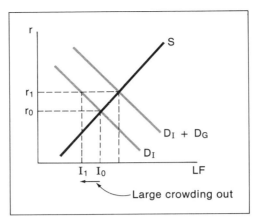

FIGURE 9–23 Large Crowding Out When Supply of Loanable Funds Is Inelastic

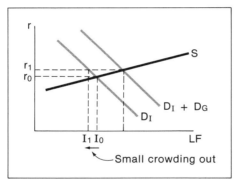

FIGURE 9–24 Small Crowding Out When the Supply of Loanable Funds Is Elastic

Some would argue that when United States interest rates are low relative to those in foreign countries, the supply of loanable funds is inelastic because much of the available funds has gone abroad for bet-·ter returns. As interest rates rise, however, more funds stay at home; and as United States interest rates become high relative to those of other countries, foreign funds flow into the country, rapidly expanding the quantity of loanable funds supplied. Above a certain level of interest, then, the supply of loanable funds becomes more elastic. But even as this flow of funds into the United States diminishes the crowding-out problem, it causes a balance of trade problem. The influx of funds results in a stronger dollar, and a falling balance of trade (X-M).

Clearly, if the crowding-out effect is large, an expansionary fiscal policy (increasing G-T) would be offset by a fall in investment (I). If an influx of foreign funds is the only reason crowding out does not occur, then the expansionary fiscal policy would be offset by a falling trade balance (X-M). In either case, the expansionary fiscal policy would not expand AD as intended, but would substitute new government spending for private investments or private spending on domestic production.

The interventionists argue that crowding out is not a major problem for policy, but the noninterventionists maintain that it is, and that it is one more reason intervention makes no sense.

This issue of potential crowding out can be avoided, however, if the President and Congress can convince the Fed to monetize the deficit. In effect, this means the Fed would expand the money supply to meet the money demand generated by a deficit.

In this case, represented in Figure 9-25, the supply of loanable funds is expanded by the action of the Fed, and this new supply is then available to meet the government's demand for loanable funds.

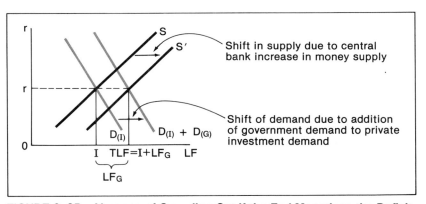

FIGURE 9-25   Absence of Crowding Out if the Fed Monetizes the Deficit

If the increase in the supply of loanable funds is exactly equal to the increase in demand, the interest rate will remain the same. The total amount of loanable funds exchanged (*TLF*) will be divided between investment (*I*) and the share to the government (*LF$_G$*). Since neither investors' (private borrowers') demand for loanable funds (*D$_I$*) nor the interest rate has changed, the amount of loanable funds that goes to investment (*I*) will remain the same. All the additional funds available will be channeled to the government.

The problem with monetization of the deficit is that if it continues, it can set off the vicious cycle of inflation demonstrated earlier. This could occur if the Fed allows the money supply to expand in an unrestrained fashion.

Furthermore, if the Fed's monetization of the deficit does set off such an inflationary spiral the economy needs more and more money to keep up with the expectations that get built into price setting. If the Fed then cuts back on the growth of the money supply, the fuel for the inflation will be removed but the inertia of the expectations will remain. The consequences of such a change are rising interest rates and rising unemployment until the inflationary expectations are squeezed out of the economy.

This is how that happens: In terms of our AD/AS analysis, the AS curve continues to rise as wage demands continue to reflect the expectations of inflation. However, since the government deficit is no longer being monetized, interest rates rise, investment slows, and AD (in the extreme case) stops rising. Such a course of events (constant AD and rising AS) will cause the unemployment rate to increase dramatically. As unemployment rises, workers' concerns turn from keeping up with inflation to keeping their jobs. Wage demands moderate, and when unemployment gets extremely high, the AS curve stops shifting up. At this point the inflationary expectations have been squeezed out of the economy.

This case is represented in Figure 9–26. We see that after condition 5 the AD, no longer fueled by money, stops rising. The AS keeps rising; but as unemployment grows, the expectationally based wage demands, and therefore the upward shifts of AS, become smaller. Finally, the expectations are squeezed out of the economy when AS ceases to rise at condition 9. In effect, the expectationally based and money-fueled inflation is eliminated by cutting off the fuel. Notice that the price of this cure for inflation is very high unemployment.

Just such a course of events took place in our economy between 1979 and 1983. Inflation, fueled by the Fed, was brought to a halt by the Fed when the growth of the money supply was reduced. The result was higher interest rates, higher unemployment, and lower inflation. The prime interest rate went from 9.0 percent in 1978 to 14.8 percent in 1982. Between 1979 and 1983 unemployment increased from 5.8 to 9.5 percent, and inflation went down from 13.3 to 3.9 percent (the effect slightly lagged).

The rise in United States interest rates also set off a capital flow into the United States and as a result the dollar strengthened. The price of a British pound, for example, fell from $2.12 in 1979 to $1.34 in 1984. This made imports cheaper, which contributed to the fall in inflation but also caused net exports (in nominal terms) to go from a $13.2 billion surplus in 1979 to more than a $66.3 billion deficit in 1984. (*Source*: *Economic Report to the President*, February 1988, Tables B-21, B-62, B-71, B-108.)

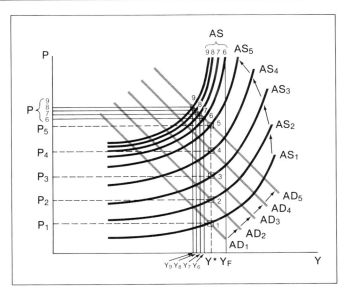

FIGURE 9–26   Fed Response to a Wage/Price Spiral: Squeezing Expectations Out of the Economy

Again, we return to the heart of the argument between the interventionists and noninterventionists. The noninterventionists claim that all this pain is proof that intervention does more harm than good. The interventionists counter that noninterventionists mistake a particular policy failure for a failure of the general policy approach. They say that laissez-faire is a simplistic approach that allows problems caused by basic distortions to persist, and argue that wise intervention is better than no intervention. The noninterventionists counter that since wisdom is a rare quality in policymaking, laissez-faire is preferable.

The noninterventionists hold consistent views with respect to monetary and fiscal policy, but in one respect the noninterventionists are more adamant in their rejection of interventionist fiscal policy. While they do not like interventionist monetary policy, they at least recognize the policymaking body as potentially coherent since the Federal Reserve Board is a small body led by a chairperson. They would not give the fiscal policy decision-making process so much credit. They would argue that not only is fiscal policy useless, the fiscal policy determination process is intrisically flawed.

The budget process is an institutional tug of war among the President, the Senate, and the House of Representatives. This contest is complicated by the fact that there are two parties in each House of Congress, with factions within each party, and that there are factions within the White House staff. On top of all this, individual members of the Senate (100) and the House (435) are tugged in 535 different directions. They must respond to the interests of their general constituency and also to the special interests of those with the power (e.g., money) to influence the course of their next election.

Here we see the potential tension between the macroeconomic (aggregate) policy with respect to the government budget position and the microeconomic (disaggregate) policy with respect to who is to benefit from the government's expenditures, who is to receive preferred tax treatment (an implicit expenditure), and who is to pay taxes and how much? Given the multiplexity of the microeconomic and macroeconomic objectives of all the interests, it is likely that these objectives will be mutually exclusive. There may, for instance, be a consensus that it would be wise macroeconomic policy for the government to reduce its deficit. Yet micro realities make that very difficult. It is hard to cut spending, because to do so means that someone loses benefits. It is hard to eliminate tax breaks, because to do so means that someone loses benefits. It is hard to raise taxes, because to do so means that someone must pay more. Yet, if the government satisfies everyone, spending rises, taxes fall, and the deficit grows— which will have undesirable macroeconomic consequences that will eventually affect everyone.

The government borrows to cover its deficit. If its needs are met by the Fed, this may ultimately set off inflation. If the Fed does not meet those needs, the government must compete with private investors for the scarce loanable funds. As a result, the cost of borrowing funds— the interest rate—rises and productive investment may be crowded out. Increased interest rates can also have a dramatically adverse effect on our balance of trade with other nations.

D. TRADE POLICY

Recall that a flow of capital into the United States increases the demand for dollars because foreign investors require dollars to make investments here. This results in a rise in the dollar relative to other currencies (e.g., the pound). Economists speak of this as a case of the dollar getting stronger (Figure 9–27).

A stronger dollar makes our goods and services more expensive to foreigners. This is true because even if the dollar price of these goods and services remains constant, it costs more foreign currency to buy

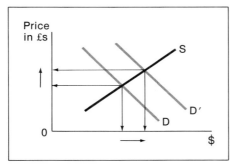

FIGURE 9-27   Strengthening Dollar

dollars. Thus it costs foreigners more of their currency to buy our products. As a result, *ceretis paribus*, our exports fall.

The stronger dollar also makes foreign goods and services less expensive for us. This is true because even if the price of goods and services in their currency remains constant, it costs us less of our dollars to buy their currency and therefore their products. As a result, *ceretis paribus*, imports rise. The net effect of this fall in exports and rise in imports is a fall in the trade balance.

We find, in fact, that in the early 1980s when the Fed's tight money policy combined with large federal deficits caused real interest rates to rise, these high United States interest rates attracted foreign capital. Consequently, the dollar became very strong and, as our model predicts, the effect was a dramatic growth in the trade deficit.

When imports rise and exports fall, the expanding trade deficit results in a decrease in the number of domestic jobs. The auto industry, the textile industry, the shoe industry—the list of industries hit hard by this shift in trade was large and the number of jobs lost was immense. The consequence was a chorus of calls for a trade policy that would protect American jobs.

Just as with monetary and fiscal policy, the government can take an interventionist or a laissez-faire approach to trade. The approach the government takes is its trade policy.

Given our nice assumptions, the only distinction between the analysis of global and the national economies is that in the former case there is one extra layer of markets that must adjust—foreign exchange markets. If these markets, along with all others, adjust quickly and efficiently with no distortions due to market power, the extension of the model causes no additional problems for the microeconomic market adjustment system. In such a case, the global economy achieves a result analogous to what happens in the national case—a global General Competitive Equilibrium with all the efficiency benefits and equity questions that such a result implies.

The justification for a laissez-faire policy rests, as we have seen, on the belief that the market system does work well. If this is true, then nonintervention allows all concerned to reap the benefits of greatest feasible gains from trade. In such an environment, if the nice assumptions are realistic, trade and capital will flow so as to benefit all (to the extent of their initial endowment), and the foreign exchange markets will adjust exchange rates so that the sum of trade and capital flows (the balance of payments) is balanced.

As with monetary and fiscal policy, the argument for intervention is that the market system does not work well and therefore may not function optimally. If this is true, the argument goes, the government should step in to correct the situation.

Let us assume that the problem is a very large trade deficit and that the government chooses to intervene. There are several ways it can do so.

The government can intervene directly in the foreign exchange market by taking dollars from its vaults and selling those dollars for foreign currencies. With this kind of intervention the government is, in effect, simply trading one kind of asset for another. By doing so, however, it expands the supply of dollars to the foreign exchange markets and thereby reduces the foreign currency (e.g., pound) price of dollars. This would make foreign goods more expensive to Americans and United States goods less expensive to foreigners, so that, *ceretis paribus*, imports would decrease and exports would increase. The net effect is a reduction in the adverse trade balance.

The noninterventionist's criticism of this trade policy is as follows: The policy distorts a market signal and therefore interrupts the market adjustment process. The action is analogous to taking painkillers for a broken foot and then continuing to walk along as if all is well. The problem is not solved, it is masked. What is more, the government hasn't got the resources to carry on this kind of intervention forever unless it is willing to simply print money. If it succumbs to this temptation, the result could be an inflationary spiral that would make the policy self-defeating. Continuing the analogy, using painkillers to mask pain can be self-defeating if one becomes addicted to the drug.

An alternative policy option is to set up barriers in order to reduce the size of imports. These can be subtle, such as making the red tape for importers such a big hassle that it raises costs; or they can be blatant, such as imposing tariffs or quotas. *Tariffs* are a direct tax on imports that by raising prices reduces quantity demanded. *Quotas* set a direct limit on the number of imports.

Again, the noninterventionists would argue that this kind of action would be counterproductive. Trading partners would probably retaliate, so the likely outcome would be a mutual increase in trade barriers. The winner in such a war would be domestic producers of goods and services that would otherwise have been produced more efficiently in another nation. The loss would be the gains from trade. Some people argue that the straw that broke the international economy's back and turned a recession into the Great Depression was the Smoot-Hawley Tariff of 1930, which dramatically raised rates.

The interventionists recognize the problems with these policies but argue that the noninterventionist solution—wait for the markets to adjust—is not an adequate response to unemployment caused by a huge trade deficit. The noninterventionists reply that the solution does not lie in distorting the international trade market.

E. THE PROBLEM WITH POLICY

A basic economic problem for the United States in the 1980s was that we began to require a great deal more capital than we were providing for ourselves. As a result, we became more and more dependent on foreign capital. The flip side of this influx of capital was a continuous weakening of our trade position. During the mid and late 1980s the Fed's intervention lowered interest rates and the dollar, but because of our continuing need for more capital than we were willing to provide for ourselves and because of foreign producers' willingness to accept smaller profit margins, the structure of our balance of payments accounts did not change dramatically.

Most NeoClassical economists believe that the solution to the trade problem of the 1980s lies not in erecting trade barriers, but rather it lies (at least in part) in lowering the government's budget deficit and increasing domestic saving. Doing so would reduce our dependence on foreign capital. This, in turn, would help reverse our trade position, because in the absence of any intervention, a reduction in capital flows into the United States would be accompanied by an improvement in our trade balance.

NeoClassical consensus on this point stems from the fact that high budget deficits are not part of a macro policy that either interventionist or noninterventionist economists would call coherent. Rather, the deficits represent a failure of the national political leadership of 1980s to resolve the conflict described above between micro- and macroeconomic policy. During the 1980s the President refused to slow or stop the increase in military spending, the Congress refused to reduce domestic spending beyond a certain level, and the President would not consider a tax increase. Thus the deficit problem went unresolved. In such an environment direct solutions to the resulting trade problems, such as tariffs and quotas, become attractive.

In the midst of this political stalemate with respect to fiscal policy, the Fed pursued a monetary policy aimed primarily at ameliorating the consequences of the stalemate. It lowered interest rates when necessary to maintain some growth in an economy that, despite the stimulus of the budget deficit, had been sluggish because of the huge trade deficit. When it could, it intervened in the foreign exchange markets in order to weaken the dollar and thereby reduce the trade deficit. Every time it did so, however, it kept a wary eye on the inflation rate, fearing that its efforts would set off a new burst of inflation and feed expectations that would further fuel inflation.

So as we enter the 1990s are we doomed to a continuation of this muddling incoherence in policy? Both the noninterventionists and the interventionists would say no, but for very different reasons.

The noninterventionists would argue that we can enforce micro/macro policy coherence by law. Specifically, they advocate a balanced budget amendment to the Constitution. The balanced budget amendment would ensure that fiscal policy is noninterventionist because the budget position $(G-T)$ would be locked in at zero. Though this is the noninterventionist prescription for fiscal policy, the actual implementation of such an amendment would be a short-term radical intervention with dramatic, but unclear, consequences for the economy. The second part of the noninterventionist prescription is a return to the gold standard. The gold standard would tie the amount of currency in the economy to the amount of gold held by the government in Fort Knox, thus eliminating the Fed's power to intervene in the economy by manipulating the money supply. Presumably also, there would be no trade barriers. This would be easy enough to ensure with respect to imports, but not with respect to exports, since access to others' markets is beyond our control.

Would this noninterventionist policy system ensure micro/macro coherence? For those who have a strong faith in the market system, the answer is yes. They envision a world of balanced budgets, benefits from international trade, and full employment. What could be more coherent?

The interventionists see this policy system as simplistic, pie in the sky and what is more, as dangerous. They argue that the nice assumptions are not realistic and that the economy is therefore not internally guided along a proper course. It must be steered. Constraining the flexibility of fiscal and monetary policymakers with a balanced budget amendment and a gold standard would leave the macroeconomy rudderless. When shocks occur that throw the economy off course, there will be no means to steer it back to the proper course.

The interventionists believe that coherent policy comes from effective leadership. At the micro level the government has hard choices to make about who should benefit from policy and who should pay for it. These choices must be consistent with the macroeconomic objectives of full employment and a steady price level. They also must be made in the context of our society's values, so that the objectives of both equity and efficiency can be realized as fully as possible. Making micro choices in a way that is consistent with macro objectives is difficult enough. Making difficult micro choices and making the macro system "work" at the same time requires leadership with wisdom, strength, and vision. According to the interventionists, wise policy is not easy, but it is possible, and we must pursue it in order to keep the economy on course.

And again, the noninterventionists respond: The interventionists are the ones who live in a fool's paradise. Such leadership is rare at best and dangerous at worst, since it can be confused with demagoguery and lead to dictatorship. Individuals know their own interests better than some politician or bureaucrat in Washington. In pursuit of those interests, guided by the invisible hand of the market coordination mechanism, individuals freely interacting with one another will produce the greatest wealth for the nation. Liberty rewards itself.

The interventionists rebut: The choice is not dictatorship or liberty. The choice is between constructive competition with justice and destructive competition with injustice. Good government can fashion a set of institutions that allows individuals to pursue their own interest, while at the same time ensuring the fairness of the competition and the justice of the outcome. In the absence of government involvement, rent-seeking behavior will get out of hand and we will all be worse off. Intervention does not imply dictatorship, it means constructive involvement.

So what are the policy problems? Today, as always, they are fears of inflation, unemployment, poverty, waste, pollution. And what is the problem with policy? At its heart, the problem is philosophical. It has to do with questions like: What kind of society do we want? What can we reasonably expect from one another as individuals, from our market system, from our political system? The way we answer these questions largely determines our views about policy. Since lots of different answers are possible, there are lots of different policy perspectives. And that is what makes it so difficult to get a consensus on policy.

The State of NeoClassical Theory

[T]hese conclusions (of mainstream economists from 1803 when J.B. Say established them until 1936 when J.M. Keynes challenges them) may have been applied to the kind of economy in which we actually live by false analogy from some kind of non-exchange Robinson Crusoe economy. . .

John Maynard Keynes
The General Theory of Employment, Interest, and Money, 1936.

THE "CONCLUSIONS" to which Keynes is referring are that markets will adjust quickly and smoothly and, therefore, that in the aggregate the economy will always move toward full employment. The point Keynes makes is that this assumes that markets coordinate a complex economy as perfectly as Crusoe's head does his simple one-person society. Keynes says that this is a "false analogy" and on that basis he rejects the notion that a laissez-faire policy is the best policy. In making this case Keynes stirred up a debate that had been dormant since the time of Malthus and Ricardo. In this chapter, we look at the background of the debate, the state of the debate, and the empirical problems that make it difficult if not impossible to resolve the debate.

A. HISTORICAL BACKGROUND—FROM J. B. SAY TO J. M. KEYNES

The interventionist versus noninterventionist debate is as old as the study of economics itself. Many people cite Adam Smith as the first economist, and the noninterventionists often treat him as their patron saint. If one reads Smith's work carefully, however, it is clear that he is not an absolute noninterventionist.

Smith wrote that "[A]ll members of society stand in need of each other's assistance, . . . [and] are likewise exposed to mutual injuries"

220

(*Theory of Moral Sentiments*, first published in 1759). He also recognized that since people are less than perfectly virtuous they might suffer such injuries at the hands of one another. For example he wrote that "people of the same trade seldom meet together, even for merriment and diversion, but the conversation ends in a conspiracy against the public, or in some contrivance to raise prices" (*Wealth of Nations*, first published in 1776).

To use modern terminology, Smith believed that rent-seeking behavior (seeking and exploiting advantage) is a weakness inherent in human nature. The weaker an individual's self-command (the self-discipline to do what is "right"), the more that person will exploit others. Given this problem, he saw the government ("the civil magistrate") as "entrusted with the power not only of preserving public peace by restraining injustice, but of promoting the prosperity of the commonwealth by establishing good discipline and by discouraging every sort of vice and impropriety" (*Theory of Moral Sentiments*). Smith recognized, however, that the quality of government intervention would be only as good as the quality of the government. Thus he stands with most economists on that vast middle ground between the noninterventionist and interventionist extremes.

The real patron saint of noninterventionism is Jean-Baptiste Say. Writing in 1803, Say popularized the idea that a market system can and does effectively coordinate all decisions, and thus it always assures that the economy will work efficiently. This belief became known as *Say's law*.

Say's law implies that the market system assures outcomes in a complex society that are analogous to those in a simple Robinson Crusoe society. Recall that in a Robinson Crusoe society the decisions of supplier and demander are perfectly coordinated because the supplier and demander are one and the same person. According to Say's law, the complex society exhibits the same perfect coordination despite the dispersion of supply and demand decisions among many people, because the market coordinates perfectly.

Say's law dominated mainstream Western economic thinking for over a century. During that time most analysis focused on the microeconomic system, because it was assumed that after any exogenous shock the macroeconomic system would adjust back to full employment and to a price level determined by the quantity of money. Hence the belief that the real mysteries lay in the micro world.

All this changed with the Keynesian revolution. John Maynard Keynes wrote a book called *The General Theory of Employment, Interest and Money* in 1936 (New York: *Harcourt Brace Jovanovich*, 1964; citations below from pps. v, viii, 18–20). He opens his Preface with the following statement:

This book is chiefly addressed to my fellow economists. I hope that it will be intelligible to others. But its main purpose is to deal with difficult questions of theory, and only in the second place with the applications of theory to practice. For if orthodox economics is at fault, the error is to be found not in the superstructure, which has been erected with great care for logical consistency, but in a lack of clearness and generality in the premises. Thus I cannot achieve my object of persuading economists to reexamine critically certain of their basic assumptions except by a highly abstract argument and also by much controversy.

And he concluded the Preface by saying:

The composition of this book has been for the author a long struggle of escape, and so must the reading of it be for most readers if the author's assault upon them is to be successful—a struggle of escape from habitual modes of thought and expression. The ideas which are here expressed so laboriously are extremely simple and should be obvious. The difficulty lies, not in the new ideas, but in escaping from the old ones, which ramify, for those brought up as most of us have been, into every corner of our minds.

Keynes identifies the "habitual modes of thought and expression" from which he must escape as follows:

From the time of Say and [David] Ricardo the classical economists have taught [Say's Law] that the supply creates its own demand. . . .

He cites some passages from J. S. Mill (1806–1873) and Alfred Marshall (1842–1924) that support this proposition, and then continues:

The doctrine is never stated to-day in this crude form. Nevertheless it still underlies the whole classical theory, which would collapse without it. . . . Post-war [World War I] economists seldom, indeed, succeed in maintaining this standpoint *consistently*; for their thought to-day is too much permeated with the contrary tendency and with facts of experience too obviously inconsistent with their former view. But they have not drawn sufficiently far-reaching consequences; and have not revised their fundamental theory.

What are the "facts of experience too obviously inconsistent with their former view" that Say's law is valid? They are the realities of the Great Depression. Keynes looks out the window in the 1930s and asks: How can a theory that is based on the belief that the market system works nicely be relevant to present experience? His point is that while such a theory may be internally consistent given our nice assumptions, in the real world those nice assumptions apparently do not hold. This is the point he is making when he writes in his Preface to the *General Theory* that "if orthodox economics is at fault, the error is to be found not in the superstructure, which has been created with great care for logical consistency, but in a lack of clearness and of generality in the premises." According to Keynes, the "Classical" model is based on strong assumptions that make it a model of a special case that does not exist in reality.

He emphasizes this point when he writes that "[T]hese conclusions [Say's law] may have been applied to the kind of economy in which we actually live *by false analogy from some kind of nonexchange Robinson Crusoe economy*" [emphasis added]. Keynes argues that the analogy is false because in a Robinson Crusoe society coordination of supply and demand intentions is perfect by definition, but in a complex society coordination is by definition a complex process vulnerable to distortions and failure.

The gist of Keynes's argument is that intervention may be necessary in order to correct breakdowns in this complex system. His model established the framework for macroeconomic analysis and his interventionist views became very influential in the economics profession. Those who have followed his direction, the Keynesians, enjoyed their greatest influence during the 1960s. Their influence waned when events of the late 1960s and the 1970s—first inflation, then stagflation—cast doubts on the wisdom of the interventionist approach.

B. THE CURRENT STATE OF NEOCLASSICAL THEORY

In the 1970s and 1980s the Keynesians were challenged on two fronts. From one side came the supply-siders, who argued that the aggregate demand–oriented policies of traditional Keynesians had produced stagflation. Instead, they contended, the emphasis should be on producing incentives for increased productivity in order to shift the aggregate supply curve to the right. The result (you can draw the graph) would be lower prices and higher employment.

Most economists would not argue with the proposition that increased productivity is desirable. The problem the supply-side approach encounters is timing and effectiveness. Traditional Keynesians argue that the benefits are very slow in arriving because changing techniques of production is not something that can be done quickly. The noninterventionists oppose the supply-siders on different grounds: they believe creating incentives for investments is as much a distortion of the market as any other kind of intervention. It skews the flow of capital into investments that are favored by the incentives rather than allowing capital to flow into investments that are warranted by market conditions. The consistent noninterventionists hold that capital will flow to where it is most productive when all government distortions—both incentives and disincentives—are removed.

The more powerful challenge to the Keynesians has come from the resurgent noninterventionists. The new banner under which they march is "Rational Expectations" or the "New Classical" approach.

The Rational Expectations version of the NeoClassical model is based on two assumptions. First, it is assumed that our nice assumptions are reasonable and that therefore the market system does work well. Second, it is assumed that all players use the information at their disposal effectively when making choices. (Recall that under our nice assumptions everyone has equal access to information.) What does this "effective information use" assumption mean?

We saw very early in our study that people make choices by comparing the present value of the expected utility produced by each option in the array of available options. We also saw that because of risk and uncertainty people can make choices that do not produce the desired result. This does not mean that the decision was wrong. The only basis for making a choice is the information available at the time of the decision. If one makes a rational choice based on the best available information, then it was the best decision at the time. No one has 20/20 foresight, but everyone has 20/20 hindsight.

"Effective information use" simply means that everyone uses the best available information to form the most accurate possible expectations in order to make the best possible choice at that time. When expectations are formed in such a manner, they are called *rational expectations*. In the Rational Expectations version of the NeoClassical model, it is assumed that expectations *are* formed this way.

When the combination of our nice assumptions and the assumption of effective information use is built into the foundation of the Neo-Classical model, several predictions follow. The first should already be clear. As we have seen, our nice assumptions insure that all microeconomic markets will clear and therefore the macroeconomy will always adjust to the natural rate of unemployment. Thus we can see that the Rational Expectationists are cut from the same cloth as the traditional (or, as Keynes referred to them, the Classical) noninterventionists. It is for this reason that Rational Expectationists are often referred to as the New Classical economists.

The second prediction distinguishes the Rational Expectationists from the traditional noninterventionists. Traditional noninterventionist theory predicts that the macroeconomy will adjust back to full employment after a shock caused by monetary and/or fiscal policy. But the Rational Expectationists argue that because people have plenty of information nowadays and know how monetary and fiscal policy decisions are made; when they go to make their choices, their expectations take into account the probable course of monetary and fiscal policy. Therefore, the Rational Expectationists predict that, unless monetary and fiscal policymakers can surprise people, interventionist policy will not shock the economy. The unemployment rate will remain at the natural rate, and all that can result from policy is a change in the price level. If this prediction is correct, it is clear that, as Rational Expectationists propose, noninterventionist policy is the correct policy for government to follow.

C. RESOLVING THE DEBATE WITHIN NEOCLASSICAL THEORY—PROBLEMS

Overview

Currently, the noninterventionist and interventionist extremes in the policy debate within Western mainstream NeoClassical theory are represented by the doctrinaire Rational Expectationists and the doctrinaire Keynesians, respectively. As we have often said, however, most NeoClassical economists do not occupy either extreme, but hold views that would place them somewhere along a continuum between absolute laissez-faire and eager interventionism. What is more, for any particular economist the position she takes along this continuum may vary as the specific policy issue under consideration varies.

It has been said that if you survey 30 economists on an issue you will get 60 opinions. Everyone will have a different view and the expression of each view will be couched in terms like: "On one hand . . . but then on the other hand . . . ." (President Harry Truman is said to have wished for a one-handed economist.) Why can't economists agree? Why doesn't someone prove once and for all that this view or that view—that any one view of the economy—is the correct view?

The problem lies in testing. Recall that at the outset of our study, when we were discussing the steps in the scientific process, the last step in the process was testing for verifiability (are the predictions consistent with what we find?) or falsifiability (can we identify an inconsistency?). It was noted then that testing in the social sciences is very difficult. The text continued:

This leads to two problems. First of all, since the testing methods are imperfect, error may escape even the eye of a perfectly unbiased observer. Second, since there are no perfectly unbiased observers . . . error is determined in the biased eye of the beholder. As a result of competing interpretations of test results, it is possible for two competing theories, each with strong supporters, to coexist.

This is what one finds in economics, wherein the two dominant theories are Neo-Classical theory and Marxist theory . . . . Neither theory has prevailed over the other because each presents evidence to support its point of view while attacking the evidence presented by the opponent as invalid because it is based on flawed testing.

Now we find that this problem not only allows NeoClassical and Marxist theory to coexist, but it also allows competing viewpoints within the NeoClassical mainstream to coexist. This problem generally frustrates interested observers of the debate within economics. The student of economics and the consumer of economic advice want answers, not more debate. We cannot resolve this problem here. We can, however, examine the source of the problem so that we can understand it more clearly.

Recall that the economist who wants to test a model must first operationalize the model. This means that she must transform theoretical, abstract definitions of the variables included into technical definitions that can be measured. She must also specify the relationship between variables exactly. After all, the predictions of a model can only be tested if the variables included can be measured and the model itself can be exactly specified. Unfortunately, this process of transforming a theoretical model into an operational model is imperfect at best and vulnerable to self-serving manipulation at worst.

Theoretical versus Technical Definitions

Consider the transformation from a theoretical to a technical definition.

The former defines a concept that is used in the model. The latter defines a set of criteria we can use to measure the concept so that the explanation and prediction of the model can be tested. Ideally, the theoretical and the technical definitions would be a perfect match. However, those who collect the data (e.g., the government) must set the criteria for the technical definition with the practical problems of data collection in mind. Because macro variables are aggregates (summations of lots of individual values) and because the microeconomy is so large and complex, technical definitions are often only poor proxies (approximate replacements) for the theoretical definitions they represent.

Take the problems with operationalizing labor-related terms. One hears a great deal in the media about the unemployment rate. It is based on the governments measures of labor force and unemployment and is calculated as follows:

$$\text{Unemployment Rate} = \frac{\text{Number unemployed}}{\text{Labor force}} \times 100\%$$

The labor force is technically defined as people from 16 to 65 years old who are not in an institution (e.g., in jail) and who are working, awaiting return to work (laid off), or actively looking for work. People who fit only the first two criteria but not the third are not counted in the labor force. We refer to this group as *voluntarily unemployed*. If you won the lottery, you might choose to be voluntarily unemployed. You would also be technically considered voluntarily unemployed if you do productive labor outside the market economy, such as housework or volunteer work, or if you have actively looked for work in the past but because of lack of success have given up in despair. The latter group is called *discouraged workers*. Some people have argued that counting houseworkers, volunteers, and discouraged workers among the voluntarily unemployed represents a problem with the technical definition of the labor force.

Those within the labor force fall into two categories: *employed* and *unemployed*. An individual is technically considered unemployed if during the reference week she is either laid off, waiting to report to work, or is available for work and has actively looked for a job during the last four weeks. Technically, you are employed if you have worked at least 1 hour for pay or at least 15 hours at the family business or farm during the week the government does its labor survey. This week, called the "reference week," includes the 12th of the month. Some believe that this is a poor measure of the employed because people who would like to be working full-time but can only find part-time work, as well as people who are working at a job that does not use their full skill level (a doctor working as a short-order cook), are counted as employed when, in fact, they consider themselves *underemployed*.

Recall that the Rational Expectationists predict that only a surprise can push the unemployment rate away from its natural rate, and even then, the economy will adjust back to the natural rate. Clearly, a test of that prediction depends on an accurate measurement of the unemployment rate. Unfortunately, as we have just seen, the measures we use are not without flaws.

The test of the Rational Expectationists' predictions also requires that the natural rate itself (the sum of structural and frictional unemployment) be accurately measured. This is, however, difficult to determine. Historically, the natural rate of unemployment has not been very high. As late as the 1960s most economists put it at around 4 percent. In the 1980s some economists argued that because of a rapidly changing economy, it rose to as high as 7 percent. What the actual natural rate is continues to be a subject of debate.

Similar problems arise when the concept of gross national product is operationalized.

The technical definition of GNP has four criteria for inclusion. First, the production must be exchanged for money. This criterion is included because a common denominator is necessary if we are going to add up apples and oranges and other components of the social product. Since money is a unit of account and market price is a representation of value in money terms, it is easy to aggregate (sum up) the value of all products that are exchanged for money. Note that this means work done in one's own home and volunteer work are not included in the measure of GNP. GNP also excludes the production done in what is called the *underground economy*. The underground economy is primarily a barter system for service exchange: You fix my car and I fix your plumbing. Such exchanges are often used as a method of escaping the Internal Revenue System (IRS) because there is no paper transaction agents can follow.

The second criterion for inclusion in technically defined GNP is that the transaction be legal. Payments for mafia hits or political bribes are not generally reported to the government. Because of the difficulty of collecting data on illegal transactions, they are excluded from GNP.

The third criterion is that the transaction be for current production. The logic here is that goods and services produced in previous years are not part of this year's product. Thus, a transaction for "old" products (e.g., a used car) is not included in GNP. It represents an exchange of preexisting product for money, not a payment for new production.

Last, only final goods are counted in GNP. The value of these products can be measured either by their market price or by the value added during each step in production, but not both. This criterion avoids double counting. If the value of a loaf of bread was measured by adding up all the money transactions that occurred in its production and final sale—farmer to miller to baker to grocery to you—the sum would overstate the value because the price you pay at the last exchange includes all the other prices. Adding them in along with the final price would be double counting.

These, then, are the technical criteria the government uses for measuring the GNP. It is plain they leave out some important things. The government has recognized this and has made some exceptions in order to include things that it has decided are too important to exclude. One example is government production. Many of the services the government provides (e.g., schools and defense) are not sold to the consumer in a marketplace for money. Thus, according to the technical criteria, this production would be excluded from GNP. Since government production is so big an item in our economy, an exception is made and the value of government production is measured by and added into GNP at the cost of producing it. But while the exceptions capture some important things, many others (such as the value of home production done by a member of a family for the family) are still excluded. Thus the technical definition of GNP is flawed.

We have examined two examples of technical definitions that are flawed. Both are of macroeconomic variables. While most macro variables suffer from such flaws, one can at least be thankful that most key macroeconomic variables are actually measured. The common problem with microeconomic variables is that there are often no measures of the values of variables relevant to the model. This is so because there are so many things to measure in a microeconomic empirical test.

For example, if an economist wanted to test her model's prediction about the factors that determine the number of hours an individual works per week, she would need information from thousands of individuals on the number of hours they work each week, their wage, education, age, race, sex, health status, experience, and any other factors the model predicts are relevant. That is a lot of numbers, and often the actual measures do not exist, so proxies (substitutes) are used instead.

For instance, there is often no measure of experience, so age minus education minus six is used as a proxy. The logic here is that one spends six preschool years and all school years outside the labor force and the rest of life in the labor force acquiring experience. The problems with this proxy variable should be obvious. It does not allow for the possibility of years outside the labor force after school, it does not account for variations in the quality and kinds of experience one can acquire, and so on. There are, in short, lots of problems with micro data, just as there are with macro data.

These problems with technical definitions contribute to the coexistence of competing theories because they make definitions malleable (adjustable). As we saw at the outset of our study, it is very difficult to disprove a theory when it is based on malleable definitions.

Regression Techniques

These definitional problems are not the only flaw in the testing process that allows competing viewpoints within NeoClassical theory to coexist. There are also testing flaws that arise in the process of specifying the relationships between variables once they are defined.

Take the hours-worked issue cited earlier. If the number of hours worked is predicted to depend on wage, education, experience, wealth, and so on, then a specification of the predicted relationship might look something like this:

$$\text{Hours} = 2.3 \text{ Wage} + 1.5 \text{ Education} + 1.5 \text{ Experience} - .5 \text{ Wealth} + \dots$$

If we plug in actual values for wage, education, experience, wealth, and so on, this specification will give us a prediction of the hours worked. Notice that this specification has hours increasing with wage, education, and experience and decreasing with wealth.

To test this prediction economists use a statistical technique called *regression analysis*. In effect, the computer is told that the relationship between hours (the dependent variable) and the independent variables that determine hours is:

$$\text{Hours} = \beta_1 \text{ Wage} + \beta_2 \text{ Education} + \beta_3 \text{ Experience} + \beta_4 \text{ Wealth} \dots$$

and the computer is given information on actual hours worked, wage, education, experience, wealth, and so on for lots of individuals.

Using this information, the computer will estimate values for the β_1, β_2, β_3 and β_4 in this specification. Clearly, if it is her own model that the economist is testing, she hopes that the computer results will be consistent with her model's predictions. Usually the economist is satisfied if the predicted sign is correct (e.g., that the sign of the β coefficient on wealth is, in fact, negative) and that all the variables that were predicted to be significant in determining the dependent variable, are, in fact, significant (the computer will report the level of significance for each independent variable).

This regression technique is widely accepted as a useful way to estimate the effect of independent variables on a dependent variable. The problem lies not so much in the technique itself as in the way it is used.

The computer can only test on the basis of the data and the model specification it is given. As we have seen, because of the use of proxy variables, the data is often suspect. Another problem is that the specification of the model can be manipulated in order to achieve desired results. If, for instance, in our hours-worked example the computer estimated a negative sign on the wage, one might change the wealth variable to wealth squared (Wealth^2) in the hope that when this is done, the sign on the wage variable will also change. Anytime the specification of the model is changed, the values, signs, and significance of all βs in the model will change.

This flexibility in testing is necessary but it also makes it possible for someone to manipulate the test until the results fit the predictions of her model.

After seeing how the testing process is flawed, it should not surprise us that conflicting interpretations of the NeoClassical model, and even entirely different models (NeoClassical and Marxist), can coexist without one ultimately prevailing.

D. CONCLUSION

It has probably occurred to you by now that the economic problems we face as a society and as a world do not stem from economies as such, but rather from us. As the old comic strip character Pogo once put it: "We have met the enemy and they are us."

We have shown how, under the correct conditions (given our nice assumptions and a "just" distribution of the initial endowments), a market system will realize an efficient and just society. As Adam Smith put it: "Human society, when we contemplate it in a certain abstract and philosophical light, appears like a great, an immense machine, whose regular and harmonious movements produce a thousand agreeable effects" (_Theory of Moral Sentiments_).

The world Smith has in mind here is the world we refer to today as a General Competitive Equilibrium. In such a world the race is fair and the competition is constructive. All individuals strive for personal excellence, and in that pursuit we each serve ourselves and one another. If all receive a fair share of the initial endowment that the institutions of society distribute (e.g., educational opportunities), the society would realize ethical and efficiency norms: justice and Pareto optimality.

Smith recognized, and we have demonstrated, that it is in fact very difficult to realize such a society because constructive competition is only possible if the competition is built on a more fundamental foundation of cooperation. For competition to be constructive, there must be universal cooperation in observing the basic standards of conduct that ensure a fair race. Smith wrote *The Theory of Moral Sentiments* to represent how these standards of conduct should be determined. He realized, however, that these standards are ideals for which we can strive, but that due to human frailty, we never have, and possibly never will, realize them. He recognized, in short, that vice exists and undermines society's efforts to realize the ideal.

Continuing the quotation cited above, Smith writes that:

As in any other beautiful and noble machine that was *the production of human art* [emphasis added], whatever tended to render its movements more smooth and easy, would derive beauty from this effect, and, on the contrary, whatever tended to obstruct them would displease upon that account: so virtue, which is, as it were, the fine polish to the wheels of society, necessarily pleases; while vice, like that vile rust, which makes them jar and grate upon one another, is as necessarily offensive.

Ironically, the rationality of individuals is the source of both virtue and vice in competition. It is the motive force for constructive competition and also for destructive competition.

We have seen that in a complex society the incentive to provide for the needs of others is most often based on a recognition that by specializing and generating a surplus, one can benefit by the gains from trade. Further, any individual will only share in the benefits if she provides a quality product at the lowest possible price.

As Smith states:

It is not from the benevolence of the butcher, the brewer, or the baker that we expect our dinner, but from their regard to their own interest. We address ourselves, not to their humanity but to their self-love, and never talk to them of our own necessities but of their advantages. (*Wealth of Nations*)

This is the virtue of rationality. Since trade only occurs when it is mutually beneficial, all involved benefit from the process.

The flip side of rationality is that unbridled self-interest leads to cheating. Individuals or coalitions of individuals often use their resources in pursuit of advantage rather than excellence. As Smith wrote:

People of the same trade seldom meet together, even for merriment and diversion, but the conversation ends in a conspiracy against the public, or in some contrivance to raise prices. (*Wealth of Nations*)

Either control of markets or control of the social and political institutions that distribute the opportunities that are paths to markets can be exploited in order to produce a rent. We have referred to this behavior as "rent-seeking", and we have seen how such behavior distorts the distribution and undermines the efficiency of the microeconomy and results in macroeconomic problems.

It is precisely this two-sided nature of rationality that makes economics such an inexact science. If the rationality of all individuals were constrained by an absolute commitment to a fair race, then in a sense both the interventionists and the laissez-faire advocates would be correct. The market system would work very nicely wherever markets existed, and the government of such a people would intervene wisely wherever markets failed. In the absence of such a perfect people, the laissez-faire advocates put faith in the market system, the interventionists put much less faith in the market system, and the vast majority of economists grope for answers in the face of the complex reality.

This text has not been written to provide all the answers. In fact, there can be no answers as to how the economy will behave until all people determine how they will behave individually. The purpose of the text is to show you the consequences of different choices. The choices you make as an individual and as a citizen will to some degree shape the future for yourself and for society. It should be clear that the choices which will shape your economic future are not simply those related to where to work and what to buy. While these are important, your choices as to what values to adopt and whom to vote for will be equally important.

Individuals do not always have the opportunity to make such choices. In a society with a totalitarian government and a command economy, there are no elections in which to choose leaders and no markets in which to choose exchanges. The dictator makes all choices. A benevolent dictator may choose justice and the efficiency of markets, but what assurance is there that the next dictator will be so benevolent? In a free society with a government of, by, and for the people, the people choose and there is the potential for justice and efficiency. However, it is only a potential. There are forces ("factions," Adam Smith called them) constantly in pursuit of control in order to benefit from exploiting the advantages control bestows.

Thus the success of a free society requires a degree of what Smith refers to as "self-command." This is necessary to rein in one's self-interest when it threatens to distort the fair race. Where self-command fails, we must turn to a collective enforcement of the fair race imposed by government. Unfortunately, government, as a human institution, is just as prone to the distortions of human frailty as any other institution.

The fact that you hold this book in your hand represents your connection to a complex society. The labor and capital of many individuals you will never meet are embodied in these pages. Complexity brings with it great benefits for those who enjoy the fruits of more productive human labor. But it does not come without costs. As Smith put it, in such a world "[a]ll the members of human society stand in need of each others assistance . . . [and] are likewise exposed to mutual injuries." The cost of complexity is vulnerability that comes with interdependence.

This, then, is the quandary of a free society made up of lesser beings than angels: Each individual must determine for himself the proper balance between self-interest and commitment to a set of social values, and society as a whole must determine the balance between individual freedom and society's right to impose rules.

Your choices, combined with those of all your fellow citizens, will determine the answer to the question: What kind of society will we have?

Appendix:
Extenders

		Found on Page	Referred from Page
E1-1	"The Road Not Taken"	237	2
E1-2	Representing Scarcity and Opportunity Cost: The Production Possibility Curve	238	2
E2-1	On the Concept of Utility	241	16
E2-2	Representing the Relationship Between Total, Average, and Margin	241	17
E2-3	Responding to the Structure of Incentives—"Spending Time" and Other Examples	248	32
E2-4	Time Preferences, Risk, Inflation, and Interest	253	37
E2-5	Risk and Insurance	255	38
E2-6	Comparative Advantage	259	44
E2-7	How Complex is our Society?	260	45
E3-1	Functional Form and Two-Dimensional Analysis	261	53
E3-2	Indifference Curve and Budget Line Analysis	265	62
E3-3	More on the Concept of Elasticity	276	73
E3-4	Demographics and Demand	286	74
E3-5	The Entrepreneur	286	79
E3-6	Demonstrating Graphically the Efficiency of Perfect Competition	290	81
E3-7	Market Production, Home Production, and Opportunity Cost	292	84
E3-8	More on Sunk Costs	293	84
E3-9	Input Substitution: Isoquant/Isocost Analysis	295	85
E4-1	Classic Examples of Violation of Our Equal Access to Information Assumption	299	96
E4-2	On Exploitation	302	100

235

Extenders (continued)

		Found on Page	Referred from Page
E4-3	Affirmative Action: Pro and Con	306	100
E4-4	Forms of Market Power	311	100
E4-5	Revisiting Our Basic Decision Rule: MC/MB Analysis	313	103
E5-1	Marketing Pollution Rights	314	110
E5-2	How Far Do We Want to Trust the Market Process?: Babies for Sale	315	110
E5-3	Price Controls: Ceilings and Floors	319	112
E5-4	On Taxes, A Microeconomic View	321	113
E6-1	Technical Definition of the CPI	324	125
E7-1	The Keynesian Cross Derivation of the AD Relationship	327	139
E7-2	The Multiplier Effect	329	142
E9-1	Money Supply	333	189
E9-2	The Discount Rate	333	191
E9-3	The Influence of the Fed	336	205
E9-4	How Independent is the Fed?	339	205
E9-5	Exchange Rate Manipulation: A Case Study	341	216
E9-6	Protectionist Legislation and Trade Wars	345	217

E1-1:   The Road Not Taken

Do the choices you make matter? Is choice really a quandary? The following poem by Robert Frost reflects the quandary of choice—and choice as an opportunity to shape your own existence. Note that our choices are all the more complicated by the fact that the ones we make today have consequences down the road, and we can't see what lies very far down the road.

The Road Not Taken

Two roads diverged in a yellow wood,
And sorry I could not travel both
And be one traveler, long I stood
And looked down one as far as I could
To where it bent in the undergrowth;

Then took the other, as just as fair,
And having perhaps the better claim,
Because it was grassy and wanted wear;
Though as for that the passing there
Had worn them really about the same,

And both that morning equally lay
In leaves no step had trodden black.
Oh, I kept the first for another day!
Yet knowing how way leads on to way,
I doubted if I should ever come back.

I shall be telling this with a sigh
Somewhere ages and ages hence:
Two roads diverged in a wood, and I—
I took the one less traveled by,
And that has made all the difference.

Source: The Collected Poems of Robert Frost,
Halcyon House, New York, 1939.

E1–2: Representing Scarcity and Opportunity Cost: The Production Possibility Curve

Economists often use graphs to represent concepts such as relationships because, as it is said, "a picture is worth a thousand words." One concept that is easily represented by a picture is scarcity.

Suppose that as a nation we have a limited set of resources and two generic items we want to produce: guns (representative of our desire for a secure nation) and butter (representative of our desire for a nation with lots of goods and services to consume). Suppose further that if we used our resources totally efficiently, we could produce G amount of guns and no butter or B amount of butter and no guns, or some combination of G and B. If we wanted to represent this case graphically, we could let the vertical axis measure the amount of guns we can produce and the horizontal axis measure the amount of butter we can produce. Thus the two extreme cases would appear graphically as in Figure E1–2A.

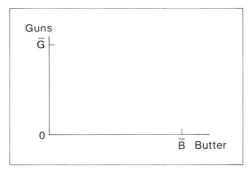

FIGURE E1–2A   Representing the Guns and Butter Tradeoff, I

The question remains, however: How would we represent all the other feasible combinations of guns and butter?

As we start the transfer of resources from gun to butter production, we would first use those resources that are worst for gun production and best for butter production. So at first the opportunity cost of butter in terms of guns given up is low. However, if we continue to transfer resources from gun to butter production, the last resources we transfer would be those that are best suited for gun production. Thus, to squeeze the last little bit of butter out of our resources would carry a high opportunity cost in guns. This kind of trade-off can be represented graphically as shown in Figure E1–2B.

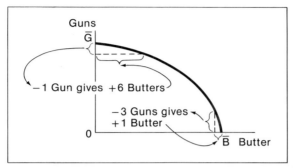

FIGURE E1–2B   Representing the Guns and Butter Tradeoff, II

The curved line from *G* to *B* represents our production possibilities. Using all our resources most efficiently, we can produce combinations of *G* and *B* represented by any point on that line, but to move from point to point means we are choosing a different combination. Thus we could choose to produce at point *J*, or *K*, or *L*, or *G*, or *B* in Figure E1-2C, but only at one, for these choices are mutually exclusive.

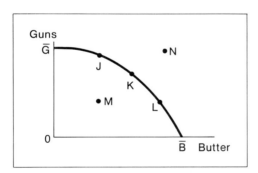

FIGURE E1–2C   Various Production Cases

Can we produce *M* as shown in Figure E1–2C? Yes we could, but given our resources, we could produce more guns and butter than the combination that *M* represents. Thus at *M* we must be producing inefficiently, not using all of our resources, or both. Can we produce at *N* as shown in Figure E1–2C? No. Given our resources and the greatest possible efficiency, the most we can produce is represented by the points along the production possibility curve from *G* to *B*. Point *N* is beyond our reach.

So we see that the production possibility curve represents the concept of scarcity: limited resources constrain our production possibilities (we can't reach *N*). It also represents opportunity cost: if, for example, we choose combination *K*, we give up the opportunity to choose any other combination.

What would happen to the production possibility curve if our resource base expanded or if we became more efficient in using that base? It would shift out as shown in Figure E1–2D

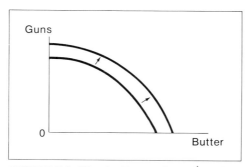

FIGURE E1–2D   An Expansion of Production Possibilities

Conversely, if we reduced our resource base or became less efficient in using it, our production possibility curve would shift in as shown Figure E1–2E.

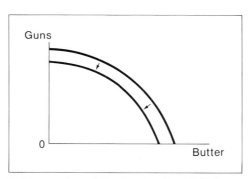

FIGURE E1–2E   A Contraction of Production Possibilities

Thus we see that with graphs we can represent the production possibilities our society faces, and the scarcity and opportunity cost issues embodied in those production possibilities.

E2-1: On the Concept of Utility

We use the concept of utility in this text as a heuristic device, a teaching tool. In fact, we cannot see or measure the satisfaction that an individual derives from a choice she makes. All that we can say about a given choice is that (assuming rationality) it reveals the individual's preference: of the available options, she chose this one, so it must be her preferred option.

We have assumed that individuals know their preference ordering so if we ask someone to rank the available options in order of preference, she could do so. The list she would generate would be an *ordinal ranking*—a ranking by order without any numerical value attached to each level in the ranking.

For the purposes of theory, an ordinal ranking of preferences is all that is required. For the presentation of the theory, however, it is sometimes useful to attach numerical values to levels of preference and to refer to these as the level of utility (measured in utils). This gives concrete form to an abstract concept.

As you read about utility, keep in mind that the numbers used are imposed on the preference ordering. We do this in order to give a *cardinal* (numerical) *ranking* to preferences that are really only ordinally ranked. If you bear this in mind, you will not be tempted to make a common mistake: interpersonal utility comparisons. Such comparisons are only possible if we can numerically measure the level of satisfaction a given choice provides. There is no such direct measure, so we cannot say that I get more satisfaction from an ice-cream cone than you do. We can only say that if we both buy cones, we must each prefer that choice to the alternative uses of the money we spent on the cones.

Again: Preferences can only be ranked ordinally. Utility is a device we use in order to give cardinal values to preferences. It is a heuristic device for giving preferences more concrete form. If we keep this in mind, utility is a useful tool for presenting the theory.

E2-2: Representing the Relationship Between Total, Average, and Margin

The total points any given student will receive on the final in this course will, holding all else constant, depend on the number of hours she studies. That "holding all else constant" phrase represents a strong assumption because clearly one's math background and lots of other factors can affect the final outcome. Such assumptions are useful, however, because they allow us to simplify the questions we examine by reducing them to two dimensions. Doing so is legitimate as long as we are explicit about what we are assuming. What is more, we can always examine the effect of other important variables in the same way. Obviously, n -dimensional analysis (allowing everything to vary at once) is more realistic, but lacking the tools to do that kind of analysis, we work in two dimensions. We can learn a lot from this simpler world.

When we work in two dimensions (or for that matter in n-dimensions), there are three different ways to measure the effect of the independent variable (where the effect comes from, the cause) on the dependent variable (where the effect is felt). We can measure the total effect, the average effect, or the marginal effect. All three measures will be important to our analysis. What we want to do now is see how we measure each effect and how these measures relate to one another.

Since a concrete example should prove useful, let us consider the following case: Total points on the final exam is a function of hours studied, holding all else (e.g., quality of study) constant.

We will assume that we have data on the relationship between hours studied and final grade, holding all else constant. They are presented in Table E2–2A. This table shows us the relationship between hours studied and total points. The total points value reflects how many points a student received for any given cumulative number of hours studied. To see how many points a given cumulative number of hours

TABLE E2-2A

H (hours studied)	TP (total points)
0	0
1	5
2	25
3	55
4	75
5	86
6	93
7	97
8	99
9	100
10	100

generated, we need only read across. We see, for example, that if someone studied four hours, she would receive 75 total points, while if someone studied seven hours, she would receive 97 total points. Thus we see that the measure of total effect (here, the total effect of hours studied on points received) is very straightforward.

The measure of average effect simply represents how much a generic unit of the independent variable (here, hours studied) effects the dependent variable (here, total points). When we measure the average effect, we treat all units of the independent variable as if their individual effects are equal. Thus, "on average," all units of the independent variable have the same effect. To calculate the value of this average effect we simply divide the number of units of the independent variable (here, the number of hours) into the number of units of the dependent variable (here, total points). Thus, in mathematical terms:

$$\frac{\text{Average points}}{\text{per hour}} = \frac{\text{Total points}}{\text{Number of hours}}$$

The value of the average effect in our test example is directly derivable from the information about the total effect presented above. Extending our table to include these values, we have Table E2–2B.

We see in this table that if someone studied four hours, she would receive 75 total points and that the average productivity of an hour would be 18.8 points. If someone studied seven hours, she would receive 97 points and the average productivity of an hour would be 13.9 points.

Notice the apparent injustice? The person who studies longer gets less return per hour. Why does that happen? The answer is that not all

TABLE E2–2B

H (hours)	TP (total points)	AP (average points)
0	0	0
1	5	5.0
2	25	12.5
3	55	18.3
4	75	18.8
5	86	17.2
6	93	15.5
7	97	13.9
8	99	12.4
9	100	11.1
10	100	10.0

hours of study are created equally. This should come as no surprise. When you start to study, you are fresh and you begin on the basics, so it is likely that you can cover a lot of material (and therefore generate a lot of points) fairly rapidly. As the night wears on, however, two things begin to slow you down. First, you get tired. When you are tired, it is harder to concentrate and therefore your rate of speed slows. This problem is compounded by the fact that as you get further into the material, it becomes more complicated. Needless to say, the more complicated the material, the slower your progress.

Our measure of total effect treats hours as a sum, so this difference between hours is obscured when we measure the total effect of hours studied on your grade. The measure of average effect treats hours as if they were all identical in their effect, so this, too, obscures the variation in productivity between different hours. In order to specifically identify this difference between the productivity of various hours, we must turn to our measure of marginal effect.

In general terms, the measure of marginal effect represents how much a *specific* unit of the independent variable (here, hours studied) affects the dependent variable (here, total points). When we measure the marginal affect, we treat each unit of the independent variable individually so that its unique impact can be specifically identified.

As with the average effect, the value of the marginal effect in our test example is directly derivable from the information about the total effect presented above. Extending our table to include these values, we have Table E2–2C. Remember, the measure of marginal effect represents how much a *specific* unit of the independent variable (here, hours studied) affects the dependent variable (here, total points).

TABLE E2–2C

H (hours)	TP (total points)	AP (average points)	MP (marginal points)
0	0	0	0
1	5	5.0	5
2	25	12.5	20
3	55	18.3	30
4	75	18.8	20
5	86	17.2	11
6	93	15.5	7
7	97	13.9	4
8	99	12.4	2
9	100	11.1	1
10	100	10.0	0

Look, for example, at the fourth hour. How much was its marginal effect? If someone studied three hours, she would receive 55 total points. If that person studied four hours, she would receive 75 total points. Clearly, the marginal effect of the fourth hour itself (i.e., the marginal points that *particular* hour generated) is 20 points. Notice that the marginal effect of the seventh hour is 4 points. clearly, the material is getting harder and the student is getting tired.

Note that there is a systematic relationship between the margin and the average. The margin guides the average, or to state the relationship in reverse, the average follows the margin. Look again at Table E2–2C. Whenever the margin is above the average, the average is rising; and whenever the margin is below the average, the average is falling. To make intuitive sense of this think about your grade point average. Your cumulative GPA, your "average" GPA for your college career, will rise whenever you have a good semester—in other words, a higher "marginal" GPA. Conversely, . . . never mind, it won't happen to you.

We can see this relationship between the margin and the average graphically by plotting the marginal and average values from our last table. What we get is Figure E2–2A.

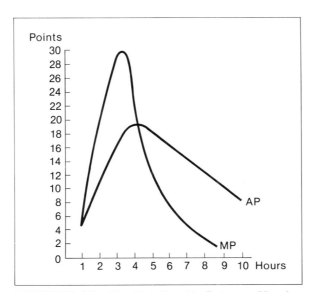

FIGURE E2–2A   The Relationship Between Margin and Average

Here we can see that where the margin is above the average, the average is rising—the margin "cuts" the average at the average's maximum,—and where the margin is below the average, the average is falling.

We can state it as a general rule that, graphically, where the margin is above the average, the average will be rising, the margin will "cut" the average at an extreme (a maximum or a minimum); and where the margin is below the average, the average will be falling. Figure E2–2B shows the first relationship and Figure E2–2C the second.

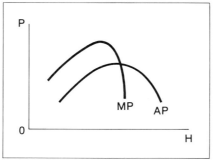

FIGURE E2–2B   Margin Cutting the Average at Maximum

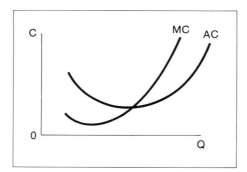

FIGURE E2–2C   Margin Cutting the Average at Minimum

We can also represent the relationship between the margin and the total graphically. Recall that in our example the marginal effect of successive hours studied increased until the third hour, which produced 30 additional points; it then fell, until the tenth hour produced no additional points. From the first to the ninth hour, even when the margin was falling, the total was increasing. In general, we can say that as long as the margin is positive, it will increase the total. Graphically, we can show the relationship between total points and marginal points as in Figure E2–2D.

What happens to the total if the margin becomes negative? Suppose

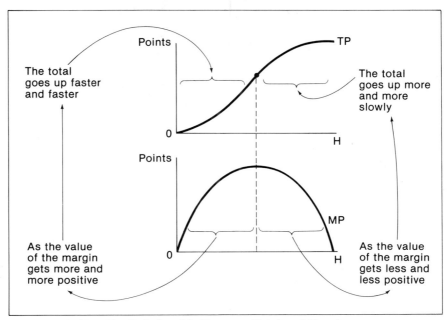

FIGURE E2–2D   The Relationship Between Total and Margin

you study so long as you are exhausting the energy you need the next day to perform on the test. The effect of those marginal hours on your performance would then be negative. You actually do worse on the test than you would have if you had quit studying and gone to sleep, because you are tired and confused. We represent this graphically in Figure E2–2E.

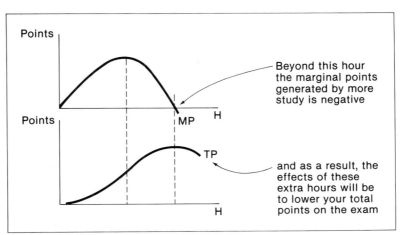

FIGURE E2–2E   The Effect of a Negative Margin on the Total

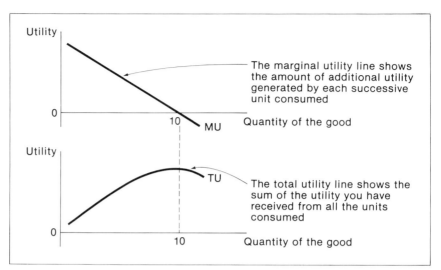

FIGURE E2–2F   Relationship Between Total and Marginal Utility

This relationship between the margin and total is very useful in identifying decision rules. Consider the following case: If a good is free, how much would you decide to consume? We have assumed diminishing marginal utility, so we can represent the case graphically as shown in Figure E2–2F. Here we see that the tenth unit gives you zero marginal utility and therefore does not add to your total utility. Furthermore, units beyond the tenth generate negative marginal utility and thus lower your total utility (e.g., too many M&Ms will make you sick). So what decision rule do you follow in consuming a free good? You consume until:

$$MU = 0$$

As long as $MU > 0$, you may be able to derive more utility from another unit, but once $MU = 0$, you know that there is no more utility to be gained from consuming that good.

E2–3:   Responding to the Structure of Incentives; "Spending Time" and Other Examples

We can demonstrate the validity of our utility maximization decision rule, set: $EPVUMP_1 = EPVUMP_2 = \ldots = EPVUMP_n$, graphically.

Suppose you have a choice between two activities, playing and working, and you have a total of six hours to spend on these two activities. Figure E2–3A shows the present value of the utility you expect to derive from each successive (marginal) hour of play and work.

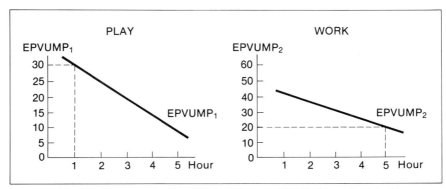

FIGURE E2–3A   Values of EPVUMP for Play and Work Given Initial Allocation of Time

Being a dedicated soul, you tentatively allocate five hours to work and one hour to play (see Figure E2–3A). For that allocation you have Table E2–3A.

Table E2–3A

	EPVUMP For Last Hour Allocated	Total Utility by Activity	
Play	30	1st @ 30	= 30
Work	20	1st @ 40 + 2nd @ 35 + 3rd @ 30 + 4th @ 25 + 5th @ 20	= 150
		Overall total utility	= 180

Is this an optimal allocation (i.e., would it maximize utility)? According to our decision rule it isn't, because currently:

$$EPVUMP_1 = 30$$
$$EPVUMP_2 = 20$$
$$\text{So } EPVUMP_1 \neq EPVUMP_2$$

Suppose you reallocated one hour from work to play. Graphically, you would have the case shown in Figure E2–3B.

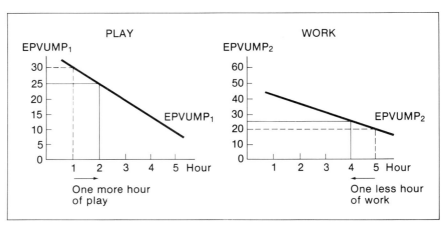

FIGURE E2–3B   Values of EPVUMP After Reallocation of Time

What did you lose by that reallocation? You lost the EPVUMP of the fifth hour of work—in other words, you lost 20 utils. What did you gain? You gained the EPVUMP of the second hour of play—in other words, you gained 25 utils. Was this reallocation a good idea? Yes. You gained 25 utils and lost 20 utils, so you had a net gain of 5 utils. Now you have Table E2–3B.

TABLE E2–3B

	EPVUMP For Last Hour Allocated	Total Utility by Activity
Play	25	1st @ 30 + 2nd @ 25 = 55
Work	25	1st @ 40 + 2nd @ 35 + 3rd @ 30 + 4th @ 25 = 130
		Overall total utility = 185

Is this an optimal allocation? According to our decision rule, it is, because currently:

$$EPVUMP_1 = EPVUMP_2 = 25$$

Suppose you doubted the rule and tried to gain even more utility by reallocating yet another hour from work to play. If you did this, would you be better off? You would lose the EPVUMP of the fourth hour of work, 25 utils, and you would gain the EPVUMP of the third hour of play, 20 utils. Thus you would suffer a net loss of 5 utils. Your overall total utility would fall to 180. We see, then, that our decision rule is the one you must follow in order to maximize your utility.

A simple example of the time allocation problem will put the concept into a personal context. Consider the following situation:

You have two exams tomorrow and you have seven hours to "spend" studying. Your preferences are such that for both exams every point you earn (produce) is worth 1 util to you (i.e., your marginal utility per point is constant at 1). As you plan your strategy for studying, you determine that your utility marginal product schedules —in other words the number of points you gain from each successive hour of study for the two exams—are shown in Table E2–3C.

TABLE E2–3C

	Exam #1								Exam #2							
Hour	#0	#1	#2	#3	#4	#5	#6	#7	#0	#1	#2	#3	#4	#5	#6	#7
UMP	0	45	25	14	10	5	1	−2	0	55	25	10	6	1	0	−3

Being rational, you plan to maximize your utility, and since the only other option available is doing your laundry, you plan on spending all seven available hours studying. How will you allocate your time? (Write down your answer before you read further.)

Given the UMP schedules shown in Table E2–3C, you find that there are several possible ways to follow our decision rule, setting $UMP_1 = UMP_2$.

$$UMP_1 = UMP_2 = 25 \qquad \text{(2 hours on both exams)}$$
$$\text{or } UMP_1 = UMP_2 = 10 \qquad \text{(4 hours on Exam \#1 and 3 hours on Exam \#2)}$$
$$\text{or } UMP_1 = UMP_2 = 1 \qquad \text{(6 hours on Exam \#1 and 5 hours on Exam \#2)}$$

You immediately recognize that the last case is not an option because it requires more time (11 hours) than you have (7 hours). It is also clear that the first case is not desirable because it uses only four of your seven available hours. Since there are no other options for time allocation that offer any utility at all, you may as well use all seven available hours to generate the utility that studying can bring. So being the dedicated soul that you are, you choose the second option, feeling confident that doing so will get you a 94 on Exam #1 and a 90 on Exam #2. Not a bad product for a night's work.

Then you go to dinner. At dinner you find yourself sitting next to a person you have been dying to meet. The conversation goes well; s/he is actually worth meeting. Now the trick is to set up another rendez-vous. S/He suggests that you go together to a movie on campus *that night*. Suddenly all prior plans must be reconsidered in light of this new opportunity. Your structure of incentives has been altered. Will your planned behavior change?

Later, as you're nodding off to sleep, you reflect on your evening. "Oh well, so I get a 70 (on Exam #1) and an 80 (on Exam #2), the rendezvous was worth it."

How many hours did you study for each exam and how many hours did you "spend" with your newfound friend? Can you make up a table representing the UMP you derived from each successive hour with your friend that is consistent with your actual behavior?

Applications of This Analysis to Public Policy Issues

Consider some other examples of the relationship between the set of opportunities (structure of incentives) one faces and the behavior one chooses that relate to social issues.

Application #1: Crime

There are people who are not in college or in a decent job. Rather, they have chosen to make a living through crime. Why have they chosen differently than you? What does their choice tell us about the structure of incentives they face whan they choose burglary and/or prostitution instead of college?

Our analysis offers one possible answer. If an individual sees many of the legitimate opportunities as being closed to him or her, then that person is much more likely to choose an illegitimate of illegal option.

What is the policy implication of this analysis with respect to crime?

Application #2: Discrimination

Clearly discrimination affects the choices of those who are being discriminated against. It reduces the set of opportunities available to them and thus limits their choices. Discrimination is a violation of our fair race assumption and, as we will see, such distortions reduce the social welfare.

For the moment, however, let's focus on a more subtle effect of discrimination that is relevant to our current discussion of the relationship between time allocation and the structure of incentives people face. Specifically, let us apply our current analysis in order to understand how the expectation of future discrimination could affect current choices.

Suppose you and a dear friend of yours are registering for your junior year of college. You have both done extremely well in essentially the same course work, and now you are discussing your respective choice of major. Both of you are seriously considering majoring in biology and declaring yourselves to be pre-meds. Your friend has no doubt that is the path he will take. You, on the other hand, have doubts because you face a very different opportunity set and thus a different structure of incentives. The year is 1950 and you are a woman. You are well aware that medical schools do not accept many women. They justify this by arguing that the training is wasted on women because they do not use the training. They get married, stay home, and have kids. They also point out that very few women apply to medical school, so the small number of women in medical schools primarily reflects women's choice rather than medical schools' policy.

Apply our analysis of the allocation of time to:

1. The quandary you face.
2. The logic of the medical schools' justification for accepting only a small number of women.

Is there a public policy issue involved here?

E2–4: Time Preferences, Risk, Inflation, and Interest

In the old Popeye cartoons Wimpy is constantly proposing that "I will gladly pay you Tuesday for a hamburger today." To an economist this is a case that embodies the issues of time preferences, risk, and interest. Suppose you are the person to whom Wimpy is making the proposal. We assume that you and Wimpy both have a time preference for current consumption—in other words, you both discount the future. Wimpy wants you to forego your current consumption of the hamburger until Tuesday so that he can have it now. In order to make such a deal worthwhile for you, he must compensate you for your sacrifice of your time preference in consumption. He must offer to repay you an amount on Tuesday that has a present value equal to one hamburger today. He must, therefore, compensate you by at least your discount rate.

There is, however, another element in this proposed exchange that must be considered. That is the risk that Wimpy will not pay up on Tuesday. He may die, he may be dishonest, he may have honest intentions and simply fail to get the necessary funds. So in proposing this deal, he is not only requesting that you forgo current consumption, he is also asking you to accept a risk. In order to make such a deal worthwhile for you, he must compensate you for accepting that risk.

The combination of these compensations for foregoing time preference in consumption and accepting risk is what economists call *interest*. The amount of interest paid per unit of time is the interest rate. Interest rates are a two way street. The borrower and the lender must both find a rate acceptable in order for the exchange to actually occur. There are lots of interest rates in society because risks vary and individuals' discount rates vary.

This compensation for foregoing time preference and accepting risk is not the only consideration when borrowers and lenders exchange money. Because the exchange has a time dimension, they must also allow for the fact that money itself may change value. If all prices rise (inflation), then a given amount of money buys less. In other words, the money has lost value.

If, owing to a combination of time preference and risk, I discount the future at 10 percent per year, then I would be willing to loan you $100 today in return for the promise of $110 in 365 days. The interest rate I am charging you is 10 percent. Let us assume the loan is made and a year later you pay me the $110, but during the year the price of everything has risen 10 percent. Have I been compensated for my sacrifice of time preferences and acceptance of risk? No. What I received at the end of the year was no more buying power than I gave up at the beginning of the year. If I had anticipated the inflation, I would have charged you 20 percent interest, 10 percent to cover inflation plus 10 percent to compensate my time sacrifice and acceptance of risk. In economics we refer to the latter 10 percent charge for compensation as the *real rate of interest*, because that is the amount one is really being compensated. Once the inflation adjustment is added on, we call the sum the *nominal rate of interest* (here 20 percent), because that is the amount actually named in the contract.

If you understand this distinction, you will be able to read graphs like the following that appeared in *The New York Times* on September 14, 1986.

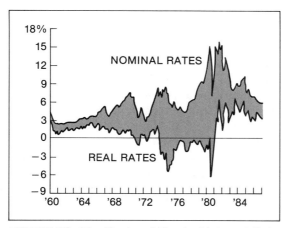

FIGURE E2–4A   Real and Nominal Interest Rates   Nominal interest rate is the monthly average rate on three-month Treasury bills; real interest rate subtracts from that rate the monthly year-to-year change in consumer prices, both in percent.

Source: _The New York Times_, 14 Sept. 1986.

E2–5:   Risk and Insurance

We all face risks—similar risks. Any of us could get cancer, be in a traffic accident, become the victim of a crime. For any population of people we can, on the basis of experience, make a prediction of the probability that a person in that population will experience one of these tragedies. What we can't know, however, is which person(s) it will be.

There are two ways that you as a member of the population can choose to cope with these risks. One is to accept the risk individually. Following this strategy, you would make efforts to reduce your personal risk by taking precaution (e.g., getting regular medical checkups, driving defensively, and buying dead bolt locks), while at the same time accepting full responsibility if by chance you are the one who is struck by disaster. If disaster does strike, it might cost you your health or your life. It would almost certainly cost you your quality of life in one significant respect: it would cost you your wealth. Thus the bet you make if you accept the risk alone is that you will be among the lucky ones. The consequence of losing the bet is catastrophe. Statistics can tell you the odds on the bet, but it is still a bet—you can lose big.

An alternative approach to dealing with risks is to share them. While statistics do not give a definitive answer as to whether you will personally be struck by disaster, they do—if properly collected—give a good prediction of what portion of the population will suffer such a fate. Thus as a population we can plan on the basis of predictable outcome. If all members of the population agree to absorb the consequences of the risk regardless of whom the disaster actually strikes, then the risk has been shared or "pooled." In such a scheme you would know approximately the financial cost of the risk to you. Should disaster strike, you have committed yourself to paying that specific share of the cost. But if you are struck by disaster, you will bear *only* that share, and everyone else in the pool will absorb the rest of the cost. Clearly there is no way to share the pain of disease or injury, but pooling the risk can ensure that the money will be there to do whatever you need to do to ameliorate your situation.

Insurance is a formal method for pooling risk. Your premium is your contribution to the pool, and payments to those who encounter disaster are drawn from the pool. Insurance companies make their money by charging fees for maintaining and managing the pool and by earning interest on loans they make from the pool. There are, however, several problems with insurance schemes.

If the pooling of risk through insurance makes you feel less vulnerable to the consequences of your actions than you would feel if you accepted the risk alone, then you might be less careful than otherwise. For instance, you are likely to be much more careful with your car if it isn't insured. This tendency to accept greater risk because the consequences are pooled is called *moral hazard*. One way insurance companies attempt to forestall this kind of behavior is to place deductibles on policies so that the first dollars spent in response to a claim come from the pocket of the policyholder.

Another problem is that when people know more about their individual risk than general population statistics imply, they can take advantage of the system. For instance, if you know that you have heart disease and yet you pay the same health insurance premium as everyone else, then you are being subsidized by the other people in the pool. With this kind of subsidy you have the incentive to buy more health insurance. Thus this assymetry of information (you know more about your risk than the company does) leads to what is called *adverse selection*. This adverse selection leads to higher costs for all policyholders. As a result, those who are low-risk members of the population are forced either to pay premiums that are out of proportion to their risk or to give up the policy and bear the risk alone.

Finally, there is a problem of information assymetry that works to the seller's advantage. The seller, the insurance company, collects and analyzes all the data on risks. If the company is able to determine that various subpopulations have different risks, it can offer policies to those with low risks and refuse to give policies to those who have high risks, leaving the latter group uncovered. This is called _skimming_. The company skims off the cream of the clients and leaves the rest behind.

Is there a public policy issue here? Does society have any responsibility to cover the risk of its high risk members (e.g., the elderly)?

The following newspaper article from _The New York Times_ (September 18, 1986) reflects the relationship between risk and insurance.

Quake Insurers Get More Cautious

By PAULINE YOSHIHASHI

LOS ANGELES, Oct. 17— Many business executives and homeowners here can no longer obtain or afford insurance policies to fully protect their property from what Angelenos call "the big one," the powerful earthquake that seismologists say will probably strike the region sometime in the next few decades.

The increasing likelihood of a huge seismic event here has added to a mood of cautious underwriting in an insurance industry that is trying to cope with rising claims of all types. That has caused insurers to rapidly raise rates for earthquake insurance, even while sharply limiting the amount of coverage they offer. That means many property owners are relying on construction engineering and on luck to see them through any disastrous shifting underground.

Full Coverage Is Rare

Few of the city's skyscrapers, from City Hall to the glistening new 41-story Citicorp Plaza, are fully covered by comprehensive earthquake insurance. Although a recently passed state law requires insurers to offer earthquake insurance with homeowner's policies, only about 11 percent of the state's homeowners have bought the increasingly expensive coverage.

"At one time, earthquake insurance was almost seen as a purchase benefit—if you bought a business package for liability, you could add earthquake coverage for very little," said John McCann, regional vice president of the Insurance Information Institute, a national trade group. "Now, many of those buildings are getting half of their previous coverage at substantially higher premiums, if at all."

Mr. McCann said that two or three years ago each $100 worth of coverage cost less than 10 cents, but it now costs as much as $1 for a typical high rise building.

Mr. McCann also said that earthquake policies do not cover the casualty, life, auto, fire or workers' compensation losses that might be sustained in an earthquake.

The Transamerica Example

The Transamerica Corporation, which owns buildings that are prominent features of the Los Angeles and San Francisco skylines, is a typical case. "Our coverage was reduced by about half in the past year, to $53 million," said William McClave, a company spokesman. "That's still substantial coverage, but because of the condition of the insurance industry it can be very expensive or simply impossible to get."

Mr. McClave said that the 48-story pyramid-shaped San Francisco building was designed to withstand a sizable quake. He declined to disclose what dollar value the company puts on it or the 28-story tower in Los Angeles.

Other property owners, especially those with older buildings, have not fared as well in the scramble for coverage.

For example, the City of Los Angeles now carries earthquake coverage on only one of its more than 900 buildings. The Los Angeles County government, which owns $1.3

billion in property, has two general insurance programs, each with sublimits of $50 million for earthquake damage.

"We only insure a property if it's required by bond funding," said Henry S. Bachrach, the county's chief of risk management. "We've got less than half the commercial coverage on the same facilities for double the premiums."

In the private sector, the Broadway Plaza, which contains a Hyatt Regency hotel, a 33-story office building and an underground shopping mall, may be forced by soaring premiums to drop its coverage when the policy is up for renewal later this year, said Richard W. Klatte, a Plaza official.

A flurry of small California earthquakes in recent months has focused attention on the insurance situation, as did the 5.4 magnitude quake in El Salvador last week. That quake was hundreds of times weaker than the 8.25 magnitude quake that is assumed by actuaries and public planners here in their disaster planning.

The passage of time is also seen as adding to the risk, since the experts contend that each year that goes by without a major quake increases the likelihood of one occurring.

Earthquakes present special problems in assessing commercial liability. Because quakes are unpredictable and cause heavy losses in a highly concentrated area, insurance experts say that underwriters limit the amount of their exposure in any particular region.

Recent statistics seem to confirm the wisdom of that strategy. According to an annual report by the state's Department of Insurance, an earthquake measuring 8.25 in the Los Angeles area, which would be similar to the San-Francisco earthquake of 1906, would cause at least $5.9 billion in insured property loss. That does not include related claims from life, health and automobile policies. A similar quake in San Francisco would cost insurers at least $4.3 billion in property damage, the report said.

"The underlying problem with commercial earthquake coverage is that most of the losses would be absorbed by the reinsurance market," said Richard J. Roth Jr., the state's assistant insurance commissioner. Reinsurance companies assume risks from primary insurers for a percentage of the premiums, particularly on large or high-risk policies.

The reinsurance industry, which is dominated by foreign-based carriers, has been battered by several problems, including the drop in interest rates, which has cut the return in investment portfolios. "The reinsurers were hit by a lot of losses, and they were scared into covering more predictable things like auto and fire," Mr. Roth said. "Our research shows that reinsurers would end up assuming 70 percent of the loss in the event of a major earthquake here."

To complicate matters, state actuaries say that the law mandating that residential policies be offered has reduced the coverage available to commercial customers. "An insurance company will only write so much earthquake coverage in a given area, whether it's commercial or residential," Mr. Roth said. "Once it reaches the limit, that's it."

Ted E. Davidson, vice president of the Robert E. Driver Company insurance agency and a specialist in commercial earthquake insurance, said that most of his clients could not find as much coverage as they would like, regardless of price. "I advise people to get what coverage they can, but I also tell them to put their money for a new building into earthquake design," Mr. Davidson said.

Industry executives say it is unclear if the insurance situation will improve in the next year or two. "We hope to see an upswing in the reinsurance market in the next few years," said James Shamberger, senior vice president of the Reinsurance Association of America. "But the fact that so much of the probable maximum loss is borne by the reinsurers is sobering, and we're not sure how quickly or to what extent earthquake insurance will return."

Source: *The New York Times*, 18 Sept. 1986

E2–6: Comparative Advantage

In the body of the text it was demonstrated that trade is beneficial if each individual specializes in the activity at which she is better. In that case, we say that each participant has an *absolute advantage* (is absolutely better) in one activity. David Ricardo demonstrated in his *Principles of Political Economy and Taxation* (published in 1817) that specialization and exchange of surpluses can be mutually beneficial to two parties even if one of them is absolutely better at doing all activities. In this case, the benefit derives from each party specializing in what is referred to as her *respective comparative advantage*. In order to understand the gains from specialization with comparative advantage, consider the following example in a simplified two-participant/two-good world.

Suppose you have an absolute advantage over me in the production of both wheat and cloth, as represented by Table E2–6A, which shows production per hour of labor.

TABLE E2–6A

	Wheat/Hour (bushels)	Cloth/Hour (yards)
Me	4	1
You	12	2

Since any hour spent on one activity is one less hour that can be spent on the other activity, we see that your opportunity cost of producing 2 yards of cloth is 12 bushels of wheat. In other words, each yard of cloth "costs" 6 bushels of wheat. For me, however, the opportunity cost of producing 1 yard of cloth is 4 bushels of wheat; each yard "costs" 4 bushels. Thus we see that while you are absolutely more efficient at producing both products, the opportunity cost of producing cloth is greater for you than it is for me. In other words, it is relatively or comparatively cheaper for me to produce cloth than it is for you to do so.

In the language of economics we say that an individual (or country) has a *comparative advantage* when she can produce a good at a lower opportunity cost. In the example we just used, you have an absolute advantage in all production, but your comparative advantage lies in wheat production, while I have a comparative advantage in cloth production. As long as such comparative advantages exist, trade is beneficial to both of us.

E2–7: How Complex Is Our Society

In *The Wealth of Nations* Adam Smith extolls the virtue of the division of labor and exchange of surpluses as follows:

It is the great multiplication of the production of all the different arts, in consequence of the division of labour, which occasions, in a well-governed society, that universal opulence which extends itself to the lowest ranks of the people. Every workman has a great quantity of his own work to dispose of beyond what he himself has occasion for; and every other workman being exactly in the same situation, he is enabled to exchange a great quantity of his own goods for a great quantity, or, what comes to the same thing, for the price of a great quantity of theirs. He supplies them abundantly with what they have occasion for, and they accommodate him as amply with what he has occasion for, and a general plenty diffuses itself through all the different ranks of the society.

He then goes on to demonstrate how incredibly complex the division of labor and exchange of surpluses can become with a simple example:

Observe the accommodation of the most common artificer or day-labourer in a civilized and thriving country, and you will perceive that the number of people of whose industry a part, though but a small part, has been employed in procuring him this accommodation, exceeds all computation. The wollen coat, for example, which covers the day-labourer, as coarse and rough as it may appear, is the produce of the joint labour of a great multitude of workmen. The shepherd, the sorter of the wool, the wool-comber or carder, the dyer, the scribbler, the spinner, the weaver, the fuller, the dresser, with many others, must all join their different arts in order to complete even this homely production. How many merchants and carriers, besides, must have been employed in transporting the materials from some of those workmen to others who often live in a very distant part of the country! How much commerce and navigation in particular, how many ship-builders, sailors, sailmakers, rope-makers, must have been employed in order to bring together the different drugs made use of by the dyer, which often come from the remotest corners of the world! What a variety of labour too is necessary in order to produce the tools of the meanest of those workmen! To say nothing of such complicated machines as the ship of the sailor, the mill of the fuller, or even the loom of the weaver, let us consider only what a variety of labour is requisite in order to form the very simple machine, the shears with which the shepherd clips the wool. The miner, the builder of the furnace for smelting the ore, the feller of the timber, the burner of the charcoal to be made use of in the smelting-house, the brick-maker, the brick-layer, the workmen who attend the furnace, the mill-wright, the forger, the smith, must all of them join their different arts in order to produce them.

This was written in 1776—a much simpler era. Consider the complexity of our own time. Pick a garment that you have on and do as Smith did—imagine all the hands that went into producing it. Your list will probably only scratch the surface, but the exercise should give you a feeling for the complexity of our world.

E3–1: Functional Form and Two Dimensional Analysis

When the value of one variable is dependent on the values of several other variables, this relationship can be represented in a mathematical shorthand called a *functional form*. For instance, your grade in this course is dependent on the quality of your effort, your background, your teacher's effort, your teacher's background, the text, the manual, your health, your support group, and a number of other variables. This relationship can be represented in functional form as follows:

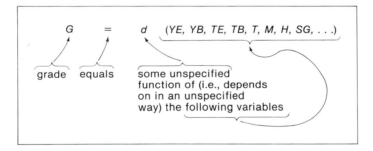

where *YE* is your effort
YB is your background
TE is your teacher's effort
TB is your teacher's background
T is the text
M is the maual
H is your health
SG is your support group
and the three points (. . .) stand for all those other (unidentified) variables that will affect your grade.

In this functional form, *G* is the dependent variable and *YE, YB, TE, TB, T, M, H, SG, . . .* are independent variables. Each of these independent variables may, in turn, be dependent variables in other functional forms.

For instance:

$$H = f(GN, N, E, EN, . . .)$$

represents the fact that health is a function of genetics, nourishment, exercise, environment, and other variables.

Functional forms are generally written without the three points. For instance, we can write:

$$H = f(GN, N, E, EV)$$

Leaving off the three points is an implicit assertion that all other variables are either constant or, if they change, their impact on the dependent variable is insignificant. Thus, as it is represented here, health (H), is primarily determined by genetics (GN), nourishment (N), exercise (E), and environment (EV). Whether or not this is a valid assertion is an emperical question (i.e., something we must resolve by data analysis).

If we want to explicitly assert that a particular independent variable is assumed constant (i.e., we are abstracting from changes in that variable), we can write the functional form as:

$$H = f(N, E, EV \mid GN)$$

The vertical line means "holding *constant* everything beyond this point." If we were examining the variables that determine the health status of genetically identical twins, we could write the functional form in the manner just shown.

So far we have looked at unspecified functional forms. In these functions the exact relationship between the dependent and the independent variables is not specified. In its specified form, a function not only says there is a relationship, it details the relationship.

For instance, the unspecified functional form representing the variables that determine the height of a plant may be written:

$$HT = g(GN, H_2O, SUN, FERT, BUG)$$

where the height is determined by genetics, water, sunlight, fertility of the soil, and the bugs that feed on it. (Notice that the symbol for the function [here g] is just a symbol and although we generally use letters, any kind of symbol will do.)

This functional relationship might be specified as:

$$H = GN^3 + 2\,H_2O^2 + SUN^2 + 6\,FERT - BUG^2$$

In this specified form, if we can plug in quantities for the independent variables, we can exactly determine the value of the dependent variable. Notice also that variables can differ in the size and direction (positive or negative) of their impact on the dependent variable.

In order to specify a functional form, the economist tries to determine which variables are important and the direction and size of the effect these variables have on the dependent variable. To do so is to construct a model. Since theory construction and model building are very difficult, rather than specifying the relationship exactly, economists must generally be satisfied with specifying whether the effect of each independent variable is positive or negative and its relative significance.

For instance, economists generally assert that individual demand functions can be written as follows:

$$Q_1 = d(P_1, P_c, P_s, I, T)$$

This says that the quantity of a commodity one demands (Q_1)— for example, beer — is a function of the price of beer (P_1), the price of complementary goods (P_C), such as peanuts or rock concerts, the price of substitute goods (P_S) such as wine, the level of income (I), and taste (T).

For reasons that should become clear as the course unfolds, the signs of P_1 and P_c are negative (i.e., as P_1 or P_c falls, Q_1 rises), the sign of P_s is positive (i.e., as P_s falls, Q_1 falls), and the sign of I is generally positive but may be negative (for goods that are defined as "inferior").

In advanced courses and in research economists apply multivariate analysis. Using calculus for theoretical study and econometrics for empirical study, this kind of analysis examines systems in which there are many functions and in which lots of variables are changing at the same time. This multivariate analysis is called "n-dimensional" because a large number of variables (n stands for that large number) are allowed to vary.

In our introductory course we simplify the analysis. We do what is called two-dimensional analysis. To accomplish this we work with functions in which only one independent variable is allowed to vary at a time. Thus, while we understand that the demand function can be written as:

$$Q_1 = d(P_1, P_c, P_s, I, T)$$

we work with demand relationships such as:

$$Q_1 = d(P_1 \mid P_c, P_s, I, T)$$

Here we are looking at the relationship between quantity demanded, Q_1, and own price, P_1, holding all else constant. We call this the *demand relationship* between a good or service and its own price.

Focusing on the demand relationship between P_1 and Q_1 has one major advantage that makes it desirable. It allows us to draw two-dimensional pictures of the realtionship (*n*-dimensional pictures are rather challenging!) so we can *see* what is going on without using calculus.

For instance, if Q_1 and P_1 are inversely related (and we will see that they are), we can draw a graph of this relationship as in Figure E3–1A.

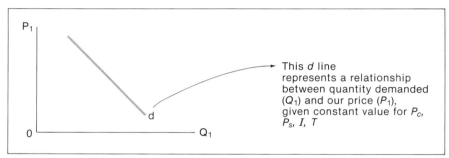

FIGURE E3–1A   The Demand Relationship

Notice that the line drawn represents how Q_1 will change as P_1 changes, holding all else constant.

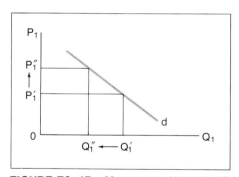

FIGURE E3–1B   Movement Along the Demand Curve

Thus, if P_1 changes from P_1' to P_1'', we see that, *all else constant*, Q_1 changes from Q_1' to Q_1''. In other words, as P_1 changes, we move along the *d* line. The *d* line does not move so long as P_c, P_s, I, and T are constant. (See Figure E3–1B.)

If, however, there is a change in any of the "given" variables (P_c, P_s, I, or T), then the position of the entire relationship line will shift left or right, depending on how the given variable affects the relationship. (See Figure E3-1C.)

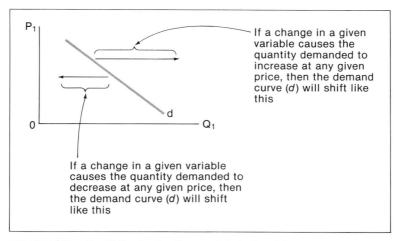

FIGURE E3-1C   Shifts in the Demand Relationship

In conclusion, this functional form notation is simply a shorthand method for expressing relationships that could be spelled out in prose. It is useful if we all agree on and understand the same shorthand because it allows us to represent relationships we want to study in a quick and efficient manner. Further, we have seen how the functional form relates to the two-dimensional graphs we will be using in this course. Behind every graph is a functional form. If you keep this in mind, you will have a shorthand method of writing out what the graph represents pictorially.

E3-2:   Indifference Curve and Budget Line Analysis: Deriving the Utility Maximization Decision Rule for Income Expenditure Graphically (Assuming a two-good world so that we can work in two-dimensions)

In order to do this we need to assemble some tools.

First we introduce the *indifference curve*. The indifference curve is a graphical representation of all combinations of two goods (e.g., X_1 and X_2) that give the same level of utility (holding all else constant) to a given consumer. Graphically, it appears as in Figure E3-2A.

If we assume that more is better, then we have an array of indifference curves representing higher levels of utility as they move further from the origin. This is called *an indifference map* and graphically it would appear as in Figure E3-2B.

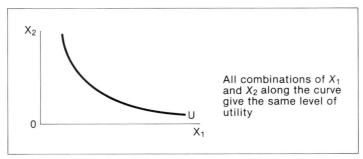

FIGURE E3–2A   An Indifference Curve

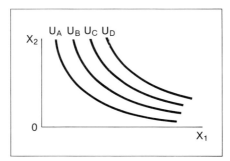

FIGURE E3–2B   An Indifference Map   Note that the indifference map tells us only that $U_D > U_C > U_B > U_A$. It does not tell us the absolute difference in utility levels. We use absolute (cardinal) measures of utility as a heuristic device (e.g., U = 15 utils), but in fact utility can only be measured ordinally where: $U_D > U_C > U_B > U_A$. This is an ordinal ranking. There are no numbers; it just shows us that U_D is most preferred and U_A is least preferred.

(*NOTE:* Given our assumptions, indifference curves can never cross. Can you explain why?)

We draw the indifference curve sloping down (negative slope) because, assuming both goods are desirable, we would only be willing to give up one if we were offered more of the other.

In order to see why indifference curves are drawn bowed to the origin, we need to derive the slope of an indifference curve. To do so, consider Figure E3–2C. Recall that as we consume more of a good, its marginal utility falls, and as we consume less of a good its marginal utility rises.

Now we know that the amount of utility we lose by giving up ΔX_2 is the units of X_2 we lost times their marginal utility (MU_2), and the amount of utility we gain by getting ΔX_1 is the units of X_1 we gain times their marginal utility (MU_1).

Since the net effect of giving up ΔX_2 and gaining ΔX_1 is zero along a given indifference curve, we can write that:

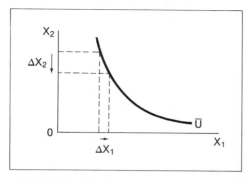

FIGURE E3–2C   Movement Along an Indifference Curve   As we give up a quantity of X_2 equal to ΔX_2 (here Δ stands for "change in"), it takes a quantity of X_1 equal to ΔX_1 to keep us at the same level of utility, $\bar{U}$.

$$\underbrace{\Delta X_1 \cdot MU_1}_{\text{gain}} - \underbrace{\Delta X_2 \cdot MU_2}_{\text{loss}} = \emptyset$$

Manipulating this equation, we get:

$$\Delta X_1 \cdot MU_1 = -\Delta X_2 \cdot MU_2$$

$$\frac{\Delta X_2}{\Delta X_1} = -\frac{MU_1}{MU_2}$$

where $\dfrac{\Delta X_2}{\Delta X_1}$ is the rise over the run, or the slope of the indifference curve. Thus

$$\text{the slope of the indifference curve} = \frac{MU_1}{MU_2}$$

Now we can understand the shape of the indifference curve. Consider Figure E3–2D.

With indifference curves we can represent our preferences graphically, However, in order to derive the utility maximization rule for income expenditure, we also need to represent our income constraint on our graph. For this we use the *budget line*. The budget line is a graphical representation of all the combinations of two goods (e.g., X_1 and X_2) that a consumer can afford given his budget (income $= I$) and the prices of the goods (P_1 and P_2), assuming all income is spent. Graphically, it appears as in Figure E3–2E.

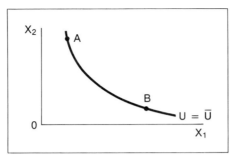

FIGURE E3-2D Slopes at Two Points Along a Given Indifference Curve   For all goods MU falls as quantity consumed increases. At point A, where quantity of X_1 is small and quantity of X_2 is large, we should have a large negative slope $\left(-\frac{MU_1}{MU_2}\right)$, and so it is. At point B, where quantity of X_1 is large and quantity of X_2 is small, we should have a small negative slope $\left(-\frac{MU_1}{MU_2}\right)$, and so it is.

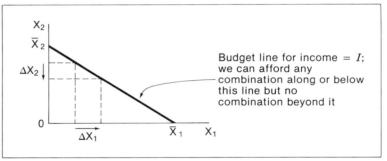

FIGURE E3-2E A Budget Line   Budget line for income $= I$, we can afford any combination along or below this line but no combination beyond it.

The budget line is downward sloping because if we buy more X_1, we can afford less X_2.

If we buy only X_2, then we can afford quantity $(\overline{X}_2)$ of it:

$$\overline{X}_2 = \frac{I}{P_2}$$

and if we buy only X_1, we can afford quantity $(\overline{X}_1)$ of it:

$$\overline{X}_1 = \frac{I}{P_1}$$

If we give up ΔX_2 of good 2, we can afford ΔX_1 more of good 1 because along a budget line:

(minus for expenditure)

$$\underbrace{+P_2\Delta X_2}_{\text{what we save}} = \underbrace{-P_1\Delta X_1}_{\text{what we can spend}}$$

Manipulating this equation we get:

$$\frac{\Delta X_2}{\Delta X_1} = -\frac{P_1}{P_2}$$

So here we see that the slope of the budget line is $-\frac{P1}{P2}$.

Now we have the tools necessary to derive our utility maximization rule. The indifference curves represent our preferences. Its slope represents our personal rate of trade-off between the two goods. The budget line represents our income or budget constraint. The slope of the budget line represents the market rate of trade-off between the two goods.

Consider Figure E3–2F.

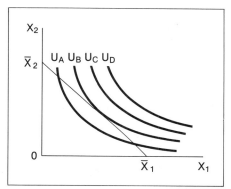

FIGURE E3–2F   Combining Indifference Curve and the Budget Line   Given our income (budget constraint), what combination of X_1 and X_2 would we choose to consume in order to maximize our utility?

Can we achieve utility levels U_C or U_D? No, all combinations of X_1 and X_2 that give this much utility are beyond our means. Can we achieve utility level U_A? Yes, but we can do better. What is the highest level of utility we can achieve given our budget constraint? We can reach the one just tangent to our budget line—in this case U_B. So what combination of X_1 and X_2 would we choose?

As noted above, the highest indifference curve we can reach is the one just tangent to the budget line. See Figure E3–2G. At the point of

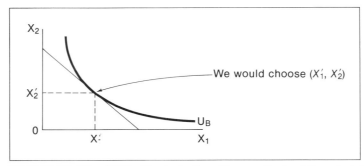

FIGURE E3–2G   Utility Maximization Given a Budget Constraint

tangency the indifference curve and the budget line have the same slope, so as we maximize our utility, we are setting:

Slope of the budget line = Slope of the indifference curve

OR

$$-\frac{P_1}{P_2} = -\frac{MU_1}{MU_2}$$

but this can be rearranged as:

$$\frac{MU_1}{P_1} = \frac{MU_2}{P_2}$$

which is exactly the utility maximization rule we derived intuitively in the text.

1. Changes in Relative Prices Are Reflected in a Shift of the Budget Line.

Suppose we have the initial condition shown in Figure E3–2H. and then the price of good 1 increases from P_1 to P_1'. Graphically, this would appear as a rotation of the budget line, as shown in Figure E3–2I.
We can explain this rotation two ways:

1. We can examine the intercepts in Figure E3–2I. The X_2 intercept remains the same because I and P_2 are constant. The X_1 intercept moves in because P_1 increases while I is constant.

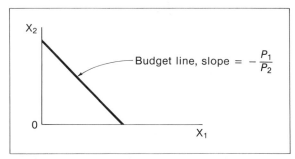

FIGURE E3–2H   Initial Budget Line

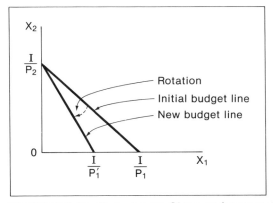

FIGURE E3–2I   Budget Line Given an Increase in P_1

2. We can examine the slope. If P_1 rises, then clearly $-\dfrac{P_1}{P_2}$ will become a steeper negative slope.

When relative prices change this way, the utility-maximizing combination of X_1 and X_2 (consumption bundle) will also change. The nature of this change depends on the degree of the relative price change and on the preferences as embodied in the indifference curves. For example, if P_2 remains constant and P_1 falls (the opposite of the earlier case), we could have the case represented in Figure E3–2J.
This figure shows that the result is an increase in the consumption of both X_1 and X_2. Given exactly the same change but different preferences, the outcome would have been as shown in Figure E3–2K

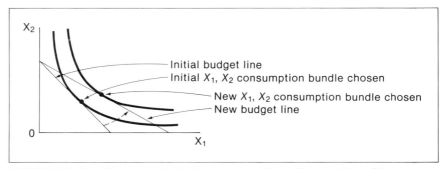

FIGURE E3-2J   Change in Optimization Condition Given a Price Change

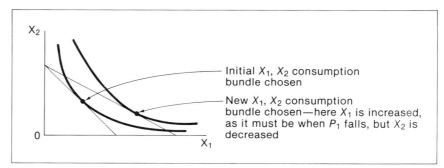

Figure E3-2K   Structure of Preferences Affects Consequences of Price Change

The representation of a change in P_2 follows the same logic. In that case, the budget line rotates with a constant X_1 axis intercept.

This analysis can be used to derive the demand curve. Assuming I, P_2, and T (tastes or the shape of the indifference curve) are constant, as P_1 rises, we can trace the result on the indifference map and then derive the demand curve. See Figure E3–2L.

2. Changes in the Structures of Preferences are Reflected by Changes in the Shape of the Indifference Map.

A. Standard Case

Our standard case looks as shown in Figure E3–2M.

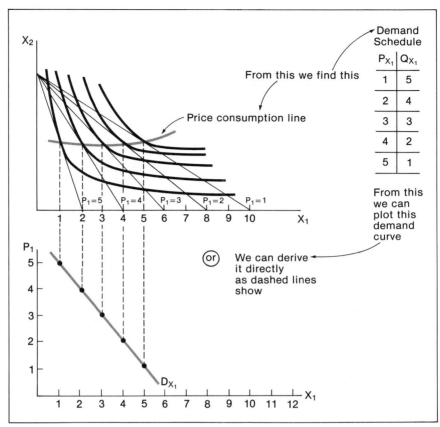

Figure E3-2L   Derivation of Demand Curve

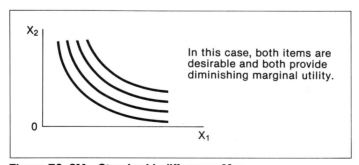

Figure E3-2M   Standard Indifference Map

If we feel much more strongly about X_1 than X_2 so that MU_1 falls very slowly while MU_2 falls very rapidly, then the indifference curve would be shaped as shown in Figure E3-2N.

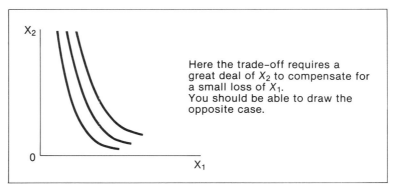

Figure E3–2N   Representing a Strong Preference for X_1

But if our preferences changed from stronger feelings for X_1 to stronger feelings for X_2 then, *ceteris paribus*, our consumption bundle would change as in Figure E3–2O.

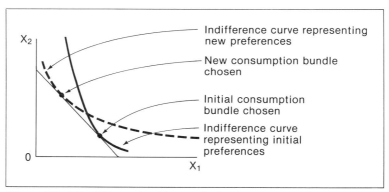

Figure E3–2O   Effect of a Change in Preferences on Consumption, *Ceteris Paribus*

B. Special Cases of Indifference Maps

1. Items desired in fixed proportions (e.g., left and right shoes) have an indifference map that looks like Figure E3–2P. (Assuming free disposal of extras.)

2. Figure E3–2Q represents preferences when one item is a "good" and one is a "bad."

3. Figure E3–2R represents preferences when two goods are perfect substitutes.

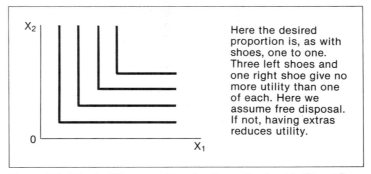

Figure E3–2P Indifference Map for Items Desired in Fixed Proportions

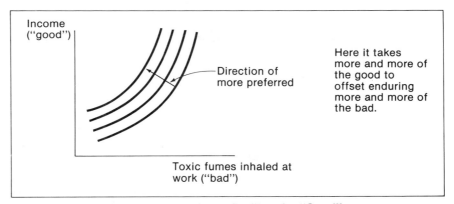

Figure E3–2Q Indifference Map for a "Bad" and a "Good"

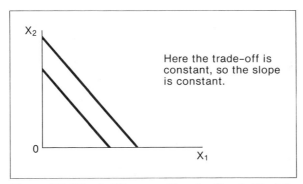

Figure E3–2R Indifference Map for Goods That Are Perfect Substitutes

We've seen that the demand curve can be derived from the indifference curve/budget line analysis. You should now be able to demonstrate graphically how a change in preference will affect demand.

E3–3: More on the Concept of Elasticity

Elasticity—General

In its functional form, we write demand as:

$$x_1 = d_1 \ (p_1 \,|\, p_2, \ldots , p_n, I, T)$$

and graphically we depict it as shown in Figure E3–3A.

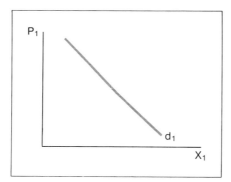

Figure E3–3A A Demand Curve

The dependent variable responds to any change in each kind of independent variable. The degree and directon of this responsiveness is called the *elasticity*.

We note three kinds of elasticity.

1. As p_1 changes, x_1 (quantity demanded) responds directly because the response is along the demand curve. The sensitivity of this response is measured by the *own price elasticity*.

2. As $p_2, \ldots , p_n$ (the price of any good or service other than x_1) changes, x_1 responds indirectly. The first response is in the entire structure of demand—the demand curve shifts (at any given price, quantity demanded changes). This, in turn, results in a change in the equilibrium quantity demanded. The direction of this response

is measured by the *cross-price elasticity*. This concept allows economists to distinguish complements and substitutes.

3. As *I* (income) changes, x_1 responds indirectly. The first response is in the entire structure of demand—the demand curve shifts. This, in turn, results in a change in the equilibrium quantity demanded. The direction and degree of this response are measured by the *income elasticity*. This concept allows economists to distinguish inferior, normal, and superior goods.

Elasticity—Own Price

Own price elasticity measures the responsiveness of the quantity demanded of a good to a change in its own price.

Own price elasticity is often represented by the symbol η.
Note: In what follows, the symbol Δ (delta) will stand for the phrase "change in."
For demand function:

$Q_1 = d\ (p_1 \mid p_2, p_3, \ldots, p_n, I, T)$
where Q_1 is the quantity of good 1 demanded
p_1 is the price of good 1
$p_2, p_3, \ldots, p_n$ are the prices of other goods
I is income
T is tastes

The own price elasticity equation is:

$$\eta = \left| \frac{\dfrac{\Delta Q_1}{Q_1}}{\dfrac{\Delta P_1}{P_1}} \right| = \left| \frac{\%\Delta Q_1}{\%\Delta P_1} \right|$$

Note: The vertical lines around the fractions are "absolute value" symbols. They simply eliminate any negative signs. For own price elasticity, we are primarily interested in the size of the effect. We generally assume the sign is negative.

For an example of own price elasticity, consider the following excerpt from a newspaper article.

The Pressure Keeps Building at Big Blue

Slowdown in Growth

Charles C. Oldenburg, general manager of computer services at the Chevron Corporation, was incredulous. It was the fall of 1984 and a group of I.B.M. customers had just been briefed about I.B.M.'s growth projections. The company had said it would grow 14 percent a year for many years; such growth rates would have made it a $100 billion company by the 1990's and a $200 billion company by the turn of the century. "I thought it was absurd," said Mr. Oldenburg. "The growth rates just had to moderate."

He was right. A survey of 500 I.B.M. users by the International Data Corporation showed that the main reason customers are not buying I.B.M. mainframes is that they simply do not need any new ones.

"In the 60's and 70's, we always needed more capacity than we could get," said Irwin J. Sitkin, vice president of corporate administration for the Aetna Life and Casualty Company. "Suddenly that's stopped." Indeed, big companies have been increasing computer capacity at a range of about 30 percent to 50 per-cent a year since the late 1970's, and no longer need so much. At Aetna, for example, Mr. Sitkin said, the newest mainframe computer, an I.B.M. 3090 "has more MIPs in one machine than we had in the whole shop in 1978." MIPs are millions of instructions per second, a common measure of computer power.

Moreover, for I.B.M. to keep growing, it must sell not only more computing power each year, but a lot more. As technology improves, computers become cheaper. The price per unit of computing power decreases by 20 percent or so each year, so I.B.M. must sell more than 20 percent more computing power each year just to keep revenues level.

So far, I.B.M. has been able to outrace the treadmill. Each price decline has spurred more than enough increases in demand to make revenues grow. But in the current downturn, demand does not appear to be as elastic as it had been earlier and price cuts have not produced the expected sales gains.

Many computer industry executives and customers think demand growth has stalled temporarily while ven-dors and users develop new uses for their machines.

At I.B.M., there are a number of new applications that could spur usage, but they are not quite ready yet. Networks are needed to link computers for electronic communications. Artificial intelligence, which would make computers easier to use and allow them to handle such things as drawing up insurance policies or offering financial advice, could lead to a new burst of computer use. I.B.M., which once shunned the field, is now getting involved in it. Image processing—moving images of documents around by computer—is another potential use. I.B.M. still has no product in this category, but customers say it is working on one. The company is also planning numerous enhancements to its mainframes.

But most of these improvements involve software, which takes a long time to develop. "They know what the problem is but they don't have the solution," said Thomas J. Crotty, president of Gartner Securities, which closely monitors I.B.M.

Source: *The New York Times*, 10 Aug. 1986.

Elasticity—Cross Price

Cross-price elasticity measures the responsiveness of the quantity demanded of a good to a change in the price of another good.

Cross-price elasticity is often represented by the symbol η_x, which means the elasticity of one good (e.g., good 1) with respect to a change in the price of some other good (e.g., good 2).

For the demand function:

$$Q_1 = d\ (p_1 \,|\, p_2, p_3, \ldots . p_n, I, T)$$

The cross-price elasticity equation for good 1 with respect to a change in the price of good 2 is:

$$\eta_x = \frac{\dfrac{\Delta Q_1}{Q_1}}{\dfrac{\Delta P_2}{P_2}} = \frac{\%\Delta Q_1}{\%\Delta P_2} = \frac{\Delta Q_1}{\Delta P_2}\frac{P_2}{Q_1}$$

We are primarily interested in whether a change in the price of a related good (e.g., P_2) will cause the quantity demanded of good 1, Q_1, to rise or fall. Therefore we are interested in the *sign* of η_x. Since p_2 and Q_1 are always going to be positive numbers, to determine the sign of η_x we need only assume some change in p_2 (e.g., let p_2 rise so $\Delta p_2 > 0$) and see how Q_1 responds.

Assume, for instance, that p_2 rises (i.e., $\Delta p_2 > 0$). Then, given the law of demand, we know that Q_2 falls, as shown in Figure E3–3B.

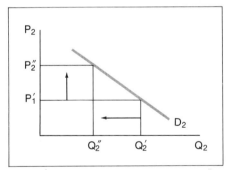

FIGURE E3–3B   A Movement Along the Demand Curve

This can, in turn, have two possible influences on Q_1:

1. If Q_1 and Q_2 are consumed together, they are called *Complements.* If this is the case, a rise in p_2 will cause a fall in Q_2, which, in turn, will reduce demand for Q_1, since Q_1 and Q_2 are consumed together. A reduced demand for Q_1 will mean a fall in the quantity of Q_1 demanded as shown in Figure E3–3C.

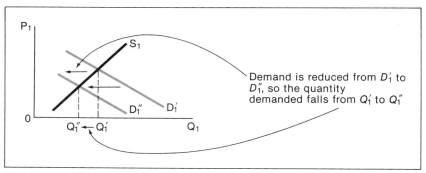

FIGURE E3–3C   A Decrease in Demand

Thus for complements we see that:

$\Delta p_2 > 0$ causes $\Delta Q_1 < 0$

Therefore, in the case of complements:

$\eta_x < 0.$

An example of complementary goods is pizza and hamburgers.

2. If Q_1 and Q_2 are items that replace one another they are called *Substitutes*. If this is the case, a rise in p_2 will cause a fall in Q_2, which, in turn, will increase demand for Q_1, since Q_1 is a replacement for Q_2. An increased demand for Q_1 will mean a rise in the quantity of Q_1 demanded, as shown in Figure E3–3D.

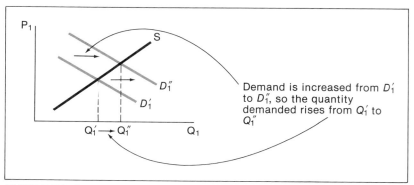

FIGURE E3–3D   An Increase in Demand

Thus for substitutes we see that

$\Delta p_2 > 0$ causes $\Delta Q_1 > 0$

Therefore, in the case of substitutes:

$\eta_x > 0$

An example of substitute goods is wine and beer.

Elasticity—Income

Income elasticity measures the responsiveness of the quantity demanded of a good to a change in income. Income elasticity is often represented by the symbol η_y.

For the demand function:

$Q_1 = d\ (p_1 \mid p_2, p_3, \ldots . p_n, I, T)$

The income elasticity equation is:

$$\eta_y = \frac{\dfrac{\Delta Q_1}{Q_1}}{\dfrac{\Delta I}{I}} = \frac{\%\Delta Q_1}{\%\Delta I} = \frac{\Delta Q_1}{\Delta I}\frac{I}{Q_1}$$

We are interested in the *sign* of η_y. Since I and Q_1 are always going to be positive numbers, to determine the sign of η_y we need only assume some change in I (e.g., let I rise so $\Delta I > 0$) and see how Q_1 responds.

Assume, for instance, that I (income) rises (i.e., $\Delta I > 0$). There are two possible influences on Q_1:

1. An increase in income can reduce demand for Q_1 at any given price. A reduced demand for Q_1 will mean a fall in the quantity of Q_1 demanded, as shown in Figure E3–3E.
In this case, $\Delta I > 0$ causes $\Delta Q_1 < 0$ and therefore $\eta_y < 0$. A good for which an increase in income causes a fall in quantity demanded is called an *inferior good*. Can you think of an example?

2. An increase in income can increase demand for Q_1 at any given

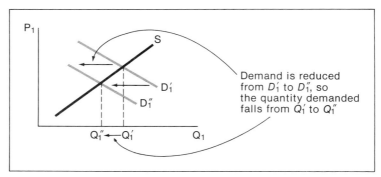

FIGURE E3-3E   A Decrease in Demand

price. An increase in demand for Q_1 will mean a rise in the quantity of Q_1 demanded, as shown in Figure E3-3F.

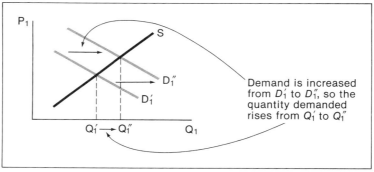

FIGURE E3-3F   An Increase in Demand

In this case, $\Delta I > 0$ causes $\Delta Q_1 > 0$ and therefore $\eta_y > 0$. A good for which an increase in income causes a rise in the quantity demanded is called a *normal good*.

Most goods are normal goods; *ergo,* the name.

> *Note:* There is a special case of normal goods for which η_y is not only greater than zero, it is greater than 1.
>
> $\eta_y > 1$ implies that $\%\Delta Q > \%\Delta I$—in other words, the quantity demanded of the good increases more than proportionally to an increase in income. Goods that exhibit this characteristic are called *superior goods.* Designer jeans may be an example of superior goods.
>
> The following excerpt from a *New York Times* article represents income elasticity in action.

Lotto's 'Lucky 21': Richer, but Still on the Job

BY SARA RIMER

A year later, not much has changed. Joe Smith, William Jon-Ming, Willy Lao, Luis Ramos, Kevin Fleming, Walter Sobolak and others, big-time lottery winners now, are still on the assembly line at the Hantscho plant in Mount Vernon, N.Y.

From 7 A.M. to 4:30 P.M., with half an hour for lunch (brown-bag or take-out from Paul's Deli nearby), they work side by side at the same gray tables under the same fluorescent light, making small parts for offset printing presses. With overtime, it brings them each about $25,000 a year.

A year ago Thursday, they got a piece of the $41 million New York State Lotto jackpot, the largest in the nation's history, when one of the 21 $1 tickets they had chipped in to buy came up a winner. With two other winning tickets—held by a waitress from Troy, N.Y., and a computer consultant from Brooklyn—the Hantscho workers' take was $13.7 million, or about $650,000 apiece. The annual installments, paid out over 20 years, come to about $24,000 after Federal withholding taxes, for each of the 21.

"I consider myself happy," said Mr. Ramos, 33 years old, from the Dominican Republic, who still lives in the same $500-a-month apartment near the Grand Concourse in the Bronx with his wife and four small children. "I got my kids, my wife and a couple dollars. In a couple more years I'll retire and go back to my country."

Mr. Ramos and the others are proudly known as the Lucky 21, two Mount Vernon natives and the others immigrants from a dozen different countries. They have been immortalized in a Lotto television commercial and a Lotto subway poster with the slogan: "Lotto Made Our American Dream Come True."

But they are still, in many ways, the men in subassembly—"a bunch of hard-working guys who know how to watch a buck," in the words of Paul Leck, vice president for personnel at Hantscho Inc.

And even as the members of the Lucky 21 look forward to receiving their second lottery checks, they have the universal complaints of working people everywhere.

"You working tomorrow?" Joe Smith, 30 years old, born and raised in Mount Vernon, asked William Jon-Ming, from Suriname, at the end of the first shift last Friday.

"Yeah," Mr. Jon-Ming, 39 years old, said, groaning at the thought of yet another Saturday of overtime. A couple of the guys, he added, were on for Sunday, too.

With the exception of Mr. Fleming, 32, the token bachelor, the members of the Lucky 21 all have wives and children to support. Their lottery checks have made them more secure, they say, but hardly millionaires.

And while they have opened tax shelters and some have bought new cars and nicer homes, they are still living in the same neighborhoods of Yonkers, Mount Vernon, the Bronx and New Rochelle.

Still Driving a '77 Van

Mr. Jon-Ming, his wife and their 13-year-old son still call home the same $450-a-month, two-bedroom apartment in Mount Vernon, near the railroad tracks. And Mr. Jon-Ming still goes to work in the same 1977 Dodge van.

"People say, 'How ya doing, millionaire?'" he said, "'You still driving the old beat-up van?'"

Steve Yung, 32, from China, gave up his post-Lotto plan to move his family from their two-bedroom apartment near Pelham Parkway in the Bronx to Yonkers. "House prices are too high," he said.

But he says he is grateful for the lottery prize that made it possible for his wife to quit her job as a seamstress in a downtown Manhattan factory and stay home with their year-old son.

A Change of Fortunes

If the lottery has transformed anyone's life, it is certainly Kevin Fleming's. Mr. Fleming, the other Mount Vernon native, had been, to put it mildly, down on his luck.

"I didn't have a checking account," he said. "I had a savings account, if you call $100 a savings account."

His one credit card had been withdrawn. He was driving or, more accurately, not driving, a 1979 Chevette that needed repairs he could not afford.

"Everybody thought it was the biggest piece of junk around," he said. "I was bumming rides to work, riding my bicycle when the weather was nice."

A Move to Yonkers

Moreover, he was still recovering, both emotionally and financially, from the deaths, within 18 months of each other, of both of his parents.

The first thing Mr. Fleming

bought after he hit the jackpot was a Chevrolet van with custom interior that cost almost $20,000. He moved from a $450-a-month "dump" in Mount Vernon, as he calls it, to a modern two-bedroom apartment in Yonkers for $513 a month. He bought a VCR, opened his first checking account and an I.R.A., hired an accountant and started thinking about reapplying for a credit card.

He wrote a check to the American Cancer Society in memory of his mother, who died of cancer. He made the longest flight of his life, to California, to visit one of his four brothers, Kenny, whom he hadn't seen in 12 years.

"Winning the lottery was second to seeing him," he said.

Welcome Attention

While Mr. Fleming is going into his ninth year at Hantscho and has no immediate plans to leave, his lottery win means that he is no longer tied to the factory as he once was. He gets two weeks and three days vacation time, five sick days and 11 holidays annually. Now, he says, he can afford to take occasional personal days without pay and turn down overtime, something his late father, Edward Fleming, who put in 18 years on the night shift at Hantscho, could never do.

"My father never took a day off in his life," Kevin Fleming said. "With four kids, he couldn't."

The lottery, Mr. Fleming and the others say, has also brought a mostly welcome attention and respect for 21 men who felt they were working their lives away in near-oblivion.

Now, as members of the Lucky 21, they are even more famous than the $13.7 million winners, Deborah Turcotte, who has retired from her waitressing job at a Troy tavern, and Joe Moore, who has moved from Brooklyn to the Upper East Side and gone into business for himself as a computer consultant.

Source: *The New York Times*, 19 Aug. 1986.

We can demonstrate the effect of a change in income graphically (Prerequisite E3–2).

Suppose we have the initial condition shown in Figure E3–3G, and

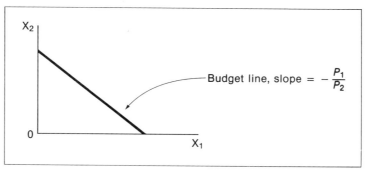

FIGURE E3–3G Initial Budget Line

then income increased from I to I'. Graphically, this would appear as a parallel shift in the budget line, as shown in Figure E3-3H. We can explain the shift shown in Figure E3-3H by examining the intercepts and the slope. First, we note that since income increased and the prices, P_1 and P_2, remained constant, the X_1 and X_2 intercepts must move out. Second, we note that since relative prices have not

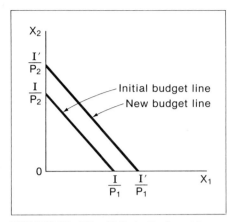

FIGURE E3-3H   Shift in Budget Line

changed the slope, $-\dfrac{P_1}{P_2}$ must remain constant and therefore the new budget line must be parallel to the initial budget line. Clearly, if income decreases, the budget line shifts inward and maintains the same slope.

When income changes this way, the utility-maximizing combination of X_1 and X_2 will also change. The nature of this change depends on the size of the income change and on the preferences embodied in the indifference curves. For example, if I rises, we could have the case shown in Figure E3-3I, where consumption of X_1 and X_2 increased as income increased—both are normal goods. Or we could have the case shown in Figure E3-3J, where the consumption of X_1 increased and consumption of X_2 decreased, so we know X_1 is a normal good but X_2 is an inferior good. Can you show the case of X_1 inferior and X_2 normal?

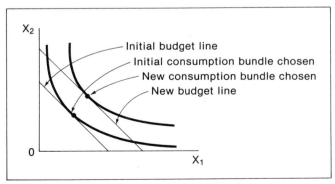

FIGURE E3-3I   Case of Two Normal Goods

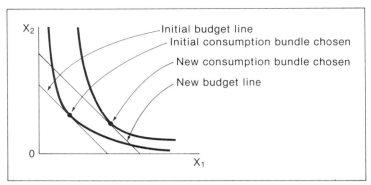

FIGURE E3-3J   Case of X_2 as an Inferior Good

The difference between the two cases just illustrated is that the preferences represented by the indifference curves varied. As we have seen, different preferences imply different shapes for the indifference curves.

E3-4:   Demographics and Demand

The following advertisement reflects the relationship between demographics and demand. After you read the ad consider the following questions: Where does your cohort (your generation) fit into the demographics of society? Is yours a large or a small group relative to other cohorts? How will the relative size of your cohort affect your personal experience as you pass through the stages of life?

E3-5:   The Entrepreneur

An *entrepreneur* is one who identifies new markets and employs resources in order to meet the demand in those markets. The benefit of being an entrepreneur is the temporary profit or rent one enjoys from being the first to enter a market—provided, that is, the anticipated demand is really there. The cost of being an entrepreneur is the resources sunk into the project.

While the costs are sunk up front, the benefits are prospective. The entrepreneur always takes a risk that the actual benefits realized will be less (possibly much less) than those she expected. Entrepreneurs are market trailblazers, and part of the nature of trailblazing is taking risks.

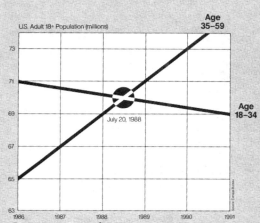

On July 20,1988
a profound change will take place
in American marketing.

And Prevention puts you
right in the middle of it.

America's purchasing power has shifted.

This year, the number of people age 35–59 will surpass the group marketers often covet, 18–34 year olds. And that gap will widen dramatically for the rest of the century.[†]

What's more, when it comes to spending, the most powerful consumers are that same group: people age 35–59. New findings show that, in category after category, they far outspend both the 18–34 and 60+ markets.[††]

For marketers who want to reach the money in the middle, *Prevention* is the answer, with a higher percentage of readers 35–59 than all the women's service and health magazines.[†††]

For more information on this new marketing opportunity, call or write our Publisher, Sanford T. Beldon for our free report, "The Money's in the Middle." 708 Third Avenue, New York, N.Y. 10017.

Sources: [†] U.S. Census Bureau [††] U.S. Bureau of Labor Statistics [†††] MRI–Fall, 1987

AMERICA'S LEADING HEALTH MAGAZINE

New York (212) 370-9643 · Chicago (312) 726-0365 · Los Angeles (213) 383-2237 (415) 398-8183 · Detroit (313) 332-9200

ARTICLE E3–4A

Source: *Prevention Magazine*

Under our nice assumptions, individuals will flow into entrepreneurial activity until all advantages from the pursuit are eliminated. We see, therefore, that even the benefit enjoyed by the market trailblazer, is ultimately reduced by competition to a normal return on the capital and labor the entrepreneur invests in a project.

Remember, however, that this discussion of the entrepreneur and the return she can hope to enjoy rests on our nice assumptions. We will see shortly that when we relax those nice assumptions the effect on income distribution can be significant.

As a preview of that discussion, consider the case of a gifted entrepreneur, one who enjoys an insurmountable market advantage because she has a "nose" for new market opportunities.

Such an entrepreneur is like a concert pianist or a professional tennis player. The only difference is the nature of the gift. The gifted entrepreneur is one who has a talent for identifying or creating a market demand and simultaneously supplying the item to satisfy that demand. Inventiveness is not enough, marketing skill is not enough; the especially successful entrepreneur must combine both of these abilities. The reward for such a gift is a rent, a return to the advantage of entrepreneurial talent. If our nice assumptions hold, the advantage and therefore the rent are short-lived. Nevertheless, to be first is an advantage as long as the competition is working to catch up. If government intervention (e.g., patents) maintains the advantage, the return to such activity is multiplied and so, too, the incentive to pursue such a path. The following articles from *The New York Times* (February 15, 1987) are about some aspiring and some successful entrepreneurs.

Treating Invention as an Art Form

Jacob Rabinow, 77, an electrical engineer, works as a part-time consultant to the National Bureau of Standards, which sets official standards for all units of scientific measurement. But he spends most of his time improving hinges or locks or "just doing something in my head." Among his inventions are the automatic regulator once used in car clocks, the letter-sorting machine used by the United States Postal Service, an improved reading machine that digitizes printed characters for use in computers and

the "straight line" phonograph, which replaces the traditional swinging arm with a system that produces better sound.

There could have been more. "I keep nine volumes of notes, with more than 2,000 ideas," he told the conference, "I invent a lot of things and throw half of them away."

By most measures, Mr. Rabinow seems a happy man. He has the leisure to invent things on a whim or because a friend wants something, like a device he recently invented, which allows one to read the

label on a phonograph record while it is turning. "It's a challenge to make a record stand still," he said. He gets genuine satisfaction from a good invention, his own or someone else's. "I believe inventions are an art form," he said. "I can look at an invention and say, 'it's gorgeous, it's elegant.'" He toyed with a nut-threader, a screw that cuts threads in nuts and then lets the nuts drop on a U-shaped bar. "The first time I saw this, I said, 'my God, this is so cute. This is beautiful.'"

But Mr. Rabinow's travails

as a businessman may be a lesson to other would-be Edisons. Although many of his ideas have found their way to market, he said, "my inventions get changed all the time, usually for the worse." Nor are they always lucrative. Mr. Rabinow made a lot of money when he sold his reading machines to the Control Data Corporation. But he said that he lost it all when, because there were no corporate takers, he tried to market his phonograph himself. By the time Bang & Olufson, the Danish phonograph-equipment maker, began to sell the invention, he says, his patent had expired. Nor could he peddle his other phonograph patent, for a device that plays both sides of a record without flipping it. Sharp Electronics eventually came out with a version of the device, he said, "but now people are buying the compact disk player, which is very cute."

Life is even harder for inventors these days, in Mr. Rabinow's view. Wall Street is favoring a handful of fashionable technologies, such as biogenetics, at the expense of others. Companies are larger and more resistant to change, as well as less impressed by inventions that may have little, if any, effect on the bottom line. "Now, whoever buys a patent, you have to throw stardust in their eyes," he said. "The chief executive today has no interest in long-range planning. Invention is not supported by people who look at quarterly reports."

Source: *The New York Times*, 15 Feb. 1987.

10% Inspiration and 90% Marketing

As the inventors told it, the biggest problem isn't coming up with ideas, or even executing them, but getting creations to market. "I have more than 200 ideas, I just need the right contacts," said Abbas Husain, a New Jersey doctor who received a patent this year for a "safer nail clipper." By the end of the conference, more than a dozen of the inventors were convinced they had found a contact on the speaker's platform, or at least someone who could help them make a connection.

Many said they got their greatest inspiration from Richard C. Levy, a 40-year-old self-styled "imagineer" who has licensed some of his own inventions and designs to the likes of Mattel, Milton Bradley and Procter & Gamble. Selling an invention is "90 percent marketing and 10 percent innovation," he told the conference. "All you have to do is look at the quality of products on the market to know that's true."

Typical of the way Mr. Levy innovates and markets is his approach to his newest product: a board game for young children about the life of the late Rev. Martin Luther King Jr. Mr. Levy got the blessing of the King estate, which will receive royalties from sales of the game, marketed by Cadaco of Chicago. He says he started thinking how to teach children about Dr. King after his 6-year-old daughter came home from school with questions about the civil rights leader.

"One night, I guess I had a dream, too," he said. "I woke up and said to my wife, 'board games are great for learning,'" The Levys put together a game in which players draw cards and move across the board, traveling through the milestones of Dr. King's life (when he goes to jail, so does the player) and death, followed by the commemoration of his birth with a national holiday. "King is unique," said Mr. Levy. "I don't believe there's another individual today who could be a successful board game."

Selling the product to a company is where the real inventiveness comes in, he told his audience. "A lot of people have trouble getting executives on the phone, he said. "I don't, I never have. I start calling at 7 in the morning. If I hit a switchboard operator or a security guard, my line is 'John told me to call at this hour.'" Once you get an executive on the line, he advised, "then you need the skills of a cop talking a jumper off a ledge."

Mr. Levy gives them his five minute sales pitch, then his 10-minute pitch, then visits the company armed with his product, advertising copy and estimated assembly costs ("they don't expect you to be correct, they just expect you to be smart enough to know there's a cost of assembly"). He also gives them operating instructions. "I write it out like a comic book," he said. "You have to put everything out in front of these people."

Source: *The New York Times*, 15 Feb. 1987.

———————————————

E3-6: Demonstrating Graphically the Efficiency of Perfect Competition (Prerequisite: E2-2)

We know, as the text points out, that a firm's MC curve is its supply curve. We also learned in an earlier extender (E2-2) that a rising MC cuts the associated AC curve at its minimum point, as shown in Figure E3-6A.

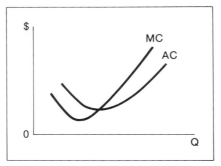

FIGURE E3-6A   Relationship Between Marginal and Average Cost

With this information we can redraw the picture representing an individual firm's relationship to the market (we assume all firms are identical, so this picture is representative of all) as shown in Figure E3-6B.

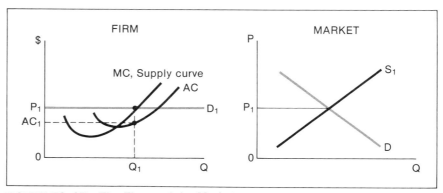

FIGURE E3-6B   The Firm and the Market

Note that under current conditions shown in Figure E3-6B the firm, a price taker, is producing quantity Q_1 selling at P_1/unit, and incurring a cost of AC_1/unit. Under these conditions, the firm's total revenue is $(P_1 \times Q_1)$ and its total cost is $(AC_1 \times Q_1)$. Since total revenue is greater than total cost (remember, costs include a normal return on the owner's labor and capital), the firm is enjoying an excess return, a profit equal to $((P_1 - AC_1) \times Q_1)$.

As we learned in the text, given our nice assumptions, a profit will attract new competitors. Their entry into the market will shift out the market supply curve and lower the market price. This process will continue until all profit is eliminated. Graphically, this dynamic is illustrated in Figure E3–6C.

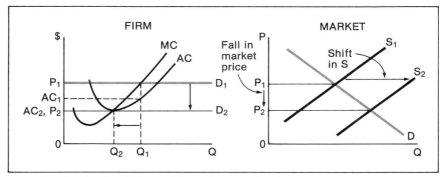

FIGURE E3–6C   The Effect of Free Entry on Profit

Figure E3–6C shows that as a result of the entry of new suppliers attracted by profits, S shifted until P_1 fell to P_2. At P_2 the firm supplies the quantity Q_2. At Q_2 the firm receives P_2/unit and incurs costs of AC_2/unit. Since $P_2 = AC_2$, the firm is breaking even. It earns a normal return on all factor inputs, but no profit. Note that if more firms entered, pushing market supply out farther and market price down more, the firm's costs would go up while its revenue would go down. In that case, the firm would be losing money, and some firms would have to exit the market until the market price rose to at least P_2. Thus we see that at $P > P_2$ there is entry and at $P < P_2$ there is exit. The market will reach an equilibrium at P_2. Notice that at the market equilibrium firms are producing at their minimum average cost. Thus we see that under perfect competition (i.e., given our nice assumptions) the dynamics of the market forces drive firms to produce at the most efficient level.

This graphical analysis can also be used to demonstrate that, given our nice assumptions, all firms must adopt the most efficient technique. Can you demonstrate that?

This analysis becomes more complicated if we relax our assumption that all costs are variable and adopt the more realistic assumption that some costs are fixed and some are variable. The efficiency argument can be made in this more complex case. Can you do it?

E3–7: Market Production, Home Production, and Opportunity Cost

As opportunities for market participation improve, at some point the opportunity cost of home production (taking care of one's own household tasks) becomes too great, so one shifts to market participation. Then one must use the return from market participation (income) to purchase market replacement for what one initially did for oneself. This article from *The New York Times* (January 29, 1987) reflects this substitution process.

No Time To Do Tasks? Agencies Can Help

BY ANDREE BROOKS

When Eileen Fink, an investment broker in Westfield, N.J., leaves her well-kept suburban home for the office each morning she carries a list of local agencies that will perform the jobs she would have done a decade ago when she was a full-time homemaker.

On the list are shops or restaurants where she can find takeout food if she is working too late to make dinner for her husband and two teenagers. Then there is the tailor's shop ("I don't even have time to do a hem anymore," she said); the home-care service for the elderly, which assists her mother-in-law, who is recovering from hip surgery; the catering service that helps with dinner parties, and the service for the swimming pool.

And if the woman who cleans her house twice a week resigns, she knows she will turn to a service to fill the job, too. "The traditional house-hold helper just isn't out there anymore," she said.

Nowadays, household-management agencies will take care of routine tasks, such as picking up and delivering the dry cleaning, and emergencies, which include caring for an ill elderly parent. These agencies, increasingly prevalent in urban areas, are becoming as common in the suburbs, in which traditionally the wife stayed at home and assumed these responsibilities.

"A lot of these women have had to work through the idea that it is not a luxury, but a necessity," said Barbara Kelly, publisher and founder of Houston Woman, a regional monthly magazine. A quarter of the magazine's advertisements promote these services. Six years ago, there were no such advertisements.

At the core of the change is an increasing number of married women who have full-time jobs outside the home. "Even women with large families are now in the labor force," said Dr. W. Keith Bryant, professor of consumer economics and housing at Cornell University. "As their wage rates rise, so does the value of their time. It's cheaper to do it this way than have the wife stay at home."

The arrangement, he noted, is parallel to that of the upper-middle-class household at the turn of the century. Skilled people such as laundresses could come in once a week and tradesmen specializing in one product would deliver. The wife was the manager rather than the provider of services as she is becoming once again.

The one-stop-shopping approach is gaining ground. The Stepford Group (the name is a satirical reference to "The Stepford Wives," a 1975 movie about perfect housewives who are really robots) was started 18 months ago by Laura Pelco and Melissa Schwartz, both former commuters, in Westport, Conn. Each felt overburdened, as most working women do, and decided a gap needed to be filled.

The Stepford staff will wait at home for repairmen, pick up and deliver dry cleaning, provide house-cleaning crews, shop for groceries, take care of business at the motor vehicle bureau, and hire caterers and gardeners. Ms. Pelco and Ms. Schwartz, each perched on a stool taking the orders in the waiting room of the Saugatuck Metro-North station in the mornings, have become an integral part of the rush-hour scene. Fees vary, but most tasks cost at least $10 an hour. The agency has about 200 regular clients. Most are married women with full-time jobs. The rest are single men who live alone. "Single mothers can't afford us," said Ms. Schwartz.

The main deterrent to faster agency growth is lack of help, not lack of clients. "I can't keep up with the demand," said Arlene Clapp, president of Maid for You, a five-year-old cleaning agency in Ridgewood, N.J.

Classification of such services in the Yellow Pages is still a puzzle. Conventional headings such as house cleaning or catering do not suggest the range of services many now supply, while homemaking is reserved primarily for nursing care for the disabled or elderly. "We actually belong under 'w' for wife," said one provider.

Even that has problems. One of the earliest all-purpose services started in Stamford, Conn., in 1981, as Rent-a-Wife, was admonished by local feminists, who maintained that the title debased an honorable status by suggesting a married woman was nothing more than a drudge.

Agency owners insist their success is equally the result of changing attitudes of domestic workers. "Those who are out there want the assurance of steady work and benefits," said Mrs. Clapp. "They don't want to lose out every time the household goes away. And even when the family is home, there's nobody to pick them up at the bus stop anymore."

Mrs. Clapp provides her workers with a car, equipment, vacation pay, medical benefits, social security and is insured and bonded.

Contributing to the growth of such agencies is the decline in the number of teen-agers helping out after school and the demise of the kaffee-klatsch network. "Our clients complain that you can't even turn to the neighbor next door anymore," said Ilene Nordle, founder and president of Sitting, an all-purpose agency in Fairfield, Conn.

The increasing numbers of single men living alone use such services. The men, many of whom are divorced and in their middle years, have high incomes and are not interested in becoming proficient in household tasks. Soon after his divorce in 1982, Harold Sherman, a lawyer who lives in Warren, N.J., began using a caterer in nearby Cranford to supply his dinner. "You quickly get tired of eating out and anyway, I hate to go out to dinner alone," he said.

Source: *The New York Times*, 29 Jan. 1987.

E3–8: More on Sunk Costs

The question we ask ourselves explicitly or implicitly as we make each choice in life is: What will be the consequence of this choice versus that choice? In order to answer that question we consider our current circumstances in light of our past experiences. The past sets the context for the present, and that context constraints and guides our choices for the future. As time passes, current choices will be past and their consequences will shape the present that once was future. In that new present new choices must be made for a new future. And so it goes with time and choice: each present choice is soon to pass and shape the future.

Whenever you make a choice, you are allocating resources. At the very least, you're allocating time to the process of choosing, and quite often the choice (e.g., to buy a pair of shoes) also requires the expenditure of money. Economists refer to the resources that you use up in the process of making and carrying out a choice as *sunk costs*. You've committed those resources to the choice; and no matter what the outcome, whether you follow through with the choice or whether you are happy with it, those resources are spent or sunk.

For example, maybe you're having second thoughts about the value of this course (I hope not). Should you drop it? Well, you've sunk a lot of time in this project already. Isn't that reason enough to see it through? An economist would say no. According to an economist, if you're going to maximize your utility, your attention shouldn't be focused on what you've put into a project already. Rather, you must focus on what you can hope to get out of the project if you stick with it. Sunk costs are just that—sunk. If you're not going to benefit from following through, then there's no point in pouring more resources into the project. Does that mean that the past is irrelevant when making present choices? No. As we noted above, the past sets the context for the present and that context constrains and guides your choices for the future. So what about that decision on dropping the course? Well, just because you've expended a lot of resources so far is no reason to go on. However, if those past expenditures have provided you with a foundation on which you can build an educational experience that will be of value, then maybe you should stick it out. The answer must be found by focusing on your expectations about the future, not by worrying about your wisdom in the past.

This is true for you and it is true for people making million-dollar decisions in the business world. For example, if a businessperson sinks millions of dollars into a plant that is, contrary to expectations, suddenly obsolete because of the emergence of alternative technology—what should she do? Should she forge ahead with the obsolete plant in order to recover those sunk costs? Of course not. To do so would be throwing more money into a losing proposition. Building the plant may have been a rational decision given the knowledge she had at the time, but given the new reality, the rational decision is to accept the consequences of that decision and use the resources she still has at her disposal on projects that appear to be more fruitful. For you and her and me and everyone, sunk costs are sunk. *C'est la vie.*

E3–9: Input Substitution: Isoquant/Isocost Analysis (Prerequisite: E3-2)

It has been demonstrated that when two goods exhibit diminishing marginal utility, an indifference curve for those two goods would appear as shown in Figure E3-9A.

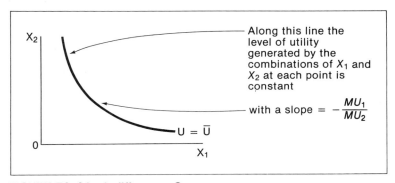

FIGURE E3–9A   Indifference Curve

By an analogous argument (an argument you should be able to make), it can be demonstrated that if two factor inputs (e.g., capital *[K]* and labor *[L]*) exhibit diminishing marginal productivity, we can draw an: *Isoquant*—a graphical representation of all combinations of two-factor inputs (e.g., K and L) that generate the same level of output (holding all else constant) as shown in Figure E3-9B.

It was also demonstrated earlier that if two goods have constant prices, the price trade-off between those two goods, given income level, can be represented by a straight budget line that looks like that shown in Figure E3-9C.

By analogous argument (an argument you should be able to make), it can be demonstrated that if two inputs *(K, L)* have constant prices we can draw an *Isocost line*—a graphical representation of all combinations of K and L that can be purchased for a fixed cost (a constant level of expenditure) as shown in Figure E3-9D.

If a firm chooses to produce output level O_1, the array of available techniques can be represented by an isoquant as shown in Figure E3-9E.

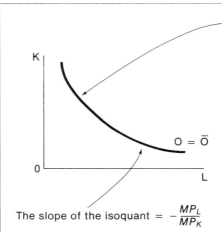

Note that at each point along the isoquant the mix of capital and labor used, or capital/labor ratio K/L is different. Thus each point represents a different technique. Those up to the left are more capital-intensive. Those down to the right are more labor-intensive.

$O = \bar{O}$ or all combinations of K and L along this curve give the same level of output

The slope of the isoquant $= -\dfrac{MP_L}{MP_K}$

FIGURE E3–9B   An Isoquant

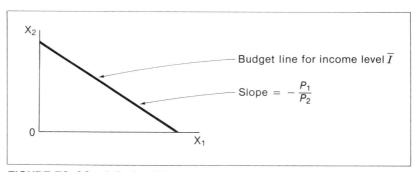

Budget line for income level $\bar{I}$

Slope $= -\dfrac{P_1}{P_2}$

FIGURE E3–9C   A Budget Line

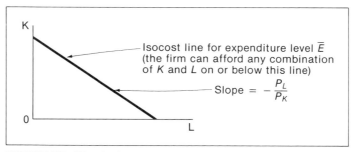

Isocost line for expenditure level $\bar{E}$ (the firm can afford any combination of K and L on or below this line)

Slope $= -\dfrac{P_L}{P_K}$

FIGURE E3–9D   An Isocost Line

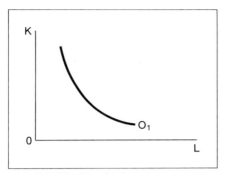

FIGURE E3-9E   An Isoquant

How does the firm determine the least-cost technique for producing O_1 given the price of factor inputs P_L and P_K? Consider Figure E3-9F. At expenditure level E_3 the firm can afford an array of techniques (from A to B) that would produce O_1; however, the firm wants to minimize cost, so it would like to spend less than E_3 if possible. Can it?

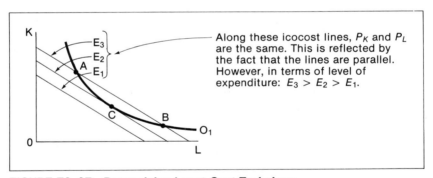

FIGURE E3-9F   Determining Least-Cost Technique

How about expenditure level E_1? That will not do. At that level of expenditure there is not an affordable technique (combination of K and L) that will produce O_1.

The lowest level of expenditure that allows the firm to produce O_1 is represented by the isocost line that is just tangent to the isoquant. In Figure E3-9F that is E_2, and the cost-efficient technique is the combination of K and L represented by point C.

Since the isocost/isoquant tangency determines the least-cost technique (capital/labor ratio), we can write a decision rule for cost minimization as setting:

Slope of isoquant = Slope of isocost

OR

$$-\frac{MP_L}{MP_K} = -\frac{P_L}{P_K}$$

OR

$$\frac{MP_L}{MP_K} = \frac{P_L}{P_K}$$

This equality between the ratio of marginal products and ratio of factor prices means that if a firm is to minimize cost, then the rate at which factors can be substituted technologically must be equal to the rate at which they can be substituted in the market.

With some manipulation, our cost minimization decision rule becomes:

$$\frac{MP_L}{P_L} = \frac{MP_K}{P_K}$$

So we see that firms minimize cost by setting the marginal product per dollar of all factor inputs equal.

Now note what happens when there is a change in the relative prices of factor inputs. For example, let P_L rise while P_K remains constant. In terms of our equation, we suddenly have (as P_L rises):

$$\frac{MP_L}{P_L} < \frac{MP_K}{P_K}$$

In order to return to our cost-minimizing condition (assuming the firm is a price taker so that P_L and P_K are set), the firm must reduce the use of labor (increasing MP_L) and increase the use of capital (decreasing MP_K) until, once again:

$$\frac{MP_L}{P_L} = \frac{MP_K}{P_K}$$

In other words, in response to an increase in the price of labor, the firm will substitute capital for labor, increasing the capital/labor ratio. That is, it will move to a more capital-intensive technique. This is demonstrated graphically in Figure E3-9G.

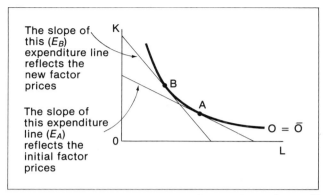

The slope of this (E_B) expenditure line reflects the new factor prices

The slope of this expenditure line (E_A) reflects the initial factor prices

FIGURE E3–9G Change in Technique as Input Costs Change Given initial factor prices, the cost-minimizing technique is *A*. As P_L rises, the slope of the iso-cost line$\left(-\dfrac{P_L}{P_K}\right)$ will get steeper. If the firm seeks to maintain output level (*O*), it must identify the expenditure line that minimizes costs at the new factor price ratio. Here that line is E_B and the cost-minimizing technique (*K/L* combo) is *B*.

We see from the figure that in response to an increase in P_L the techique changed from *A* to *B*—a change that reflects substitution of capital for labor.

Can you demonstrate the effect of a change in P_K?

E4–1: Classic Examples of a Violation of Our Equal Access to Information Assumption

The following two newspaper articles represent real life examples of how information access can be distorted and/or exploited to the advantage of some and the detriment of others.

Housing Study Reveals Wide Discrimination

John Yinger, a professor of economics at the Maxwell School of Citizenship and Public Affairs at Syracuse University, recently had a paper published in the American Economic Review that concluded that housing agents who discriminate against minorities do so for economic reasons.

His findings were based on analysis of fair housing audits conducted in Boston in 1981.

He spoke with Post-Standard business reporter Alberto Bianchetti about the techniques and findings of his study.

POST-STANDARD:
How did the study come about?
YINGER:
The study actually has a long history. There are three parts to it. The first part is that a technique has been developed in the last 20 years. It was started by fair hous-

ing groups to investigate fair housing complaints and it was picked up by a bunch of researchers at the U.S. Department of Housing and Urban Development in 1977. They did a big study in 40 different cities.

The HUD placed a bunch of requirements on Boston in order for it to receive its Community Development Block Grants. One of the requirements was to hire a bunch of experts to look at what was going on in the city.

I was one of the people that got involved. I have been a consultant to HUD for a long time, including on the methodology for this particular technique. The people who did the study gave me the data and I wrote a paper based on their data.

POST-STANDARD:
How are the tests carried out?
YINGER:
The technique is actually the central thing to get across. It is a very simple technique. You take a black person and a white person, but the technique can be applied to compare the treatment of any two groups—it has been used to study the treatment of Hispanics.

In this case you take a black person and a white person and you select people of the same age and the same sex, you give them both rigorous training so they behave in a similar way and you assign them similar family histories to use when they go in to talk to a housing dealer.

You send them successively to a landlord or real estate broker to inquire about some housing that has been advertised.

Because of the design of this audit they differ only in race. They don't differ significantly on anything else, so if there is some difference in treatment they receive from the agent—if one of them is told about three units and another is only told about one available unit— then the difference must be because of their race. So it is a very carefully controlled, almost an experimental, technique that is used to isolate differences in treatments due to group distinctions, in this case race.

POST-STANDARD:
Were real estate agents aware that the study was going on in their industry —was the study publicized when the money was granted?
YINGER:
They were not aware that this was going on. In fact, avoiding detection is a very important part of this technique.

If the brokers know that something is going on then they can change their behavior temporarily and not alter their discriminatory patterns.

POST-STANDARD:
What types of discriminatory patterns did you find?
YINGER:
The studies examine a very wide range of behavior, including the number of units that people are told about; the number of units they are invited to go look at; the number of available units; the number of houses they actually go visit; the prices they are quoted; whether they are encouraged to get a mortgage and given help in getting a mortgage; and others.

I think the main conclusion that comes out, not just of this study but of other studies done in other cities, is that the

most common way to discriminate is simply to not tell black customers about units that are available.

So, typically in Boston, the whites learn about almost twice as many available units as the blacks. So a black has to spend a lot more time searching to see as many houses.

Now, some of the patterns that exist are much more complicated than that and they are a little more unique to individual cities.

For example, there is some evidence that blacks are steered into certain areas and whites are steered into others. There is some evidence that in the sales market whites are told about all kinds of creative financing devises and blacks are not told about anything.

So there are other kinds of discrimination, but the main thing is blacks simply aren't told. And if they aren't told what there is, they can't go look at it to try and rent it or purchase it.

POST-STANDARD:
How do you arrive at those conclusions?
YINGER:
There are two things I do in my study. The first thing is to simply measure how much discrimination there is and the results are very strong. They have been found in quite a few other studies now.

The study of 40 cities HUD did in 1977 and also studies in Dallas and Denver and several other places find a very high level of discrimination against blacks. That is the first and most dramatic point to make.

Discrimination has not disappeared in U.S. housing markets, despite strong language in our civil rights laws. But the civil rights laws have very weak enforcement mechanisms.

The second point, and this is one of the reasons that I undertook the study, is to try to understand why real estate agents and landlords discriminate.

What is it that motivates them to behave that way. There are very different theories about why they discriminate.

One theory is that landlords and real estate brokers in white communities are catering to the prejudices of their white customers, they know that if they rent or sell to blacks, then they will lose customers, some of their white tenants will leave, or some of their potential white buyers will not come into their real estate offices.

And so to protect their economic reputation with white customers they discriminate against blacks. That theory suggests that discrimination will take place strongly in largely white areas, but once a neighborhood starts to change from all white to all black, as neighborhoods sometimes do,

then the housing seller will no longer have an incentive to discriminate, because the white customers are all leaving, and the agent can't be blamed anyway because the process has already started.

A second theory is that the landlords and brokers are themselves prejudiced and they just don't want to deal with blacks.

And a third theory is that the housing sellers are trying to predict what their customers will want so they don't show blacks houses in white neighborhoods because blacks will not want to buy those. That may not be true but that is what the agents assume is true.

I tested all of those theories in the paper and I find very strong evidence to support the first theory, mainly that housing sellers cater to the prejudice of their white customers.

I find a little bit of evidence to support the theory that some real estate agents and landlords are prejudiced themselves. And I find strong evidence to reject the theory

that housing sellers are simply trying to predict the preferences of their customers.

POST-STANDARD:
What do you think the findings of your study mean for other cities?

YINGER:

Every study finds a high level of discrimination. It doesn't matter what city you are in, there is discrimination everywhere. Again, it is not the blatant and vicious discrimination, at least typically not, that was observed often in the 1950s, but blacks simply aren't told about available housing units.

POST-STANDARD:

In your opinion what remedies are there to better enforce the spirit of the Civil Rights Act?

YINGER:

Well, there are remedies at a lot of different levels. The most striking thing about housing discrimination is that despite the Civil Rights Act of 1968, which prohibits racial discrimination in housing, there is no criminal penalty for discriminating.

Source: _Syracuse Post Standard_, 9 Feb. 1987.

Insider Trading: A Matter of Trust

WASHINGTON—Gary Lynch, director of enforcement at the Securities and Exchange Commission, has a rule of thumb for defining illegal insider trading. If an investor has reason to suspect—only suspect—that a stock tip is based on private corporate information and that the stock price would be affected

if the public knew about it, it would probably be illegal for him to trade in the stock. In fact, the person giving him the tip might be subject to S.E.C. charges as well.

As the S.E.C. has interpreted the law, illegal insider trading often involves the misappropriation—stealing, some call it—of confidential infor-

mation. An employee who learns his company has entered into takeover negotiations would violate the law if he bought its stock; the information is not legally his, the S.E.C. says, and he is in effect stealing from shareholders the profits they might otherwise earn.

In addition, an employee

who has a fiduciary responsibility to his corporation could be charged with breaching that duty just for giving others the information. People outside a company can also commit such breaches: An investment banker retained by a corporation would do so if he told investors about a planned merger, even if he did not trade in the stock.

Dennis B. Levine, an investment banker, and Ivan F. Boesky, the arbitrager, made huge profits when Mr. Levine breached his responsibility and both men misappropriated his inside knowledge of planned takeovers. But a reporter and a lawyer have been charged with insider trading for passing on information, even though they personally made no money.

So the next time a neighbor passes on a hot investment tip, ask him how he knows. If the source of his information is not on the public record, following his advice could be illegal.

Source: *The New York Times*, 23 Nov. 1986.

E4–2:   On Exploitation

If we define exploitation as the exercise of an advantage in order to generate a distributive benefit (a rent), we can identify a number of cases of exploitation that do or have existed in society.

An obvious example of the exploitation of a naturally occurring advantage is the gifted entrepreneur or professional athlete. Clearly, the multimillion-dollar income some such entrepreneurs and athletes enjoy is a return to hard work, practice, working conditions, and giftedness. Since equivalent hard work, practice, and working conditions in other lines of work don't generate incomes remotely close to the gifted entrepreneur's or athlete's millions, the predominant source of that huge return must be the exploitation of an advantage derived from a naturally occurring gift. In this case, the individual does not "take advantage"; rather, the luck of the genetic draw has given her an advantage.

Of course it is possible for people to take advantage of one another. In terms of economic theory, we can understand this case as follows. Individuals or groups of individuals may enjoy an increased distributive share generated by the exploitation of artificially created advantages. A classic case of this kind of exploitation is the apartheid system that currently exists in South Africa. The white minority has used the power of the government to create barriers to market and information access by black people. This institutionally created violation of our fair race assumptions gives the white minority market power. The consequences of that market power are easy to see: the average white South African enjoys a standard of living that is equivalent to that of an upper-middle-class American, while the average black South African endures a standard of living that is equivalent to that suffered by the poorest of Americans.

Our theory not only explains the distribution of income in South Africa, it allows us to identify a sad irony of the situation there. Recall that the creation and maintenance of advantage (rent seeking and rent protection, as we have called these activities) use up resources that could have been used in productive rather than exploitative ways. For example, millions of dollars' worth of resources are allocated to the police and military activities necessary to enforce apartheid. Furthermore, the system denies blacks the opportunity to use their physical and intellectual potential to its fullest. Therefore many billions of dollars' worth of human effort, sacrifice, and creative genius are being wasted because the people in whom that potential is embodied are being denied the opportunity to realize it.

Now consider the counterfactual case, the one that doesn't exist but that is feasible. In a South Africa under our nice assumptions—that is, with a fair race in which all of the country's human potential is nurtured and realized—no resources would be wasted on exploitation and all resources would be used most efficiently. Such a South Africa would have an output many times greater than the output of actual South Africa.

The size of the pie in Figure E4–2A represents the full South African output; the shares to whites and blacks are represented by the size of the W and B slices, respectively.

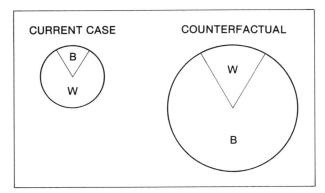

Figure E4–2A: Cases

As the two pies demonstrate, the elimination of apartheid would reduce the whites' relative share but, it is possible that because of the productive benefits of the fair race, increase their absolute share. In short, the whites' might enjoy a higher standard of living in the absence of apartheid. So why don't they use their power to move from the current case to the fair race case? Because they know the benefits of the current system, but they can't be sure about what the future would hold if they were to give up their power. The fair race counterfactual is just one possible outcome. There are others that are less attractive to the whites.

Thus the white South Africans are trapped in a difficult situation of their own making. They created a system of advantage that has generated many years of benefits for them. But now black resistance is strong, and as that resistance grows, the costs of maintaining the benefits of white control will also grow. Thus the net benefits (benefits minus costs) diminish. The more difficult the blacks make it for the whites, the smaller the net benefit of apartheid. The South African government's response has been to crack down on dissent in the most efficient manner possible—they have outlawed the organizations that lead the resistance, thus making coordinated black opposition more difficult. In response, the black community has looked for leadership to its one remaining legal resistance institution: the church.

In the following piece from *The New York Times* (March 14, 1988), Archbishop Desmond Tutu, head of the Anglican Church in Southern Africa and 1984 Nobel Peace Prize winner, makes a statement on human rights. Note as you read this article that the most powerful form of nonviolent resistance available to the blacks has been "strikes, rent strikes, and consumer boycotts." (This last form of resistance, the consumer boycott, was what propelled Dr. Martin Luther King, Jr., to leadership in the American civil rights movement. He led a bus boycott in Montgomery, Alabama, that won blacks the right to desegregated bus seating.) The response cited by Bishop Tutu is predictable given our model: the white government is resorting to "surrogate forces" ("cheaper" than spending white lives) and banning the resistance.

South Africa—a Lebanon?

By DESMOND M. TUTU

CAPE TOWN—Black South Africans have exercised the most remarkable patience in pressing for their human rights.

In the 1950's, they launched a nonviolent defi-ance campaign. In 1960, their peaceful protests were met with the bullets of Sharpeville and the banning of the African National Congress and the Pan-African Congress. With nothing to show for half a century of pleading, the black leadership went underground or into exile to begin an armed struggle.

But the peaceful campaigning went on, with Steve Biko and other young black intellectuals forging a new philosophy of black consciousness that helped people assert their humanity and self-respect. The uprisings of 1976 began as peaceful protests by our children against their fifth-rate education and turned violent only in reaction to police bullets.

In the 1980's, the pattern has continued. While increasing numbers, the young in particular, have chosen violence as a last resort, many of us still explore every last possible peaceful avenue for change. We have developed a range of organizations (the largest of which is the United Democratic Front, a coalition of about 600 antiapartheid groups) whose purpose is to resist a Government that in 1984 went so far as to incorporate apartheid into the Constitution by creating separate chambers of Parliament for different races.

We have used many nonviolent ways of trying to bring change, such as strikes, rent strikes and consumer boycotts. The authorities have responded by declaring states of emergency and tightening emergency regulations. They ban peaceful protest, they detain our children and they ban our leaders. Step by step, since 1985, President P. W. Botha's Government has closed off avenue after avenue of peaceful political change— most recently, last week's ban on the newly formed Committee for the Defense of Democracy.

At the same time, Mr. Botha isn't even delivering the "reforms" he promised us. A few years ago, many claimed that the Government's "final solution"—its policy of uprooting people from their homes and dumping them to starve in the bantustans in pursuance of its aim of segregation—had been abandoned. Now we hear otherwise. In Mr. Botha's old parliamentary seat, the authorities want to remove the people of a small place called Lawaaikamp. When the people appealed, he told them he was opposed to forced removal "unless it is accompanied by the provision of better living standards."

Just over a fortnight ago, the Government removed nearly all effective means of working for true change by peaceful means when it prohibited political activity by 18 organizations and banned 18 leaders.

What other church leaders and I found particularly horrifying were the restrictions placed on two leaders of the United Democratic Front who had been advocates of peace in two of the most desperate crisis areas of our land—at a squatter camp in Cape Town and the townships around Pietermaritzburg in Natal province.

In an unusually strong statement, we argued that when we saw the banning of these leaders, the harassment of peacemakers, the Government's failure to arrest people against whom there is clear evidence of murder and assault, we could only conclude that "the authorities are deliberately obstructing peace in our country and encouraging violence among our people."

"Their purpose," we said, "is to use surrogate forces to smash effective opposition to their heretical policy of apartheid, and to insure as fast as possible that it is the blood of black people, and not of white people, that is spilled in pursuance of their aim."

If allowed to continue, the deliberate incitement of violence in our country will turn it into a Lebanon-like wasteland.

We felt so strongly about this that on Feb. 29 we tried to proceed to Parliament to present a petition calling on the Government to turn from the path it had chosen. The most creative response to a peaceful act of Christian witness that the Government could come up with was to arrest us all.

It has become abundantly clear the present Government has chosen a military option for the future. The Law and Order Minister, Adriaan J. Vlok, has spoken openly of the need to "eliminate radicals and revolutionaries."

Not only does the Government threaten the security and lives of the people of South Africa, it is destabilizing the whole of Southern Africa and threatening the interests in the region of its major trading partners, including the United States, Britain and West Germany. Even if its most extravagant claims of offering a power sharing deal with blacks were to be believed, they offer nothing more than token black faces in the Cabinet. The Government has no intention of relinquishing control.

As one who believes that one ought never to resort to violence under any circumstances, I also believe there can come a time—as when the Nazis invaded Europe— when it is justified to take up arms to overthrow an unjust system. I can therefore sympathize with those South Africans who have already decided that violence is justified.

For myself, though, I agree with Dr. Allan Boesak, head of the Dutch Reformed Mission Church and a patron of the United Democratic Front, when he says that we must not descend to the Government's level in responding to its latest actions with violence. That is the reason that a number of us in Cape Town formed the Committee for the Defense of Democracy to fight peacefully against the Government's suppression of its

Desmond M. Tutu, Nobel Peace Prize winner in 1984, is Anglican Archbishop of Cape Town and head of the Anglican Church in Southern Africa.

opponents. And now, the Government has chosen to ban even this group.

It should come as no surprise, therefore, that those of us who ask desperate people to take nonviolent action are filled with despair when they learn that the U.S. and Britain have once again vetoed international attempts to do the same. The American and British decisions to veto sanctions in the U.N. Security Council were all the more staggering in the light of the South African representative's arrogant challenge to the Security Council to "do your damndest."

I want to issue a challenge to the American, British and West German Governments. You say you are against apart-

heid. If you are, then make three demands of the South African Government:

First, the state of emergency must be lifted.

Second, last month's restrictions against our peoples' organizations and leaders must be lifted.

Third, detainees, particularly children, must be tried in open courts or released.

If the Government does not meet these demands, you must cut diplomatic ties. That would not be a radical step to take in the circumstances. It's not going to cost jobs and lives. It would be a gesture, but a dramatic one with profound psychological consequences for those who wield power in South Africa.

Or do you want another Lebanon?

Source: *The New York Times*, 14 Mar. 1988.

Our model helps us understand the actions of both sides in the dispute. What should the role of our own government be? Should it pursue a laissez-faire or an interventionist policy? Your answer to that question will depend, as it does for virtually all economic policy choices, on your values, on your faith in the market system to realize those values, and on your faith in the government's ability to determine and carry out a policy that is effective and consistent with your values.

E4–3: Affirmative Action: Pro and Con

The following articles from *The New York Times* (February 26, 1987, and March 26, 1987) report decisions of the United States Supreme Court on affirmative action cases. As of 1987, these decisions determined the law of the land with respect to affirmative action. What do you think of the majority positions? The minority positions? How would an economist argue for and against each position? The makeup of the Court has changed since these decisions. Has the court's position changed since these rulings?

High Court Backs Basing Promotion on a Racial Quota

By STUART TAYLOR JR.

Justices Split 5-4

Temporary Use Allowed in Alabama Because of Severity of Case

WASHINGTON, Feb. 25—A sharply divided Supreme Court, rejecting the Reagan Administration position, ruled today that judges may order employers to use strict racial quotas temporarily in promotions as well as hiring to counter severe past discrimination against blacks.

By 5 to 4, the Court upheld a Federal district judge's orders in 1983 and 1984 requiring Alabama to promote one black state trooper for each white state trooper, assuming qualified blacks were available, until the state could develop a promotion procedure acceptable to the judge.

The decision reinforced and partly expanded three major rulings last year in which the Court rejected the Administration's broad attack on all use of racial preferences to remedy past job discrimination and approved use of temporary, limited hiring preferences.

In its affirmative action decision, the Court made clear for the first time that courts, at least in extreme cases, may order racial preferences in promotions as well as in hiring, and may use highly specific numerical "catch-up" quotas to bring an employer's work force quickly into line with the percentage of qualified members of minority groups in the available labor pool.

Reagan Appoints Dissent

The majority also said a court order requiring that black employees be promoted ahead of whites with higher test scores, like a hiring preference, did not have so severe an impact on the whites as would a requirement that whites be laid off before less senior blacks

The decision also confirmed speculation that President Reagan's naming William H. Rehnquist as Chief Justice last summer and appointing Antonin Scalia as an Associate Justice would not swing the Court dramatically toward the Administration's position on affirmative action.

Both men dissented today, as expected, siding with the Administration view that the quota order was not a good remedy for the discrimination. But this did not represent a change in the overall voting lineup.

Mr. Rehnquist, as an Associate Justice, consistently opposed affirmative action preferences. While Warren E. Burger, who retired as Chief Justice last summer, was less consistent in opposing affirmative action, he sided with the Administration in all three of last year's cases.

Solicitor Called It Arbitrary

In the Alabama case, Solicitor General Charles Fried had assailed the one-for-one promotion quota as "profoundly illegal" and "wholly arbitrary." The Court upheld it in light of the Alabama state trooper force's long history of racial discrimination and resistance to court orders. The state had totally excluded blacks from the force until it was forced to hire some by a 1972 court order.

Deborah Burstion-Wade, spokeswoman for Assistant Attorney General William Bradford Reynolds, head of the Justice Department's Civil Rights Division, said the decision was not surprising after last year's rulings and "didn't break any new ground."

Justice William J. Brennan Jr.'s opinion, which was joined by only three other Justices, rejected arguments by the Administration and the dissenters that the one-for-one quota was not "narrowly tailored" enough to pass muster under the standards the Court laid down last year.

'Astonishing' View Cited

He termed "astonishing" what he called Mr. Fried's suggestion that after years of unfulfilled promises by the state that it would adopt procedures to comply with court orders, "in 1983 the district court was constitutionally required to settle for yet another promise."

Mr. Fried said through a spokesman today that he was disappointed with the ruling and agreed with the dissenters. Civil rights groups hailed the decision in the case, United States v Paradise, No. 85—999.

Barry Goldstein, a lawyer for the NAACP Legal Defense and Educational Fund, stressed the majority's rejection of "rigid limitations on affirmative action."

He said the decision showed that Mr. Fried had been wrong in asserting that last year's rulings meant racial preferences could "hardly ever" be used.

Justice Brennan, citing last year's decisions, said "it is now well-established that government bodies, including courts, may constitutionally employ racial classifications essential to remedy unlawful treatment of racial or ethnic groups subject to discrimination."

'Race-Conscious Relief' Needed

He added that "the pervasive, systematic and obstinate discriminatory conduct of the department created a profound need and a firm justification for the race-conscious relief ordered by the district court."

Justice Brennan's 34-page opinion was joined by Justices Thurgood Marshall, Harry A. Blackmun and Lewis F. Powell, Jr.

Justice Powell said in a concurring opinion that the state "had engaged in persistent violation of constitutional rights and repeatedly failed to carry out court orders" and that the one-for-one promotion quota had been enforced by the district court on only one occasion, when it ordered the promotion of eight blacks and eight whites to the rank of corporal in 1984.

He also said that unlike affirmative action plans requiring layoffs of whites before less-senior blacks, which a majority of the Court disapproved last year as imposing a harsh burden on white employees, the district court's promotion quota "does not disrupt seriously the lives of innocent individuals," even though the promotions of some white troopers would be delayed.

Justice John Paul Stevens concurred in the decision but did not join Justice Brennan's opinion. He stressed that Federal courts had broad discretion to order racial preferences in cases in which past discrimination had been proved.

Justice Steven's opinion seemed to endorse judicial use of affirmative action to remedy past discrimination even more broadly than did Justice Brennan's opinion.

Citing the Court's endorsement of "broad and flexible" judicial authority to remedy constitutional violations in the context of school desegregation cases, Justice Stevens said judicial authority to remedy job discrimination should be equally broad.

Unlike affirmative action plans voluntarily adopted by state and local governments, Justice Stevens said, those imposed by Federal judges need not be "narrowly tailored to achieve a compelling governmental interest." Rather, they need only be within the bounds of "reasonableness."

O'Connor Writes Dissent

Justice Sandra Day O'Connor dissented, joined by Chief Justice Rehnquist and Justice Scalia. Justice Byron R. White dissented separately.

Justice O'Connor, like Mr. Fried argued that even though Alabama was guilty of an "egregious history of discrimination," the lower court's quota was not sufficiently "narrowly tailored," and was unduly burdensome on innocent white troopers seeking promotions.

She faulted the district court for imposing "a racial quota without first considering the effectiveness of alternatives," such as imposing "stiff fines or other penalties" on the Alabama Department of Public Safety until it adopted adequate procedures for promotion of blacks.

"The one-for-one promotion quota used in this case far exceeded the percentage of blacks in the trooper force. and there is no evidence in the record that such an extreme quota was necessary," Justice O'Connor wrote.

About 25 percent of the people qualified to be state troopers were blacks. Justice Brennan said temporary use of the 50 percent "catch-up" quota for promotions was justified to speed the day when blacks would occupy something like 25 percent of the department's upper positions.

Pressure on Department Sought

He said the promotion quota was "narrowly tailored" to the legitimate goals of eliminating the effects of past discrimination, "inducing the department to implement a promotion procedure that would not have an adverse impact on blacks," and eliminating the effects of the department's long delay.

The lower court had found the procedures previously adopted by the department inadequate because they included examinations on which blacks had scored much lower on average than whites.

Justice Brennan also termed the quota "flexible in application" because it applied only to the extent that qualified black troopers were available and the department needed to make promotions, and because it would be lifted whenever the department adopted adequate procedures of its own.

Source: *The New York Times*, 26 Feb. 1987.

Supreme Court, 6-3, Extends Preferences in Employment for Women and Minorities

By STUART TAYLOR JR.

Setback to Reagan

Rights Groups Hail Step as a Major Victory—Dissent is Sharp

WASHINGTON, March 25—In a broad extension of its decisions on affirmative action, the Supreme Court ruled today that employers may sometimes favor women and members of minorities over better-qualified men and whites in hiring and promoting to achieve better balance in their work forces.

The 6-to-3 decision upholding a California city's affirmative action plan for employees who are women and minority group members was a major defeat for the Reagan Administration and was hailed as a major victory by women's rights and civil rights groups. It was written by Justice William J. Brennan Jr.

The ruling was the Court's first involving an affirmative action plan giving job preferences to women over men. The Court rejected a civil rights suit by a man who said he had been the victim of illegal sex discrimination when he lost a promotion to a woman.

Balance With Population

The ruling also marked the first time the Court had unambiguously held that without any proof of past discrimination against women or minorities by a particular employer, the employer may use racial and sexual preferences in hiring and promotions to bring its work force into line with the makeup of the local population or labor market.

In a blistering dissent, Justice Antonin Scalia said the Court's "enormous expansion" of prior decisions upholding affirmative action had completed its conversion of a 1964 antidiscrimination law into an "engine of discrimination" against men and whites, especially the "unknown, unaffluent, unorganized."

Supporters of the decision jubilantly predicted that it would increase the percentage of women in jobs historically held by men. Opponents said it would prompt employers to discount merit as the basis for hiring and promotions.

Dispatcher Job at Issue

The Court rejected a suit by a man whom the Santa Clara County Transportation Agency passed over in 1980 for a promotion to the job of dispatching road crews, in favor of a woman with a slightly lower score in a competitive interviewing process.

Justice Brennan said that under Title VII of the Civil Rights Act of 1964, the Federal job discrimination statute, the same standards that the Court has laid down to assess the legality of racial affirmative action plans should be used in assessing sex-based affirmative action plans. And the standards laid down today for sex-based affirmative action plans would also apply in the racial context, he said.

Experts said the Court's interpretation of Title VII would have a broad impact, strengthening the incentives of both public and private employers around the country to adopt voluntary affirmative action plans.

Terry Eastland, the chief Justice Department spokesman, said:

"We're disappointed that the Court has departed from the moral principle of nondiscrimination for all Americans that is the basis for our civil rights law. This principle holds, and teaches, that employment decisions should not be made on the basis of race or sex."

The transportation agency, which a lower Federal court found had not discriminated against women in the past, adopted its affirmative action plan in part to achieve "the long-term goal of a work force that mirrored in its major job classifications the percentage of women in the area labor market," Justice Brennan noted.

But he also stressed that the plan considered sex or race as only one of several factors in individual employment decisions, that "the agency has no intention of establishing a work force whose permanent composition is dictated by rigid numerical standards," and that in the immediate case "any difference in qualifications" between the plaintiff and the woman who got the promotion "were minimal."

"In determining whether an imbalance exists that would justify taking sex or race into account," Justice Brennan said, "a comparison of the percentage of minorities or women in the employer's work force with the percentage in the area labor market or general population is appropriate in analyzing jobs that require no special expertise."

Many, and perhaps most employers have smaller percentages of women and minorities in major job categories than the percentages of those groups in the local labor market or population.

Past Discrimination Issue

Such employers risk being sued for past discrimination by women and minorities on the basis of statistical evidence if they fail to adopt affirmative action plans, even if the employers believe themselves innocent of past discrimination.

Today's decision in Johnson v. Transportation Agency, No. 85–1129, minimizes the risk that they will be sued for "reverse discrimination" by men or whites if they do adopt affirmative action plans.

Justice Brennan's majority opinion was joined by Justices Thurgood Marshall, Harry A. Blackmun, Lewis F. Powell Jr. and John Paul Stevens, who also wrote a separate concurrence.

Justice Sandra Day O'Connor voted to uphold the promotion of the woman, Diane Joyce, on much narrower grounds, criticizing Justice Brennan as having "an expansive and ill-defined approach to affirmative action by public employers."

Justice Scalia's dissent was joined by Chief Justice William H. Rehnquist and in part by Justice Byron R. White.

In its 1978 decision in Steelworkers v. Weber, the Court ruled, somewhat ambiguously, that private employers may sometimes give job preferences under voluntary affirmative action plans "to break down old patterns of racial segregation and hierarchy."

That decision clearly approved voluntary use by an employer of racial affirmative action preferences to remedy past discrimination by that employer. But it was unclear until today whether the Court would apply the same logic to sexual affirmative action or to governmental employers.

The Weber decision was also somewhat ambiguous on whether the Court would uphold an employer's use of racial or sexual preferences to produce a statistically balanced work force, in the absence of proof of prior discrimination by that employer.

In today's decision, Justice Brennan stressed language in the Weber decision that supported the transportation agency's affirmative action plan, which he described as a "moderate, flexible" and gradual approach to bringing women into historically male job categories that would not harm men unduly.

Thus, he said, the decision was "consistent with Title VII's purpose of eliminating the effects of employment discrimination," and did not improperly "dictate mere blind hiring by the numbers" without regard for the limited availability of qualified women in the area's labor pool.

Without questioning a Federal district court's finding that the county agency had not discriminated against women, Justice Brennan also stressed that "as for the job classification relevant to this case, none of the 238 skilled craft worker positions was held by a woman" when the affirmative action plan was adopted in 1978.

One question left unanswered by Justice Brennan's opinion was whether the Court might apply a more exacting legal standard in evaluating a constitutional challenge to a governmental employer's affirmative action plan than it used in today's case.

Today's decision established a Title VII standard considerably looser than the constitutional standard the Court laid down last year when it struck down a racially based layoff plan in Wygant v. Jackson Board of Education. While the dissenters argued that the two standards should be the same, Justice Brennan responded that the Court need not consider the Wygant standard in a Title VII case.

The constitutionality of the transportation agency's affirmative action plan was not directly an issue in today's case because Paul E. Johnson, the passed-over male employee, chose to base his suit on Title VII alone.

Justice Scalia said in his dissent that the Court had distorted Title VII, which was aimed at eradicating racial and sexual discrimination, to promote "the quite incompatible goal of proportionate representation by race and sex in the work place.

"The only losers in this process are the Johnsons of the country, for whom Title VII has been not merely repealed but actually inverted," Justice Scalia said. "The irony is that these individuals—predominantly unknown, unaffluent, unorganized—suffer this injustice at the hands of a Court fond of thinking itself the champion of the politically impotent."

Justice Scalia, and Justice White in his brief separate dissent, both called for overruling Weber, as broadened by today's decision, as a perversion of Congress's intent in Title VII. Justice White was in the majority in Weber, but said the Court had overextended it today.

Justice Scalia also said today's decision "effectively requires employers, public as well as private, to engage in intentional discrimination on the basis of race or sex."

Previous decisions, he said, "subject employers to a potential Title VII suit whenever there is a noticeable imbalance in the representation of minorities or women in the employer's work force."

After today's decision, which insulates employers who adopt affirmative action plans against "reverse discrimination" suits, he said, it would be "economic folly" in many cases for employers not to engage in reverse discrimination.

"A statute designed to establish a color-blind and gender-blind work place has thus been converted into a powerful engine of racism and sexism," he said.

Justice Scalia asserted that in today's case, "there was no prior sex discrimination to remedy," and that the reason women had been under-represented in road maintenance and dispatching was because they had not in the past viewed such jobs as desirable.

He dismissed as "patently false" the majority's assertion that its approach would insure consistency with Title VII's goal of eliminating the effects of past discrimination.

"It is the alteration of social attitudes, rather than the elimination of discrimination, which today's decision approves as justification for state-enforced discrimination," he said.

Source: *The New York Times,* 26 Mar. 1987.

E4–4:   Forms of Market Power

Economists have terms for the two forms in which power is exerted at the market: unshared power and shared power.

Case 1: Unshared Power

If a single participant has complete power over one side of the market, we say that participant is a *monopolist* when the control is exerted over the supply side and a *monopsonist* when the control is exerted over the demand side. If a single firm provides all the electric power in town, it is a monopoly. If a single firm is the only employer in town, it is a monopsony.

The benefits that come from having a monopoly or a monopsony depend first and foremost on conditions on the other side of the same market. If you are a monopolist and there is no demand, or a monopsonist and there is no supply, your power won't generate any benefits. If you're a monopsonist who faces a monopolist, then your power positions are at odds and undermine one another.

The benefits that come from having a monopoly or monopsony also depend on the substitution possibilities. To the degree that it's easy to

substitute for the supply or the demand of a monopolist or monopsonist, respectively, the benefit of the monopoly or monopsony is
undermined. For example, Procter and Gamble has a monopoly over
the sale of Crest toothpaste, but if one needs toothpaste, one doesn't
have to buy Crest. Thus, while P&G has a monopoly, it is not one that
can be intensively exploited because there is plenty of competition
from similar products. We call this case *monopolistic competition*.
Monopolistic competitors generally compete for market share by
advertising the distinction of their products. The more intense this
competition, the more it eats up the benefits—the profits—that come
from the monopolistic advantage. Similarly, there could be monopso-
nistic competition.

Case 2: Shared Power

If several participants share power over one side of a market, we say
they are *oligopolists* when the control is exerted on the supply side
and *oligopsonists* when the control is exerted on the demand side. In
its heyday the Organization of Petroleum Exporting Countries (OPEC)
was a successful oligopoly. Professional baseball team owners have
the potential to act as an oligopsony vis-à-vis players.

As with monopoly and monopsony, the benefits of having a oligopoly or oligopsony depend on the condition on the other side of the
same market and on the conditions in related markets. The key distinction between the monopoly/monopsony case and the oligopoly/
oligopsony case is that the latter, involving by definition shared
power, requires cooperation. This, in turn, gives rise to one of the
classic characteristics of the ologopoly/oligopsony case: the cooperation required to maintain the benefit of shared power is inherently
unstable. The reason for this instability is simple: everyone benefits if
all cooperate, but any individual can benefit more if she cheats while
everyone else cooperates. This was in part the cause of OPEC's
demise. By agreeing on production quotas, the OPEC countries constrained the supply and thereby increased the price of oil. Eventually,
however, some members couldn't resist the temptation to cheat—
seduced by the high price, they sold more than their quota. The action
of each member of an oligopoly affects all other members. In this
case, increasing the supply of oil benefited the cheaters but hurt
everyone else because it lowered the price of oil.

The instability of cooperative agreements when there are benefits
to cheating is represented in game theory by the *prisoner's dilemma*.

In this game there are two participants and each can choose to cooperate or cheat. Table E4–4A shows the four possible outcomes based on the two choices available to each participant. (The first number in each pair is the payoff to participant I and the second number is the payoff to participant U.)

Table E4–4A: Prisoner's Dilemma

		Participant U'S Choice	
		Cooperate	Cheat
Participant I's	Cooperate	(10,10)	(2,12)
Choice	Cheat	(12, 2)	(5, 5)

We see from Table E4–4A that if U and I cooperate we both get a payoff of 10. However, if I cooperate and U cheat, U get a payoff of 12 and I get only 2. Conversely, if I cheat and U cooperate, I get a payoff of 12 and U get a payoff of 2. Thus we see that there's a high price for cooperating if the other participant cheats. Given the structure of the payoffs, in the absence of complete trust, fear of being exploited by the other participant would drive both participants to cheat. The payoff to both parties is lower (5,5) than mutual cooperation would provide (10,10), but without any device that could ensure cooperation, this mutual cheating is the dominate strategy. It is precisely this dilemma that makes oligopolies and oligopsonies such unstable arrangements.

E4–5: Revisiting Our Basic Decision Rule: MC/MB Analysis

If we assume that at the margin the benefits of doing anything eventually begin to diminish and the opportunity costs eventually begin to rise, we can represent that case graphically as shown in Figure E4–5A. If, as we assume, your objective is to maximize your utility, at what point should you cease this activity?

Consider: For every successive unit of activity up to L_o the benefit is greater than the cost, or $MB>MC$. Thus each of these adds to your utility. For successive units beyond Lo, the cost outweighs the benefit, or $MC>MB$. Thus each of these subtracts from your utility.

We see then that you will continue to pursue this activity—for example, rent-seeking—up to L_o. You cease at L_o because at that unit you find that there is no more net utility to be had from this activity.

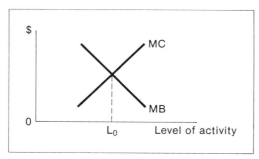

Figure E4–5A: Marginal Cost/Marginal Benefit Graph. For simplicity, we assume that we can put a dollar value on benefits and costs.

E5–1: Marketing Pollution Rights

The following article from *The New York Times* (September 14, 1986) reports on a California experiment in marketing pollution rights:

Playing the Market in Pollution Rights

By NICHOLAS D. KRISTOF

LOS ANGELES A proposed plant that would generate electricity by burning old tires has many people angry in Rialto, a growing community 50 miles east of Los Angeles. Its sponsors say the plant would employ 240 people and save 545,000 barrels of oil a year; its critics point out that it would also create more haze in the San Bernardino Valley, which has some of the worst air pollution in the nation.

But beyond the usual issues, the proposal is a test of an Environmental Protection Agency policy that permits businesses to buy and sell the right to pollute the air.

Under this "bubble policy," which the E.P.A. adopted in 1979, state and local regulators concern themselves with the total amount of pollution spewed into the atmosphere in a designated region. So long as any increase in pollution from one plant is offset by reductions at another, the industries do not face penalties or curbs.

Because the Rialto tire-burning plant would produce 640 tons of pollutants a year, for example, its developers must by "smog credits" from companies willing to cut back on pollution in San Bernardino County and surrounding areas. They could do so by paying other companies to cut production and therefore pollution or by paying them to install air-cleaning equipment, then buying the resulting emission credits.

"It's a heck of a good idea," said John C. Brewer, chairman of Garb Oil & Power Corporation, the Salt Lake City company that wants to build the tire-burning plant. "Otherwise, you'll stop growth entirely. And if you stop growth, who will feed the people?"

When Garb Oil applied for a permit to build a plant last year, waste-to-energy facilities did not have to obtain all the credits they might otherwise need, provided they made a good-faith effort to do so. But the California Legislature repealed that exemption, effective Jan 1.

While the Rialto plant may have qualified for the exemption because it had filed applications for a permit before the provision's repeal, Mr. Brewer argued that the change would make it virtually impossible to build other waste-to-energy plants. The problem, he said, is that smog credits are simply unavailable; his company negotiated with 2,000 other concerns in Southern California, he said, but was able to acquire only one-fourth of the credits it would have needed without the exemption.

The exception for the energy plants was enacted in 1981, when oil prices were high and new sources of energy and jobs seemed more important than improved air quality. Today, with California's ecomony strong and oil prices plunging, the mood has changed, legislators say. "Before you recover resources, you have to breathe." said Robert Presley, a state senator opposed to the Rialto plant.

Promoting Methanol

Some hope that a novel provision adopted earlier this month by the South Coast Air Quality Management District, which administers the bubble policy here, will derail Garb Oil's proposal. The district's plan would require certain waste-to-energy facilities to earn all their smog credits. They could obtain these, however, by buying methanol-powered buses for cities. Methanol, a form of alcohol, burns more cleanly than gasoline or diesel fuel, and California encourages efforts to increase its use. Emissions from cars, not industries, are the principal reason why the pollution in many areas of Southern California exceeds Federal clean air standards about 150 days each year.

Environmentalists contend that the bubble policy is too lax. Among other things, they say, it undercuts the benefits of pollution controls that would have been installed anyway.

In addition, Senator Presley said, a factory in an area with clean air can sell emission credits to one in a town like Rialto that has dirty air. The California system reduces the value of emission credits used some distance from where they were obtained, but it does not disallow them, he noted. Thus it might take 150 credits from a Long Beach factory to allow a Los Angeles company to emit 100 pounds of pollutants.

A recent study by the Conservation Foundation, an environmental group, concluded that the policy had saved industry money while—in a few cases, at least—reducing pollution more than Government regulations might have.

But the study also determined that the system had failed to fulfill a main objective: encouraging industry to create more effective ways of controlling pollution. "The bubble policy," it said, "has inspired virtually no technological innovation."

Does this experiment appear promising? If you were in charge, how would you adjust it to make it more successful? If you think it is doomed to failure, what, if anything, would you propose in its place?

E5–2: How Far Do We Want to Trust the Market Process?

Are market solutions the right solution for every choice coordination process, or should government step in and dictate how some decisions are coordinated? Consider the case of the baby market. Because of changes in technology, the normal source of supply is dwindling. If demand remains constant, then, as we see in the following article from *The New York Times* (April 5, 1987), the price will rise.

Adoption Market: Big Demand, Tight Supply

By ROBERT LINDSEY

SAN FRANCISCO, April 4 —The legal battle over Baby M that was settled this week in a New Jersey courtroom has focused attention on a widening gap between the number of infertile American couples who want children and the number of babies available for adoption.

Out of desperation for a baby, couples are increasingly placing advertisements in college and urban newspapers seeking an unwed mother willing to surrender her child. Some couples have even sought infants by placing notices on cars at shopping center parking lots and on park benches and railroad overpasses.

Federal officials say the rising demand has also led to a proliferation of organized rings that smuggle babies, some of them kidnapped, across the Mexican border and then sell them to the highest bidder in this country.

Competing for Babies

"It's a bad business," said Clifton J. Rogers, deputy district director of the Immigration and Naturalization Service in San Diego. "It's one thing to smuggle an adult who will go to work in this country. It's another to prey on the deep suffering and need that people have for a baby."

Although physicians say that growing numbers of childless couples like William and Elizabeth Stern, the New Jersey couple awarded custody of Baby M, are contracting with surrogate mothers or trying to conceive a child through laboratory fertilization methods, most first try to adopt a child in a marketplace in which there is far more demand than supply.

And those who compete in this marketplace say the experience can be frustrating, painful and emotional.

"The frustrating thing is there aren't the number of babies out there that there used to be," said Helen Barbato of Pleasanton, Calif., who, with her husband, Gary, is among thousands of Americans who send letters, make phone calls and use whatever other strategies they can to find an infant or a pregnant woman willing to give up her unborn child.

"We came close this weekend, right in our own neighborhood, when we heard about a girl who was pregnant," Mrs. Barbato said. "But people are telling her, 'You can get money for your baby.' It's illegal, but you have to compete with people who are willing to buy a baby."

According to the National Committee for Adoption, an association of 130 private adoption agencies, the number of adoptions between unrelated people in the United States declined to 50,720, from 82,800, from 1971 through 1982, the last year for which complete statistics are available.

The 38 percent decline is attributed principally to a diminishing pool of children available for adoption because of more abortions, a greater use of contraceptives and a lessening of the social stigma faced by single parents.

Some experts, however, estimate that the number of adoptions has risen about 10 percent since 1982, primarily because of successful efforts by Roman Catholic groups to persuade some unmarried pregnant women not to have abortions and, more important, a sharp increase in the number of children brought to this country legally, generally by public and private agencies, for adoption by American families.

The number of foreign-born children adopted in the United States rose from 4,868 in the 1981 fiscal year to 9,945 last year. Of those, 6,188, almost two-thirds, came from South Korea.

Baby Boom Generation

Despite the apparent recent increase in the availability of infants for adoption, social workers and family counselors say the demand for babies is growing faster than the supply. They say the main reason is that many members of the postwar baby boom generation, after previously postponing parenthood, have discovered they are infertile and are now seeking to adopt children.

"We have 12 to 15 prospective parents for every easy-to-place baby," said Raymond Chirosky, an official in California of the Children's Home Society, a national private adoption agency, referring to what he and others describe as the most sought-after child: a white infant with no physical or mental handicaps.

According to adoption specialists, the widening gap between supply and demand has spurred not only the smuggling of growing numbers of babies from Mexico and other Latin countries but also the creation of a new kind of entrepeneur who helps couples find a baby, usually for a large fee. Officials say many are swindlers who exploit the desperation of childless couples with promises of infants that never materialize.

Payments of $10,000 or More

In Petaluma, a city about 45 miles north of here, for example, police officials last month charged Annette M. Tonkin and Lewis E. Reid with taking $3,500 from a couple after telling them Miss Tonkin was pregnant and the child could be theirs if they paid Miss Tonkin's maternity and delivery expenses. Investigators have alleged that Miss Tonkin and Mr. Reid bilked other couples the same way at least twice before.

In another case, the authorities in Athens, Ala., said Tuesday that they were investigating the 1980 slayings of two young mothers who they say were killed by an itinerant couple from Washington State. That couple, the authorities said, then sold the women's children to couples who wanted to be parents.

Social workers say the willingness of many childless couples to pay $10,000 or more for a child is also attracting lawyers to a field once monopolized by public adoption agencies and private groups

such as the Children's Home Society. Independent adoptions handled by lawyers now account for more than one-third of the adoptions nationally and a substantially larger proportion in some states, particularly California.

Serving as Adoption Brokers

In a few cities, such nonprofit groups as Friends in Adoption in Pawlet, Vt., and the Independent Adoption Center in Pleasant Hill, Calif., offer counseling services, usually for a small fee, that are intended to teach couples how to find infants without having to use a lawyer. But social workers say the great majority of independent adoptions are handled by lawyers.

Although they emphasized that many lawyers specializing in adoption act ethically and responsibly, the social workers contended that some, in effect, serve as little more than brokers at an infant auction, often encouraging would-be parents to offer a "gift" to the pregnant woman in exchange for her child.

William L. Pierce, president of the National Committee for Adoption, said that in some cases lawyers and other entrepreneurs placed classified advertisements purporting to be from eager couples seeking a woman willing to give up her

child. But he said the majority of such advertisements appear to be legitimate.

While conceding that physicians, lawyers, and other third parties have acted as intermediaries between unwed mothers and childless couples for decades, Mr. Pierce said, "It's much bigger now because the profits are greater and the desperation has gotten greater."

Making 'a Business of It'

This week the personal columns of The Salt Lake City Tribune contained seven advertisements soliciting pregnant women for their children.

In telephone interviews, several of the would-be parents who placed the advertisements said they had received what appeared to be promising, legitimate calls from women willing to give up their babies, but they said they were troubled by some of the calls.

A 39-year-old woman from Long Island said she had received a call from one young woman demanding $30,000 for her unborn child. "I told her I didn't want to buy a baby, I wanted to adopt one."

After receiving several similar calls, a Los Angeles woman said, "I think there are some girls who get pregnant just to make a business of it."

One creative strategy that entrepreneurs have developed for meeting the demand is surrogate parenting. Surrogate fathering (with sperm banks as intermediary) has long been an accepted practice in the United States. However, as the following article from *The New York Times* (April 1, 1987), reflects, surrogate mothering is stirring a fierce debate. As you read the article, consider: What do you think of surrogate mothering as a market solution? How about surrogate fathering? Is there a justification for government intervention here? What about in other areas of technological advance such as genetic engineering? What should the role of government be?

Seven-Week Trial Touched Many Basic Emotions

By ROBERT HANLEY

HACKENSACK, N.J., March 31—Beyond the walls of Judge Harvey R. Sorkow's courtroom here, experts in philosophy, law and psychiatry wrestle with social, cultural and ethical questions about surrogate parents that go far beyond the Baby M custody case.

In the weeks before the trial involving Baby M's mother, Mary Beth Whitehead, and father, William Stern, there were many calls for swift legislative action to prevent similar fights over children born of artificial insemination for a fee. The intent appeared to be to regulate the practice.

But after the seven-week trial of raw emotion and anguish, the mood appears to be one calling for caution and careful study, stricter guidelines and thoughtful reflection.

"I haven't heard any outpouring of people who think this might be a good thing," a professor of legal issues in pediatrics at the Yale Medical School, Angela R. Holder, said. "I think more people are against it than before."

"Only in the last month has the full impact of surrogacy been understood," William Pierce, president of the National Committee for Adoption and a foe of surrogacy, said. "Many people who saw surrogacy as ethically neutral and socially neutral and legally neutral are having second thoughts."

In the aftermath of the trial and Judge Sorkow's ruling, it appears that surrogacy is poised for the wide-ranging examination that the judge specifically barred in his exploration of whether the Sterns or the Whiteheads were the more suitable parents to meet the "best interests" of Baby M.

The primary focus of the trial was a harsh concentrated attack on Mrs. Whitehead's personality and emotional state and the stability of her home and marriage.

But surrogacy and its ramifications — including the very concept of motherhood — are more profound, according to experts. Does an acceptance of surrogacy mean that American society is ready for two types of mother — the biological mother, who provides half the baby's genes and surrenders the infant at birth for a fee, and the psychological, or care-giving mother, the wife of the biological father?

"This case shakes the certainty of defining the term 'mother,'" Dr. Arthur Caplan, a philosopher at the Hastings Center, a research institute on biomedical ethics in Briarcliff Manor, N.Y., said "It's socially and culturally disturbing. It takes away a reference point.

"This case chips away at our certainty of understanding our concept of mother. Is it the environmental and social shaper or the person who provides the hereditary blue-

print?"

Dr. Caplan sees other disturbing problems. He asked how impoverished overpopulated third-world countries would view one segment of American society's ignoring thousands of children available for adoption and indulging in costly reproductive technology, while another segment undergoes 1.5 million abortions a year?

He also raised questions about couples who could not afford the $30,000 in surrogate costs for a child and whether surrogacy should remain private, excluding the poor. Or, he added, should health insurers underwrite its cost?

Mr. Pierce brought up the possibility of an artificially inseminated child being born severely retarded or handicapped. "Will the biological father or the surrogate mother eventually dump these kids on society and have the states pay $18,000 to $20,000 a year for their institutional care?" he asked.

Another issue is whether surrogacy creates an exploited breeder class of women — the poor and educationally disadvantaged carrying and bearing children for the prosperous.

"We don't want breeders for people in a different financial strata," Dr. Doris Jonas Freed, co-chairman of the surrogate-parenting committee of the New York State Bar Association, said. "The money has to be played down."

Another question is who is entitled to use a surrogate. Some advocates insist new laws must restrict it solely to married heterosexual couples who are medically certified as infertile.

But if, as some lawyers argue, the Constitution insures the right to reproduce, how can homosexual men and women be legally barred from using a surrogate or other forms of reproductive technology to obtain a child? And how, asked Myra T. Peterson, chairwoman-elect of the family law section of the New Jersy Bar Association, can courts prevent career-oriented women from hiring a surrogate out of simple convenience?

"Another thing the trial's brought out is the effect of surrogacy on the baby's half siblings," Ms. Peterson said. "What does it do to those children when they see a child being given away or sold?"

During the Baby M trial, Judge Sorkow routinely ruled out testimony on emotional ties Mrs. Whitehead's two children had for the baby. He said the feelings had no bearing on the baby's best interests.

Most important, experts said, no one knows what psychological scars will be inflicted on Baby M — or other children of surrogacy — when they learn their origins and, in Baby M's case, of the bitter fight throughout her first year of life.

"The whole case is just a tragedy for the child," Professor Holder said, because of both the publicity and the litigation. "If they go to the Supreme Court of the United States, this child will be in first grade before she knows her ultimate destination."

"For the rest of her life, she'll be the famous Baby M," a clinical professor of child psychiatry at Columbia University, Richard A. Gardner, said. "If the court had acted decisively and with finality in the first month of this, there wouldn't be the psychological traumas there will be now."

Source: *The New York Times*, 1 Apr. 1987.

E5–3: Price Controls: Ceilings and Floors

Price controls are a common method of government intervention. In their most common form price controls are administered selectively; that is, on a single good, service, or factor. We have analyzed the effect of a selective price ceiling. Here is an example of one that was reported in *The New York Times* (August 24, 1986).

U.S. Agency Cites Low Pay in Nurse Shortage

WASHINGTON, Aug. 23 (AP) —The National Institutes of Health, unable to recruit enough skilled nurses to work under a Government pay scale that is $5,000 below Washington-area standards, says it has been forced to close 5 percent of the beds in its world-renowned clinical research center.

"There is difficulty in recruiting professional nurses and technical workers, and we happen to be in one of the acute phases," said Tanya Crow, acting associate director for nursing services at the institutes' Warren G. Magnuson Clinical Center.

Colleen Henrichsen, a spokesman for the center, said Friday that the institutes had closed 19 hospital beds for cancer patients, which is more than 15 percent of the beds reserved for patients undergoing cancer therapy in research projects conducted by the institutes.

The clinical center has also closed six beds in its intensive care units because of nurse shortages, Ms. Henrichsen said. The clinical center has about 500 beds.

Up to 70 Nursing Vacancies

The center ordinarily employs the equivalent of about 700 full-time nurses, and as many as 70 of those slots at a time have been vacant because of the recruiting difficulties, Ms. Crow said.

When problems are severe the center is "not able to go full steam ahead with some of the research as quickly as some of the investigators would like to do," she said, adding, "In the aggregate, yes, it would be slowing the effort of the institute."

Ms. Henrichsen said the institutes offer beginning registered nurses $18,000 a year, in contrast to $23,000 to $24,000 by other institutions in the Washington area. The center pays head nurses $31,500 a year, while the going rate in the area is $35,000 to $38,000. Federal personnel laws do not allow the institutes to raise their pay level to compete.

The competition is expected to get stiffer as time goes by, Ms. Crow said.

'The Pool is Diminishing'

"The pool is diminishing," she said. "The number of nurses going into professional training is decreasing, so the pool that is coming out is less than it has been."

Ms. Crow said she was still successful in recruiting many nurses by offering them the chance to work alongside some of the world's leading scientists conducting research on the frontiers of medicine.

But, she acknowledged, prestigious research hospitals abound in the Washington area, so a skilled nurse does not necessarily have to choose between pay and challenge.

The Washington Post, which reported the problem Friday, said the shortage of nurses was particularly severe in the cancer wards because of the special training required and because nurses working there tended to exhaust themselves more quickly as a result of the emotional strain of dealing with critically ill patients.

Source: *The New York Times*, 24 Aug. 1986.

Now consider the effect as shown in Figure E5–3A of a selective price floor. A price floor sets a downward limit on price. If a price floor is above that price to which the market would independently adjust, the consequence would be an excess supply.

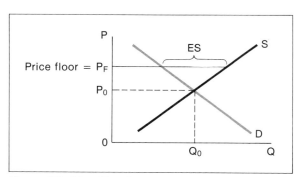

Figure E5–3A: The Case of Excess Supply We call P_F an effective price floor because it does have an effect on the market. If P_F were below P_0, it would not be effective. Why?

Price floors are common in agriculture. In response to equity considerations or to rent-seeking by agricultural interests (the interpretation depends on the commodity involved and your perspective), price floors have been established for products like milk and sugar. In order to avoid illegal dumping of the excess supply on the market (which would undermine the price floor), the government sets the floor and buys up the excess supply generated at that price. Then the government has the problem of disposing of the surplus. The efficiency implications should be obvious. First, there is the waste of resources to produce a level of output that will not be sold. Second, there is the cost of disposing of the excess supply.

The policy also has intermarket implications. As we have seen, a product's demand becomes more elastic over time as new substitutes come to the market. This process occurs more quickly if a product's price is artificially high. Thus the development and substitution of margarine for butter and of corn sweeteners for cane sugar was quickened by price supports that kept the prices of butter and cane sugar artificially high.

Price controls can also be imposed generally. This was done in the United States during World War II and during the early 1970s. In both cases, the price controls were a response to inflation and fears of greater inflation. Inflation, a rise in general level of prices, is a macroeconomic concept we will examine shortly. However, general price controls have microeconomic implications that we should note here. When all prices are frozen, this stops inflation, but it also stops the mechanism—the adjustment of relative prices—on which our market system depends for coherent coordination of supply and demand decisions. Thus a simple solution to a macroeconomic problem creates a very complex microeconomic problem: If prices are not able to coordinate decisions, how will they be coordinated?

E5-4: On Taxes; A Microeconomic View

As noted in the text, the imposition of a tax changes the structure of incentives facing individuals and therefore alters their pattern of behavior. The government has the power to tax and thus to manipulate behavior. There are lots of ways for government to tax. What we want to do here is examine one kind of tax in order to demonstrate how complicated taxation policy can be.

Suppose the government decided to impose a flat tax (fixed amount) on every bottle of beer produced. Suppose, further, that the purpose of this tax was to discourage the consumption of alcohol and thereby to reduce drunk driving and the related deaths and injuries.

The effect of the tax would be to shift up the supply curve. Specifically, the price that suppliers would charge at any given quantity supplied would go up by the amount of the tax, as shown in Figure E5–4A.

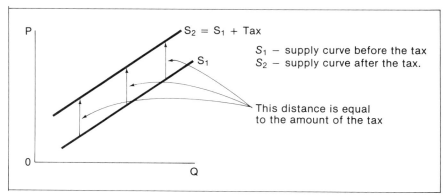

Figure E5–4A   A Flat Tax per Unit Supplied

The tax shown in the figure affects the supply curve, but the effect of the tax on the market depends on the interaction of supply and demand. So in order to know the effect of the tax, we must know the nature of demand. We well consider two extreme cases: perfectly elastic and perfectly inelastic demand.

If demand is perfectly inelastic, the market picture representing the imposition of the tax will look as shown in Figure E5–4B.

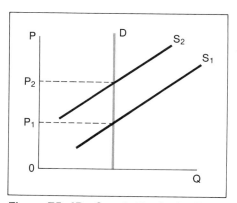

Figure E5–4B   Supply Tax in the Face of Perfectly Inelastic Demand

We can say several things about the effect of a tax in this case. In light of the objective of the government policy, this tax plan is a total failure. The purpose of the tax was to discourage consumption, but given a perfectly inelastic demand, consumption remained exactly the same. Note, however, that the government did gain tax revenue equal to the tax $(P_2 - P_1)$ times quantity exchanged (Q_1). Who paid the tax? Not the suppliers, because they are still receiving P_1 for their product. The demanders paid the entire tax, because now they are paying P_2 $(P_1$ + the tax) for the same quantity. Economists refer to this as the *tax incidence*. Incidence identifies the actual location of the tax burden. In this case, the suppliers appear to pay the tax, because they pay the tax as they produce each bottle. However, they recapture the cost of the tax when each bottle is sold, so the actual tax burden, the incidence of the tax, is on the consumer.

Now consider the case of a perfectly elastic demand shown in Figure E5–4C.

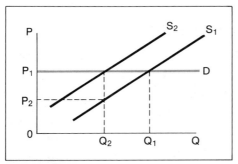

Figure E5–4C   Supply Tax in the Face of Perfectly Elastic Demand

Here the government policy apparently works. The imposition of the tax reduces the quantity of beer exchanged significantly because the demand for beer is perfectly elastic. If, however, this is so because other alcoholic beverages are perfect substitutes for beer, reducing beer consumption does not reduce alcohol consumption or alcohol-related accidents. Whether or not the policy works, the government again gets revenue from the tax, though in this case the revenue is less. While the level of the tax is the same (here $P_1 - P_2$), the imposition of the tax caused the quantity exchanged to fall. The same tax with a smaller quantity means less revenue.

What is the tax incidence? In this case, the demanders pay P_1 before and after the tax. It is the suppliers who bear the tax burden because the amount they actually receive per bottle goes down from P_1 to P_2.

Due to the perfect elasticity of demand, the supplier is unable to transfer any of the tax burden to the demander.

We see then that the effect of taxes (including incidence) depends on the elasticities in a given market and these elasticities reflect the relationship between that market and other markets. Thus the imposition of a tax anywhere in the system has a ripple effect that is felt throughout the system. Things get all the more complicated if we consider income elasticities, because any tax affects someone's income and income taxes affect everyone's income.

How would the example above change if the tax was imposed at the time of purchase (i.e., a sales tax) and if demand was less than perfectly elastic or inelastic? Consider the cases of perfectly elastic and inelastic supply.

As you can see, tax analyses can be very complex. It is also very important. For this reason, lots of economists spend their careers studying the incidence and effects of taxes.

E6-1: Technical Definition of the CPI

Conceptualizing a price index in theory is a lot easier than establishing one in practice. The latter requires a technical definition, one that can be operationalized. When calculating the CPI, the two key questions that must be answered in order for the index to be operationalized are: What is a "normal" household like? and What does a normal household consume? In the following article from *The New York Times* (February 26, 1987) you will see how changing social patterns (e.g., family size, labor force participation) and consumption patterns require adjustments in the technical definition of the CPI.

Updating the Market Basket

By ROBERT D. HERSHEY Jr.

WASHINGTON, Feb. 25 — More money for cable television, legal fees and dinners away from home. Less for car repairs, red meat, dry cleaning and pastry.

A herculean $45 million effort has reapportioned the Consumer Price Index's bas-ket of goods and services to reflect a decade's worth of changes in the nation's spending patterns.

"What it does," Patrick C. Jackman, an official of the Labor Department, said of the revision, "is update people's expenditure patterns from the 70's to the 80's."

The revision, which is to be formally introduced on Friday when the index figures for January are released, will directly or indirectly affect almost every American household, or "consumer unit," the term now preferred by the statisticians.

Among other uses, the index is the basis for changes in payments to 38 million Social Security beneficiaries, 20 million food stamp recipients, more than four million workers covered by contracts with escalator clauses and millions of Federal retirees.

The index also affects income tax brackets and the cost of school lunches for 23 million children. In the private sector, it influences a variety of payments, such as for royalties, alimony and child support.

Service Sector Expands

The latest revision — the first since 1978 — records at least one momentous change. For the first time, the service sector accounts for more than half of all spending — 52 percent in 1982–1984, up from about 46 percent in 1972–1973. Spending on commodities and goods has slipped to 48 percent.

One implication of this now well-established trend, economists say, is that wages, fees and salaries will be the dominant influence on future inflation levels.

Other changes in the price index reflect the increased numbers of two-earner families and elderly people; more spending on physical fitness; new products such as compact disk stereo equipment; the impact of energy conservation, and the population gains of the Sun Belt.

Although the index is often referred to as a measure of the cost of living, it measures only the price of a basket of goods and services in a mix that must be periodically adjusted. If consumers change their buying habits because, say, the price of gasoline rises sharply or certain types of foods decline in popularity, the market basket must be changed to keep the index a reliable barometer of the overall price level.

To aid in making comparisons, for the next six months the index will be calculated using both the old and new baskets.

Among the index's categories, food has shown a substantial long-term decline in relative importance. In 1939, food and beverages accounted for more than one-third of the market basket; under the latest revision, food fell to 17.8

Behind the New Price Measurement
Changes in expenditures by urban consumer units in the seven major categories and selected subcategories for the Consumer Price Index. Many factors contributed to the changes, including differences in consumer buying habits as well as prices, population shifts in age and location, new technology and products, and new category definitions.*

Expenditure Category	Former Average Expenditure	Former Relative Importance	Revised Average Expenditure	Revised Relative Importance
ALL ITEMS	$22,065.00	100.000	$19,362.65	100.000
Food and beverages	4,380.12	19.851	3,454.36	17.840
Food at home	2,776.44	12.583	1,962.94	10.138
Food away from home	1,352.14	6.128	1,189.82	6.145
Alcoholic beverages	239.85	1.087	301.60	1.558
Housing	8,318.95	37.702	8,255.57	42.637
Residential rent	1,367.59	6.198	1,099.66	5.679
Homeowners' 'rent'**	3,029.08	13.728	3,519.20	18.175
Apparel and upkeep	1,116.71	5.061	1,263.23	6.524
Transportation	4,772.88	21.631	3,620.03	18.696
New vehicles	851.49	3.859	1,064.36	5.497
Used vehicles	1,014.77	4.599	246.08	1.271

	Former		**Revised**	
Expenditure Category	Average Expenditure	Relative Importance	Average Expenditure	Relative Importance
Motor fuel	1,215.34	5.508	929.49	4.800
Public transportation	347.97	1.577	269.67	1.393
Medical care	1,383.25	6.269	928.58	4.796
Entertainment	931.58	4.222	848.02	4.380
Other goods and services	1,173.64	5.319	992.85	5.128

* A consumer unit is a household, individual or group of individuals that form an economically interdependent unit. Formerly, a unit was 2.8 persons; revised, it is 2.6.
** What an unfurnished home could be expected to rent for, excluding utilities.
Source: Bureau of Labor Statistics

The New Consumer Profile
Changes in demographic characteristics of urban consumer units in calculation of the Consumer Price Index.*

	Former	**Revised**
Income of consumer unit, before taxes	$12,332	$23,183
Per capita income, before taxes	$4,404	$8,917
Size of consumer unit (persons)	2.8	2.6
Number of earners	1.3	1.4
Number of children	1.0	.7
Age of reference person**	47.3	46.2
Sex of reference person: Male	75.9%	66.5%
Female	24.1%	33.5%
Percent reporting homeownership	55.8%	59.5%

* A consumer unit is a household, individual or group of individuals that form an economically interdependent unit.
** The person first mentioned by respondents in the consumer price survey when asked "the name of the person or one of the persons who owns or rents" the home.
Source: Bureau of Labor Statistics

percent, from 20.5 percent a decade earlier.

The latest revision reflects a decline in consumption of red meat, but increased popularity for poultry. Even so, beef remained "the meat of choice" although many consumers have substituted ground beef for roasts.

The sugar and sweets component has also fallen sharply, a change attributed to health-consciousness and to shifts in the age mix of the population. Children and teen-agers are the biggest buyers of confectionery products, and the trend toward smaller families reduces the importance of these items in family budgets, analysts at the department explained.

That population trend also altered meal patterns. Fewer children mean a decline in school lunches, so dinners-away-from-home rose in importance relative to lunches-away-from-home. That occurred despite the rise in the number of two-earner families in which women were eating lunch away from home.

The Transportation Sector
The weighing for transportation fell about three-tenths

of a percentage point, to 18.7 percent of spending. A significant factor there was a decline in the number of miles driven and a rise in the fuel efficiency of vehicles. Those factors produced a 23.2 percent drop in gasoline consumption per consumer unit during the decade, the department reported.

Consumers were also keeping cars longer, but that did not raise proportional spending for repair and maintenance bills. Factors cited include improvements in car quality, such as better protec-

tion against corrosion; the 55-mile-an-hour speed limit and more do-it-yourself maintenance.

A component that did post a significant rise during the decade was housing—to 42.6 percent, from 38.2 percent. This was caused mainly by an increase in rents, the department said.

The share of spending devoted to medical care fell slightly, a seeming anomaly for a category that has seen sharp rises in actual prices. The key here is in the method

of payment—much of those costs are borne by employee-benefit plans or by the Government and such payments are not reflected in the Consumer Price Index. That makes the index particularly misleading as a gauge of the cost of medical care.

Overall, the new index, covering 1982–84 spending patterns, is already somewhat out of date, even though the monthly price changes themselves will, of course, be current.

Source: _The New York Times_, 26 Feb. 1987.

E7-1: The Keynesian Cross Derivation of the AD Relationship

We derived the AD relationship in the text mathematically by combining Equation (1):

$$\frac{\text{AE}}{\text{P}} = Y$$

where $Y = Y_I$ or real income ,

Equation (3):

$$AE = C + I + (G{-}T) + (X{-}M) ,$$

and Equation (5):

$$C = a + b\,(PY) .$$

We can accomplish the same derivation graphically. Let us begin by making the simplifying assumption that AE is measured in real terms and the price level is at $P_0 = 1$, so our three equations become:

$$AE = Y$$
$$AE = C + I + (G{-}T) + (X{-}M)$$
$$C = a + bY$$

Next we define a space with axes AE and Y both on the same scale —AE is measured in real term. If we plot the relationship:

$$AE = Y$$

on that graph we get a 45° line. When $AE = 1$, then $Y = 1$; when $AE = 2$, then $Y = 2$; and so on. These points (1,1), (2,2), (3,3), etc., plot a 45° line. Now we also plot:

$$AE = C + I + (G{-}T) + (X{-}M)$$
$$\text{where } C = a + bY$$

Substituting C into the first equation, we could rewrite this:

$$AE = bY + (a + I + (G{-}T) + (X{-}M))$$

We see that this is the equation of a line with a vertical axis intercept equal to $a + I + (G{-}T) + (X{-}M)$ and a slope of b. Plotting this, we have the two lines shown in Figure E7–1A.

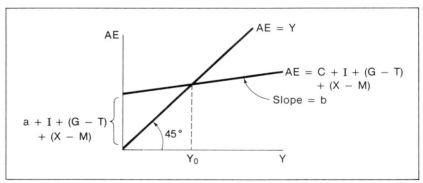

Figure E7–1A   Aggregate Expenditure Function   This graph is called the Keynesian cross because it was developed on the basis of the work of John Maynard Keynes.

Now we know that both the:

$$AE = Y$$

and the

$$AE = C + I + (G{-}T) + (X{-}M)$$

equations hold simultaneously, so the piont of their intersection (where they are both satisfied) must represent the current condition in the macroeconomy. We see in Figure E7–1B that when, as we assumed, the price level, P_0, equals 1, the real income or the real GNP demanded equals Y_0.

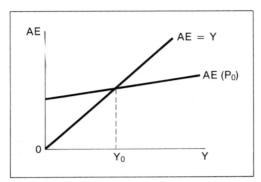

Figure E7–1B   Aggregate Expenditure at Initial Price Level P_0

Now, by allowing the price level to change, we can demonstrate in Figure E7–1C the relationship between price level and the real GNP demanded. There we see graphically, using the Keynesian cross, how the AD curve is derived.

E7–2:   The Multiplier Effect (Prerequisite: E7-1)

A given change in any of our exogenous variables (I, G, T, X, or M) actually increases real GNP demanded at any given price level by a multiple of the initial exogenous change. This multiplicative result is called the _multiplier effect_. The multiplier effect can be demonstrated most easily with the the Keynesian cross diagram introduced in the previous extender.

Let us assume that b and the price level are constant, while a, I, $(G-T)$, $(X-M)$, or some combination thereof changes. Then the AE intercept changes while the AE slope remains the same, as shown in Figure E7–2A.

Take, for example, an increase in G ($\Delta G > O$), which is shown in Figure E7–2B.

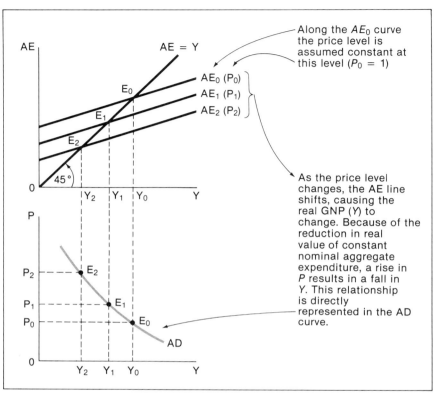

Figure E7–1C   Deriving Aggregate Demand from Aggregate Expenditure

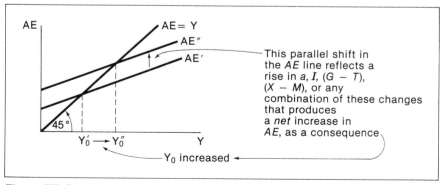

Figure E7–2A   Increasing Aggregate Expenditure

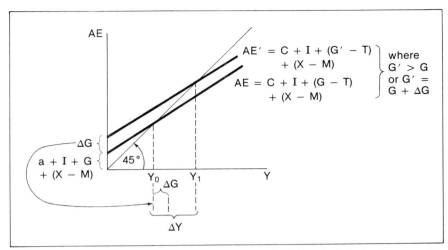

Figure E7–2B   An Increase in G   Notice at the initial level of desired aggregate expenditure (*AE*) the real GNP demanded was Y_0. When *AE* increased to *AE'* by a factor ΔG (the change in desired government expenditure—all else being constant), the real GNP demanded increased by a factor ΔY to a new level, Y_1.

We can see from the figure that the change in desired *AE* was multiplied in its effect on *Y*. As it is drawn above, ΔG caused a ΔY more than two times the initial ΔG itself. This effect is called the *Multiplier*.

Our equation (8) from the text:

$$Y = \frac{1}{1-b}\frac{a}{P} + \frac{1}{1-b}\frac{I}{P} + \frac{1}{1-b}\frac{G-T}{P} + \frac{1}{1-b}\frac{X-M}{P}$$

reflects the size of the multiplier effect. If we assume for the moment that *P* is constant, then any change in an exogenous variable (e.g., ΔG) is multiplied by $\frac{1}{1-b}$ in its effect on *Y*. Thus $\frac{1}{1-b}$ is a measure of the multiplier effect.

When any exogenous variable (*I*, (*G–T*), or (*X–M*)) changes, the multiplier effect occurs because a change in any one of these variables affects *Y* in two ways:

1. *Directly*: A change in *I*, (*G–T*), or (*X–M*) will change *AE* and, in turn, *Y* by an equal amount.
2. *Indirectly*: This occurs because the initial change in *Y*, set off directly by a change in *I*, (*G–T*), or (*X–M*), will initiate a feedback

cycle through C (remember that $C = a + bY$), which extends the effect. It is this indirect feedback cycle that gives rise to the multiplier.

Consider the example in which G changes (ΔG). The feedback cycle is reflected in Figure E7–2C.

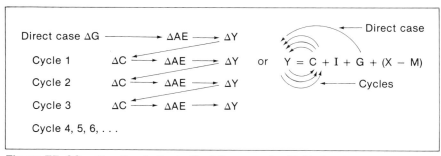

Figure E7–2C   Feedback Cycle That Creates the Multiplier Effect

The only thing that keeps this feedback cycle process from going on forever (thus making the multiplier infinite) is that the ΔC that begins each new cycle is diminished by a factor $(1\text{-}b)$ (the amount subtracted for savings) from the ΔY which ended the previous cycle. Thus with each new cycle the effect diminishes until it goes to zero.

We see, therefore, that the size of the multiplier depends on b, the marginal propensity to consume out of national income. The greater b (i.e., the less Y held back for savings), the larger the feedback and the longer it will last.

What we have demonstrated is that an increase in any exogenous variable will increase real GNP demanded by a multiple, $\frac{1}{1\text{-}b}$. In other words, an increase/decrease in I, G, T, X, and/or M will shift out/shift in AD by more than the initial increase itself. This does not imply, however, that multiplying the changes in these variables times $\frac{1}{1-b}$ will represent change in the actual real GNP. Shifts in real GNP demanded (i.e., shifts in AD) affect both the actual real GNP and the price level, and the distribution of this effect is a point of debate among economists. As we will see, some have argued that a shift in AD ultimately has no effect on actual real GNP; it only affects the price level.

All we can say about the effect of a change in I, G, T, X, and/or M on the actual real GNP is that it is somewhere between zero and $\dfrac{1}{1-b}$ times the exogenous change. Thus the multiplier we have calculated shows us the maximum real effect we can expect.

E9-1: Money Supply

There are actually three primary concepts of money supply that economists keep track of : M–1, M–2, M–3. As the chart on the next page shows, each of these is a successively broader definition of the money supply.

E9-2: The Discount Rate

The following article from *The Syracuse Post Standard* (September 23, 1986) is about the Federal Reserve Board's manipulation of the discount rate. As the graph shows, the Fed was lowering the discount rate for most of the period from May 1981 to August 1986. The drops were particularly dramatic during the period July 1982 to December 1982.

The article suggests that this policy was pursued to stimulate the economy, but that it gives some people jitters about inflation whenever the Fed embraces such a policy. As you read on in the text, you should see why manipulating the discount rate is considered stimulative and why it would make some people nervous about inflation.

Once we have covered all aspects of the policy, you should be able to analyze it in the context of the events and economic conditions of that period. You should also be able to trace the course of events from August 1986 to the current period. What has the Fed been doing with the discount rate since August 1986 and why has it done so?

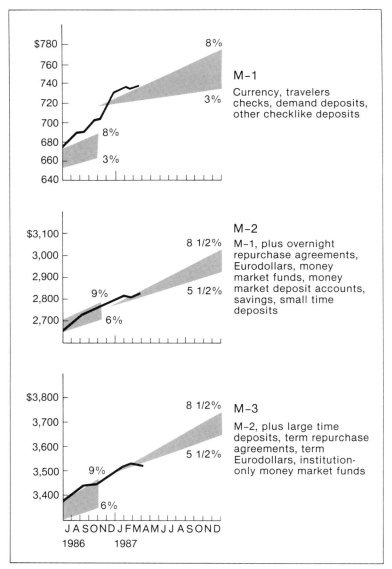

Figure E9–1A Money Supply Growth And Targets Money supply monthly averages, in billions, seasonally adjusted. Shaded areas indicate target zones for money growth.

Source: *Federal Reserve Board. The New York Times*, 17 April 1987.

Analysts: Fed Unlikely to Push Interest Rates Lower

WASHINGTON (AP) — The Federal Reserve Board, which has been aggressively pushing interest rates lower this year to prop up a sluggish economy, is unlikely to ease credit conditions further, because of concern over renewed inflation and signs of economic revival, analysts said Monday.

While economists said they doubt the central bank will go the other way and tighten up on interest rates, they said the steep slide that pushed rates to the lowest levels of this decade is over.

Policymakers at the Fed, who meet eight times a year to map monetary strategy, will

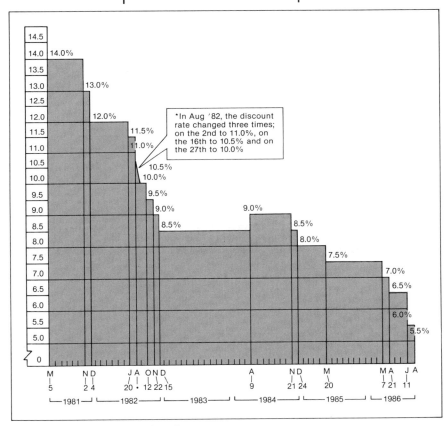

*In Aug '82, the discount rate changed three times; on the 2nd to 11.0%, on the 16th to 10.5% and on the 27th to 10.0%

Source: *Federal Reserve Board*

The dropping discount rate The discount rate is the interest rate charged by the Federal Reserve Board when lending funds to banks. It is used by the federal government to spur growth by encouraging banks to loan money.

FEDERAL RESERVE DISCOUNT RATE Interest rate, by date of first bank change.

convene behind closed doors today. The 12-member group, known as the Federal Open Market Committee, is composed of the seven members of the Federal Reserve Board, headed by Chairman Paul Volcker, and five of the 12 presidents of Fed regional banks.

After the past two FOMC meetings in July and August, the Fed announced reductions in its discount rate, the interest it charges on loans to member financial institutions. It was the most dramatic signal the central bank can send of intentions to push interest rates lower.

In all, the Fed has cut the discount rate four times this year to its current level of 5.5 percent, the lowest rate since the summer of 1977.

A variety of other rates have fallen as well as the central bank tried to use its power over interest rates to get U.S. economic growth back on track.

The economy, as measured by the gross national product, rose at a dismal annual rate of just 0.6 percent in the April–June quarter, its weakest performance since the last recession ended in 1982.

But analysts noted signs that the economy will perform better in the final six months of the year. Unemployment dipped to 6.8 percent in August, its third monthly decline, while industrial production has risen as well.

If the economy does pick up strength, the Fed would not be under the same pressure to ease credit conditions to stimulate economic growth.

Another factor weighing against further loosening moves. analysts said, was the recent jump in the price of gold and other commodities, which have raised fears that inflation is headed higher.

Those increases already have driven up long-term bond yields by more than one-half percentage point since Labor Day as investors began demanding higher yields to

guard against a renewed inflation threat.

"In light of the improvement in economic statistics and the substantial degree of concern in the bond market about renewed inflation, I think the Fed is likely to hold where it is and not move toward either further easing or restraint," said Lyle Gramley, chief economist of the Mortgage Bankers Association and a former Fed board member.

Tom Megan, an economist for Evans Economics in Washington, said the Fed is being torn in two directions. On one hand, the sluggish economy and rising trade deficit would argue for furthur easing, but the jump in gold prices and rapid expansion of the money supply argue for tighter credit conditions, he said.

"With the political realities of the November elections coming up, tightening isn't in the cards," Megan said. "I think for now they will decide to stand pat and not change policy."

Source: *Syracuse Post Standard*, 23 Sept. 1986.

E9–3: The Influence of the Fed

The following series of articles reflects the powerful influence of the Fed on the loanable funds markets.

The first article is from *The New York Times* (November 10, 1986). Recall that in the last extender we saw that from May 1981 to August 1986 the Fed reduced the discount rate. In the following article we find that the mere hint of a change in policy "jolted" the loanable funds markets. This reflects the market's respect for the Fed's power to manipulate interest rates.

Credit Markets Jolted by Fed Monetary Summary

By MICHAEL QUINT

The credit markets, already reeling from a heavy supply of new Treasury securities, were jolted late Friday by a reminder that Federal Reserve monetary policy is a two-edged sword that can send interest rates higher as well as lower.

A summary of the Sept. 23 meeting of the Fed monetary policy officials released late Friday said that a tighter monetary policy was possible if money supply growth did not subside. Although no tightening of policy was enacted, the mere mention of the possibility was enough to send prices of Treasury notes and bonds sharply lower and raise some Treasury bill rates more than an eighth of a percentage point.

The steep drop in Treasury note and bond prices means that securities dealers are facing large potential losses on the $29 billion of new Treasury issues auctioned last week. The extent of the losses depends on the degree to which dealers' purchases were hedged with offsetting transactions. But by the end of last week, dealers agreed there were some large losses and that investors were interested in the new issues only at prices well below the averages at last week's auctions.

"There has been no change in monetary policy, but the Fed's willingness to consider a tightening of policy was still a big surprise because it showed they are looking at monetary policy differently than earlier this year," said John Silva, a financial economist at Kemper Financial Services, Chicago.

By the time trading stopped in New York the new Treasury issues were at their lowest levels of the day, and well below the lows set in morning. . . .

Although Fed officials clearly remain concerned about the pace of economic growth and voted by an 11-to-1 margin to keep monetary policy unchanged, the language of the summary showed "a bias towards tightening if monetary aggregates failed to slow down," analysts at Ried Thunberg & Company noted. One part of the summary said the monetary policy "should be especially alert to the potential need for some slight firming of reserve conditions, particularly if monetary growth did not slow in line with expectations."

As events unfolded, there was no tightening of Fed policy after the September meeting, and money supply growth did subside. The annualized growth rate for the M–2 money supply measure fell to 7.4 percent in September from 11 percent in August, while M–3 growth fell to 8.8 percent from 8.9 percent.

Source: *The New York Times,* 10 Nov. 1986.

The next article (*The New York Times,* April 21, 1987) reflects the particularly powerful position of the Fed's chairperson. When the chairperson speaks, people listen.

Interest Rates Rise Sharply

Report About Volcker View Is Key Factor

By H. J. MAIDENBERG

Government bond prices plunged, in some cases by nearly two points, and interest rates soared yesterday on an unsubstantiated report that Paul A. Volcker, the Federal Reserve Board's chairman, favored tightening credit.

The credit markets were shaken last week only to recover on short covering typical before a long holiday weekend. They were worried both by the rise in the prices of precious metals and the belief that the relative stability in the dollar last Wednesday and Thursday was only temporary,

The strongest blow yesterday was in a syndicated column in newspapers by Rowland Evans and Robert Novak

that said Mr. Volcker favored tightening credit both to bolster the dollar and to reduce the risk of inflation. The bellwether Treasury long bond quickly soared 18/32, despite the absence of any market guidance from European mar-

kets, which were closed for Easter Monday.

A member of the Fed's board, Wayne D. Angell, said yesterday that Mr. Volcker was not at odds with the panel's Reagan-appointed majority about whether interest rates should rise.

Source: *The New York Times*, 21 Apr. 1987.

Indicative of the power of the chairperson is the following cartoon (*Syracuse Herald-Journal,* February 22, 1987)

Source: *Syracuse Herald–Journal.* 22 Feb. 1987.

and a front-page article from the *New York Times* (June 3, 1987) about the transfer of power at the Fed.

Volcker Out After 8 Years as Federal Reserve Chief; Reagan Chooses Greenspan

Markets Surprised
Bonds and Dollar Slump—No Drastic Shifts in Policy Expected

By ROBERT D. HERSHEY Jr.

WASHINGTON, June 2 — President Reagan nominated Alan Greenspan today to succeed Paul A. Volcker as chairman of the Federal Reserve Board, thus ending speculation over the reappointment of one of the most powerful economic policy makers in the nation's history.

The immediate reaction of economists and other analysts was that in succeeding to the job sometimes called the nation's second most influential after the Presidency itself, Mr. Greenspan was unlikely to pursue a monetary policy markedly different from the one that could have been expected from Mr. Volcker.

Source: *The New York Times*, 3 June 1987.

E9–4:   How Independent Is the Fed?

The Federal Reserve Board is supposed to be an independent agency. The president and Congress can try to shape the Fed's philosophy by the appointments they respectively make and approve, but once an individual joins the board, he or she is a member for 14 years and accountable to no one except his or her conscience. So is the Fed really beyond influence? The following article (*The New York Times*, April 17, 1987) reports how a member of the Executive Department tried to influence the Fed. It reflects this individual's reaction to rumors that in April 1987 the Fed was considering reversing its policy and pushing interest rates up.

Federal Reserve Warned On Rates by Budget Chief

Rising Interest, Miller Says, Could Lead to a Recession With 'Political' Impact

By ROBERT PEAR

WASHINGTON, April 16 — President Reagan's budget director, James C. Miller 3d, warned the Federal Reserve today not to raise interest rates, saying such action could cause a recession next year.

Amid deepening concern that the eroding dollar and tensions over trade could provoke a global slump, Mr. Miller seemed to be putting the Administration in position to blame the Federal Reserve if a recession occurs in the election year 1988 after more than four years of economic growth.

Paul A. Volcker, chairman of the Federal Reserve Board, has indicated that the central bank might have to consider pushing up interest rates to combat the dollar's fall in the currency markets. But Mr. Miller said the Federal Reserve was overreacting.

Concern About Overreaction

"Our greatest danger is overreaction," the budget director said at a breakfast meeting with reporters. "I'm concerned about the Fed's overreaction. I'm concerned about what I see in recent data showing a substantial fall in the money supply." Tightening the money supply would mean scarcer credit and higher interest rates.

Mr. Miller also said: "I am concerned that overreaction today on inflation numbers may portend a substantial slowdown a year from now.

"I need not tell you that has political consequences. My fear is that if we get into a recession we are in deep soup, and there is no question about it." As he said this, Mr. Miller banged the table twice for emphasis.

Although there is often tension between administrations' political agendas and those of the independent Federal Reserve, the candor and tone of Mr. Miller's remarks drew surprise.

Stephen H. Axilrod, who was staff director for monetary and financial policy at the Federal Reserve from 1976 to 1986, said, "It is inappropriate to inject political considerations into monetary policy, and there is no evidence that the Fed accommodates its policies to an election-year cycle."

No Comment by Central Bank

Joseph R. Coyne, a spokesman for the Federal Reserve, said there would be no comment on Mr. Miller's remarks.

The nation's central bank cherishes its independence and has gone to great lengths to affirm that is is not subject to the will of any Administration. Over the years officials of the executive branch have often tried to apply pressure through public statements in the exercise known as jawboning.

Mr. Miller said he had not cleared or coordinated his remarks with other Administration officials who make economic policy. He said he was speaking for himself but knew his comments would be perceived as a statement by the Administration.

His criticism of the Federal Reserve was reminiscent of comments made by Donald T. Regan as Secretary of the Treasury and later as the White House chief of staff. Edwin L. Dale Jr., a spokesman for Mr. Miller, said he doubted that the budget director saw himself as a "Fed basher." He was just "warning" the Fed, Mr. Dale said.

Source: *The New York Times*, 16 Apr. 1987.

Such blatant Administration attacks on the Fed's independence are not considered appropriate by the Fed itself or by Congress. Sensitive to this, the Administration acted quickly to disassociate itself from the remarks of its budget director. *The New York Times* reported the Administration's reaction on April 18 as follows:

Disclaimer On Miller's Remarks

White House Distances Itself

By STEVEN V. ROBERTS

SANTA BARBARA, Calif., April 17 — The White House today attempted to disassociate itself from comments by James C. Miller 3d, the budget director, who warned the Federal Reserve on Thursday that raising interest rates could lead to a recession.

Marlin Fitzwater, the President's spokesman, read a statement today saying that Mr. Miller was "speaking personally and not for the Administration."

The budget director's comments, Mr. Fitzwater said, "didn't reflect the Administration's position."

"The markets are very sensitive to any economic statement by the Administration, and we want to make sure they're accurate," the spokesman said in an interview after briefing reporters here, about 30 miles from the mountaintop ranch where President Reagan is vacationing.

But Mr. Fitzwater declined to say whether the Administration would support any move by the Fed to tighten the money supply and raise interest rates.

Referring to Mr. Miller, Mr. Fitzwater said: "We don't want him speculating on the future, and we won't, either. That's the whole point."

The spokesman said the two days of comments were not part of any grand Administration plan, and that officials here were definitely displeased with Mr. Miller for speaking out.

Source: *The New York Times*, 18 Apr. 1987.

Disclaimer notwithstanding, the administration's position had been made clear. Whether it influenced Fed policy is not clear. The point is that while the Fed is nominally independent, it is not immune to attempts by nonmembers to influence the direction of its policy.

E9–5: Exchange Rate Manipulation: A Case Study

The expansionary monetary policy pursued by the Fed between November 1984 and August 1986 (see graph in E9–2) lowered United States interest rates. This, combined with the administration's policy of "jawboning," was intended to weaken the dollar in order to improve the United States trade balance. The dollar was successfully weakened, but the trade deficit did not respond as much as had been hoped. This lack of response was due in part to the willingness of foreign producers to absorb the exchange rate changes in the form of lower profits rather than lose market share, and in part to the continuing attractiveness of the United States as a place to invest, as the following *New York Times* article (April 7, 1987) points out.

Japanese Funds Still Pour In

Little Affected By Dollar Fall

By LOUIS UCHITELLE

Over the past two years, the dollar's unrelenting decline has cost Japanese investors huge paper losses in the value of their various holdings in this country. But they are not selling off.

Quite the contrary, according to the Commerce Department, the Japanese are step- ping up the flow of their money into the American economy. This is happening even as Americans fear that a continuing decline of the dol- lar might finally prompt the Japanese to pull out funds that have been a vital prop to the economy. That fear became especially strong after President Reagan's announce- ment of trade sanctions against some Japanese prod- ucts sent the dollar into a new plunge last week.

The Japanese themselves say that over the long run they will continue to invest in the United States because this country represents a haven and the best long-term return obtainable anywhere for their earnings from trade with this country.

Portfolio Shifts

The dollar's fall, however, is drastically changing the mix of American bonds, corporate stocks, factories and property that the Japanese hold.

Source: *The New York Times*, 7 Apr. 1987.

In the face of this resistance of the trade deficit to respond to the falling dollar, the administration redoubled its efforts. *Newsweek* reported this new attack (January 26, 1987):

Where Will the Buck Stop?

The United States stages a rapid fall for the dollar

The cease-fire in the cur- rency wars didn't last long. after allowing the U.S. dollar to drop 40 percent in 20 months against the Japanese yen and the West German mark, the Reagan administra- tion declared a truce last October—and then waited hopefully for the results. It expected a pronounced decline in the U.S. trade defi- cit, spurred in part by a change in the export-at-all- costs policies of the Germans and Japanese. It got neither, and last week the administra- tion went back to war.

There was no formal call to arms, just a leak to the press: the administration had de- cided that the dollar's value needed to decline even more to restore the competitiveness of U.S. industry. With that, the relative calm in the currency markets turned to chaos. The dollar dropped suddenly and sharply, plunging 2 percent in a single day. The Japanese and German central banks bought dollars in an unsuc- cessful effort to counter the free fall. By the weekend, the dollar was 8 percent below its level in December. And to hear administration officials tell it, the assault will con- tinue. NEWSWEEK has learned the Treasury Department believes 1.70 marks and 140 yen per dollar are now "appropriate" exchange rates —a startling 50 percent below the dollar's peak levels just two years ago.

Source: *Newsweek*, 26 Jan. 1987.

The following graph reflects the effectiveness of the attack.

Unfortunately, as the article notes, these efforts created chaos in the currency markets. The dollar suffered some precipitous drops in January and March 1987.

To stabilize the currency the Federal Reserve intervened in the foreign exchange market. That intervention is described in the following article from the May 30, 1987, *The New York Times*.

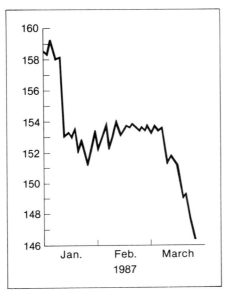

Article E9–5C   The Dollar's Plunge   Daily closes of yen to the dollar since the yearend.

Source: *The New York Times*, 31 Mar. 1987.

Jump in Dollar-Buying by Fed

By KENNETH N. GILPIN

The Federal Reserve Bank of New York reported yesterday that its purchases of dollars during the three months ended April 30 were the largest in nearly a decade.

In its role as foreign exchange agent for the Government, the New York Fed bought more than $4 billion in the foreign exchange markets in the most recent period, up from $50 million during the previous three months. The overwhelming bulk of the activity was in Japanese yen.

Sam Y. Cross, executive vice president at the New York Fed, said at a news conference yesterday that the main part of the intervention occurred during a two-week period in late March and early April, a time of extraordinary turmoil in the foreign exchange and fixed-income markets. It is not the central bank's policy to comment on its current activities in the markets; however, Mr. Cross hinted that the New York Fed's foreign exchange

activities had fallen off sharply this month.

"There has been a clear lessening of pressure in the foreign exchange market in May," he said. The recent sharp rise in interest rates had also played a significant role in stemming the dollar's decline, he added.

Over all, Mr. Cross said that the United States Treasury and the Federal Reserve sold the equivalent of $3.96 billion in Japanese yen and $99 million in West German marks. All of the intervention in the period was financed out of foreign currency balances at the Treasury and the Fed.

In terms of purchases of the dollar, "this is the highest level of intervention in several years," Mr. Cross said. "There were periods in the 1978–1979 period where we intervened in greater magnitudes than this." And, Fed officials said, activity was greater in the three months from November 1980 through January 1981, when intervention totaled $4.4 billion, but at that time the Fed was selling, rather than buying, dollars.

The recent intervention was conducted, Mr. Cross said, in a coordinated fashion with other central banks and was in keeping with the currency stabilization accord reached in Paris in late February. That agreement, signed by the United States and five other major industrial countries, called for the dollar to stabilize "at current levels."

Mr. Cross said yesterday that the intervention efforts "have been positive," in spite of the fact that the activity was not enough to prevent the dollar from sliding against the yen. At the time of the February meeting, the dollar was worth roughly 153 yen. Yesterday, it was worth 143.75 yen.

Mr. Cross declined to say exactly how many dollars foreign central banks had bought to support the currency. He did say that they were "very heavy" purchasers.

The Fed did disclose that the latest three-month period was the busiest quarter in terms of foreign exchange activity by the leading central banks since the current system of floating exchange rates was instituted in 1973.

Margaret L. Green, senior vice president in charge of the New York Fed's foreign exchange operations, said that records of the so-called Group of 10 countries, which includes the United States and other major industrial countries, showed that the central banks bought and sold $73.5 billion worth of foreign currencies during the three-month period. Those figures include intervention undertaken to support the dollar. During the previous three months, gross intervention by the group's central banks totaled $44 billion.

The Government's foreign exchange activities were conducted to satisfy political and economic objectives, but statistics released by the New York Fed showed that, for the latest three months at least, the yen and mark sales also generated a tidy profit. For the period ended April 30, the New York Fed said, it recorded a gain of $688.1 million as a result of its foreign exchange operations. The Treasury's exchange stabilization fund recorded a gain of $571.9 billion during the same period.

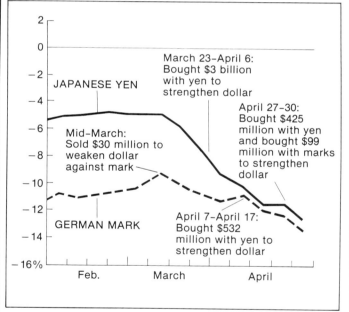

Intervention by the Federal Reserve A look at how the interventions by the U.S. Treasury and the Federal Reserve affected the Japanese yen and the West German mark. Percentage change of weekly average rates from the week ending Oct. 31, 1986. Figures calculated from New York noon quotations.

Source: *Federal Reserve Bank of New York*

What's going on now? What's the status of the trade deficit, the dollar, interest rates, the budget deficit? What policies are being pursued?

E9–6: Protectionist Legislation and Trade Wars

The classic case of a trade war that seriously injured the combatants was the Smoot-Hawley Tariff Act of 1930. The following article from *Time* magazine reflects the fact that the protectionist mentality that gave us Smoot-Hawley is difficult to avoid in times when our trade position suffers. Consider as you read, what would you do if you were a member of Congress during such a time?

Shades of Smoot-Hawley

As the bill moved through Congress, formal protests from foreign countries flooded into Washington, eventually adding up to 200 pages. Both houses voted aye nonetheless. While the legislation sat on the President's desk, 1,028 American economists called for a veto. Herbert Hoover made it the law of the land anyway, swallowing his own reservations and, on June 17, signing the Tariff Act of 1930.

Known as Smoot-Hawley after its legislative sponsors, the bill promptly fulfilled the worst fears of critics. A new panic seized the already battered stock market; the slide continued for two years. In raising import duties on scores of items, in some cases to 50%, the measure provoked angry retaliation by 25 of the nation's trading partners. U.S. exports fell by nearly two-thirds in just two years.

How did Hoover, a President well versed in international commerce, fall into such a trap? In part, he was bound by the 1928 Republican platform, which promised tariffs to help the ailing farm economy. A crisis atmosphere took hold a year later with the stock market crash and the onset of the Great Depression. For decades the Republicans had been sympathetic to protectionism; now they saw trade barriers as a means of placating demands that the Government do something concrete to fight unemployment.

Willis Hawley of Oregon chaired the House Ways and Means Committee, and Reed Smoot of Utah headed the Senate Finance Committee. Both were fiscal experts with more than 20 years of service on Capitol Hill. But, responding to pressure from organized labor and some sectors of industry, they transformed what was to be an agricultural measure into a comprehensive increase in tariffs.

Hoover was hemmed in by tradition and the G.O.P. platform. Henry Ford spent an evening at the White House pleading for a veto of what he called "an economic stupidity." Other automobile executives backed Ford. But no President had ever vetoed a tariff measure, and Hoover was not about to be the first. "With returning normal conditions, our foreign trade will continue to expand," he said hopefully.

In 1932, with international trade in collapse, Franklin Roosevelt denounced Smoot-Hawley as ruinous. Hoover responded that Roosevelt would have Americans compete with "peasant and sweated labor" abroad. Then, as now, protectionism had a strong if superficial political appeal: by election eve, F.D.R. had backed down, assuring voters that he understood the need for tariffs. Protectionist politicking, however, could not save the Republicans in 1932. Smoot and Hawley joined Hoover in defeat. The Democrats dismantled the G.O.P.'s legislative handiwork with caution, using reciprocal trade agreements rather than across-the-board tariff reductions. The Smoot-Hawley approach was discredited. Sam Rayburn, House Democratic Speaker from 1940 until 1961, insisted that any party member who wanted to serve on the Ways and Means Committee had to support reciprocity, not protectionism.

Though some legislators today might be reluctant to make such a promise, no one in Congress is seriously proposing anything as drastic as Smoot-Hawley. Still, the pro-tariff mania that swept Washington 55 years ago remains a danger. "What we are afraid of," says S. Bruce Smart, Under Secretary of Commerce for International Trade, "is that people are so emotional that they will do something that they know is foolish, just to do something."

Not since Smoot-Hawley days had Washington witnessed such an explosion of demand to limit imports as occurred in August and early September 1985. Fretted Sir Roy Denman, Ambassador of the European Community to Washington: "We have seen protectionist sentiment before, but never anything like this."

Many factors combined to produce that surge. The figures on the trade deficit seemed to cry for action. Last spring the International Trade Commission found that the shoe industry was being crippled by competition from low-priced imports and recommended that Reagan impose a strict quota on foreign footwear. But in August the President refused, warning of a trade war and renewed inflation if he acquiesced. His action convinced many on Capitol Hill that the Administration would not help even

the most severely affected industries unless Congress forced his hand.

In addition, some Congressmen, particularly Southern Democrats representing textile-producing areas, got their ears burned when they went home during the August recess. In Sycamore, Ala., Congessman William Nichols convened a gathering in the spinning room of a closed mill. A constituent who said he was a Korean War veteran complained, "I had no way of knowing that when I put my life on the line back then, I would be fighting for a country that was going to put me out of a job." He was referring to heavy textile imports from South Korea.

Many Congressmen returned from the August recess convinced that stopping imports was the cause of the hour. Democrats in particular thought that they had hit on an issue that might at last win back the blue-collar workers, especially Southern whites, who had been deserting them in droves. Some read great significance into a special congressional election in the first district of Texas in August. Democrat Jim Chapman, an advocate of protection, defeated Republican Edd Hargett, who said that he did not understand "what trade policies have to do with bringing jobs to east Texas." Later analysis suggested that many voters were bothered less by Hargett's stand on trade than by a feeling that he might not be especially bright, but at the time Democrats were convinced they had hit political pay dirt. Said California Congressman Tony Coelho, chairman of the House Democratic Congressional Campaign Committee: "The issue is there.

Texas One [the First District] proved that." More than a few Republicans suspected that the Democrats could very well be correct, politically if not economically. Wyoming Congressman Dick Cheney, a member of what he described as "a small band of brothers" favoring free trade, was afraid that the issue of curbs on imports provided "an opening for Democrats to reestablish their ties to the blue-collar voter. It's the Iranian hostage crisis in reverse." His meaning: now it was a Republican Administration that looked weak in the face of foreign hostility.

The protectionist surge, indeed, has been pushing some legislators into action against their better judgment. Florida Democrat Sam Gibbons, chairman of a Ways and Means subcommittee on trade, returned in early September from a 24-day swing through Asia alarmed by the prospects of foreign retaliation against American exports, especially farm products, if the bill restricting U.S. textile imports became law. "The Chinese told us without any equivocation, 'If we can't sell you our products, we can't buy your products,'" reported Gibbons. His conclusion: the bill is "about as horrible a piece of legislation as you can imagine." Still, he made no attempt to bottle up that "horrible" bill in his subcommittee; he let it be passed on to the full Ways and Means Committee. Why? Says Gibbons: "Bad as it is, there could be worse things ahead if Congress is not allowed to vote on it. I have a whole host of my colleagues who say, 'Sam, you are right, but I have serious district problems on this matter.'" Meanwhile, Gibbons has written an import-restricting bill of his own. It would impose penalty tariffs on natural resources, such as minerals and natural gas extracted from government-owned land in foreign countries, that are shipped to the U.S. at subsidized prices. This bill, along with the textile bill, the Rostenkowski-Gephardt-Bentsen 25%-surcharge proposal and the two Danforth reciprocity bills, are among the measures most likely to get serious considerations.

Though the protectionist push has begun to worry increasing numbers of Congressmen, it has by no means petered out. So many Senators and Representatives have committed themselves to the textile bill that it is nearly certain to pass, though probably not by margins large enough to override a Reagan veto.

Source: *Time*, 7 Oct. 1985.

As the article points out, political realities often make protectionist legislation a very appealing short-run response to the demands for action from those who have lost their jobs because of imports. This reflects the point made in the text that micro motives often drive macro policy—sometimes in directions that all participants agree are foolish from a macro perspective.

What's going on now? Is trade more or less free than it was in October 1985? Are we in the midst of a trade war or have we been able to solve the trade deficit problem without protectionist legislation?

Index

A

Acid rain, 102–3
Adverse selection and
    insurance, 256
Affirmative action, 98, 306
Aggregate demand (AD):
    defined, 133
    relationship derived,
        135–39
    sources of shocks, 141–42,
        152–68
Aggregate expenditure (AE):
    defined, 134
    major components, 136
Aggregate supply:
    long run (LAS), 142–44
    short run (AS):
        described, 144–45
        sources of shocks,
        146–47, 169–70
Allocation 3, 22 (*See also*
    Factor)
Apartheid:
    and market power, 97
    as exploitation, 302
Arrow, Kenneth, 49, 89
Asset, 191
Assumption:
    defined, 6

    most basic scientific, 6
    relaxing strong, 12
    role in scientific process, 8
Assymetric information:
    and insurance, 256–57

B

Balance of payments:
    accounts, 161–62, 164
    role of exchange rate, 160
Banks (*See also* Financial
    intermediary):
    run on (*See also* Panic),
        193
Barter, 45
Box of tools, 7
Budget line, 267
Bush, George, 187

C

Capital (*See also* Money
    capital)
    defined, 22
    human, 22

Capital *(continued)*
  intensive technique (*See
    also* Elasticity of input
    substitution), 85
Cardinal ranking (*See also*
    Ordinal ranking), 241
Carter, Jimmy, 185–86
Ceteris paribus, defined, 12
Circular flow, diagramed, 51
Command economy, 40
Comparable worth, 84–85
Comparative advantage, 259
Competition (*See*
    Destructive or
    Constructive)
Complements (*See also*
    Elasticity, Cross price),
    72, 279
Complex society:
  reason for, 41–45
  role of money, 45–46
  types, 39–41
Constructive competition,
    48, 100
Contractionary policy (*See*
    Fiscal; Monetary policy)
Consume:
  defined, 16
  time bias, 32
Consumer price index (CPI):
  described, 125–26
  technical definition,
    324–27
Consumption (C):
  defined, 136
  function, 137–38
Coordination mechanism:
  centralized system
    (command economy),
    40
  decentralized system
    (market economy), 40
  simple system (Crusoe
    economy), 38
  traditional system (custom
    economy), 40
Crowding out effect, 208–10
Crusoe, Robinson, 15
Current account, 161

D

Decision rules, basic, 25
Deflation, defined, 124
Defoe, Daniel, 15
Demand (*See also* Elasticity;
    Quantity demanded):
  curve introduced, 52–53
  derived, 85
  excess, 56
  role of tastes, 71
Demand-deficient
    unemployment, 122
Demand deposit account,
    191
Demographics and demand,
    286
Depression (See also Great
    Depression), 121
Destructive competition, 48,
    100
Discount (micro concept):
  defined, 32
  rate, 32–33
Discount rate (of Federal
    Reserve), 191, 333–36
Discouraged workers, 227

Discrimination, 13, 97, 252,
  299, 307–11
Distribution, basic micro
  question, 3
Division of labor, 43–45
Drugs, illegal, economic
  analysis of policy,
  113–15

E

Earthquakes and insurance,
  257
Economics:
  basic questions, 3
  connection to other social
    sciences, 101–2
  defined, 1
Economies of scale, 94
Efficiency:
  basic question, 3
  standard (*See also* Pareto
    optimality), 88
  trade-off with equity, 112
Elasticity of demand, 276
  cross-price (*See also*
    Complements;
    Substitutes) 72–73, 278
  income (*See also* Inferior;
    Normal; Superior
    goods) 71–72, 281
  own price, 63, 277
  cases, graphically, 69
  conditions that
    determine, 63
  elastic, defined, 64

inelastic, defined, 64
  relationship to total
    expenditure/revenue,
    65–66
  unitary elastic, defined,
    64
Elasticity of input
  substitution, 85, 245
Elasticity of supply, 76
Employed, technical
  definition, 227
Entrepreneur, role in the
  economy, 286
Equilibrium (*See also*
    General equilibrium):
  changes in market, 58–60
  defined, 57
  price, 57
  quantity exchanged, 57
Equity:
  standards, 88
  trade off with efficiency,
    112
Ethics, relationship to
  economic analysis, 88
Exchange rate (*See also*
    Trade policy; Balance of
    payments), 159, 341–45
Exogenous
  shock, defined, 141
  variables, defined, 141,
    145–46
Expansionary policy (*See*
    Fiscal; Monetary policy)
Expectations, role in
  economy, xiii, 37–38,
    154, 185, 203, 212
Expected utility (*See also*
    Risk), 38
Exploitation, defined, 302

Externality:
acid rain case, 102–3
described, 101–2
graphical analysis, 105
policy example, 314

F

Factor market, 51, 81, 87
Factors of production (*See also* Elasticity of input substitution):
defined, 21
market for, 51
types, 21–22
Fair race assumption (no market power), 47–48
Federal Deposit Insurance Corporation (FDIC), 193
Federal Open Market Committee (FOMC), 190
Federal Reserve (*See also* Discount rate; Monetary policy):
external influence on, 339–41
influence of, 336–39
reserve requirement, 193
system described, 189–90
Financial intermediary, function, 192
Firm, role of, 50
Fiscal policy (*See also* Government policy):
contractionary, 205
crowding out, 209–10
defined, 205

expansionary, 205
macroeconomic influence described, 205–14
problem of micro/macro tension, 213–14
Ford, Gerald, 185–86
Foreign exchange market, 157–59
Fractional reserve system (*See also* Reserves):
described, 192
money creation, 194–96
Free rider, 106
Frictional unemployment (*See also* Unemployment), 122
Friedman, Milton, 107
Frost, Robert, 237
Full employment (*See also* Natural rate), defined, 122
Functional form, 261

G

Gains from trade (*See also* Division of labor), 44
General equilibrium (GE):
general competitive equilibrium, (GCE), 13
determinates of, 86–87
determines, 86
efficiency of, 88
equity of, 89
special case of GE, 92
standards, 88
General equivalent, defined, 46

Gold standard, 218
Good, distinguished from
     service, 16
Government budget:
  balanced budget
     amendment to the
     Constitution, 218
  deficit:
     defined, 208
     financing, 190, 208
     monetizing, 211
  determination, in theory,
     165–66
  net government budget
     position, described, 136
  surplus, defined, 208
Government policy (*See also*
     Fiscal; Intervention;
     Monetary;
     Nonintervention):
  background on the
     macroeconomic debate,
     111, 179, 187–88
  example of difficulty at
     microeconomic level,
     108–10, 112, 113–15,
     321–24
  macroeconomic debate,
     200–14
  microeconomic debate,
     107–8, 110–13
  problems resolving the
     debate, 225–31
Great Depression, 123,
     155–56, 193
Great Society, 184
Gross National Product
     (GNP), (*See also* Real
     versus nominal):
  defined, 120–21
  determinants of real full
     sustainable (*See also*
     Full employment), 142
  gap, 172
  social welfare, 121
  sources of growth in real
     full sustainable, 143
  technical criteria for
     measurement, 228
  exceptions to criteria,
     229
  theoretical definition, 120
Growth, basic question, 3

H

Hahn, Frank, 50
Household:
  defined, 16
  role, 50
Human capital, xii, 22
Hyperinflation (*See also*
     Inflation), 124, 204
  German experience, 204

I

Ideology, role in the
     scientific process, 9
Indexing (*See also* Price
     index), 125
  of wages, 185
  role in inflation, 185

Indifference curve, 265
Inferior good (*See also*
    Elasticity, income), 72,
    281
Inflation (*See also*
    Hyperinflation):
    costs of, 124
    defined, 124
    effect on interest rate, 253
    expectations, role in, 185
    hyperinflation, 124
    measuring, 126
Inflationary gap, 175
Initial endowment:
    changes in, 21
    defined, 21
    distribution of, 49
Insider trading, 301
Insurance, economics of,
    255
Interest rate:
    real versus nominal, 254
    reasons for, 253
International capital flow
    (See also Money capital),
    161, 199, 212, 214, 341
Intertemporal choice (*See
    also* Discount; Present
    Value), 35–36
Interventionist policy (*See
    also* Government
    policy), Underlying
    assumptions, 108, 188
Invest, microeconomic
    concept defined, 32
Investment (I),
    macroeconomic
    concept:
    defined, 136
    effect of expectations, 154

level determined (*See also*
    Crowding out), 153–54
Invisible hand metaphor, 41,
    80
Isocost line, defined, 295
Isoquant, defined, 295

J

Johnson, Lyndon, 184

K

Kamps, Celia, x
Keynes, John Maynard, xxi,
    220–23
Keynesian:
    cross analysis, 327
    policy, 223

L

Laissez-faire (*See also*
    Noninterventionist),
    defined, 108
Labor force:
    technical definition, 227
    theoretical definition, 121
Labor-intensive technique
    (*See also*
    Capital-intensive),
    defined, 85

Liability (*See also* Asset),
defined, 191
Liquidity, defined, 192
Loanable funds market,
153–54, 208–9
Long run (*See also,* Very
long run), defined, 142

M

Money capital:
account, 161
international flow, 161
Macroeconomics:
basic questions, 118
conditions, graphically
represented, 147–51
connection to
microeconomics,
171–79
contrasted with
microeconomics, 118
defined, 3
policy (*See also*
Government policy):
heart of the debate, 188
preview of the debate,
119
problems, defined, 181–87
Malthus, Thomas Robert, 152
Margin:
defined, 17
described, 244
relationship to average
and total values, 241
Marginal:
analysis, NeoClassical
theory as, 17

diminishing:
product, 22–23
utility, 17
propensity to consume
(*See also* Multiplier
effect), 137, 332
Market:
demand as sum of
individual demands,
73–75
factor, 81
failure (*See also*
Externality; Free rider;
Public good), 48, 101
gains from trade, 44
power, 48, 93–101
artificially created,
95–98
forms, 311–13
naturally occuring, 94
and PACs, 99
and patents, 98
seeking, 99
product, 61
role of, 49
signal, 57
supply as sum of
individual supplies,
75–79
system as coordination
mechanism, 41
Marshall, Alfred, xx
Microeconomics:
basic questions, 3, 90–91
defined, 2
Micro/macro connection,
171–79
Misery index, 186
Model (*See also* Scientific
process), 4

Monetary policy (*See also*
   Government policy):
defined, 189
macroeconomic influence,
   described, 196–205
tools of, 189–196
Money:
basic questions, 2
characteristics of good, 46
commodity, 46
emergence of, 46
fiat, 46
multiplier, 192–96
roles of, 46
supply:
   manipulation of (*See
   also* Federal Reserve;
   Monetary policy),
   190–91
   measurement of, 333
Monopolist, defined, 311
Monopolistic competition,
   312
Monopoly, 94
artificial, 95
natural, 94
Monopsonist, defined, 311
Moral hazard, and insurance,
   256
Multiplier effect (*See also*
   Money multiplier),
   329–33

N

National product (*See also*
   Gross national product),
   basic questions, 3, 120

Natural rate of
   unemployment (*See also*
   Full employment), 122
NeoClassical:
as marginal analysis, 17
western mainstream
   analysis, 10, 12
Net exports (*See* Trade
   balance)
New Classical economists
   (*See* Rational
   expectations)
Nice NeoClassical
   assumptions, 48, 92
Nominal, versus real values,
   127–30
Noninterventionist policy
   (*See also* Laissez-faire),
   underlying assumptions,
   108
Normal goods (*See also*
   Elasticity, income), 72
Normal returns, 80
Nurses, marker for, 82

O

Occam's razor, 11
Oligopolist (*See also*
   Prisoner's dilemma),
   312
Oligopsonist, 312
One period time horizon
   (*See also*
   Intertemporal), 26
Open market operations,
   190–91

Opportunity cost:
  defined, 2
  example, 292
  represented, 238
Ordinal ranking (*See also*
  Cardinal ranking)
  defined, 241
Organization of Petroleum
  Exporting Countries
  (OPEC), 165

P

Policy (*See* Government
  policy)
Pareto, Vilfredo, 88
Pareto optimality, 88
Patents, and market power, 98
Perfect competition, 47–48,
  290–92
Phillips curve, 183–84
Political action committees
  (PACs), and market
  power, 99
Pollution:
  as externality, 102–3
  marketing rights, 314
Portfolio, defined, 191
Preference ordering, 16
Preferences (*See* Demand,
  Tastes)
Present value (*See also*
  Discount rate), 32–33
Price:
  as market signal, 57
  controls, ceiling and floor,
  319
  freeze, general, 321
  index, 125

  level, defined, 124
  taker, defined, 81
Prisoner's dilemma (*See
  also* Oligopoly), 312
Process of production,
  defined, 21
Product market, 51, 61, 87
Production (*See* Factors of;
  Process of)
Production possibility curve,
  238
Productivity, 43, 45
Profit:
  as signal of advantage,
  79–80
  defined, 79, 94
  role under perfect
  competition, 79
Proxy, use in testing, 229
Public good, 106

Q

Quandary of choice, 1–2
Quantity demanded (*See
  also* Demand), 53
Quantity supplied (*See also*
  Supply), 54
Quotas, trade (*See also*
  Government policy,
  trade), 216

R

Rational behavior, defined, 16
Rational expectations, 224,
  228

Reagan, Ronald, 186–87
Real, versus nominal, 127–30
Recession, defined, 121
Regression analysis, 8, 230
Rent, defined, 94
Rent-seeking:
    defined, 99
    and regulation, 110
    and social welfare loss, 100
Reserves (*See also* Federal
        reserve):
    bank reserves defined, 192
    fractional reserve system,
        192–93
    full reserve system, 192
Resources (*See also*
        Allocation), 21
Ricardo, David, 152
Risk (*See also* Uncertainty):
    defined, 37
    role in insurance, 255
    role in interest rate, 253
Robbins, Lionel, 1
Run, on banks, 193

S

Sargent, Thomas, 204
Save, defined, 32
Savings function, 138
Say's law, 221
Scale of production, 94
Scarcity, source of, 21
Schumpeter, Joseph, 6, 131
Scientific process:
    coexistence of competing
        theories, reason for, 10
    flaws, where they enter,
        9–10
    ideology, role of, 9
    standards, 10–12
    steps in, 5–8
    testing, problems in, 9
Service, distinguished from
        good, 16
Short run, defined, 144
Signal (*See* Price)
Signaling theory, xiii
Simple society, summary,
        38
Smith, Adam, xx, 5, 41–45,
        47, 92, 93, 220–21,
        231–32, 260
Smoot-Hawley Tariff Act of
        1930, 217, 345
Social choice, 89
Social welfare, 100, 121
South Africa, 97, 304
Specialization (*See also*
        Division of labor), 43
Stagflation, defined, 185
Structural unemployment
        (*See also*
        Unemployment), 122
Substitutes (*See also*
        Elasticity, cross price),
        72, 280
Sunk costs, 84, 294
Superior good, defined,
        282
Supply (*See also* Quantity
        supplied):
    curve introduced, 53
    excess, 55
Supply-side macroeconomic
        policy (*See also*
        Government policy), 223

Supreme Court, United
States, 307–11
Surplus (*See* Division of
labor)

Truman, Harry, 225
Tutu, Archbishop Desmond,
304

T

Tariff (*See also* Trade), 216,
345–47
Tax incidence, defined, 323
Taxes (T) (*See* Government
budget position)
Technical definition, versus
theoretical, 226
Technique of production
(*See also* Capital
intensive; Elasticity of
input substitution; Labor
intensive; Technology),
22, 85
Technology (*See also*
Technique), defined, 22
Theoretical definition,
versus technical, 226
Theory (*See also* Scientific
process), defined, 4
Time preference, 32, 253
Trade balance (X-M):
defined, 136
determined, 156–65
Trade policy (*See also*
Government policy),
tools, 214–17
Transmission mechanism,
described, 196–97
Treasury department, role in
government finance, 190

U

Uncertainty (*See also* Risk),
defined, 37
Underemployment, defined,
227
Underground economy, 228
Unemployed, technical
definition, 227
Unemployment (*See also*
Demand deficient;
Frictional; Natural rate;
Structural):
basic questions, 3
kinds, defined, 122
rate, 123
Utility, 16, 241
Utility marginal product
(UMP), defined, 26–27

V

Value, basic microeconomic
question, 3
Value of the marginal
product, 85
Velocity of money (V),
defined, 199

Venter, Lize, 97
Very long run (*See also* Long
 run), defined, 143
Vietnam war, 184
Vision (*See also* Scientific
 process), defined, 6
Voluntarily unemployed, 121

W

Wage indexing (*See*
 Indexing)
Wage-price spiral, 184
World War II, 165, 167–68,
 321